Virginia Woolf
Reading the Renaissance

ELEPHANT AND CASTLE.

Virginia Woolf
Reading the Renaissance

Edited by

Sally Greene

Ohio University Press

ATHENS

Ohio University Press, Athens, Ohio 45701
©1999 by Ohio University Press
Printed in the United States of America
All rights reserved

Ohio University Press books are printed on acid-free paper ♾

05 04 03 02 01 00 99   5 4 3 2 1

Excerpts from TO THE LIGHTHOUSE by Virginia Woolf, copyright 1927
by Harcourt Brace & Company and renewed 1955 by Leonard Woolf,
reprinted by permission of the publisher.

Excerpts from THE WAVES by Virginia Woolf, copyright 1931 by Harcourt
Brace & Company and renewed 1959 by Leonard Woolf, reprinted by
permission of the publisher.

For permission to reprint copyright material, grateful acknowledgment is
made to the Society of Authors as the literary representative of the estate
of Virginia Woolf.

Library of Congress Cataloging-in-Publication Data

Virginia Woolf : reading the Renaissance / edited by Sally Greene.
    p.   cm.
    Includes bibliographical references (p.   ) and index.
    ISBN 0-8214-1269-8 (acid-free paper)
    1. Woolf, Virginia, 1882–1941—Knowledge—Literature. 2. European
literature—Renaissance, 1450–1600—History and criticism—Theory,
etc. 3. European literature—Renaissance, 1450–1600—Appreciation—
England. 4. English fiction—European influences. 5. Renaissance
in literature. I. Greene, Sally.
PR6045.O72Z8947 1999
823'.912—dc21
                                     98-32062
                                         CIP

For Paul and Tucker, Renaissance men

Contents

Part 2: Rewriting the Renaissance

⌒ Preface

This collection of essays represents several years of "thinking in common" about Virginia Woolf and the Renaissance, beginning with a special session on the subject at the 1994 convention of the Modern Language Association and including a panel at the Sixth Annual Conference on Virginia Woolf, in 1996. I am grateful first and most of all to the contributors for their consistently fine work as well as their cheerful cooperation. We have learned much from each other, and that has been half the fun. Further, since the project is an outgrowth of my dissertation, which I wrote with the support of an American Fellowship from the American Association of University Women, special thanks are due to that very special organization.

Among the many other people who have been helpful along the way, I'd like particularly to thank my editor, Gillian Berchowitz, for steady patience and unfailingly good advice, and my manuscript editor, Nancy Basmajian. Thanks also to Reid Barbour, Ilona Bell, Kateri Carver-Akers, Melba Cuddy-Keane, Michelle Deal, Juliet Dusinberre, Craufurd Goodwin, William Harmon, Howard Harper, Mark Hussey, Dudley Marchi, Karen Robertson, Louise Schleiner, Pauline Scott, Ellen Tremper, Pierre-Éric Villeneuve, Joe Viscomi, Linda Wagner-Martin, Tae Yamamoto, Alan M. Greenberg of Integrity Indexing, and two anonymous readers for Ohio University Press whose knowledge appropriately spans the centuries. For less direct but nevertheless crucial support, I am grateful to the entire community of Woolf scholars, an uncommonly generous group.

Important groundwork for all of us writing in this collection was established by Alice Fox in *Virginia Woolf and the Literature of the English Renaissance* (Oxford, 1990). Although she died before I could thank her personally, I hope the book honors the spirit of her meticulous labor and insightful speculations.

The cover illustration is Duncan Grant's *Venus and Adonis* (1919), which was inspired by his earlier "free translation" (Roger Fry's term) of the so-called *Simonetta Vespucci* (sometimes called *Cleopatra*) by the early Italian Renaissance artist Piero di Cosimo. According to Richard Shone in *Bloomsbury Portraits* (Phaidon, 1976), Grant commented that the painting was "not in any way an illustration of the subject, but a rhythm which came out of the subject"—a statement that could easily apply to Woolf's "free translations" of her Renaissance sources. The painting is housed in the Tate Gallery; I am grateful to Art Resource for permission to reproduce it.

For the illustrations in chapter 2, thanks to Nina Beskow for permission to use Giselle Freund's photo of Woolf and to Giraudon/Art Resource for permission to reproduce the portrait of Montaigne. For the portrait of Elizabeth I in chapter 3, thanks to Alinari/Art Resource. For the drawing of the layout of the British Library Reading Room in chapter 4, thanks to the British Library; and in the same chapter, thanks to the University of Chicago Press for the use of the illustrations of Bruno's memory system and Camillo's memory theater.

For the Blake illustration from *Comus* in chapter 5, thanks to the Museum of Fine Arts, Boston. For permission to use Mark Severin's woodcut illustration to *Circe and Ulysses* in chapter 7, thanks to the Associated University Presses, acting on behalf of the Golden Cockerel Press.

With the authoritative textual editing of Woolf's work so much of the "present moment," a brief discussion of my choice of texts is in order. The Shakespeare Head Press is publishing the novels in beautiful, high-quality editions. The series is not complete, however, and the published volumes are not easily available in America. Therefore I have chosen to use the popular Harcourt Brace paperback editions readily available in print. For the Hogarth Press, Andrew McNeillie has published four of his projected six volumes of Woolf's essays, extending to 1928. In America these volumes are being published by Harcourt Brace, but the fourth volume has not yet appeared. Because it is more complete, I have cited the Hogarth edition (the pagination is the same). But since the fourth volume is not yet available in America, I have usually not cited essays in the fourth volume if the same essay can also be found in a more easily available authoritative source—for example, in McNeillie's edition of *The Common Reader* or in any of the posthumous collections of Woolf's essays that Leonard Woolf assembled and edited—*The Captain's Death Bed and Other Essays, The Death of the Moth and Other Essays, Granite and Rainbow* (unfortunately out of print), or *The Moment and Other Essays.*

For Renaissance texts, contributors have, for considered reasons of their own, made independent choices among modern and older editions.

For letters and diary entries I have used the authoritative multivolume editions. And like many grateful Woolf scholars I have consulted the *Bibliography of Virginia Woolf,* in the welcome new fourth edition prepared by B. J. Kirkpatrick and Stuart N. Clarke (Oxford, 1997), for assorted crucial details.

Finally, I should point out for readers not familiar with Woolf scholarship that, following what is by now a convention, I have retained Woolf's idiosyncratic spelling and punctuation, even the use of the ampersand for quotations from her diaries, letters, and other handwritten sources—even though, as others before me have noticed, the typographical ampersand comes nowhere close to capturing the "flight of the mind" that her handwriting had the difficult job of tracking.

Introduction

~ Sally Greene

"*D*id women have a renaissance?" Joan Kelly asked in 1977. The challenge issued in that question—which, as Kelly recognized, went against "the widely held notion of the equality of Renaissance women with men" established by Jacob Burckhardt and followed even by some general histories of women[1]— has animated Renaissance feminist studies for the next twenty years, up to the present day. But after rediscovering, as Virginia Woolf had already dramatized in *A Room of One's Own,* that "there was no renaissance for women—at least, not during the Renaissance,"[2] feminist critics working in the literature of the sixteenth and seventeenth centuries began to take a closer look. The answer to Kelly's question today, a qualified but enthusiastic yes, is apparent in the dozens of anthologies and critical studies that have succeeded in bringing to attention the lives and literary works of Mary Wroth, Aemilia Lanyer, Mary Sidney, Elizabeth Cary, and others.[3]

The scholars involved in this recovery work have at times taken aim at Woolf, who seems, through the rhetorical success of *A Room of One's Own,* to have been a coconspirator in the silencing of these women's voices. The winter 1996 issue of the *Shakespeare Quarterly,* for example, titled "Teaching Judith Shakespeare" in ironic tribute to Woolf's most memorable fictional character, is

1

dedicated to demonstrating how factually mistaken were the doubts she expressed about the possibility of women's writing in the Renaissance.[4] As Margaret Ezell had earlier pointed out, however, the source of the misunderstanding that feminist Renaissance critics are working to correct lies not so much in Woolf's text as it does in the recent outpouring of anthologies of women's writing. Charmed to persuasion by Woolf's text, the editors of these anthologies have wholeheartedly embraced the tentative theories proposed in *A Room of One's Own* and melded them into their evolving understanding of the facts.[5]

In thinking back to Woolf's 1929 work, it is hard to separate the extent to which she lacked evidence from that to which she consciously manipulated the available facts in the service of a larger "truth" about women ("Fiction here is likely to contain more truth than fact," her narrator warns).[6] From her other writings we do know that she deeply wished to trace a line of women writers and readers as far back as possible. Her essays touching the Renaissance attempt to imagine the inner lives, for example, of women ranging in social status from Anne Clifford, one of John Donne's patrons, to Mercy Harvey, the milkmaid sister of Gabriel Harvey. But, as Juliet Dusinberre demonstrates in her recent study *Virginia Woolf's Renaissance: Woman Reader or Common Reader?* we have to look to the period just following what is traditionally called the Renaissance to spy her engaging with a strong tradition of literary and literate women. According to Dusinberre's analysis, which might have been predicted from Kelly's, Woolf's personal "renaissance," while encompassing Montaigne and Donne, in important ways finds its center in the later works of the seventeenth century, including the letters of Dorothy Osborne and Madame de Sévigné as well as the writing of a working-class "outsider" named John Bunyan.[7]

This collection of essays proposes a different approach. Rather than examining Woolf's successes or failures in finding (and thus creating) a Renaissance tradition of women writers, the scholars whose work appears in the following chapters are primarily interested in tracing Woolf's footsteps as a reader and reinterpreter of the canon of Renaissance literature as it was conceived in her time—those works written by authors whose names were well known. It is not only Woolf the literary historian who is examined here—the prophetic feminist critic—but also and perhaps more so Woolf the creative writer, to whom the Renaissance offered a living fund of working materials. While acknowledging that her attitudes toward her male predecessors were ambivalent—that in striking ways these literary "fathers" functioned as censors, much like the Oxbridge beadle who instructs a certain woman to keep off the grass—the critics writing in this collection complicate the picture by shifting the focus from psychological influence to intertextuality.[8] Through an "awareness of intertextuality, of language as a tissue of inherited discourses," as Dusinberre says in her consideration of Woolf and Montaigne, she was able to "remake the language of men in her own image."[9] As these essays demonstrate, Woolf needs to be reckoned with, along with T. S. Eliot, James Joyce, W. B. Yeats, and Ezra Pound, as a major modernist writer who significantly reconceived the Renaissance in the early twentieth century.

The four essays in part 1, "Rereading, Remembering the Renaissance," approach Woolf's Renaissance broadly as a way of remarking the depth of her engagement with it. In "Michelet, Woolf, and the Idea of the Renaissance" I note that the sense of the period that she inherited from the Romantics and the Victorians was less ideologically rigid than, in hindsight, recent criticism tends to assume. Woolf was influenced hardly at all, I argue, by Burckhardt, the nineteenth-century historian who is now considered largely to blame for having invented the "Renaissance man" in all his imperious glory. Rather, her Renaissance is aligned with the visionary Romanticism that characterizes the Renaissance of Michelet—a revolutionary narrative forged in the fires of 1789. In his retelling, the "heroic" sixteenth century arises *sua sponte* from dying medieval embers, bringing forth the creative likes of Galileo, Brunelleschi, Van Eyck, and especially Leonardo da Vinci. Michelet places us in the gallery of the Louvre, face-to-face with the works of Leonardo, and forces us to confront "the genius of mystery and discovery" as we contemplate "the unknown abyss of the ages." "[W]hat do you wish of me?" Michelet bids Leonardo's silent figures to ask us, urging us collectively into a reinvented future. The democratic promise of Michelet's Renaissance, like that of the French Revolution, remains unfulfilled; yet the possibility is sustained through glimpses of "harmony." Correspondingly Woolf's prophetic Renaissance is articulated, for example, in *Night and Day*, in which Ralph and Katharine (two romantic moderns) are drawn together by visions of "new worlds" that they can only begin to describe, resorting finally to abstract sketches of the pen, "blots fringed with flames meant to represent— perhaps the entire universe."

A key Renaissance figure with whom Woolf kept up a lifelong conversation is Montaigne; and here we catch her in the act of re-creating her material. At an earlier moment in *Night and Day,* Ralph spies Katherine reciting, "'It's life that matters, nothing but life—the process of discovering—the everlasting and perpetual process, not the discovery itself at all.'" The narrator says "she had twisted the words of Dostoevsky to suit her mood."[10] Whether Woolf as novelist knew that she was twisting Montaigne's words, not Dostoevsky's, is a baffling question, given that, as Nicola Luckhurst tells us in "'To quote my quotation from Montaigne,'" she surely did at other times get the author right, while she just as surely persisted in reshaping the quotation to suit her moods. Contrasting Woolf's reading with Leonard Woolf's more "schematic" one, Luckhurst sees Woolf echoing Montaigne's insistence on process, even using this quotation to cope with her own mortality. Like Michelet and Pater, Woolf emphasizes Montaigne's skepticism—she treats him as a "contemporary" for practicing what Pater calls "suspended judgment."[11] But what interests Luckhurst more is Woolf's study of Montaigne's verbal "self-portrait" as a spur to "drawing her own self-portrait," which she pursues with the understanding that his "*Essais* are more a mirror than a self-portrait of their author." A rewritten Montaigne, Luckhurst argues, "'come[s] out' in Woolf's public writing," particularly in her attempts toward "women's autobiography."

Part of Woolf's autobiographical project involved an abiding identification with Queen Elizabeth. In "Rough with Rubies: Virginia Woolf and the Virgin Queen," Reginald Abbott argues that Woolf conceives of the queen, and figures her fictionally, as a woman of artistry as well as authority. Abbott's careful attention to Woolf's reflections and refractions of the queen's image through the image of the ruby—a strictly private, not historical, association— deepens our understanding of the subjectivity of her Renaissance. Rather than a historical Elizabeth, Abbott demonstrates, Woolf constructs an imagined Elizabeth out of personal associations that coalesce in "a daring new inscription of a tradition of female power." These depictions, moreover, at least reflect a fundamentally accurate understanding of the queen's authority; and thus her portrait differs from those of her academic contemporaries. The professor Walter Raleigh, for example, deals with Elizabeth's power by denying it: "There is an old saying that it is better to have a queen than a king, for under a queen the country is ruled by men, and under a king by women." And when, as

Abbott reminds us, Woolf credits Elizabeth with the "long thin hands of an artist," she contradicts Lytton Strachey's statement, in *Elizabeth and Essex,* that her "extraordinarily long hands" suggest "a touch of the sinister."[12] Yet there is something productively "sinister" in the Elizabeth types that appear, sometimes as crones, within the novels. In the end, Abbott shifts our attention from Woolf's private identification with Elizabeth, most fully achieved in *Orlando,* to a highly public (and hardly genteel) reinscription discernible in the productive tension between Mrs. Manresa and Miss La Trobe in *Between the Acts.*

Following chapters highlighting Woolf's creative memory, Anne E. Fernald in "The Memory Palace of Virginia Woolf" addresses this subject specifically. Situating us beside Woolf's characters in the Reading Room of the British Library—whose design resembles that of the Renaissance memory systems of Bruno and Camillo—she discusses Woolf's ambivalent relationship to cultural memory. The Reading Room is all Enlightenment: a stone edifice embodying an "ambition of completeness," it reifies one version of literary history. Emphasizing the Renaissance beginnings of the "development of the system" of memory, the Victorians spurned "all of the art of memory that was personal and idiosyncratic." Woolf, in contrast, resists the collective memory invoked by the circle of men's names inside the Reading Room's dome and emphasizes what the Victorians ignored: the neoplatonist desire for a flexible set of tools with which to build a personal "memory palace." Fernald reads the "cartwheel" blots that Woolf's persona in *A Room of One's Own* creates out of her anger, like the unfathomable "mark on the wall" in the story of the same name, like Eleanor's doodles in *The Years* (like Ralph and Katherine's vision of flaming blots), as symbols of Woolf's purifying, "antimemorial" urge. Meaning is to be suspended, put to provisional use, in ways Bruno would have understood. And yet, as Fernald acknowledges, Woolf capitulates to the writer's impulse to create memorable scenes: the Elephant and Castle where Judith Shakespeare is buried; Whitehall, scene of a "splitting off of consciousness." Perhaps a way to think of this paradox is to place Woolf, paradoxically, at the intersection of Walter Benjamin's "novelist," who "perpetuates" memory, and his "storyteller," who leaves a story sufficiently untold that it becomes a new creation in the listener's memory and experience.[13]

The six essays in part 2, "Rewriting the Renaissance," focus on individual works. Consistent with Woolf scholarship today as a whole, they (like the first four) reflect an abiding interest in her life as background and intertext. In no case does the critic reduce the work to a function of the life, however. At the hands of these critics the works have a way of slipping off in highly unpredictable directions. But inevitably, as Benjamin writes, "traces of the storyteller cling to the story the way the handprints of the potter cling to the clay vessel." And again in this phenomenon we can see an aspect of Woolf's Renaissance. When we read her works with an eye toward the edges, we are reading the way she read Thomas Browne, whom she called the first writer to prompt "the whole question, which is afterwards to become of such importance, of knowing one's author."[14]

If Milton, as Fernald reminds us, is a monumental cultural icon whom the narrator of *A Room of One's Own* prefers to forget, Woolf did not always find Milton forbidding, as Lisa Low points out in "'Listen and save': Woolf's Allusion to *Comus* in Her Revolutionary First Novel." Unlike most modernists—with the relevant exception of Joyce—she considers him useful for his Puritan "denunciation of a clerical hierarchy that can fetter the minds of a citizenry."[15] *Comus,* a work quite different from *Paradise Lost,* represents in *The Voyage Out* the possibility of the victory of female "freedom of mind" over patriarchal oppression. By weaving traces of the triumphant story of the Lady of *Comus,* who is saved by another woman, into the fateful story of Rachel Vinrace, Woolf both engages the taboo subject of sexual abuse (including the abuse she herself "suffered but cannot tell") and radically suggests "that only a community of women can save women." While male academic readers of her time were threatened by the *"self-regarding"* nature of the Lady's virtue,[16] Woolf embraced *Comus* for its resistance to a "culture of violence," thus extending, as Low notes, a tradition of appreciative female readers. As she adds, *The Voyage Out* prepares the way for Alice Walker and others to deal openly with sexual abuse.

Taking up Woolf's use of a Shakespearean song from *Cymbeline,* Diana E. Henderson argues in "Rewriting Family Ties: Woolf's Renaissance Romance" that this play functions throughout *Mrs. Dalloway* as "a model worth revising" by a modern female novelist seeking to get beyond the plots of traditional romance and imperial domination. Against the background of a struggle for empire, *Cymbeline* resolves conventional plots of love and marriage and lost siblings under a "providential cosmos in which certain social relations are seen as natural." Reuniting Clarissa with Sally Seton and Peter Walsh, either of whom could be seen as a sibling or a love interest, yet refusing romantic closure, *Mrs. Dalloway* "ironizes the relations" among Shakespeare's plot elements as well as "the naturalness of each." Further, the link between Clarissa and Septimus forged through Shakespeare's dirge suggests, if not an easy resolution to issues of war and class difference, then at least a recognition of their intractability. Within an argument that also addresses Woolf's conscious self-positioning as "Shakespeare's sister," Henderson proceeds to explore her love and grief for her brother Thoby, against whom she tested her first critical reactions to *Cymbeline*. A discussion of Septimus's shifting interpretations of *Othello* recalls Woolf's comment that "[t]o write down one's impressions of *Hamlet* as one reads it year after year, would be virtually to record one's own autobiography, for as we know more of life, so Shakespeare comments upon what we know."[17] Here Woolf echoes the Romantics, who found their own thoughts anticipated in Shakespeare;[18] within the logic of Romanticism, she uses him, in Henderson's reading, as "both an alternative source of British authority and a fluid construct" helpful in "keeping the imperial patriarchs at bay."

Fundamentally, Henderson argues, *Cymbeline*—which is both a history play and a romance—provides a suitable, if unstable, generic framework for *Mrs. Dalloway,* which similarly hovers between war story and romance. Further addressing the way Renaissance sources invade Woolf's fiction even on the level of genre, Kelly Anspaugh in "Circe Resartus: *To the Lighthouse* and William Browne of Tavistock's *Circe and Ulysses* Masque" considers an early seventeenth-century source for *To the Lighthouse*. Browne's masque is itself a "feminist" revision of Homer's episode of Ulysses and a wicked Circe: this Circe wishes only "love." Countering Ulysses' announced expectation of ill treatment, she retorts, "'Thinges farre off seene seeme not the same they are.'" And indeed, as the masque ends in revels and "a chastisement of Time," the "enemy of all festivity," no one seems interested in leaving. Claiming Mrs. Ramsay as a version of Browne's Circe, Anspaugh traces the masque throughout the novel (even reads the novel's structure as a masque) as he marks Woolf's further revisions. She transforms Browne's malevolent Triton, for example, into a "benevolent demigod" in the figure of Mr. Carmichael as he watches over Mr. Ramsay's trip to the lighthouse. By this time Lily Briscoe has assumed Circe's mantle; her painterly attention to perspective becomes a reiteration of Circe's claim about "[t]hinges farre off seene"—a Woolfian "ethical perspectivism" suggesting that one's single view is not sufficient. Finally, positing that Milton conceived of *Comus,* with its emphasis on chastity, in part "as a Puritan reaction against Browne's Epicureanism," Anspaugh argues that "Woolf brings together the antagonistic vision" of the two, "establishes harmony between them, unites them in her own artistic visioning." Such time-defying "harmony," one might add, echoes Michelet's Renaissance while it reinforces Woolf's modernist formalism.

In Anspaugh's reading of Browne's masque, the "Eternal Masculine" and the "Eternal Feminine" meet as equals. Reading *A Room of One's Own* as commentary on Petrarchan notions of "woman"—taking advantage of fluidities that recent criticism has detected in the superficially stable "male" and "female" of the Elizabethan sonnet—Rebecca Laroche in "Laura at the Crossroads: *A Room of One's Own* and the Elizabethan Sonnet" devotes attention to Woolf's "occupying, inverting, and subverting" of the sonnet as a means of "open[ing] literary history to new and female voices." Aligning the persona of a frustrated female scholar with the would-be female writer and further with the "adored and objectified" female beloved of the sonnets, Laroche first identifies a type within Woolf's text, a composite figure that seizes upon the claim of the (Petrarchan) Lady of *Comus* that "[t]hou canst not touch the freedom of my mind." Further, she reads "Judith Shakespeare" as the absent "female beloved" poet imagined and sought out by the female scholar; Judith Shakespeare is the "speculative" counterpart to Sidney Lee's all too "solid" biography of Shakespeare. Laroche argues that, "instead of throwing out the sonnet form," Woolf presents a theory of the sonnet—indeed a theory of literature—that must stay "flexible, slippery, and negotiable" if Judith Shakespeare is to "'walk among us in the flesh.'"

Laroche elucidates Woolf's ability "'to read over [male-authored] Renaissance texts . . . as if for the first time'" in order to find possibilities for female subjectivity.[19] Such "over-reading" is also important to Diane F. Gillespie in "Through Woolf's 'I's': Donne and *The Waves.*" Woolf's interest in Donne was influenced by Herbert J. C. Grierson's edition, which also inspired T. S. Eliot and an entire generation of academics. But where Eliot saw a unity of opposites, Gillespie writes, Woolf detected "multiple contradictions." Approaching fifty, questioning "what constitutes a self and what gives life meaning," she deepened her identification with Donne's "rebelliousness" while she revised him to articulate female experiences to which he could only allude. Gillespie cites the Hampton Court dinner scene as a charged "converging [of] historical moments"—the scene of the conference that resulted in the King James Bible, important to Donne's religious crises, becomes for Woolf's characters the site of reflections on "aging and loss." Conscious of the setting's three-hundred-year participation in the history of the empire, the characters nonetheless "undermine" that history, as well as their significance in it, by attending to larger forces—"'the whirling abysses of infinite space.'" Woolf's conception of Donne's "complex and fluid trajectory" meets her interest in the dynamic fields of physics and natural history to produce in *The Waves* "a ritual, an offering, an attempt to communicate the experience not only of individual but also of communal living, aging, and dying."[20]

Focusing on *Between the Acts* and the unfinished essay "Anon," David McWhirter in "Woolf, Eliot, and the Elizabethans: The Politics of Modernist Nostalgia" further investigates Woolf's project—intensified in the perilous year 1939—of envisioning a historical and literary tradition that could honor the communal and the marginal. Like Gillespie, he sees a sharp contrast between Eliot's notion of "order," forged in relation to the Renaissance, and Woolf's perception within the Elizabethan past of "an image or 'pattern' of a culture that she finally saw as celebrating difference and dialogue." Both participate, in McWhirter's reading, in what Perry Meisel termed the "myth of the modern"—each author "belatedly invest[s] the Elizabethans with a myth of original coherence and plenitude," thus positioning "modernism as a quest to regain a cultural wholeness and unity that have been lost." But Eliot wants to "refus[e] history," whereas Woolf "discover[s] in the Elizabethans a flexible vehicle for engaging the real historical crises of her time." McWhirter illustrates by comparing the Reverend Streatfield—whom he reads *as* Eliot—to Miss La Trobe, who looks to Elizabethan drama for help in "resisting [history's] current, ominous trajectory." The pageant's "chaotic" conclusion "is less a reflection of a fragmented modernity than an image of the wholeness of historical process" and a "parody of Eliot's nostalgia." Acknowledging that Woolf's Renaissance is "historical fantasy," McWhirter finds the self-consciousness with which she presents it to be productive. Although the "common voice" of "Anon" that she seeks to resurrect inevitably dies, it is reborn in "the reader"—and "it is only the birth of the reader that allows us to shape and reshape history at all."

Thus, the final chapter leaves us in Woolf's Renaissance, which could be Michelet's, "reach[ing] toward an always unconcluded future." As illustrated by her study of "Anon," the late medieval "outsider" who, as McWhirter notes, left the church to find "[t]he old Gods . . . hidden beneath the new," Woolf by the late, urgent 1930s was extending her view of "the Renaissance" along lines still consistent with Michelet's. Like the man who has been called "the first great democratic historian by virtue of his feeling for the people and his hatred of all tyranny," she persisted in seeing in the Renaissance—a time she hopefully if mistakenly called "far more elastic" than her own—the roots of an unfulfilled promise of democratic equality.[21] But on the brink of a second world war, Woolf found it difficult to muster even Michelet's wavering confidence. Having described the physical integrity of the self-supporting dome Brunelleschi designed for the cathedral in Florence, Michelet pauses to declare, "Art and reason reconciled, here is the Renaissance, the marriage of the beautiful and the true."[22] In "Craftsmanship" (1937), Woolf asks, "How can we combine the old words in new orders so that they survive, so that they create beauty, so that they tell the truth?"[23] Is it possible to join the beautiful to the true, and could something so fragile survive into the precarious future?

When Woolf in *Between the Acts* places us beside her characters and compels us to consider our own reflections, we may feel, as Michelet may make us feel in the gallery of the Louvre, that the "reality" is "too strong."[24] *What do you wish of me?* ask Leonardo's paintings. *What do you wish of yourselves?* demands Woolf's text. The mirror scene is a metaphor for, among other things, the act of reading the Renaissance—an act that links the past to the "present moment" in all its turmoil or serenity. Such a movement "*through* time via dynamic change and development" is not altogether favored in recent Renaissance criticism. American new historicism and its British counterpart, cultural materialism, share a "tendency to move *across* time" synchronically, as Margreta de Grazia writes, to probe selected moments from afar, resisting all temptation to bridge the historical gap. "We trust in fragments now instead of in wholes, in sites of dispersal rather than in continuous movement," de Grazia reflects. Diachronic readings are likely to suggest "totalities" that "might be the instruments of political totalitarianism." Since Woolf's encounters with the Renaissance, the period has been "demystified," as Barthes says in a relevant context, and subjected to "a new type of political analysis."[25]

The following chapters read Woolf reading the Renaissance differently; they find her embarked on a personal, public, and political search within literary history for "a system that [does] not shut out."[26] As resources for the study of the historical Renaissance, they will not do. But as episodes in the long history of reading the Renaissance—and as contributions to the challenge of understanding Woolf's elusive genius—they constitute fertile ground on which specialized and common readers alike may happily trespass.

∽ Notes

1. Joan Kelly, "Did Women Have a Renaissance?" in *Women, History, and Theory: The Essays of Joan Kelly* (Chicago: University of Chicago Press, 1984), 19–50, 20, 20 n. 1; Jacob Burckhardt, *The Civilization of the Renaissance in Italy* [1878]; 2d ed., revised and translated by S. G. C. Middlemore (New York: Oxford University Press, 1945). In "The Social Relations of the Sexes: Methodological Implications of Women's History," in *Women, History and Theory*, 1–18, 3, 3 n. 3, Kelly cites Burckhardt's volume as having influenced even Simone de Beauvoir's *The Second Sex* (1952) (*La Deuxième Sexe*, 1949).

2. Kelly, "Did Women Have a Renaissance?" 19.

3. Mary Wroth, *The Poems of Lady Mary Wroth*, edited by Josephine A. Roberts (Baton Rouge: Louisiana State University Press, 1983); Naomi J. Miller and Gary Waller, eds., *Reading Mary Wroth: Representing Alternatives in Early Modern England* (Knoxville: University of Tennessee Press, 1991); Aemilia Lanyer, *The Poems of Aemilia Lanyer: Salve Deus Rex Judaeorum*, edited by Susanne Woods (New York: Oxford University Press, 1993); Margaret P. Hannay, *Philip's Phoenix: Mary Sidney, Countess of Pembroke* (New York: Oxford University Press, 1990); on Elizabeth Cary and others, see Barbara Kiefer Lewalski, *Writing Women in Jacobean England* (Cambridge, Mass.: Harvard University Press, 1993). For further reading, see Kim Walker, *Women Writers of the English Renaissance* (New York: Twayne, 1996); and Louise Schleiner, *Tudor and Stuart Women Writers* (Bloomington: Indiana University Press, 1994).

4. Elizabeth H. Hageman and Sara Jayne Steen, eds., "Teaching Judith Shakespeare," *Shakespeare Quarterly* 47, no. 4 (1996).

5. Margaret J. M. Ezell, in "The Myth of Judith Shakespeare: Creating the Canon of Women's Literature in the Twentieth Century," chap. 2 of *Writing Women's Literary History* (Baltimore: Johns Hopkins University Press, 1993), cites the 1985 *Norton Anthology of Literature by Women,* edited by Sandra Gilbert and Susan Gubar, as the most influential of these anthologies.

6. Virginia Woolf, *A Room of One's Own* (1929; reprint, with a foreword by Mary Gordon, New York: Harcourt Brace Jovanovich [Harvest], 1989), 4.

7. Juliet Dusinberre, *Virginia Woolf's Renaissance: Woman Reader or Common Reader?* (Iowa City: University of Iowa Press, 1997).

8. Harold Bloom's theory of "anxiety of influence" has been applied to Woolf, most notably by Sandra Gilbert and Susan Gubar in *Madwoman in the Attic: The Woman Writer and the Nineteenth-Century Literary Imagination* (New Haven, Conn.: Yale University Press, 1979), but also by Perry Meisel in *The Absent Father: Virginia Woolf and Walter Pater* (New Haven, Conn.: Yale University Press, 1980). For an argument that such an analysis is not necessarily appropriate to a modernist reading the Renaissance, see Reed Way Dasenbrock, *Imitating the Italians: Wyatt, Spenser, Synge, Pound, Joyce* (Baltimore: Johns Hopkins University Press, 1991), esp. 8–9. For a helpful discussion of "intertextuality" versus "influence," see Susan Stanford Friedman, "Weavings: Intertextuality and the (Re)Birth of the Author," in *Influence and Intertextuality in Literary History,* edited by Jay Clayton and Eric Rothstein (Madison: University of Wisconsin Press, 1991), 146–80, esp. 152 for the concept of "active negotiation."

9. Dusinberre, 45.

10. Woolf, *Night and Day* (1919; reprint, New York: Harcourt Brace Jovanovich [Harvest], 1973), 130, 135.

11. "Suspended Judgment" is the title of a chapter in which Montaigne appears in Pater's unfinished novel *Gaston de Latour* [1896], edited by Gerald Monsman (Greensboro, N.C.: ELT Press, 1995).

12. Walter Raleigh, "The Age of Elizabeth," in *Shakespeare's England* (Oxford: Clarendon Press, 1916), 1:4; Lytton Strachey, *Elizabeth and Essex: A Tragic History* (New York: Harcourt, Brace, 1928), 16.

13. Walter Benjamin, "The Storyteller" (1936), in *Illuminations,* edited and with an introduction by Hannah Arendt, translated by Harry Zohn (New York: Schocken Books, 1969), 98, 91.

14. Ibid., 92; Woolf, "Reading" (1919), in *The Essays of Virginia Woolf,* 4 (of 6) vols. to date, edited by Andrew McNeillie (London: Hogarth Press, 1986–94), 3:141–61, 156.

15. Patrick Colm Hogan, *Joyce, Milton, and the Theory of Influence* (Gainesville: University Press of Florida, 1995), 63; thanks to Lisa Low for this reference.

16. See Herbert J. C. Grierson, *Cross Currents in English Literature of the XVIIth Century* [1929], rev. ed. (London: Chatto and Windus, 1958), 244–45, endorsing the sentiment of C. H. Herford in *Dante and Milton* (1924).

17. Woolf, "Charlotte Brontë" (1916), in *Essays,* 2:26–31, 27.

18. See S. Schoenbaum's chapter on the Romantics in *Shakespeare's Lives* [1970], rev. ed. (New York: Oxford University Press, 1991), 181–89.

19. Carol Thomas Neely, suggesting new directions for contemporary Renaissance feminism in "Constructing the Subject: Feminist Practice and the New Renaissance

Discourses," *English Literary Renaissance* 18 (1988): 15, quoted in Barbara L. Estrin, *Laura: Uncovering Gender and Genre in Wyatt, Donne, and Marvell* (Durham, N.C.: Duke University Press, 1994), 15.

20. Woolf's curiosity about new discoveries in physics and the natural sciences is the ongoing subject of Gillian Beer's perceptive criticism; see generally *Virginia Woolf: The Common Ground* (Ann Arbor: University of Michigan Press, 1996).

21. Wallace Ferguson, *The Renaissance in Historical Thought: Five Centuries of Interpretation* (Cambridge, Mass.: Riverside Press, 1948), 174; Woolf, "The Niece of an Earl" (1928), in *The Second Common Reader* [1932], edited by Andrew McNeillie (New York: Harcourt Brace Jovanovich [Harvest], 1986), 214–19, 218. Michelet's commitment to France as *patrie*, however, was more pronounced than Woolf's love of her country, complicated as her feelings were by her pacifism and feminism.

22. Jules Michelet, *Renaissance et Réforme. Histoire de France au XVIe siècle* [1855–56], with a preface by Claude Mettra (Paris: Robert Laffont, 1982), 64: "L'art et la raison réconciliés, voilá la Renaissance, le mariage du beau et du vrai." Translation mine.

23. Woolf, "Craftsmanship" (1937), in *The Death of the Moth and Other Essays*, edited by Leonard Woolf (1942; reprint, New York: Harcourt Brace Jovanovich [Harvest], 1974), 198–207, 204.

24. Woolf, *Between the Acts* (1941; reprint, New York: Harcourt Brace Jovanovich [Harvest], 1970), 179.

25. Margreta de Grazia, "*Fin-de-Siècle* Renaissance England," in Fins de Siècle: *English Poetry in 1590, 1690, 1790, 1890, 1990*, edited by Elaine Scarry (Baltimore: Johns Hopkins University Press, 1995), 55 (emphasis in original); Roland Barthes, citing the rise of Marxism to "separate us" from Michelet, in "Michelet, Today" (1972), in *The Rustle of Language*, translated by Richard Howard (Berkeley: University of California Press, 1989), 205–6.

26. Woolf, *The Diary of Virginia Woolf*, edited by Anne Olivier Bell and Andrew McNeillie, 5 vols. (New York: Harcourt Brace Jovanovich, 1977–84), 4:127 (2 October 1932).

Rereading,
Remembering the
Renaissance

1

~

Michelet, Woolf, and
the Idea of the Renaissance

~ Sally Greene

On or about September 1980, with the introduction of Stephen Greenblatt's *Renaissance Self-Fashioning* into college classrooms, our conception of the Renaissance changed. The very name for the period of European history that in Britain roughly coincides with the sixteenth century was "supplemented," as Leah Marcus recalled in 1992, by the term "early modern." The new designation was intended to establish a purifying distance from the period that was once—naively, it had come to appear—considered "a time of re-naissance, cultural rebirth, the reawakening of an earlier era conceived of as (in some sense) classic." For Marcus, who spoke for a generation "redrawing the boundaries" of scholarship, the word's stale connotations of "rebirth and renewal" evoked merely some "marvelous ideas" bought "at too great a price—the neglect of other cultural currents and forms of cultural production, a vast sea of human activity and misery that *Renaissance* either failed to include or included only marginally."[1]

As Marcus had written in her 1988 study of Shakespeare, the once progressive claim that literature had the power to enlighten something called "human nature" had become, after the political turmoil of the 1960s and 1970s, identified with a lifeless formalism: "For many scholars and students of that era, the formalist enclosure of art was not just barren but reckless and irresponsible." The "transcendent subject" for which Ben Jonson's construction of Shakespeare as "author" had so successfully argued no longer speaks to us, according to Marcus, for "we have developed an appetite for dissonance, for an art which is multicentric, shifting, provisional, implicated in other things."[2]

As fruitful as it has been for the current generation of Renaissance scholars, the sea change initiated by new historicism and other varieties of materialist criticism was launched as a reaction to a very different Renaissance from that which Virginia Woolf imagined. Although she could write of human nature, the literary classics, and even the transcendent genius of Shakespeare without embarrassment or qualification, she was also acutely conscious of what Melba Cuddy-Keane usefully calls "the varieties of historicist experience." Woolf approached the past with more questions than assumptions; her historical sense, Cuddy-Keane points out, was "dynamic."[3] Further, the Renaissance as Woolf found it, beginning with the obscure "Elizabethan prose writers" whom she "loved first & most wildly,"[4] was less monolithic than recent criticism implies. Certainly it was open to liberal as well as conservative interpretations, and its relevance to the revolutionary project of modernism (or to what she often called simply the "present moment") was a given. Perhaps most important for understanding Woolf's purposes, it had hardly solidified into a "period" at all.

If we are to appreciate the depth and significance of Woolf's creative interventions in the debate over the ever-changing meaning of "the Renaissance," we need first to consider the numerous ways in which the period was being understood when she came to it as a rebellious child of the Victorians. It was not the writing of Jacob Burckhardt, the most commonly cited source for the now discredited notion of a not-so-universal "Renaissance man,"[5] so much as the infinitely more slippery works of Jules Michelet—himself a child of the French Revolution—that significantly colored her understanding. The following brief consideration of Renaissance historiography in the nineteenth and early twentieth centuries, followed in turn by a discussion of the strongly romantic, visionary Renaissance of Michelet, as Woolf received and reconceived it, will help us to see how avant-garde her idea of the Renaissance was and, perhaps, continues to be.

Although credit for the notion of a "renaissance" as a rebirth of cultural knowledge after a long period of benightedness usually goes to Petrarch, it was not until nineteenth-century historians employed the term that it began commonly to apply to a whole historical period, as opposed to various movements in the arts and sciences. In England, the consolidation of "the Renaissance," together with its denomination as the site of the birth of the Burckhardtian "individual," occurred as part of the larger process of historical periodization that also began in the nineteenth century. Lately periodization itself "has become somewhat unfashionable," as Margreta de Grazia mildly puts it, thanks to our renewed understanding of at least some of the political and social forces that motivated it.[6] In particular, Burckhardt's promulgation of the Renaissance as "'the beginning of the modern era'" is today seen by de Grazia and others as a "nervous response" to historical movements "that were shaking the subject at its foundations." And yet, as J. B. Bullen reminds us in *The Myth of the Renaissance in Nineteenth-Century Writing*, Burckhardt's *Civilization of the Renaissance in Italy*, published in 1860 but not translated into English until 1878, was neither the first nor the last word.[7]

When the term "Renaissance" entered the English language from the French, around 1860, a battle over its meaning had already been imported. This "highly politicized" Renaissance reflected divisions in post-Revolutionary France between conservative defenders of state-sanctioned Catholicism, accentuated by the Jesuits who were by 1843 campaigning for control of the schools, and the liberal intellectual community, represented by Michelet and another historian, Edgar Quinet. As Bullen writes, "For the Church party it appeared to be an aggressively secular movement and the embodiment of religious infidelity" following the piety of the Middle Ages, while "to the secular wing it epitomized man's successful and heroic struggle against repressive dogmatism."[8] In England the controversy continued, although the force of Protestantism—especially vocal around 1850 when the Roman Catholic hierarchy was reinstated[9]—complicated the question of whose side God favored. John Ruskin and Walter Pater, both nominally Protestant, exemplified the opposite extremes. In fact, despite strong religious overtones, in England the issue was joined more on political, cultural, and even personal grounds. Those who, like Pater, embraced the Renaissance were reacting less against Catholicism than against "moral orthodoxies which were felt to be repressive, dogmatic, and conformist."[10]

Moreover, these debates were explicitly public, not academic. Not until John Addington Symonds's multivolume treatment of the period, which began appearing in 1875, did the "polemicization" of the Renaissance in England begin its gradual turn toward "professionalization" in the universities.[11] But in spite of the creeping professionalism, even into the early twentieth century the defining of the Renaissance was largely the province of novelists and "men of letters" writing to influence wide audiences. On the one hand was Ruskin, for whom the Renaissance "towers . . . like some terrible incubus in the history of the West."[12] On the other were the generative uses of the period in the historical novels of Charles Kingsley, George Eliot, and others, culminating in Pater's aesthetic embrace of "the Renaissance" as a "complex, many-sided movement" that represented the "outbreak of the human spirit."[13]

An important characteristic shared by these emerging "Renaissances" is that they are "mythic," in the sense in which Hayden White has taught us to understand the term. They are, as Bullen observes, "intimately dependent upon rhetorical strategies and literary devices."[14] Accordingly, Ruskin's Renaissance begins not in Rome or Florence but, idiosyncratically, in Venice, a city to which he had a "personal, psycho-sexual attachment"; he pictures the city as a fallen woman who "in her decline" is "the source of the Renaissance."[15] The Renaissance, in turn, becomes a "foul torrent" that "swept . . . away" the edifices of the Middle Ages, spoiling "all unity and principle." Or it is even colder, more barren: "the Renaissance frosts came, and all perished."[16]

Ruskin's vivid depictions, despite their negative cast, were turned to positive advantage by writers eager to attempt the popular genre of historical fiction. Through their engagement with the Renaissance, in fact, Victorian novelists combined explorations of British nationhood with the investigation of a topic of increasing, if vexed, importance—the emergence of "the self" as "a complex organism with the power to transcend its organic roots."[17] In contrast to Ruskin's curiously "unpeopled" Renaissance, these writers are often aligned with Burckhardt, who was to say that in Italy "a thousand figures meet us each in its own special shape and dress." Having had "individualism" thrust upon them, in Burckhardt's reading, by the conditions of feudal despotism, these people "were forced to know all the inward resources of their own nature." If individualism "[i]n itself . . . is neither good nor bad, but necessary," there was at least the possibility of turning it to the good in a new atmosphere of "worldliness" that "was not frivolous, but earnest, and was ennobled by art and poetry."[18]

In particular it was a new edition of Hakluyt's *Voyages* that inspired Kingsley to set *Westward Ho!* (1855) in the heroic Elizabethan age.[19] Against the contemporary contexts of the Crimean War, which he supported, and the revival of the Catholic hierarchy, which as an Anglican cleric he opposed, Kingsley revisits the nation's defining moment in the defeat of the Armada. The conflict between Protestant England and Catholic Spain is played out in an epic tale of high-seas adventure. Rose Salterne, the heroine, disappoints her several suitors by eloping with a Spanish officer who, although respecting her Protestantism, cannot protect her from a duplicitous English Jesuit. She dies in the Inquisition. But Amyas Leigh, the stalwart English hero, has the privilege of executing the bishop who had ordered her death, and his participation in the rout of the Armada ensures a providential ending. Kingsley's message, one critic writes, is that "individuals and nations doing their duty serve a cause larger than they can realize."[20]

George Eliot, while resisting the notion that "the individual" burst forth in the Renaissance, makes in *Romola* (1862–63) an intensive investigation of selfhood in the ambivalent context of the private lives of characters caught up in the public controversies of late fifteenth-century Florence. As suggested by its psychologized treatment of Savonarola—a perplexing figure about whom it was hard, even in Eliot's day, to be neutral[21]—this novel is preoccupied not with religious differences (or with English nationalism) but with human dilemmas arising from the period's "new liberty of thought and behavior."[22] Romola, the one character capable of channeling her will within a sympathetic engagement with others, must confront her father, an idealistic scholar whose narrowness is symbolized by his blindness; her husband, a handsome but cunning Greek who becomes "'the mere instrument of changing schemes'";[23] and Savonarola, whose righteous but dogmatic proclamations lead her to some lonely soul-searching. For all its period detail, *Romola* brings to the Renaissance distinctly nineteenth-century questions (as Leslie Stephen early recognized). And its prophetic, romantic end, in which Romola advocates "wide thoughts, and much feeling for the rest of the world," suggests an equally nineteenth-century solution: a longing, even through a dark period, for society's "egotism" to turn to "altruism."[24]

Eliot was among those whose interest in the Italian Renaissance was per-versely inspired by Ruskin.[25] But it was Pater who most thoroughly revised Ruskin's moral disapproval (as well as Matthew Arnold's) in ways that would prove particularly fruitful for Woolf and others of her generation.[26] His *Studies in the History of the Renaissance* (1873, 1877, 1888, 1893) reflected what was already "a highly personal myth" of the period.[27] In "Coleridge's Writings" (1866) he associates the Renaissance, as Quinet and Michelet had, with progres-sive resistance to medieval scholasticism: "The Catholic church and humanity are two powers that divide the intellect and the spirit of man." The Renaissance becomes for Pater "a 'movement' rather than a specific period," writes Bullen, with "profound implications for the present."[28] Indeed, the implications of his own theories led him away from the idea that the Renaissance was defined by a clean break from the Middle Ages. The outlines of *The Renaissance* suggest that "the Renaissance" was a process of discovery that could happen any time.[29]

Like Michelet (as we shall see) and in direct opposition to Ruskin, Pater undertakes a biographical approach. Pico della Mirandola, for example, is seen to have contributed in his oration on "the dignity of man" to "that rehabilita-tion of human nature, the body, the senses, the heart, the intelligence, which the Renaissance fulfils." And biography quickly becomes psychobiography: Leonardo da Vinci both embodies and depicts a series of mental states. His subjects, "[n]ervous, electric, faint always with some inexplicable faintness," appear "to feel powers at work in the common air unfelt by others, to become, as it were, the receptacle of them, and pass them on to us in a chain of secret influences." [30]

Pater's attention to these moments of revelation is what leads, in the con-clusion of *The Renaissance,* to his famous pronouncement on the flaming "gem-like" quality of life at its fullest, the steadily "inward" movement of our "im-pressions" until, finally, "[n]ot the fruit of experience, but experience itself, is the end."[31] And yet, having in one sense succeeded in severing the ties of art to society, by so emphasizing the subjectivity of interpretation Pater posed a challenge to late Victorian culture—a rationalist culture that would not easily give way to this modern view.[32] In the early twentieth century, Pater's hopeful Renaissance existed side-by-side with Ruskin's perception of it as a time of cultural decline, as replayed in the late works of Arnold and again in T. S. Eliot; and with Kingsley's patriotic reenactment of the fall of the Armada, as revisited, for example, in a book portraying fallen World War I soldiers as *The New Elizabethans*.[33] It is surely relevant that *Westward Ho!* was reissued in the United States in 1941, the year of Pearl Harbor.

No reader of Virginia Woolf needs to be told where in this debate her sympathies lay. Her disappointment in the emerging professionalism of Renaissance studies is evident in a disenchantment with the professor Walter Raleigh, who devolves from esteemed editor of Hakluyt to a pedant satirized across three centuries in *Orlando*.[34] In *Orlando*'s opening scenes, Woolf burlesques Ruskin's "frosty" Renaissance, melting the frozen waters of the Thames into a liberating "torrent" of energy. That this episode also draws on Thomas Dekker's reportorial account of strange icy weather on the Thames only begins to suggest the ways in which her uses of the Renaissance are layered, even overdetermined—and marked by loving, playful embrace.[35] (Such a dangerous trifle was *Orlando* that E. M. W. Tillyard began his wartime polemic *The Elizabethan World Picture* by dismissing it.)[36]

Too modern, too self-conscious of the difficulties of historical reconstruction to write conventional historical fiction, Woolf uses the Renaissance— overtly in *Orlando*, more subtly elsewhere—as a testing ground for a series of radical reconceptions of Western culture. Perhaps under the broad influence of Burckhardt, whose ideas are echoed by writers as varied as Lytton Strachey, Walter Raleigh, and H. G. Wells, to name a few of her contemporaries, she seems to have taken somewhat seriously the suggestion that "the individual" began with the Renaissance. Not only are the long-lived Orlando and Judith Shakespeare both "Elizabethans" by birth; both the first and the second volumes of *The Common Reader* begin with essays, written for those collections, that explore Elizabethan literature as a basis for moving chronologically toward the contemporary moment.[37] But Woolf's Renaissance, as I have already suggested, is not Burckhardt's. White has successfully argued that his history is ironic "satire," that for Burckhardt "there was no *progressive* evolution in artistic sensibility." "The truths taught by history were melancholy ones. They led neither to hope nor to action."[38] Woolf's Renaissance—in the tradition of George Eliot's, Pater's, and especially Michelet's—is "romantic." That is to say, among other things, that it has not yet fully come to pass.

Thanks to books by Alison Booth and Perry Meisel, Woolf's debts to Eliot and Pater are firmly established. In a perceptive comparison of *Romola* and

Orlando, Booth usefully cites Elizabeth Barrett Browning's Italy as an intertext shared by "the erudite historical romance and the belletristic *jeu d'esprit.*"[39] And when Meisel reads Pater on Michelangelo beside Woolf on Gibbon, he aptly finds both to be "unmooring their respective subjects from the particularities of time, place, and even symbolism" as they seek to "trace" a "movement of temperament" from these subjects into their own consciousness, finally to "record," in Woolf's famous phrase, "the atoms as they fall upon the mind."[40] But beyond this inclination toward a pure aesthetics, I believe Woolf relished Pater's understanding of the Renaissance as productively "uncertain" in a social sense. Calling it "that movement in which, in various ways, the human mind wins for itself a new kingdom of feeling and sensation and thought, not opposed to but only beyond and independent of the spiritual system then actually realized," Pater adds that "within the enchanted region of the Renaissance, one needs not be for ever on one's guard," for "there are no fixed parties, no exclusions."[41] Similarly, Woolf saw the Renaissance as a founding yet also renewable moment; its liberating spirit supported her feminist politics as well as her modernist aesthetic.

In passages such as those above, paeans to "that outbreak of the reason and the imagination, . . . that assertion of the liberty of the heart," Pater best illustrates the influence of Michelet, whose Renaissance in turn is colored by the radical fervor of the French Revolution.[42] Woolf also read widely in Michelet's *Histoire de France,* drawn to it again and again over a period of thirty years. In 1915 she declared, apparently referring to his volumes on the Renaissance and the Reformation, that his work was "superb, and the only tolerable history." She intuited much that has since been theorized about the poetic or performative nature of historical narrative: in 1928 she wrote to her nephew Julian Bell, "I am reading Michelets History of France—God knows why. I find it fascinating, but wholly fictitious. Do you think any history is even faintly true?"[43] Striking parallels between her work and his leave no doubt that the makeup of what I have elsewhere called Woolf's Renaissance imaginary is deeply influenced by Michelet's visionary reconstructions.[44] In the end, it is a Renaissance of her own. But of its many cultural backdrops, the most compelling is Michelet's "heroic" sixteenth century.

With a chair in *histoire et morale* at the Collège de France, Michelet (1798–1874) was certainly a professional scholar, but that status tells us little today. He was a passionate public intellectual who, as Linda Orr writes, envisioned history prophetically "as a new, dynamic genre" through which he might "instill in a new generation the forgotten ideals of 1789."[45] Indeed the rhythms of his writing life, like those of his career, are tied to successive outbreaks and suppressions of republicanism. In the first volumes of the *Histoire de France,* for example, he had romanticized the Middle Ages as a period of *haute harmonie,* in consonance with his optimism following the July Revolution of 1830. But the "citizen king" Louis Philippe responded to further insurrections by adopting repressive measures, including the Jesuit play for control of the schools mentioned earlier.[46] In 1843 Michelet suspended his epic history project in order to write a history specifically of the Revolution, which came out in seven volumes, concluding in 1853. By then the republicans had seen yet another triumph, the Second Republic of 1848, dashed by Louis Napoleon's December 1851 *coup d'état* and the resulting Second Empire. Having lost his job for rejecting Napoleon's loyalty oath, Michelet returned to the *Histoire de France.* At this point the Renaissance emerges as a release from the Catholic *Moyen Age,* which has become "a world of illusion."[47]

Michelet's Renaissance is the saga of repeated attempts of the human spirit to wrest itself from oppressive medieval systems. Although much of its delight stems from a merciless irony deployed against insufferable scholastics, the overriding "mode of emplotment," to use White's term, is that of romantic comedy.[48] For Michelet, the moment of comic release had happened in 1789. With the promise of that *éclat* slipping painfully away, he seeks solace and inspiration elsewhere. "Ce livre . . . n'est pas écrit pour faire peine aux mourants," he writes, alluding to his revised Middle Ages. "C'est un appel aux forces vives." His new subject encompasses "la découverte du monde, la découverte de l'homme," and consequently that of the power of human will. "L'histoire, qui n'est pas moins que l'intelligence de la vie," Michelet writes, "elle devait nous vivifier, elle nous a alanguis au contraire, nous faisant croire que les temps est tout, et la volonté peu de chose."[49] The Renaissance, because of its sporadic progress, offers ample illustration of *la volonté* at work. "La révolution du XVIᵉ siècle, arrivée plus de cent ans après le décès de la philosophie d'alors, recontra une mort incroyable, un néant, et partit de rien," he writes. "Elle fut le jet héroïque d'une immense volonté." Indeed, "Le xvie siècle est un héros."[50]

The Renaissance ought to have begun in the twelfth century, in Michelet's reading, but something separated the classes and the "voix du peuple" became drained of emotion: "on ne songe plus à l'oreille, mais plutôt aux yeux. On écrit pour le cabinet," he complains, in words echoed by Woolf as she describes Victorian as opposed to Elizabethan drama.[51] Through "[d]es abdications successives de l'indépendance humaine," only tedious scholasticism endures. To save itself, "[l]'esprit . . . se mit à voler. Il s'appuya des puissances d'amour et de seconde vue qui permettent au génie d'atteindre la vérité lointaine et d'anticiper l'avenir."[52] The first coup of the Renaissance occurs, according to Michelet, in the field that could most easily elude the surveillance of the church: art. Giotto "avait laissé les types consacrés, les insipides et muettes figures du Moyen Age, pour peindre ce qu'il voyait, d'ardentes têtes italiennes, de belles et vivantes madones." In Florence Brunelleschi revolutionizes architecture by applying the laws of physics, while to the north Van Eyck "fait flamboyer la vie dans cette brûlante peinture qui pâlit l'autre, et l'envoya, ombre ennuyeuse, dormir près de la scolastique."[53]

Turning to Leonardo da Vinci, Michelet invites us to experience the powerful attraction that has claimed his own imagination. "Entrez au Musée du Louvre," he bids us: "à gauche vous avez l'ancien monde, le nouveau à droite." The "défaillantes figures du frère Angelico de Fiesole," who with their "regards malades et mourants semblent pourtant chercher, vouloir," are opposed to Leonardo's pictures, which impart "le génie de la Renaissance, en sa plus âpre inquiétude, en son plus perçant aiguillon. Entre ces choses contemporaines," Michelet asserts, "il y a plus d'un millier d'années." And he commands our direct confrontation with this scene:

> Bacchus, saint Jean et la Joconde dirigent leurs regards vers vous; vous êtes fascinés et troublés, un infini agit sur vous par un étrange magnétisme. Art, nature, avenir, génie de mystère et de découverte, maître des profondeurs du monde, de l'abîme inconnu des âges, parlez, que voulez-vous de moi? Cette toile m'attire, m'appelle, m'envahit, m'absorbe; je vais à elle malgré moi, comme l'oiseau va au serpent.[54]

But following this seductive internal dialogue, he shifts abruptly to point out that the day is not yet won. "Galilée est loin encore." Leonardo—with Brunelleschi and Van Eyck, with Gutenberg and Columbus—suffers for his "grande solitude." "Un abîme reste évidemment entre ces cinq ou six hommes, les héros de la volonté, et la foule, misérablement entravée et arriérée, qui ne peut se soulever du Moyen Age gothique et de l'aplatissement du XVe siècle."[55]

The one significant mass event that has taken place is the rise of the bourgeoisie, "rien qu'une classe amphibie, bâtarde, servilement imitatrice, qui ne veut que faire fortune et devenir une noblesse." With their prosperity comes anxiety, followed by a destructive frivolity. When the church service is adorned by the *serpent,* a baroque instrument noisier than a dozen drunkards, is it any wonder that thoughts fly elsewhere? "Croyez-vous donc, idiots, qu'on retienne lié dans un sac l'insaisissable lutin, l'éther de la pensée humaine?" The answer to such a dangerous question Michelet denies having uttered; "non, l'homme que voici est loin, très loin, partout aileurs." At the fairy oak, he safeguards "l'indépendante tradition des cultes que vous croyez éteints." Quietly, the human spirit has retreated to "la consolante mère, la Nature."[56]

But whether it is the nature of "la blanche Diane" or that of one of the more obscure "faux dieux" is uncertain; the narrative's moral outlines become precarious here. As we follow the favorite prey of the Inquisition, the *sorcières,* as they answer to "justice" under the terrorism of the German monk Sprenger, it is reassuring to know that even Roland Barthes admits that, while "intelligible on the level of each sentence," Michelet's prose can be frustratingly "enigmatic on the level of discourse."[57] Clearly Michelet sympathizes with woman, who "est dans la réalité la victime de ce monde sur laquelle tous les maux retombent." He understands why "elle rôde sur la prairie déserte, . . . le fiel au coeur et maudissante." When "Dieu ne lui parlait qu'en latin, en symboles incompréhensibles," the Devil, who "parlait par la nature," became a more amiable companion. But as her "volonté violente," her "infini de haines," leads her to perform "l'avortement que subit la dédaigneuse qui la regarde avec dégoût," as a "royauté de terreur" courses through her, the text induces a kind of vertigo, to use a favorite word of Michelet's.[58] Only after much confusion between what Barthes identifies as "the three great historical states of the witch: latent (the serf's wife), triumphant (the priestess), decadent (the professional)" does Michelet point out that the belief that the Devil can enter human form is itself a falling off from the *bon sens* of the twelfth century. The scandal of more recent times—in Michelet, who translated Vico, it is often impossible to pinpoint the time—is that humanity's "faibles yeux ne font pas la différence de la nature créée de Dieu à la nature créée du Diable. . . . Une terrible incertitude planera sur toute chose."[59]

Across the four volumes of Michelet's history of the Renaissance and the Reformation, its *incertitude* remains. But also constant is his theory of why its achievements are so singular: "Les efforts des héros, des hardis précurseurs, sont restés individuels, isolés, impuissants" because "[l]e peuple n'est pas né qui eût pu les soutenir." Michelet's history is something other than a Carlylian pageant of "great men"; it is a call, issuing out of the past to the present, for the living spirit of *la Renaissance* to rise up collectively, *as a body*. Do not give up, Michelet admonishes the age, figured female now dramatically as well as grammatically. "Non, va, marche, sois confiante, entre [l'avenir] sans t'effrayer. Qu'un seul mot te rassure: *Un monde d'humanité commence, de sympathie universelle.*"[60]

In the conclusion to the fourth volume, the still prophetic narrative of the *héros* turns intimate, contradictory. Luther and Calvin are paired against Rabelais and Copernicus as "deux rameaux d'un même arbre" bearing "la Réforme et la Renaissance, aïeules des libertés modernes." Together this imagery comprises "l'unité moderne du XVIᵉ siècle." In the end, "il est une personne. On a pu tracer son portrait." Further, in the aftermath of the corporate martyrdom of the Saint Bartholomew's Day Massacre, there emerges—in ways not imagined by the unsuspecting Catholic church, complacent in its victory—a new Protestantism "qui embrasse le monde même, celui de la raison, de l'équité, de la science."[61] Michelet's final trope, however, retreats from the openly political to a lyrical *éternel retour* as it recalls the lost songs of the late Middle Ages.[62] Writing about Palestrina, his last example of the isolated genius of the Renaissance, he claims to find again "[l]'*harmonie*, le chant en parties, la concorde des voix libres et cependant fraternelles, ce beau mystère de l'art moderne." But the new music of Palestrina lacks a following. "Ses mélodies mélancoliques" are "prisonnières" in the Sistine Chapel, only to be misunderstood by Michelangelo's watchful figures. "Ils l'écoutent et gémissent, les géants indomptables. . . . Ces accents ne sont pas les leurs. Leur génie tout viril rayonne d'un bien autre avenir." The century's dominant theme has become religious war, and Michelet is left bitter. Yet he is not hopeless. "Tuer quinze millions d'hommes par la faim et l'épée, à la bonne heure, cela se peut. Mais faire un petit chant, un air aimé de tous. . . . Ce chant peut-être à l'aube jaillira d'un coeur simple, ou l'alouette le trouvera en montant au soleil, de son sillon d'avril."[63]

With the promised resurrection of Judith Shakespeare among a growing sisterhood of professionals—laboratory scientists as well as writers—Woolf continues Michelet's reasonable dream. "Elle se cherche à tâtons, elle ne se sait pas, ne se tient pas encore," says Michelet of *la Renaissance;* Woolf's narrative anticipates the time when "the dead poet who was Shakespeare's sister will put on the body which she has so often laid down." Like Michelet, Woolf celebrates—with all the accuracy of poetry—the possibility of individual achievement, while holding that genius is the result of "many years of thinking in common, of thinking by the body of the people."[64] And like Michelet, who scorned the socialism of his time, she has at times been criticized for not being political enough. She could claim that the roots of change "lie not so much in Acts of Parliament as in a [Shakespearean] song or two."[65] Hearts and minds are to be swayed individually, not through institutionalized approaches.

And in this regard she shares with Michelet a particular conception, now almost foreign to academic readers (but perhaps not to common readers), of "the self," of its ethical obligation to itself and to others.[66] In the unfinished essay "Byron and Mr. Briggs," Woolf seats Terence Hewet, "alone in a tumultuous frame of mind," before Shakespeare's *Troilus and Cressida,* where he must use "the utmost agility of imagination" as he faces the "thousand questions" that will confront him. Though he will fail to find "the lesson," he will participate in a shared quest for the means "to live more fully and completely." Woolf's notion that "the writers of England and the readers of England are necessary to one another" reflects a belief that "we make a world of literature and that this world is inseparable from the world of the hearth rug and of the pavement."[67]

Woolf's Renaissance, as Alice Fox has shown, begins like Kingsley's with the Elizabethans, as depicted in Hakluyt and providentially interpreted in Froude.[68] But those sixteenth-century voyages, so easily translated to later military conquests made in the name of divine providence, in Woolf take revolutionary turns in other directions: ultimately she blends Michelet's Romanticism into a modernist vision of her own. The contrast between her twentieth-century Renaissance and that of the Victorians is clearly seen, for example, in the early novel *Night and Day* (1919).[69] Against Mr. and Mrs. Hilbery, who prefer Ruskin to living writers, who uphold a Burckhardtian "civilization" in the face of modern barbarities, are set Katharine Hilbery and Ralph Denham, drawn together by their dreams. Ralph rejects "the worship of greatness in the nineteenth century" (20) in favor of "strange voyages," dreams in which "he figured in nimble and romantic parts, but self-glorification was not the only motive of them. They gave outlet to some spirit" by which he thought "he could set flowering waste tracts of the earth, cure many ills" (127). Katharine's "dream state," set specifically in Elizabethan England, "was a place where feelings were liberated from the constraint which the real world puts upon them." Joined by a "magnanimous hero, . . . they swept together among the leaf-hung trees of an unknown world" (141). She and Ralph agree that their "'notion of perfect happiness'" would be a cottage with "'the sea not very far off, so that one could hear the waves at night. Ships vanishing on the horizon'" (334).

What shifts their romantic vision toward a modern conception of the Renaissance is their awareness of illusion—of the illusion of all dreams, even, or perhaps especially, the dream of perfect love: "The fragmentary nature of their relationship was but too apparent" (473). (William Rodney, meanwhile, treats Katharine as a Shakespearean Rosalind; he writes her sonnets.) In an urgent attempt to overcome the "lapses" (473) that mar their conversations, Ralph writes her a note defending an ideal of "communication," such "communion" being at least a window upon other worlds, even "a world such as he had had a glimpse of the other evening when together they seemed to be sharing something, creating something, an ideal—a vision flung out in advance of our actual circumstances." Finally he resorts to "draw[ing] little figures in the blank spaces, heads meant to resemble her head, blots fringed with flames meant to represent—perhaps the entire universe" (487). Katharine responds only to the "'little dot with the flames around it,'" saying, "'Yes, the world looks something like that to me too'" (493).

The resolution of this comic novel is deferred, as it must be if it is to be faithful to Woolf's open-ended vision. Katharine and Ralph "lack[] the unity of phrases fashioned by the old believers." But out of this loss comes an achievement. "Together, they groped in this difficult region, where the unfinished, the unfulfilled, the unwritten, the unreturned, came together in their ghostly way and wore the semblance of the complete and the satisfactory" (506). Just as Pater's Michelangelo "gains by leaving nearly all of his sculpture in a puzzling sort of incompleteness," by compelling the viewer to imagine the "spirit in the thing [that] seems always on the point of breaking out,"[70] so Woolf poises us on the brink of our own discoveries. As in Michelet's France, in *Night and Day* and throughout Woolf's work the imagined future threatens to break in, "more splendid than ever from this construction of the present" (506).

In our own poststructuralist present, when historians, philosophers, and literary critics scrupulously and with ample reason suppress even the desire for a "unity of phrases," for fear that such an impulse might imply a closed totality of meaning, we need to ask one final question: Does Woolf's idea of the Renaissance have anything valuable left to offer, or is it simply a relic, though an interesting one, of a quirky strain of modernism, the underside of Eliot?[71] Some recent impatience with the reliance of materialist criticism on the synchronic method—in which a discrete textual passage is analyzed in its immediate context, with the distance and at times the dispassion of a scientist—suggests that Woolf, with her insistence on the direct bearing of Renaissance literature (indeed all literature) upon the living moment, indeed has substance to add to contemporary conversations.

"Is it not possible to think of historicity as a relation less discretely periodized, one that emerges over time between any text and subsequent generations of readers?" asked Wai Chee Dimock in 1997 as she proposed, as an alternative to the synchronic, "a diachronic historicism." Woolf herself had observed, in approaching Sidney's *Arcadia* some three hundred years after its creation, that "[e]ach [intervening reader] has read differently, with the insight and the blindness of his own generation." Able "to read through multiple historical lenses," as Cuddy-Keane puts it, Woolf recognizes that distance may invite usable new meaning even while it distorts the old. Dimock's "theory of resonance," which "allows texts to be seen as objects that do a lot of traveling: across space and especially across time" and therefore supports her claim for "literature as a democratic institution," is anticipated in Woolf's essay "Craftsmanship." There she praises the "highly democratic" way in which words elude definition: "they hate anything that stamps them with one meaning or confines them to one attitude, for it is their nature to change."[72]

Further, Woolf's dialogic theories of reading, often worked out in her essays in relation to Renaissance literature,[73] are implicitly endorsed in Isobel Armstrong's recent work. Challenging us to "rethink the power of affect, feeling and emotion" in our reading, she argues that the subjective element is never absent, however strongly it may be denied by some materialist critics. A new "paradigm of reading" that "does not construct the text as one of the *objects* of our knowledge" but instead refuses the binary construction of "feeling" versus "thought" would, in her analysis, help to prevent potentially destructive dynamics of power.[74]

If reading is conceived of as "a reciprocal network without being involved in subject/object positions," Armstrong theorizes, "[t]he interactive network which is text and reader" is freed to "creat[e] new possibilities of meaning." Once we are "caught up with . . . the structure of the text's processes," she argues, we will cease to read "for mastery" but instead will enter a more productive relationship with it, something like a cooperative relationship with another person. Or, by becoming the writer's "fellow-worker and accomplice," she might have said with Woolf, a reader may influence the direction of literature: "The standards we raise and the judgments we pass steal into the air and become part of the atmosphere which writers breathe as they work." Reading and writing are interdependent, in Woolf's view; both are crucial to "freedom of mind," a concept that Milton, among others, taught her to cherish.[75]

In *Small World,* David Lodge's wicked send-up of the ultraprofessionalized Anglo-American academy of the early 1980s, a young Irish professor—an academic ingenue—accidentally commits himself to writing a book about the influence of Eliot on Shakespeare. He means it as a joke. But is it? Certainly *Hamlet* has never been quite the same after Eliot.[76] Woolf's conceptions of the Renaissance have had a lesser impact, in part because they are more subtle, not so insistent. The provisional subjectivity of Woolf's Renaissance, however, is strategic: her revisions invite further turns as she practices upon her readers what Cuddy-Keane calls "the trope of the twist."[77]

Defending the new historical emphasis on "local readings" of Renaissance texts, Leah Marcus describes it as "part of a major epistemological shift whereby we free ourselves from a demanding allegiance to the 'Truth'" to be distilled from an "original" text. After the failure of the search for universals, the critical goal has become to "rework received opinion . . . in order to find—even to celebrate—new, less rigidly positivist vantage points."[78] These late twentieth-century interpretations seek primarily to recover the multiple contexts of a text's first readership. But they do not foreclose fresh insights, and they clearly aim for relevance to the "present moment." If we dare to infiltrate the historicist and materialist projects of contemporary Renaissance criticism with a touch of Woolf's passionate, mischievous engagement, we may be led, even now, to pastures new.

∿ Notes

1. Leah S. Marcus, "Renaissance/Early Modern Studies," in *Redrawing the Boundaries: The Transformation of English and American Literary Studies,* edited by Stephen Greenblatt and Giles Gunn (New York: Modern Language Association, 1992), 41–43.

2. Leah S. Marcus, *Puzzling Shakespeare: Local Reading and Its Discontents* (Berkeley: University of California Press, 1988), 31–32.

3. Melba Cuddy-Keane, "Virginia Woolf and the Varieties of Historicist Experience," in *Virginia Woolf and the Essay,* edited by Beth Carole Rosenberg and Jeanne Dubino (New York: St. Martin's, 1997), 61.

4. Virginia Woolf, *The Diary of Virginia Woolf,* edited by Anne Olivier Bell and Andrew McNeillie, 5 vols. (New York: Harcourt Brace Jovanovich, 1977–84), 3:271 (8 December 1929).

5. See, for example, the introduction to *Rewriting the Renaissance: The Discourses of Sexual Difference in Early Modern Europe,* edited by Margaret W. Ferguson, Maureen Quilligan, and Nancy J. Vickers (Chicago: University of Chicago Press, 1986).

6. Margreta de Grazia, *"Fin-de-Siècle* Renaissance England," in Fins de Siècle: *English Poetry in 1590, 1690, 1790, 1890, 1990,* edited by Elaine Scarry (Baltimore: Johns Hopkins University Press, 1995), 55. On the troublesome concept of periodization generally, see *The Challenge of Periodization: Old Paradigms and New Perspectives,* edited by Lawrence Besserman (New York: Garland, 1996).

7. Margreta de Grazia, Maureen Quilligan, and Peter Stallybrass, introduction to *Subject and Object in Renaissance Culture,* edited by Margreta de Grazia (New York: Cambridge University Press, 1996), 4, quoting Burckhardt, by way of Felix Gilbert, *History: Politics or Culture? Reflections on Ranke and Burckhardt* (Princeton, N.J.: Princeton University Press, 1990), 61. J. B. Bullen, *The Myth of the Renaissance in Nineteenth-Century Writing* (Oxford: Clarendon Press, 1994), 2. My understanding of Renaissance historiography is also indebted to Wallace Ferguson's valuable book *The Renaissance in Historical Thought: Five Centuries of Interpretation* (Cambridge, Mass.: Riverside Press, 1948).

8. J. B. Bullen, 11; see also 162.

9. See John R. Reed, "The Victorian Renaissance Self," *Clio* 17 (1988): 197.

10. J. B. Bullen, 300.

11. Ibid., 297–98; see also 15–16. For more on J. A. Symonds's *The Renaissance in Italy,* see Peter Allan Dale, "Beyond Humanism: J. A. Symonds and the Replotting of the Renaissance," *Clio* 17 (1988): 109–37.

12. J. B. Bullen, 124.

13. Walter Pater, *The Renaissance: Studies in Art and Poetry,* edited by Donald L. Hill (Berkeley: University of California Press, 1980), xxii–xxiii. My sense of the Victorian novelists' uses of the Renaissance is informed by Reed's helpful essay.

14. J. B. Bullen, 3. Bullen's understanding of the various "myths" of the Renaissance is indebted to Hayden White's theories as articulated in *Metahistory: The Historical Imagination in Nineteenth-Century Europe* (Baltimore: Johns Hopkins University Press, 1973), *Tropics of Discourse: Essays in Cultural Criticism* (Baltimore: Johns Hopkins University Press, 1978), and elsewhere.

15. J. B. Bullen, 141; also 147, quoting from the first volume of *The Stones of Venice* (1853), in *The Works of John Ruskin* (New York: Longmans, Green, 1903–12), vols. 9–11, 9:46–47.

16. Ruskin, *The Seven Lamps of Architecture* (1846), in *Works,* 8:97–98; Ruskin, *The Stones of Venice,* in *Works,* 9:278. For fuller discussion, see, in addition to J. B. Bullen, Wendell V. Harris, "Ruskin and Pater—Hebrew and Hellene—Explore the Renaissance," *Clio* 17 (1988): 173–85.

17. Reed, 188.

18. J. B. Bullen, 12, comments on Ruskin's "unpeopled" Renaissance versus Burckhardt's position on the question of selfhood. The subsequent quotes are from Burckhardt, *The Civilization of the Renaissance in Italy* [1878], 2d ed., revised and translated by S. G. C. Middlemore (New York: Oxford University Press, 1945), 129–30, 455, 492.

19. Charles Kingsley, *Westward Ho!* (1855; reprint, New York: Dodd, Mead, 1941). According to Larry F. Uffelman in *Charles Kingsley* (Boston: Twayne, 1979), 96, it was the historian James Anthony Froude who prompted Kingsley to read Hakluyt; Froude was reviewing a new edition, probably the 1850 Hakluyt Society edition of *Divers Voyages Touching the Discovery of America and the Islands Adjacent.*

20. Uffelman, 102; see also Reed's helpful discussion, 195–98.

21. See J. B. Bullen's discussion (223–29) of Eliot's intervention into the debates about Savonarola.

22. Reed, 199.

23. George Eliot, *Romola* [1862–63], edited by Andrew Brown (New York: Oxford University Press, 1994), 498.

24. Leslie Stephen, *George Eliot* (London: Macmillan [English Men of Letters], 1902), 136–37; see also Reed, 200–201; for further discussion of Stephen's reading, see Alison Booth, "Trespassing in Cultural History: The Heroines of *Romola* and *Orlando,*" chap. 5 of *Greatness Engendered: George Eliot and Virginia Woolf* (Ithaca, N.Y.:

Cornell University Press, 1992), 172–73. G. Eliot, 547. J. B. Bullen, 214, from his extended discussion (214–38) of Eliot's indebtedness to the Comtean positivism.

25. See J. B. Bullen, 232, 238.

26. Arnold's views of the Renaissance became progressively negative; see J. B. Bullen, 241–52. For further discussion of Pater's work as responsive to Arnold's, see J. B. Bullen, 278, and especially Dennis Donoghue, *Walter Pater: Lover of Strange Souls* (New York: Knopf, 1995), 120–28.

27. The textual history of Pater's *Renaissance* is documented in Donald L. Hill's authoritative edition. For discussion of Pater's "highly personal myth," see J. B. Bullen, chap. 12 (273–98), esp. 273.

28. Pater, "Coleridge's Writings," quoted in J. B. Bullen, 277; J. B. Bullen, 278.

29. For this point see W. V. Harris, 183.

30. Pater, *The Renaissance*, 31, 91.

31. Ibid., "Conclusion," 186–90.

32. As Perry Meisel points out in *The Absent Father: Virginia Woolf and Walter Pater* (New Haven, Conn.: Yale University Press, 1980), 1–5, Leslie Stephen was among those who publicly opposed Pater's aesthetic.

33. E. B. Osborn, *The New Elizabethans: A First Selection of the Lives of Young Men Who Have Fallen in the Great War* (London: John Lane, 1919). T. S. Eliot was unimpressed with this book; see his unsigned review, "The New Elizabethans and the Old," *Athenaeum*, 4 April 1919, 135–37.

34. In *Orlando* (1928; reprint, New York: Harcourt Brace Jovanovich [Harvest], 1973), the Renaissance poet Nick Greene becomes a nineteenth-century version of Professor Raleigh; with a doctorate and a knighthood, he is the prototypical critic of the age. For Woolf's views on Raleigh, see her admiring "Trafficks and Discoveries" (1906), in *The Essays of Virginia Woolf*, 4 (of 6) vols. to date, edited by Andrew McNeillie (London: Hogarth Press, 1986–94), 1:120–24, reviewing his edition of Hakluyt's *English Voyages of the Sixteenth Century*, followed by a trenchant review of his letters, "Walter Raleigh" (first published in *Vogue* in 1926 as "A Professor for Life"), in Virginia Woolf, *The Captain's Death Bed and Other Essays*, edited by Leonard Woolf (1950; New York: Harcourt Brace Jovanovich [Harvest], 1978), 87–93.

35. On Woolf's re-creation of the "great frosts" of the first decade of the seventeenth century as recorded by Thomas Dekker, see Reid Barbour, *Deciphering Elizabethan Fiction* (Newark: University of Delaware Press, 1993), 143.

36. E. M. W. Tillyard, *The Elizabethan World Picture* (1943; reprint, New York: Vintage, n.d.), 1–2.

37. I have found no evidence that Woolf read Burckhardt. But Burckhardtian ideas are present, to cite some examples, in Strachey's *Elizabeth and Essex: A Tragic History* (New York: Harcourt, Brace, 1928); Raleigh's "The Age of Elizabeth," in *Shakespeare's England* (Oxford: Clarendon Press, 1916), 1:1–47; and H. G. Wells's *The*

Outline of History [1920], 3d ed. (London: Macmillan, 1924), chap. 34, "The Rena-scence of Western Civilization." See also Leslie Stephen's Burckhardtian musings in *English Literature and Society in the Eighteenth Century* (1903; reprint, New York: Barnes and Noble, 1955), 22–23; and Stephen, *George Eliot*, 132.

    38. White, *Metahistory*, 230.

    39. Booth, 203.

    40. Meisel, *The Absent Father*, 41–43, quoting Woolf, "Modern Fiction" (first pub-lished in 1919 as "Modern Novels"), in *The Common Reader: First Series*, edited by An-drew McNeillie (New York: Harcourt Brace Jovanovich [Harvest], 1984), 146–54, 150.

    41. Pater, *The Renaissance*, 5, 20.

    42. Ibid., 18. Pater's reading of vol. 7 of Michelet's *Histoire de France*, on the Re-naissance, is especially evident in his treatments of Abelard and Joachim de Fiore; see Donoghue, 134–37.

    43. Many thanks to Pierre-Éric Villeneuve for pointing out Woolf's fondness for Michelet, which she would have read in French. Her references to reading Michelet begin with a 1909 letter to Lytton Strachey, in *The Letters of Virginia Woolf*, edited by Nigel Nicolson and Joanne Trautmann, 6 vols. (New York: Harcourt Brace Jovanovich, 1975–80), 1:398, and end with a 1939 letter to Ethel Smyth, in *Letters*, 6:312. In her diary of 30 January 1915 (*Diary*, 1:31), she complains that she "cannot get on with Michelet's middle ages"; but two weeks later she is "reading a later volume of Michelet, which is su-perb, and the only tolerable history" (*Diary*, 1:34, 14 February 1915). In the letter to Strachey, she reports being "absorbed in Michelet. . . . It is thus that I should write the history of the Restoration," she writes, surely meaning the Reformation, "if I were a man." The letter to Bell is dated 26 February 1928 (*Letters*, 3:465). Michelet also provides another intertext linking Woolf and George Eliot (see J. B. Bullen, 212).

    44. See my "Entering Woolf's Renaissance Imaginary: A Second Look at *The Sec-ond Common Reader*," in *Virginia Woolf and the Essay*, edited by Beth Carole Rosen-berg and Jeanne Dubino (New York: St. Martin's, 1997), 81–95.

    45. Linda Orr, *Jules Michelet: Nature, History, and Language* (Ithaca, N.Y.: Cornell University Press, 1976), 3. For more on Michelet's place within the French tradition of public intellectual practice, see Lionel Gossman, *Between History and Literature* (Cam-bridge, Mass.: Harvard University Press, 1990), 162ff.

    46. See Gossman, 176, 173.

    47. Michelet, quoted in Gossman, 176.

    48. See White's "Michelet: Historical Realism as Romance," chap. 3 of *Metahistory*, 135–62. Michelet's history of the Renaissance and the Reformation takes up vols. 7–10 (1855–56) of his *Histoire de France* (Paris: Chamerot, 1835–67). Those four volumes are published as one volume, *Renaissance et Réforme. Histoire de France au XVIe siècle*, with a preface by Claude Mettra (Paris: Robert Laffont, 1982). Subsequent quotations in the text are from the one-volume edition; the translations are my own.

49. Michelet, 34, 35, 34: "This book . . . is not written to torment the dying. It is an appeal to the living forces." His subject encompasses "the discovery of the world, the discovery of man." (Burckhardt elaborates on these "striking expressions" of Michelet's; see his part 4, "The Discovery of the World and of Man," esp. 308, 308 n. 1.) "History, which is nothing less than the intelligence of life, ought to breathe life into us; to the contrary it has weakened us, making us believe that time is everything, that the will is nothing."

50. Michelet, 38: "The revolution of the sixteenth century, having arrived more than a hundred years after the demise of the philosophy of that time, encountered an incredible death, a nothingness, and took off from nothing." "It was the heroic spume of an immense will." "The sixteenth century is a hero."

51. Michelet, 40–41: The "voice of the people" is drained; "one no longer has the ear in mind but rather the eyes. One writes for the study." Cf. Woolf, "Notes on an Elizabethan Play" (1925), in *The Common Reader*, 48–57, 50.

52. Michelet, 42, 46: Through "successive abdications of human independence," scholasticism endures. "The spirit . . . puts itself to flight. It supports itself in the powers of love and the intuitive insight that permits genius to await distant truth and to anticipate the future."

53. Michelet, 60–61: Giotto "had abandoned the consecrated types, the insipid and mute figures of the Middle Ages, to paint what he saw, flamboyant Italian heads, beautiful and lively madonnas." Van Eyck "made life flame in this ardent painting style that paled the other and sent it, wearisome shadow, to sleep near the scholastic."

54. Michelet, 65–66: "Enter the Louvre . . . : to the left you have the ancient world, the new to the right." The "faltering figures of Fra Angelico of Fiesole," who with "their sick and dying looks seem to be perhaps searching, longing," are opposed to Leonardo's pictures, which impart "the genius of the Renaissance, in its most harsh uneasiness, in its most piercing sting. Between these contemporary things, there is more than a thousand years."

> Bacchus, Saint John and *la Joconde* [*Gioconda,* the Mona Lisa] direct their looks toward you; you are fascinated and troubled, an infinity takes hold of you by a strange magnetism. Art, nature, the future, the genius of mystery and discovery, master of the profundities of the world, of the unknown abyss of the ages, speak, what do you wish of me? This canvas attracts me, calls me, invades me, absorbs me; I go to it despite myself, as the bird goes to the serpent.

Cf. J. B. Bullen's discussion of this passage, 179–80.

55. Michelet, 66–67: "Galileo is still far away." Leonardo, with the others, suffers for his "great solitude." "An abyss clearly remains between these five or six men, the

heroes of the will, and the masses, miserably shackled and backward, who are unable to rise from the gothic Middle Ages and the flattening of the fifteenth century."

56.   Michelet, 69–71: The bourgeoisie is "nothing but an amphibious, mongrel, servilely imitative class, which wishes only to make a fortune and to become nobility." "Therefore, do you believe, idiots, that one holds bound in a sack the unassailable imp, the ether of human thought?" "[N]o, the man who speaks is far, very far, anywhere but here," safeguarding "the independent tradition of cults that you believe to be extinguished." The human spirit has retreated to "its consoling mother, Nature."

57.   Michelet, 71ff.: "the white Diana" . . . "false gods." Roland Barthes, "Michelet, Today," in *The Rustle of Language,* translated by Richard Howard (Berkeley: University of California Press, 1989), 195.

58.   Michelet, 71–72: Woman "is in reality the victim of this world on which all evil falls again." Michelet understands why "she prowls on the deserted prairie, . . . bile in her heart and cursing." When "God spoke to her only in Latin, in incomprehensible symbols," the Devil, who "speaks by Nature," became a more amiable companion. But as her "violent will," her "infinity of hatreds," leads her to perform "the abortion experienced by the disdainful woman who regards her with disgust," as a "reign of terror" courses through her, the text induces a kind of vertigo.

59.   The quote from Barthes is from his essay on Michelet's *La Sorcière* (1862), a book that amplifies ideas sketched in vol. 7 of his *Histoire de France.* Barthes, *"La Sorcière,"* in *Critical Essays,* translated by Richard Howard (Evanston, Ill.: Northwestern University Press, 1972), 107. Michelet, 79: humanity's "dim eyes cannot make out the difference between nature created by God and nature created by the Devil. . . . A terrible uncertainty hovered over everything."

60.   Michelet, 209–11: "The efforts of heroes, of bold precursors, remained individual, isolated, powerless" because "the populace was not yet born that could have supported them." "No, go, march, be confident, enter [the future] without being frightened. Let one sole word reassure you: *A world of humanity begins, of universal sympathy"* (emphasis in original). Michelet's important concept of *le peuple* is difficult to translate; see Barthes, "Michelet, Today," 206–7, for further discussion.

61.   Michelet, 795: Luther and Calvin are paired against Rabelais and Copernicus as "two branches of the same tree" bearing "the Reformation and the Renaissance, grandparents of the modern liberties." Together this imagery comprises "the modern unity of the sixteenth century." In the end, "it is one person. We can trace the portrait." There emerges a new Protestantism "that embraces the world itself, that of reason, of equity, of science." Cf. Woolf's essay "Montaigne" (1924), in *The Common Reader,* 58–68, which similarly responds to the biographical lure of "portraiture" in Renaissance art: she admires Montaigne's way, for example, of "giving the whole map, weight, colour, and circumference of the soul in its confusion" (58)—a habit

that, as Nicola Luckhurst explores in chap. 2 of this volume, "'To quote my quotation from Montaigne,'" she appropriates for her own use.

62. In his introduction to Michelet's *Renaissance et Réforme,* 27, Claude Mettra compares Michelet's method to that of Mircea Eliade's *Mythe de l'éternel retour* (1949).

63. Michelet, 799–800: "*Harmony,* the song in parts, the concord of free yet fraternal voices, this beautiful mystery of modern art" (emphasis in original). Palestrina's "melancholy melodies" are "imprisoned" in the Sistine Chapel. Michelangelo's figures "listen to it and moan, these uncontrollable giants. . . . These accents are not theirs. Their genius, all virile, shines of a completely different future." "To kill fifteen million men by starvation and the sword, fine, that is possible. But to make a little song, an air loved by all. . . . This song perhaps at the dawn will burst forth from a simple heart, or the skylark will find it going up to the sun, away from its April furrow."

64. Michelet, 211: "She feels her way gropingly, she does not know herself, she does not stand up yet." Woolf, *A Room of One's Own* (1929; reprint, with a foreword by Mary Gordon, New York: Harcourt Brace Jovanovich [Harvest], 1989), 114, 65. Michelet's words "L'histoire est une résurrection" are inscribed on his tombstone in the Père Lachese cemetery above a figure of a female body rising from the mortal male body.

65. Woolf, "'Rebels and Reformers'" (1917), in *Essays,* 2:196–98, 197. On Michelet and socialism, see Gossman, 181ff.

66. As Reed writes, "self-examination becomes the basis for social action; right conduct is evoked by consulting one's best self, not by blindly following a religious or social code" (188).

67. Woolf, "Byron and Mr. Briggs" (typescript c. 1922), transcribed and reprinted in *Essays,* 3:473–99, 496–99, 490.

68. Alice Fox, *Virginia Woolf and the Literature of the English Renaissance* (Oxford: Clarendon Press, 1990), chap. 2, "Hakluyt's *Voyages.*"

69. Woolf, *Night and Day* (1919; reprint, New York: Harcourt Brace Jovanovich [Harvest], 1973). Subsequent references included parenthetically in the text are to this edition.

70. Pater, *The Renaissance,* 53.

71. On the relationship of Woolf's Renaissance to Eliot's, see David McWhirter, "Woolf, Eliot, and the Elizabethans: The Politics of Modernist Nostalgia," chap. 10 of this volume.

72. Wai Chee Dimock, "A Theory of Resonance," *PMLA* 112 (1997): 1061, 1060. Woolf, "The Countess of Pembroke's *Arcadia,*" in *The Second Common Reader* [1932], edited by Andrew McNeillie (New York: Harcourt Brace Jovanovich [Harvest], 1986), 40–50, 40; Cuddy-Keane, "Virginia Woolf," 71. Woolf, "Craftsmanship" (1937), in *The*

Death of the Moth and Other Essays, edited by Leonard Woolf (1942; reprint, New York: Harcourt Brace Jovanovich [Harvest],1974), 198–207, 206.

73. As an illustrative discussion, see Juliet Dusinberre, *Virginia Woolf's Renaissance: Woman Reader or Common Reader?* (Iowa City: University of Iowa Press, 1997), chap. 2, "Virginia Woolf and Montaigne: Them and Us."

74. Isobel Armstrong, "Textual Harassment: The Ideology of Close Reading, or, How Close Is Close?" *Textual Practice* 9 (1995): 403, 407, 409–10.

75. Ibid., 409–10. Woolf, "How Should One Read a Book?" in *The Second Common Reader,* 258–70, 259, 269. On Woolf's reinscription of Milton's phrase, from *Comus,* see Rebecca Laroche, "Laura at the Crossroads: *A Room of One's Own* and the Elizabethan Sonnet," chap. 8 of this volume.

76. David Lodge, *Small World: An Academic Romance* (New York: Macmillan, 1984). That the professor's accidental book proposal is eventually accepted indicates Lodge's understanding of the retroactive power of strong readings.

77. Melba Cuddy-Keane, "The Rhetoric of Feminist Conversation: Virginia Woolf and the Trope of the Twist," in *Ambiguous Discourse: Feminist Narratology and British Women Writers,* edited by Kathy Mezei (Chapel Hill: University of North Carolina Press, 1996), 137–61.

78. L. Marcus, *Puzzling Shakespeare,* 50; see also her epilogue.

2

"To quote my quotation from Montaigne"

～ Nicola Luckhurst

$\mathcal{B}$oth Virginia and Leonard Woolf sustained a long reading relationship with the prolific sixteenth-century French essayist Michel de Montaigne. They made the literary pilgrimage to Montaigne's tower in the Périgord several times, forti-fied, as Virginia's postcards boast, by "a whole paté de foie gras" and a bottle of Monbazillac.[1] In the twenties both reviewed translations of Montaigne's *Essais*.[2] And in 1929 the Hogarth Press published Trechmann's translation of *The Diary of Montaigne's Journey to Italy*. Yet their readings differed markedly. That the title and, strikingly, the last sentence of the fifth and final volume of Leonard's autobiography, *The Journey Not the Arrival Matters*, should allude to Mon-taigne's essay "Of Vanity" suggests a strong personal appropriation;[3] yet Woolf in fact records in this volume his reading of Montaigne as a liberal and a humanist in a historical not personal context. Leonard's Montaigne signals the beginning of civilization; he is "the first completely modern man in his intense awareness of and passionate interest in the individuality of himself and of all other human beings."[4] For Virginia Woolf, on the other hand, Montaigne's *Essais* both are appropriated in a deeply personal way and constitute an aesthetic model with a political point. According to this model, straight readings, such as

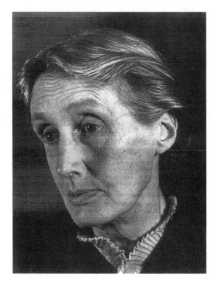

Portraits of Woolf and Montaigne: "subtle, half smiling, half melancholy." Virginia Woolf, photograph by Gisèle Freund, © Gisèle Freund/Agence Nina Beskow. Michel de Montaigne, copy of an original of the seventeenth century, private collection; by permission of Giraudon/Art Resource.

Leonard's, by which one thing is simply made to stand for another, are somewhat suspect. Leonard is not so much "reading" Montaigne, not even quoting him, but making of him, by conflating text and author, a symbol with which to mark part of a large schematic argument. We might say, then, that Virginia Woolf's reading is peculiarly modern in its appreciation of Montaigne's dialogic and digressive aesthetic.[5]

The *Essais* do, of course, invite this "Woolfian" approach—for their rhetoric repeatedly returns to the point that if they wander conversationally from their point, then it is all to the good of the argument, that if other voices speak it is because there are many points of view. Such an aesthetic fosters—might even be said to demand—a particular art of reading, namely one that is prepared to stay with the digressions, to follow them as the conscious construction of the essayist, rather than dismiss them as the ramblings of an untidy mind. "Je m'esgare, mais plustot par licence que par mesgarde," warns Montaigne in "De la vanité."[6] Dialogue is also privileged, both in terms of the conversations held between the many voices of Montaigne within the *Essais* and as the invitation to the reader to engage in conversation with the text.

These conversations could be redescribed according to the concerns of recent literary theory—the text's own multiple voices seen as an example of the Bakhtinian "dialogic," the text-reader dialogue becoming a Barthesian complicity between writer and reader as "producteur du texte."[7] Yet such redescription risks blunting the particular style of Montaigne's dialogic, which is a mode at once generous and challenging:

> La parole est moitié à celuy qui parle, moitié à celuy qui l'escoute. Cettuy-cy se doibt preparer à la recevoir selon le branle qu'elle prend. Comme entre ceux qui jouent à la paume, celuy qui soustient se desmarche et s'apreste selon qu'il voit remuer celuy qui luy jette le coup et selon la forme du coup.[8]

This art of reading is, in a sense, set before the reader as both an invitation and a provocation, which is not to say that all readers have complied. Not until the nineteenth century did readers of the *Essais,* broadly speaking, respond, and with increasing warmth, to Montaigne's invitation.[9] Theirs was in part a more personal response to the text's autobiographical elements, in part a recognition of the *Essais'* dialogic quality as rhetorically performative of their philosophical position—subjectivity, relativism, and suspended judgment.[10] Sainte-Beuve provides a wonderfully vivid image of the conversation inspired by the *Essais,* in which Montaigne's funeral is attended by his future readers (among them Rousseau and La Bruyère), all of whom are eagerly engaged in conversation: "on y cause du défunt et de ses qualités aimables et de sa philosophie tant de fois en jeu dans la vie, on y cause de soi."[11] The network of conversations I will be tracing in this essay is in a sense made possible by this larger conversation, which was first conceptualized by the late nineteenth-century reception.

Virginia Woolf's developing conversation with Montaigne and with others will be explored here through the art of reading suggested by the *Essais.* For thinking through digression and dialogue will also enable a more fruitful reading of Leonard Woolf's apparently schematic, humanist approach. It is no coincidence that both he and Virginia were drawn above all to the essay "Of Vanity"—their writing about reading Montaigne is the trace of an intimate and ongoing conversation.

But to begin with I would like to digress. In her diary, Virginia Woolf records her reading of Proust and the effect it has on her writing. More accurately, she writes to mark how reading Proust prevents her from writing. Proust puts her out of temper with her own sentences, she records on 8 April 1925.[12] Experienced as at once familiar and alien, Proust seems to get under Woolf's skin—the skin of her writing self. But we might also and more plainly say that reading Proust makes Woolf write differently; she makes an entry in her diary; he puts her out of temper, perhaps, with her public writing self, rather than with the private. It is the writerly/readerly nature of Woolf's diary that enables us to catch her so close to the *process* of reading. We seem to glimpse her at that moment when, prompted by her reading, she becomes a writer again. And where Proust figures as a block to writing, Montaigne both enables it and provides a model for how to write.

Movingly, Montaigne is also a salve to a particular form of writing—notably to writing about death. Quoting her Montaigne quotation is what Woolf does in her diary in response to this painful experience. It is a form of mourning. Both Proust and Montaigne figure in the entry of 8 April 1925, in which Woolf's reflection on her success as a writer—"I wonder if this time I have achieved something? Well, nothing anyhow compared with Proust, in whom I am embedded now"—is part of a reflection on the recent death of Jacques Raverat:

> Jacques died, as I say; & at once the siege of emotions began. I got the news with a party here—Clive, Bee How, Julia Strachey, Dadie. Nevertheless, I do not any longer feel inclined to doff the cap to death. I like to go out of the room talking, with an unfinished casual sentence on my lips. That is the effect it had on me—no leavetakings, no submission—but someone stepping out into the darkness. [. . .] More & more do I repeat my own version of Montaigne "Its life that matters."[13]

Here the quotation—"Its life that matters"—is described simply as "my own version," for Woolf has in fact taken Montaigne's argument in the essay "Of Vanity" and distilled it to this rather commonplace, even banal statement.[14] And as such the first appearance of the quotation in the diary easily escapes notice, for it is unacknowledged. Woolf's entry of 5 May 1924 records the anniversary of her mother's death:

> I think it happened early on a Sunday morning, & I [. . .] could fill a whole page & more with my impressions of that day, many of them ill received by me, & hidden from the grown ups. [. . .]
> But enough of death—its life that matters.[15]

That Montaigne goes unacknowledged here suggests further the intimate, even coded use Woolf is making of her "quotation"; that she proceeds to record in this same entry her return to Rodmell, gardening, the danger of depression—"the fidgets"—that London diverts her from this and is therefore equated with life and better for writing because it "upholds one"—all of these suggest also that the phrase is talismanic, allowing the marking of loss and mourning, but also protecting the writing, allowing it to move on.

Later references to this phrase as "my quotation from Montaigne" might more aptly be taken as Woolf quoting herself, so much has the text from which this distillation comes been appropriated. In the diary entry of 2 September 1933, Woolf reflects at once on the severe illness of Francis Birrell and on her own mortality:

> Curious how all ones fibres seem to expand & fill with air when anxiety is taken off; curious also to me the intensity of my own feelings[. . .]. Partly selfishness, of course, this horror, that it means another extinction of one's own life: brings death nearer. But let us think no more of death. Its life that matters, to quote my quotation from Montaigne.[16]

Woolf's talismanic use of the "Montaigne quotation" in her diary sends her back toward "life." Or rather, it acts as a pivot, allowing her to move back toward *writing* about life. If recording the death of others as events in her own life means mourning their loss, it also endangers a form of writing that Woolf was at pains not to allow to linger on the soul, on brooding self-analysis or melancholia. In his essay "Modernism and Mourning," John Mepham describes how death and lament figure in Woolf's novels:

> It is striking[. . .] that death is never incorporated into plot and
> never functions as the termination of a story.[. . .] Death is never
> the culmination of the action, the event around which closure is
> achieved[. . .] Death is always an event in the lives of the living. It
> is in itself without sense[. . .] It is pure contingency.[. . .] In
> mourning one closes around oneself a protective covering of incan-
> tation ("fear no more the heat of the sun" chants Clarissa
> Dalloway). One performs valedictory ceremonies, if one can find
> the right form of words.[17]

These observations can be revealingly applied to the topics of death and lament
in Woolf's diary. The deaths of others figure as events in her written life that are
pure contingency—they leave not only her own life, but also the life of her diary
"lessened[. . .] less porous & radiant."[18] Yet, unlike the tags from Shakespeare
used in the novels as a form of lament, and also found occasionally in her
diaries, the Montaigne quotation is not valued for the beauty of its formulation;
it is not even a tag as such, since Montaigne never writes "It's life that matters."
Woolf never quotes the original French, although her style may (as it does in
her essay on Montaigne) become porous to the passage to which she alludes.[19]
For most often the Montaigne phrase appears as Woolf's quotation, "Its life that
matters"; as such it allows death to be set in the context of life.

Woolf's sense of her own mortality is registered most keenly in her diary,
and, as the coupling of Raverat's death and Proust's writing in the entry quoted
earlier indicates, this sense tends to invoke the posterity of her writing. "But
what is to become of all these diaries, I asked myself yesterday," she writes on
20 March 1926. "If I died, what would Leo make of them? He would be
disinclined to burn them; he could not publish them. Well, he should make up
a book from them, I think; & then burn the body."[20] The ambiguity of the book
and the body here recalls those moments at which Woolf fears for the life of
her diary, as if it were another living self. Whose body is it Leonard should
burn? That "[w]e are nauseated by the sight of trivial personalities decompos-
ing in the eternity of print," as Woolf wrote in "The Modern Essay,"[21] demands
such a strong corporeal equation of body and book. And the corpus returns
us—by another route—to Montaigne, who claimed, "[J]e suis moy-mesmes la
matiere de mon livre," that he is himself consubstantial with his book.[22]

It is useful to contrast this kind of readerly writing, Woolf's intimate use of Montaigne, with her public essay on his *Essais,* which she published as a review in the *Times Literary Supplement* and again in *The Common Reader.* The connections between the essay-writing of Woolf and Montaigne have been documented in Juliet Dusinberre's study *Virginia Woolf's Renaissance* and by Judith Allen, who describes the "anti-generic qualities" of the essay as "perfect for Woolf," since "[they] serve to express and enact a poetics we would desig-nate as feminine [that is to say, one] which emphasizes multiple voices, con-tingency, and process over product."[23] What I would like to do here instead is to consider what it meant for Woolf to put Montaigne at the head of the list when in her diary she planned her own first collection of essays[24] and subse-quently to place him as the subject of the first single-author essay of *The Common Reader.*

Woolf's focus for her Montaigne essay is the project of self-portraiture, thereby mirroring Montaigne's own construction when, in the preface to the *Essais,* he describes them as a portrait of himself to be left to his friends, as, in fact, a memento mori. Woolf's choice of self-portraiture, where one might have expected her to focus on the stylistic and discursive qualities of his essays or, say, on Montaigne's discussions of literature, is curious. It suggests, perhaps, her own presence in the essays to come; by that I mean not Virginia Woolf's presence per se, but rather that her exposition of the process of reading and critiquing, "revealing contradictions, enthusiasm, and misgivings," expresses the affective involvement of the thinking self.[25] And Montaigne, in this respect, is a tutelary figure, a protector. The canonical status of the *Essais,* indeed their position as the origin of the genre,[26] allows Woolf to reclaim that aspect of his work which best suits her project, notably the inscription of the self—in this case the common reader who as Dusinberre argues is "transparently *female*"[27] —within the claimed discursive topic, an inscription that might otherwise be easily dismissed as too personal, subjective, that is too "feminine":

> This talking of oneself, following one's own vagaries, giving the whole map, weight, colour, and circumference of the soul in its con-fusion, its variety, its imperfection—this art belonged to one man only: to Montaigne. As the centuries go by, there is always a crowd before that picture, gazing into its depths, seeing their own face

reflected in it, seeing more the longer they look, never being able to say quite what it is that they see.[28]

What is doubly curious about Woolf's essay on Montaigne is that it at once bears the imprint of his style (so much so that it at first reads as a pastiche) and the imprint of his ideas—she often appears to be summarizing the key concerns of the *Essais*. Yet she might equally be seen as drawing her own self-portrait. She rehearses contradictory impulses of the *Essais* that were also preoccupations of her diary. Dusinberre notes that Woolf "delicately satirises Montaigne's attitude to *le vulgaire*, which is as ambivalent as her own."[29] Further, Montaigne's dislike of authority, his exploration of the soul, feminine in French but feminine too according to Woolf's usage, even his physiognomy—might as well be hers as Montaigne's. He is, she writes, "subtle, half smiling, half melancholy," with "heavy-lidded eyes" and a "dreamy, quizzical expression."[30] Yet Woolf had already warned us at the very outset of this essay that generations of readers have seen themselves in Montaigne, that the *Essais* are more a mirror than a self-portrait of their author. Her writing enacts this notion that the *Essais* encourage individual readers to recognize themselves; yet beyond this, she indicates that Montaigne's very concept of selfhood is complex and subtle, peculiarly modern in its drawing attention to generic instability and the multiplicity of the self.

Woolf's Montaigne quotation also finds its place in this essay: "But enough of death; it is life that matters. / It is life that emerges more and more clearly"[31] is the conclusion she draws from a rehearsal of this familiar *topos* of his *Essais*— which is at once Montaigne's own conclusion and the reader's, for the *Essais* are indeed, as Woolf points out, more and more taken up by questions of life as they reach "not their end, but their suspension in full career."[32] Woolf's own reading experience would seem to have followed this pattern. She speaks of not being able to "skamp" Montaigne, as he is getting "better & better," which might simply describe her growing enthusiasm for the *Essais* but could also express her experience of the increasing vigor of Montaigne's self-portrait.[33] The physicality of this portrait in the later editions of and additions to the *Essais* is at once an admission and a defiant inscription of mortality. Metaphors of physicality, notably that by which Montaigne is the substance or stuff of his book, become more outspoken, bawdier, as, in the later essay "Of Vanity," where he declares: "Ce sont icy, un peu plus civilement, des excremens d'un vieil esprit, dur tantost, tantost láche, et tousjours indigeste."[34] And the literal transcription of the body— Montaigne's final essay in particular catalogs his habits and ailments—simply adds more substance to the argument inherent in Montaigne's and, indeed, in Woolf's style, that body and soul, the physical and the spiritual, cannot easily be separated out. As Woolf comments of Montaigne, "Observe how the soul is always casting her own lights and shadows; makes the substantial hollow and the frail substantial."[35]

Diary entries around the time of the composition of this essay indicate that Woolf's writing about Montaigne has become a point of articulation between public and private. Her allusive reference to the *Essais* as an aesthetic model (on 17 August 1923) is not connected with her practice of quoting Montaigne and mourning. Yet the description does occur in the more intimate context of the diary, not, as might be expected, in her reading notebooks. Broadly speaking, this diarizing about Montaigne reveals the process of how he is to "come out" in Woolf's public writing. And the key to this process lies in Montaigne's displacement. The displacement of Woolf's Montaigne essay from the *head* of her diary plan for *The Common Reader* is echoed by the displacement of a Montaigne-inflected reflection on how to assemble a book of essays, to its more covert assimilation. Woolf's description of how "a trial should be made," itself a verbal echo of Montaigne's essayism, is part of a reflection on how to "make a book," rather than simply a "collection of articles," which she considers "an inartistic method."[36] Only the phrase "make a book" appears as a quotation in this entry, and, although this is not documented, it seems likely that Woolf is quoting herself again—one can imagine her discussing with Leonard what might, quite literally, "make a book" for the Hogarth Press. But "make a book" also brings to mind Montaigne's notion of the physicality of the *Essais*.

The *Essais* were originally conceived as a substitute for conversation with, and also a memento mori of, Montaigne's friend La Boétie.[37] Montaigne further describes them in "Consideration sur Ciceron" as a substitute for correspondence with La Boétie, suggesting that the impulse toward dialogue ("Il me falloit, comme je l'ay eu autrefois, un certain commerce qui m'attirast, qui me soustinst et souslesvast")[38] has been incorporated in the style and form of the *Essais* themselves. What might be said to make of them a book is that they originated as a conversation between the writing self and his quotations, entitled *Essais de Montaigne,* becoming *Les Essais* once they had developed into a conversation between the writing selves of the three different principal editions, written over a period of twenty years (from 1572 to 1592). Woolf's articles were at first to become a book through the device of conversation between members of the fictional Otway family:[39] "The brilliant idea has just come to me of *embedding* them in Otway conversation. The main advantage would be that I could then comment, & add what I had had to leave out, or failed to get in[. . .] to have a setting for each would 'make a book.'"[40] This dialogic style is perceived by Woolf as pleasurable and as allowing a more personal expression—both qualities noted as characteristic, defining even of the genre in her essay "The Modern Essay."[41] "I should graze nearer my own individuality," she writes; "I should mitigate the pomposity & sweep in all sorts of trifles. I think I should feel more at my ease. So I think a trial should be made."[42] For Montaigne uses the dialogic in part to essay different points of view, removing the weight of authority from the single voice of the writer, allowing the ideas to be provisional, experimental, also allowing the smuggling in of views that might otherwise be subject to censorship. Woolf's plan to assign voices to characters, who then engage in conversation, is a laying bare of this dialogic mode.

These reflections on structuring *The Common Reader* are all noted in the diary entry for 17 August 1923. There are repeated attempts in the diary entries around this time to record conversation; and Woolf's openly dialogic essay, "Mr. Conrad: A Conversation," in which Conrad is discussed by Penelope Otway and "her old friend David Lowe," appeared in *The Nation* on 1 September 1923. The "purely negative" reception it received prompted Woolf to reassess her conception of the conversational mode for *The Common Reader.* "To curtail, I shall really investigate literature with a view to answering certain questions about ourselves—Characters are to be merely views: personality must be avoided at all costs. I'm sure my Conrad adventure taught me this. Directly you specify hair, age, &c something frivolous, or irrelevant, gets into the book."[43] Woolf's reaction echoes Montaigne's claim that an essayistic exploration of quite diverse topics, in this case literature, necessarily entailed an exploration of the self. But what this entry also points up are the difficulties and even risks involved in such an enterprise—namely, how is conversation to be embodied; hence Woolf's reclaiming of Montaigne as a protector; hence too her return to a more covert form of the dialogic in *The Common Reader*.[44] The Otways become the voices of readers and texts, their physical presence translated into the acts of reading and being read.

I suggested at the beginning that Woolf's dialogue with Montaigne might be seen as part of a different conversation, a three-way conversation. She was not reading the *Essais* in isolation, but alongside Leonard, sometimes in sympathy, as their publishing of Trechmann's translation of *Montaigne's Journey to Italy* and their own visits to Montaigne's tower indicate, sometimes using the other's approach better to demarcate their own. When Leonard reviews Trechmann's translation of the *Essais* in *The Nation* he takes a short passage from "Of Vanity," the essay to which both he and Virginia are constantly alluding, for the purposes of comparing the original French with translations by Florio and Trechmann. But he goes on to describe his preference for a politicized reading of Montaigne, who, "[b]eneath the surface of his Essays [. . .] had a definite and persistent purpose," namely to "attack the religious beliefs which were making life in France intolerable."[45] Leonard contrasts this reading with an approach that sounds peculiarly like Virginia's, even inasmuch as it retraces the portrait sketched in her review:

> There are[. . .] two Montaignes. One is the man and writer[. . .] who asks the question : "Que sçay-je?" and wrote a masterpiece in not answering it; the great egoist who translated himself, body and mind, into a work of art, and whom we can still see and hear, sitting in his library at the chateau de Montaigne in Périgord, with a half-smile on his lips, watching, reading, reflecting, or engaged in that "exercise of the mind" which, he said, was "the most profitable and natural," the occupation "more agreeable" to him "than any other in life"—conversation. This is, no doubt, the greater of the two Montaignes.[46]

Despite his apparent deference, Leonard clearly preferred the politicized Montaigne, who was being established by the latest French scholarship[47] and was accessible only through "considerable attention," to what looks suspiciously like the Montaigne of Virginia's common reader. Leonard's review is the germ of what will, in his autobiography, become an all-encompassing argument about civilization; here already he claims Montaigne as "one of the most humane, rational, and civilized men that have ever lived," already he describes the "temper of his mind" as "the same as that of Erasmus, but even finer and subtler and stronger."[48] Leonard's later reading becomes more starkly delineated as part of a reflection on the World War II—Montaigne marking the beginning of modern civilization, the war its end. And this reading was to become still more extreme in later life. But the autobiography in which this schematic argument is set shares certain Montaignian characteristics that affect its persuasiveness.

The Journey Not the Arrival Matters is highly digressive, addressing social and political questions as well as telling the story of an individual life. What is questionable is how these more general reflections relate to the individual story: intentionally or not, Leonard's digressive style connects the personal and the political, or, to borrow Virginia's phrase, the general reflections answer "certain questions about ourselves."[49] Strikingly, the chapter in which Leonard's extended reading of Montaigne occurs also records Virginia's death, thus remaking her connection between Montaigne and mourning. And the narration of everyday life at the outbreak of World War II that follows on from Leonard's reading of Montaigne already painfully anticipates her suicide. The writing process is rarely recorded in Leonard's autobiography; here, exceptionally, it is described as this "recollection of misery":

> The umbilical cord which had bound *Roger Fry: A Biography* to Virginia's brain for two years was, as I said, finally cut when she returned the proofs to the printer on May 13, 1940; 319 days later on March 28, 1941, she committed suicide by drowning herself in the River Ouse. Those 319 days of headlong and yet slow-moving catastrophe were the most terrible and agonizing days of my life.[50]

Everything that occurs between this anticipation and its eventual narration must in a sense be considered a digression. Digression that is in the negative sense of deviation, a departure from the main subject toward a topic of lesser importance. But if we read the narrative between anticipation and realization as a digression in the essayistic style, it begins to signify differently.

There is one digression within this intermediary period that particularly stands out; indeed it is marked to stand out by Leonard's commentary:

This kind of tragedy, essentially terrible, but in detail often grotesque and even ridiculous, is not uncommon in village life. At the
time its impact upon me was strong and strange; somehow or
other it seemed sardonically to fit into the pattern of a private and
public world threatened with destruction.[51]

The digression tells the story of Leonard's involvement with the retarded son
of the Wests, a local Rodmell family. The Woolfs already had some connection
with the family because Mrs. West was the mother of their servant, Louie
Everest. In Leonard's account, however, the Wests remain anonymous. The
account is given as follows: a working-class man, referred to as Mr. X, was
living in Rodmell with his wife and family; his youngest son was "completely
'retarded,'" and the mother devoted her life to looking after him. In 1940, the
eldest son of the family approached Leonard Woolf and asked him to see if he
could persuade their mother to "send the boy to a mental home, as he and the
rest of the family thought that his mother was ruining her life by immuring
herself with the child." He was successful in doing so, and the child was moved
to a home. Only two weeks later, Mrs. X contacted Leonard Woolf, claiming
that her son was "being starved and ill-treated, was getting very ill, and must
be given back to them." "Then," Woolf's account continues, "one morning Mr.
and Mrs. X appeared in my garden dressed in their Sunday clothes. They had
hired a taxi and asked me to accompany them to the Medical Officer and
demand the child." The child, "obviously ill," was collected, and "a week or ten
days later he died." The verdict of the inquest was death from natural causes.

The story is, as Woolf writes, "a tragedy"—but his perception of how it
fits into "the pattern of a private and public world threatened with destruction," that is to say, his reading of the significance of the digression, is unexpected. He writes that "[t]he passionate devotion of mothers to imbecile children, which was the pivot of this distressing incident, always seems to me a
strange and even disturbing phenomenon," and further that "there is something horrible and repulsive in the slobbering imbecility of a human being."
The implications of this account are, to say the least, uncomfortable. The
language, plainly outdated for us now, makes for a more squeamish response
to Leonard's repulsed and repulsive commentary. But it is by virtue of the very
placing of the digression between the private and the public, that is, between

the arguments about Montaigne and civilization and the death of Virginia Woolf, that this digression gains its peculiarly disquieting resonance.

In itself, the story of "old Mrs. West and her idiot boy" raises general, though complex, moral questions, as, for example, who should determine the limits of physical and mental health? What justification is there for viewing these individuals as a group who collectively must be put away? How does one gauge the infringement on the well-being of another? Leonard's account, with its reference to the Wests in their Sunday clothes, indicates his role as the necessary middleman between the working class and the authorities, sanctioned as such by his education and social standing. Yet this digressive account also connects with Leonard Woolf's own life, and in particular with the episode he is about to narrate. Indeed, the answers he and Virginia had found to such questions had to a great extent shaped their life together. How was she to be cared for during her periods of illness and breakdown? Should she be nursed at home or handed over to the care of a professional institution? If she had children, might they be "imbecile"?[52] The West story must have returned Leonard to problems that were deeply personal, that had been rehearsed but ultimately not laid to rest. He chose not to put Virginia into professional care when she seemed close to a nervous breakdown in 1941; his feelings of guilt when she committed suicide must have been overwhelming. In contrast, he helped the Wests have their son put into care, and this decision too resulted in a tragic death.

Narrating this episode as part of the story of his own life, Leonard does not make these personal connections. In fact he makes no connections in this paradoxically digressive and paratactic account. He neither personalizes the digression, nor does he reflect generally on it, by thinking back to the obvious point of connection, that is, his argument a few pages before about the rights of the individual. There are even verbal echoes between the episode and the Montaigne argument. Leonard describes in the latter how he first recognized the moral necessity of the rights of others when as a child he saw puppies being drowned;[53] his narration of the West incident, on the other hand, makes a literal contrast between healthy animals and imbecile children, in favor of the former. For Leonard clearly found this episode both troubling and, in some unutterable way, deeply significant, as the detail with which it is narrated attests. For the reader the suggestion of significant links and echoes that run through Leonard's narrative are irresistible. We want to make sense of what is going on, to link the digressions and the paratactic episodes, particularly since Leonard stresses his own desire and incapacity to do so. Yet his style of narration is perhaps the precondition for any kind of recall; perhaps only through free-association could the pain of revisiting and recording these events be endured. Ultimately Woolf does offer an interpretation of this "anecdote" or "digression," but only on a wide historico-political scale, as representative in some vague sense of the sickness of the age. Beyond this Woolf is helpless to understand the "meaning" of his digression, just as he was helpless before the tragedy of the West boy's death and Virginia's suicide. Neither a more personal interpretation, nor one that connects with the earlier arguments about civilization and human rights, is possible. The reflective, "civilized" style of Leonard Woolf's autobiography resists the incorporation of the bodily and the irrational, yet painfully recognizes that these narratives not only must be told, but further are of a terrifying significance, at once personal and political.

In a letter to Ethel Smyth, Virginia Woolf refers briefly to the West story:

> Its a good thing to have books to believe in—and any number of little drudgeries: food to order: a village play to rehearse; and old Mrs West and her idiot boy—they took an hour this afternoon. We shant I suppose be killed; but I think of Montaigne, let death find me planting cabbages. A disease has struck our gooseberries.[54]

From the 1930s on, Virginia Woolf had become increasingly preoccupied with the question of writing women's lives. She urged her friends to write their autobiographies and she began to write her own. Her correspondence with Ethel Smyth is sustained by these questions; what it is possible for women to write, what still cannot be said. And I would like, in conclusion, to suggest that in this correspondence a new style of Montaignian conversation emerged at about the time when Leonard and Virginia Woolf's readings were diverging. Woolf's Montaigne quotation is reworked in the above letter for Smyth, who shared her enthusiasm for the *Essais*. But the twist, "Its life that matters," is replaced by an image from an earlier essay, "Que philosopher, c'est apprendre à mourir": "Je veux[. . .] que la mort me treuve plantant mes choux, mais nonchalant d'elle, et encore plus de mon jardin imparfait."[55] By wittily extending the quotation into her own gardening, Woolf has not only extended the meta-phoric to the literal, but has also transplanted the coded quotation from her diary into a context of conversation. Although in a tantalizing echo of the Montaigne conversation between the Woolfs Ethel tells Woolf of her intention to write a "chapter on Vanity," the promise is misleading and also unfulfilled.[56] Their correspondence was no meditation on death, but quickly had as its focus life-writing, or rather the writing of their lives, and of women's lives in general.

Woolf had already read, and greatly admired, Smyth's memoirs. She ap-preciated their openness, their brashness even, their physicality—but recog-nized that even an apparently uninhibited account such as Ethel's left much unsaid:

> I'm interested that you cant write about masturbation. That I understand. What puzzles me is how this reticence co-habits with your ability to talk openly magnificently, freely about—say H. B. I couldn't do one or the other. But as so much of life is sexual—or so they say—it rather limits autobiography if this is blacked out. It must be, I suspect, for many generations, for women; for its like breaking the hymen—if thats the membrane's name—a painful operation, and I suppose connected with all sorts of subterranean instincts.[57]

These, as Woolf calls them, "sexual speculations" constitute the background to her much quoted phrase "There's never been a womans autobiography." The hesitations and provisos of her remarks reinforce their speculatory note and might seem to allow her a somewhat ironic distance on the subject—but they in fact preface an autobiographical account of the sexual abuse she experienced as a child. For the conversation that Smyth and Woolf established in their correspondence provides the context in which such life-writing might occur. The Montaignian overtones are unmistakable. Without her "affec-tions," Woolf claims, "[a]ll my entrails, light, marrow, juice, pulp would be gone. [. . .]Take away my love for my friends and my burning and pressing sense of the importance and lovability and curiosity of human life and I should be nothing but a membrane, a fibre, uncoloured, lifeless to be thrown away like any other excreta."[58]

In letters to her other intimate female correspondents, she reports with relish this new open and sometimes bawdy style. Writing to Vita Sackville-West, she describes attending a concert at the Austrian Embassy and how "in the slow movement she [Ethel] said 'This is like the movement of ones bowels' —at which the attache's sitting by us, jumped."[59] And in a slightly later and elaborated version to her sister, Vanessa, Ethel is reported as saying "'Isn't this slow movement sublime—natural and heavy and irresistible like the movement of one's own bowels.' All the dapper little diplomats blushed."[60] And this bawdiness is not just related to bodily functions that, although ungendered, are traditionally read as male. Metaphors referring to menstruation, to the loss of virginity, as in the letter above, or to her sister's miscarriage, and anecdotes about sanitary towels, illustrate how fully this conversation is based on the experience of the woman's body. And this facilitates other narratives, accounts of the world as perceived through physical illness, such as "the history of my spine": "One day I'll write the history of my spine: I think I can feel every knob: and my whole body feels like a web spread on the knobs, and twitchy and sagging and then sinking into delicious rest."[61] It is worth noting that *On Being Ill*, originally published in 1926, was republished by the Hogarth Press in November 1930.[62]

But the conversation also yielded quite straightforwardly autobiographical stories, on Woolf's part about her marriage to Leonard, her writing, her madness. What I am suggesting is that from this basic frankness about the body, and by extension through accounts of her illness and its relation to the mind, or, one could say, the novelist's imaginary, Virginia Woolf was able to give the fullest account of her own life. And it seems likely that she was quite aware of this progression—or connectedness—and of its persistently problematic character. If their intimate conversation in this correspondence facilitated a new kind of life-writing, could such writing be made public? Her desire to write a book about the sexual life of women is born in an appropriately Eureka-like moment: "the very last morning in my bath I had a sudden influx of ideas," she writes to Ethel on 24 January 1931.[63] "The very last morning" refers to the day before her joint appearance with Ethel at a meeting of the London National Society for Women's Service, in which they both spoke, not about sex, but about professions for women. Yet the title of Woolf's projected book is also "Professions for Women," suggesting that it might well be a reflection on the question of public writing about women's experience (as outlined above), rather than an account of the experience as such.[64] And the book that grew out of this revelation was *Three Guineas,* not an account of the sexual life of women, but a polemical feminist essay that might make possible the publishing of such accounts in the future and that has itself been read as a "collective autobiography."[65]

Writing and publishing a woman's life remained problematic, as Woolf reflects in this letter of 24 December 1940 to Ethel Smyth:

> I was thinking the other night that there's never been a womans
> autobiography. [. . .]Chastity and modesty I suppose have been
> the reason. Now why shouldnt you be not only the first woman
> to write an opera, but equally the first to tell the truths about her-
> self? Isnt the great artist the only person to tell the truth? I should
> like an analysis of your sex life. [. . .]More introspection. More
> intimacy.[66]

Montaigne did not set out to write autobiography, but the essayistic mode as he fashioned it was capacious enough to allow for its beginnings. His growing and overriding sense of the newness of his *Essais* is bound up with the discovery of an autobiographical discourse.[67] Rather than telling his life as linear history, Montaigne increasingly inscribes himself into the text, as is captured by Woolf's remark that the *Essais* "reach not their end, but their suspension in full career."[68] And the style of self-inscription—incorporating the writing and the physical self; indeed, the writing self as the physical self—mirrors Woolf's own preoccupation with how to body forth voices, with a literature of embodiment.

"C'est le seul livre au monde de son espece," writes Montaigne of his *Essais.*[69] As a consequence much of his rhetoric of self-portraiture describes these beginnings, both anxiously and with pride, as much to express the author's developing sense of his project as to prepare his readers. "There's never been a womans autobiography," writes Virginia Woolf four hundred years later. It is perhaps the circularity, the self-deprecatory rhetoric, the subversive yet insistent insertion of the personal and physical—that is, all of those characteristics that mark Montaigne's essay as nascent—that appealed to Woolf in her own criticism. And they may have suggested possibilities for how to compose that new genre—which itself might look remarkably like an *essai*—women's autobiography.

Notes

Many thanks to Julian Maddison, who continues to take beautiful photographs illustrating my work. I am extremely grateful for the advice of my two Renaissance readers, Terence Cave and Angela Scholar. Finally, particular thanks are due to Kathy Laing and Alice Staveley, more than common readers, their knowledge and friendship inscribed in my essay.

1. Postcards to Ethel Smyth, 23 April 1931, and Vita Sackville-West, 23 April 1931, and a letter to Vanessa Bell, 24 April 1931, all describe this visit. Woolf, *The Letters of Virginia Woolf,* edited by Nigel Nicolson and Joanne Trautmann, 6 vols. (New York: Harcourt Brace Jovanovich, 1975–80), 4:317–19.

2. Virginia Woolf reviewed the Navarre Society edition of Charles Cotton's translation of 1685 (edited by William Carew Hazlitt, 5 vols., 1923); her review appeared in the *Times Literary Supplement,* 31 January 1924, and she included it, with minor revisions, in *The Common Reader: First Series,* edited by Andrew McNeillie (New York: Harcourt Brace Jovanovich [Harvest], 1984), 58–68. Leonard Woolf reviewed E. J. Trechmann's translation of *The Essays of Montaigne,* 2 vols. (London: Oxford University Press, 1927) for the rubric "The World of Books" in *The Nation and Athenaeum,* 17 September 1927, 778. I quote from Trechmann's translation throughout, in part simply for reasons of clarity, in part because of his connection with the Woolfs (through their publication of his translation of *The Diary of Montaigne's Journey to Italy*), but, perhaps most important, because his translation of the *Essais* was contemporaneous with the reception I am discussing. For details of the editions of the *Essais* read by Woolf, see Andrew McNeillie's notes, in Woolf, *The Essays of Virginia Woolf,* 4 (of 6) vols. to date, edited by Andrew McNeillie (London: Hogarth Press, 1986–94), 4:80.

3. "'But at such an age you may never return from so long a journey.' What do I care? When I start upon it I think neither of the return, nor of the goal. I only undertake it to keep myself on the move, as long as I like movement." *Essays of Montaigne,* 2:444. In fact, Leonard Woolf concludes the last two chapters of the final volume of his autobiography with variations on the refrain "The journey not the arrival matters." *The Journey Not the Arrival Matters: An Autobiography of the Years 1939 to 1969,* vol. 5 of *The Autobiography of Leonard Woolf* (1969; reprint, New York: Harcourt Brace Jovanovich [Harvest], 1975), 172, 210.

4. Leonard Woolf, *The Journey*, 18–19.

5. "Just as the novels break up the habitual progressions of narrative through easily identifiable beginnings, middles and ends, so, in her essays, Woolf tends to write in a way that is consciously exploratory, seeming to move from one point to the next in a tangential fashion rather than to develop logically in the traditional form of an argument." Rachel Bowlby, introduction to *A Woman's Essays* (1992), in *Virginia Woolf: Introductions to the Major Works,* edited by Julia Briggs (London: Virago, 1994), 252. Bowlby's introduction includes a close reading of the digressive style of "The Patron and the Crocus." Describing Woolf's essayistic style with particular reference to Montaigne, Juliet Dusinberre remarks how "Woolf silently enlists Montaigne in the politics of discourse." *Virginia Woolf's Renaissance: Woman Reader or Common Reader?* (Iowa City: University of Iowa Press, 1997), 45.

6. Montaigne, *Essais,* edited by Alexandre Micha, 3 vols. (Paris: Garnier Flammarion, 1969), 3:207. Trechmann's translation reads: "I go out of my way, but rather through licence than inadvertence." *Essays,* 2:464.

7. Roland Barthes, *S/Z* (Paris: Éditions du Seuil, 1970), 10.

8. Montaigne, *Essais,* 3:299. Trechmann's translation reads: "Speech is half his who speaks, and half his who hears. The latter must prepare to take it according to the impetus it receives. As with tennis players, he who takes the ball must shift his position and make ready according to the movement of the striker, and according to the nature of the stroke." *Essays,* 2:567.

9. This statement is intended to give a broad characterization only—subject of course to striking exceptions. In his study of Montaigne's reception in France, *Montaigne in France 1812–1852* (New York: Columbia University Press, 1940), Donald Frame argues that the style and self-portraiture of the *Essais* came to be more generally appreciated only among the nineteenth-century readership (previous readers having tended to view Montaigne as a moralist and a skeptic, whose prose style was at best regrettable). "The years 1812–1852," Frame argues, "may be called the period of birth and development of the modern attitude that regards Montaigne from the threefold viewpoint of personality, ideas, and style" (vii).

10. Walter Pater has been identified as a key figure in the nineteenth-century English reception of Montaigne, establishing "the *Essays* as an essentially modernist work: one of dynamic, provisional writing in the service of relative understanding." Dudley M. Marchi, "Virginia Woolf Crossing the Borders of History, Culture, and Gender: The Case of Montaigne, Pater, and Gournay," *Comparative Literature Studies* 34 (1997): 3.

11. Sainte-Beuve, *Les Grands Ecrivains français. XVIe siècle: Les prosateurs* (Paris: Garnier, 1926), 252. "People are talking about the departed, about his endearing characteristics and his philosophy which over the course of his life was so often called into question; people are talking about themselves" (my translation).

12. Woolf, *The Diary of Virginia Woolf,* edited by Anne Olivier Bell and Andrew McNeillie, 5 vols. (New York: Harcourt Brace Jovanovich, 1977–84), 3:7 (8 April 1925).

13. Ibid., 7–8. (Here and throughout the chapter, square brackets around an ellipsis indicate Luckhurst's elision, in contrast to an ellipsis standing in the quoted text.—*Ed.*)

14. Although "De la vanité" is in large part a meditation on death, this topic is not, as it is in earlier *essais* on the same subject, overtly stated in the title. In this respect this essay might be seen to follow the digressive principle of the *Essais:* "Les noms de mes chapitres n'embrassent pas toujours la matiere" (3:207). Trechmann's translation: "The headings of my chapters do not always embrace the matter of them" (*Essays,* 2:464). Yet, more important in this case, the naming of the essay is part of a rhetorical performance of Montaigne's argument about death—that death need not be announced as such, for being inseparable from life, the *Essais* will necessarily speak of it when speaking of any topic related to the human condition. This argument is particularly true of the later essays, in which Montaigne felt more keenly his own approaching death. Woolf necessarily condenses the argument into her coded "Montaigne quotation," since no single quote could encompass the argument of this essay. Just as Montaigne's philosophy allows him to move between life and death without ceremony in this and other essays, so Woolf's Montaigne quotation allows her to move between death- and life-writing in her diary.

15. Woolf, *Diary,* 2:300–301 (5 May 1924).

16. Ibid., 4:176 (2 September 1933).

17. John Mepham, "Mourning and Modernism," in *Virginia Woolf: New Critical Essays,* edited by Patricia Clements and Isobel Grundy (London: Vision; Totowa, N.J.: Barnes and Noble, 1983), 149–51.

18. Woolf, *Diary,* 4:193 (7 December 1933).

19. Dusinberre, *Virginia Woolf's Renaissance,* 16, notes that Woolf's 1903 diary contains "much evidence of her imitations of Montaigne." Woolf had received a copy of the *Essais* from her brother Thoby as a birthday present that year.

20. Woolf, *Diary,* 3:67 (20 March 1926).

21. Woolf, "The Modern Essay" (published in 1922 as "Modern Essays"), in *The Common Reader,* 211–22, 217.

22. Montaigne, *Essais,* "Au lecteur," 1:35. "Je n'ay pas plus faict mon livre que mon livre m'a faict, livre consubstantiel à son autheur, d'une occupation propre, membre de ma vie; non d'une occupation et fin tierce et estrangere comme tous autres livres" (2:36). Trechmann's translation reads: "I have no more made my book than my book has made me; a book consubstantial with its author, concerned with me alone, a part of my life; not dealing with and aimed at other and third persons, like all other books." *Essays,* 2:116.

23. Judith Allen, "Those Soul Mates: Virginia Woolf and Michel de Montaigne," in *Virginia Woolf: Themes and Variations: Selected Papers from the Second Annual Con-*

ference on Virginia Woolf, edited by Vara Neverow-Turk and Mark Hussey (New York: Pace University Press, 1993), 192.

24. Woolf, *Diary,* 2:261 (17 August 1923).

25. Anne E. Fernald, "*A Room of One's Own,* Personal Criticism, and the Essay," *Twentieth Century Literature* 40 (1994): 169.

26. For Montaigne the term *essai* refers to his method (the trying out or "essay-ing" of various topics); "essay" is subsequently coined by Francis Bacon as a generic title, retrospectively making Montaigne's *Essais* the origin of the genre. See Hugo Friedrich's discussion of this point in *Montaigne* [1949], translated by Robert Rovint (Paris: Gallimard, 1968), 353–58.

27. Juliet Dusinberre, "Virginia Woolf and Montaigne," *Textual Practice* 5 (1991): 220. The questionable gender of Woolf's reader/Woolf as reader—"Woman Reader or Common Reader?"—underpins Dusinberre's more general discussion of Woolf's reading of the Renaissance, but see in particular Dusinberre, *Virginia Woolf's Renaissance,* 11–16.

28. Woolf, *Essays,* 4:71.

29. Dusinberre, *Virginia Woolf's Renaissance,* 56.

30. Woolf, *Essays,* 4:73.

31. Ibid., 77.

32. Ibid.

33. Woolf, *Diary,* 2:282 (3 January 1924).

34. Montaigne, *Essais,* 3:159. Trechmann's translation reads, "Here, a little more de-cently, you have the excrements of an old mind, now hard, now loose, and always un-digested." *Essays,* 2:409.

35. Woolf, *Essays,* 4:78.

36. Woolf, *Diary,* 2:261 (17 August 1923).

37. See his essay on friendship, "De l'amitié," in *Essais,* 1:231–42; *Essays,* 1:182–95.

38. Montaigne, *Essais,* 1:304. Trechmann's translation reads, "I needed what I once had, a certain interchange of ideas that would lead me on, that would sustain and lift me up." *Essays,* 1:249–50.

39. "The Otways, perhaps, inherited their love of reading from the ancient drama-tist whose name they share, whether they descend from him (as they like to think) or not. [. . .] Her [Penelope Otway's] father's library, though strong chiefly in the litera-ture of the East, had its Popes, its Drydens, its Shakespeares, in various stages of splendour and decay; and if his daughters chose to amuse themselves by reading what they liked, certainly it was a method of education which, since it spared his purse, deserved his benediction." "Mr. Conrad: A Conversation" (1923), in *The Captain's Death Bed and Other Essays,* edited by Leonard Woolf (1950; reprint, New York: Harcourt Brace Jovanovich [Harvest], 1978), 76–81, 76.

40. Woolf, *Diary,* 2:261 (17 August 1923, emphasis mine).

41. Woolf, "The Modern Essay," in *The Common Reader*, 211–12, 216–17.

42. Woolf, *Diary*, 2:261 (17 August 1923).

43. Ibid., 265.

44. For a wider analysis of Woolf's use of the dialogic in her essay-writing, see Melba Cuddy-Keane, "The Rhetoric of Feminist Conversation: Virginia Woolf and the Trope of the Twist," in *Ambiguous Discourse: Feminist Narratology and British Women Writers*, edited by Kathy Mezei (Chapel Hill: University of North Carolina Press, 1996), 137–61.

45. Leonard Woolf, "Montaigne," in *The Nation and Athenaeum*, 17 September 1927, 778.

46. Ibid.

47. Notably the work of Arthur Armaingaud, who was at this time establishing a new edition of the *Essais* (6 vols. Paris: L. Conard, 1924–27).

48. Leonard Woolf, "Montaigne," 778.

49. Woolf, *Diary*, 2:265 (5 September 1923).

50. Leonard Woolf, *The Journey*, 44.

51. Ibid., 51. The full text of this digression, from which subsequent references are taken, is at 49–52.

52. Hermione Lee describes how Leonard considered admitting Virginia Woolf to a "home" after her suicide attempt of September 1913. *Virginia Woolf* (1996; New York: Knopf, 1997), 325–26. Further, Virginia's decision not to have children "may have been forced upon her in the same way that she felt 'forced' into rest-homes and rest-cures" (331).

53. Leonard Woolf, *The Journey*, 20–21.

54. Woolf to Ethel Smyth, 17 May 1940, in Woolf, *Letters*, 6:399.

55. Montaigne, *Essais*, 1:134–35. And in Trechmann's translation: "[I] hope that Death may find me planting my cabbages, but indifferent to him and still more to the unfinished state of my garden." *Essays*, 1:83.

56. Woolf to Ethel Smyth, 9 March 1931, in Woolf, *Letters*, 4:297.

57. Woolf to Ethel Smyth, 12 January 1941, ibid., 6:459–60.

58. Woolf to Ethel Smyth, 19 August 1930, ibid., 4:203.

59. Woolf to Vita Sackville-West, 30 October 1930, ibid., 4:240.

60. Woolf to Vanessa Bell, 2 November 1930, ibid., 4:244.

61. Woolf to Ethel Smyth, 4 September 1930, ibid., 4:208.

62. Curiously, *The Art of Dying*, "an anthology of 'last words' edited by Francis Birrell and F. L. Lucas, was also published [by the Hogarth Press] in this year." See Woolf, *Letters*, 4:220 n. 2.

63. Woolf to Ethel Smyth, 24 January 1931, in Woolf, *Letters*, 4:280.

64. See Woolf, *Diary*, 4:6 (20 January 1931).

65. See Georgia Johnston, "Women's Voice: *Three Guineas* as Autobiography," in

Virginia Woolf: Themes and Variations: Selected Papers from the Second Annual Conference on Virginia Woolf, edited by Vara Neverow-Turk and Mark Hussey (New York: Pace University Press, 1993), 321–28.

66. Woolf, *Letters,* 6:453 (24 December 1940). Significantly, at this key moment in her discussion of "life-writing," Woolf invokes Rousseau rather than Montaigne. And, although this chapter is not the place to begin an exploration of Woolf's reading of Rousseau, that is an area that undoubtedly touches on and may further illuminate many of the issues raised here in connection with Montaigne.

67. See, for example, Montaigne's discussion of autobiography, which begins, "Nous n'avons nouvelles que de deux ou trois anciens qui ayent battu ce chemin; et si ne pouvons dire si c'est du tout en pareille maniere à cette cy, n'en connoissant que les noms. Nul depuis ne s'est jetté sur leur trace. C'est une espineuse entreprinse, et plus qu'il ne semble, de suyvre une alleure si vagabonde que celle de nostre esprit." *Essais,* 2:48. Trechmann's translation reads, "We hear of only two or three of the ancients who have trod this path, and yet we cannot say that it was quite after this manner, knowing only their names. No one since has followed their track. It is a thorny undertaking, and more so than it seems, to follow so vagrant a course as that of our mind." *Essays,* 1:365.

68. Woolf, *Essays,* 4:77. Her remark also suggests the irony that Montaigne should discover autobiography toward the end of his life, an irony on which the *Essais* themselves also reflect: "J'ay choisi le temps où ma vie, que j'ay à peindre, je l'ay toute devant moy: ce qui en reste tient plus de la mort." *Essais,* 3:268. And in Trechmann's translation: "I have chosen the time when my whole life, which I have to portray, lies before me; what remains of it is more allied to death." *Essays,* 2:532.

69. *Essais,* 2:56. Trechmann's translation reads: "It is the only book of its kind in the world." *Essays,* 1:373.

3

Rough with Rubies
Virginia Woolf and the Virgin Queen

⚘ Reginald Abbott

$\mathcal{I}$n his study of period representations of Elizabeth I, Roy C. Strong identifies an idealized concept of the queen that could be called "the Elizabethan icon," for a specifically religious iconographic tradition informs his analysis of "the cult images of the *Diva Elizabetha*": "The remote and expressionless mask with its calm and never-ending vision, the face of *divina majestas,* of the God-ordained ruler of the Middle Ages, lives on and is indeed, through the Elizabeth-cult, revitalized in the hieratic icon-like images of the Virgin Queen."[1] Virginia Woolf's own Elizabethan icon—expressed specifically as the historical Elizabeth in the essays "Reading" and "Waxworks at the Abbey" and in *Orlando,* or as types of Elizabeth in other novels—becomes, over the course of a writing career, an idiosyncratic dual representation of power: woman as ruler and woman as artist. Ultimately, in *Between the Acts,* these two halves of an icon of female power are presented in a complex, but not competitive, proximity to each other as two distinct characters: Mrs. Manresa and Miss La Trobe.

My concept of the Woolfian double icon as it culminates in *Between the Acts* has little to do with critical analyses of the novel within the context of Woolf's pacifism (in the last chapter of this collection, David McWhirter

Queen Elizabeth, attributed by Roy Strong to Cornelius Ketel, alternatively to
Federigo Zuccaro. The sieve symbolizes the queen's chastity and discernment, but her
"long thin hands" are bare. Pinacoteca Nazionale, Siena. By permission of Alinari/
Art Resource.

discusses Woolf's response in *Between the Acts* to T. S. Eliot's reactionary politics and aesthetics), and it may even strike some readers as a violation of established feminist interpretations of Woolf's feminist agenda. Further, my identification of this Woolfian double icon (or diptych) is not a historical study of the Virgin Queen, although it begins with the real queen and always points back, one way or another, to the historical Elizabeth. Woolf's iconic interpretations of the queen are no more accurate than the extant pictures of Elizabeth are realistic: rather, they are a composite of what she observed to be the hallmarks of royal female power. The most significant symbol of this power derives from a tangible and important element of Woolf's own past that is, not incidentally, one of the most frequently mentioned precious stones in all of her writings: the ruby.

Jewelry is not considered important in Virginia Woolf's writing or thought to have much interested her personally. Alex Zwerdling writes that her "contempt for finery—fashionable clothes, jewelry, dressing for dinner, stylish furnishings—was so extreme that it amounted to a declaration of independence." An attentive reading of her diaries and letters, however, disproves this hasty summation. Throughout her life, Woolf had a complex and contradictory fascination with jewelry, and jewelry imagery recurs throughout her writings, especially in her fiction. In *Orlando,* for instance, Orlando receives an emerald ring from Queen Elizabeth, compares Sasha to the "green flame [that] seems hidden in the emerald," and survives a metamorphosis in the Middle East by selling segments of an emerald and pearl chain. All these emeralds are historically plausible details in a novel that Woolf decided "should be truthful; but fantastic."[2]

A "fantastic" detail in *Orlando,* or, more correctly, an anachronistic detail, is Orlando and Sukey's love-making "among the rubies" captured from "Spanish ventures": the New World rewarded sixteenth-century Spanish explorers not with rubies but with emeralds. Another anachronism occurs later when Woolf refers to Elizabeth's taking snuff—a habit that developed in the seventeenth century, with usage of the word for powdered tobacco appearing, according to the *OED,* around 1680.[3] But, as Melba Cuddy-Keane and Gillian Beer among others have demonstrated, history and the historical are problematic (if not downright unsatisfactory) terms when applied to Woolf's writings.[4]

Beer, for example, argues for history in Woolf's writings as "a matter of textures (horse-hair or velvet), changing light (flambeaux or gas-light), not of events or 'dominant figures of the age,'" and claims that Woolf has an "acute sense of the shifts in material and intellectual circumstances," while human beings "stand in for each other across the centuries."[5] But it should be noted that Woolf hardly demonstrates "an acute sense of the shifts in material . . . circumstances" when she gets the historical "textures" wrong, as seen above, in *Orlando*. Further, Beer neglects Woolf's consistent interest in at least one "dominant figure" of an age; indeed, this dominant figure became the name-sake of an age that captured Woolf's imagination. Perhaps it would be helpful, then, to take the example of Woolf's interest in Elizabeth as a means of investigating, at least in one instance, how and to what purposes she manipulates history. As the following discussions will demonstrate, Woolf's prose portraits of Elizabeth do contain, as noted above, historically inaccurate details—but details that are important to her own experience and, in turn, to a daring new inscription of a tradition of female power.

In an early book review, the queen makes her entry, quite dramatically, into Woolf's critical writings: "Thus, splendid and inscrutable, she rode through London on the day of her Coronation; arches, pyramids, and fountains stood in her way, from which boys sang greeting, a fine snow kept falling over her, but the gems and the golden collars shone clearly through the whiteness." This sentence, which concludes Woolf's review of Frank A. Mumby's *The Girlhood of Queen Elizabeth* (1909), is her first personal portrait of Elizabeth. We know it is her own portrait because the text on which the passage is based differs significantly. Mumby translates in full an original document of the period, Il Schifanoya's letter to the Castellan of Mantua, that describes in some detail Elizabeth's coronation procession: "On the morning of Saturday the 14th, as in the afternoon Her Majesty was to make her state entry into London, the whole Court so sparkled with jewels and gold collars, that they cleared the air, though it snowed a little." In Mumby's transcription of an eyewitness account, it was Elizabeth's court that shone with gems and gold collars, not the queen herself. Woolf's subtle revision denotes an early and significant connection between the person of Elizabeth as sovereign queen and the presence of many sparkling gems.[6]

As Horace Walpole observed, pictorial tradition associates Elizabeth with many gems, specifically with "a bushel of pearls": "Elizabeth appears like an

Indian idol, totally composed of pearls and necklaces. A pale Roman nose, a head of hair loaded with crowns and powdered with diamonds, a vast ruff, a vaster farthingale and a bushel of pearls are features by which everyone knows at once the picture of Elizabeth." Yet, although the Elizabethan era for its costume and jewelry has been christened the "Age of Pearls," Woolf's concept of Elizabeth does not highlight them. Returning to the subject ten years later, in the unpublished, deeply subjective essay "Reading" (1919), she depicts Elizabeth with many ruby rings:

> Whether some tinted wax-work is the foundation of my view, I do not know; but she [Elizabeth] always appears very distinctly in the same guise. She flaunts across the terrace superbly and a little stiffly like the peacock spreading its tail. She seems slightly infirm, so that one is half inclined to smile; and then she raps out her favourite oath . . . when, far from being infirm, she shows a masculine and rather repulsive vigour. Perhaps, under all that stiff brocade, she has not washed her shrivelled old body? She breakfasts off beer and meat and handles the bones with fingers rough with rubies.[7]

Strong's study of the many "icons" of Elizabeth documents that, although rich in jewelry, costume, and allegorical and historical references, the icon created and perpetuated by Elizabeth and her court does not include hands "rough with rubies." Indeed, relatively few rings are visible in the famous, and not so famous, portraits of Elizabeth, and no rings set with stones that are clearly meant to be rubies. Various descriptions of Elizabeth during her reign do describe her exceptionally beautiful hands, of which she was quite vain. Still, in Mumby's book for example, the details of Elizabeth's coronation procession do not include any references to rings on her fingers. In the passage that influenced Woolf's book review, the eyewitness states that the queen had "nothing in her hands but gloves."[8]

Thus, the prose portrait found in "Reading" will disappoint those who are looking for historical accuracy. Rather, it establishes the Elizabethan icon in Woolf's imagination and points to its development in her fiction. For Woolf, Elizabeth was a (female) historical subject approached by (male) historians with different emphases but with a similar historical method—a method that we have only to turn to *A Room of One's Own* to appreciate. Accordingly, her understanding of Elizabeth involves a metaphorical projection of the queen as a malleable substance—wax—capable of being shaped and exploited by different hands—female—and known differently. For this unapologetically personal, flagrantly subjective, and frequently anachronistic (re)forming of the historical Elizabeth, wax or a waxwork—not perishable, but not permanent; paintable, but not painterly; sculpturesque, but not sculptural—is an apt metaphor. Although this "tinted wax-work" imagery resurfaces for further critical exposition in Woolf's "Waxworks at the Abbey" (1928), to which I will return, it is also the basis for a Woolfian impression of queenly power and artistry manipulated in her fiction through "ruby" and "Elizabethan" images.

As a memoirist, Woolf recalled witnessing an "intense" love between Stella Duckworth and Jack Hills that was also a "respectable" or "official" engagement: "And it was through that engagement that I had my first vision—so intense, so exciting, so rapturous was it that the word vision applies—my first vision then of love between man and woman. It was to me like a ruby; the love I detected that winter of their engagement, glowing red, clear, intense." Later in the passage, Woolf states that she can connect this ruby-ringed "first vision" of love only "with respectable engagements; unofficial love never gives me the same feeling." The passage, a poignant tribute to Stella and Jack's passion, appropriately picks up the cultural and historical associations between the color red and love: the blood of Christ and the martyrs was shed for human redemption; amorousness was produced by the sanguine humor—and, to cite an example dearer to Woolf than either of those, in Shakespeare's *Cymbeline* Cytherea's kisses become "rubies unparagoned."[9]

This blood-red ruby love, however, is only a recollection of Stella and Jack's socially sanctioned union. In *Night and Day,* a novel reflecting the events surrounding that tragic marriage but also based on Vanessa's untraditional marriage with Clive Bell and Woolf's own conflicting emotions regarding both her sister and her brother-in-law, the first important ruby ring in Woolf's fiction underscores the failure of the conventions of a "respectable" engagement while drawing on the power of the ring as a social sign representing the engagement. In fact, *Night and Day* could be called the story of an engagement ring in search of its rightful owner.

Legally and in marriage etiquette William Rodney owns the ring, but he never has it and never asserts a claim for it. His reluctant fiancée Katharine Hilbury wears it, but it jars—logically and syntactically—with Ralph Denham's simile about her: "her softness was like that of some vast snowy owl; she wore a ruby on her finger." The ring does not fit her properly, and, in an encounter with Ralph in which he finally confesses his love for her, it slips off her hand easily. Katharine proceeds to spin the ring on the table, and she then asks Ralph what she should do with it. The ring is claimed by Ralph only to be reclaimed by Katharine. At the novel's end, Katharine tells Cassandra Otway, the more proper object of William's affection, that the engagement ring will fit her without "'any alteration.'" In this extraordinary turn of events, absent William's first fiancée "proposes" to his second—a shockingly presumptuous exchange that violates marriage etiquette and simultaneously subverts heterosexuality as it reinforces more suitable heterosexual unions amongst the novel's characters. Cassandra receives the ring from Katharine but then gives it back—she wants William himself to give it to her. But it is Ralph who again steps forward to assert some form of ownership as he validates its transfer to Cassandra: "'everything's perfectly all right.'"[10]

The improbable physics of the ring's spinning on the table before Ralph and Katharine suggests a roulette wheel, a Wheel of Fortune, or even a dreidel as its possession determines the characters' relationships. This element of chance regarding remarkably passionless heterosexual relationships expresses Woolf's romantic inner conflicts around the time of the novel's creation—how rarely true passion (Stella and Jack's) can merge with societal approval. It further suggests the contradictions or counterindications that cluster around a public sign of love that is, for Woolf, a private symbol of "official love." Like Richard Alardyce's poetry, the ruby ring in *Night and Day* is misapprehended by a respectable world. The most important union being formed in the novel is not the publicly announced one of William and Katharine—the match her parents thought she was making—but that of Ralph and Katharine.

The novel appears to end, however, with "the force of habit" (498) as Mr. Hilbery picks up the dropped ruby ring that has rolled to his feet. His bow to Cassandra as he returns the ring he has been told is hers "release[s] automatically feelings of complaisance and urbanity" that are soon supplemented by a Ruskin-like escape from issues of human passion into a question about art (the date of the first performance of *Hamlet* [499]), which, for Mr. Hilbery in particular, pours "over the raw ugliness of human affairs its soothing balm." Shortly before Mr. Hilbery's entrance, Mrs. Hilbery has invoked Shakespearean "balm" with her musings on the bard's tomb, remarks that earlier "seemed to contract the enormously wide circle in which they were soaring to alight, airily and temporarily, upon matter of immediate moment" (497). Thus, the entire closing scene is one not of resolution, but of comic upheavals, spinnings, circlings, and rollings as various characters rise and sit simultaneously, speak simultaneously, and feel two emotions at once. Everything appears "official" but is actually loose and unresolved.

Similarly, "unofficial love" in *Mrs. Dalloway*—either heterosexual or homosexual—fails to match the "glowing red, clear intensity" of the ruby. A ruby ring enters the novel as something foreign and wild, tainted by scandal and blood, not English and not conventional—like its heir, Sally Seton: "Sally always said she had French blood in her veins, an ancestor had been with Marie Antoinette, had his head cut off, left a ruby ring. Perhaps that summer she came to stay at Bourton, walking in quite unexpectedly without a penny in her pocket. . . . There had been some quarrel at home. She literally hadn't a penny that night when she came to them—had pawned a brooch to come down." Interestingly, Woolf gives the character Sally Seton not only her own French ancestry but also virtually all the details of that inheritance: the Chevalier Antoine de l'Étang at the court of Versailles and a ruby ring said to have been given to him by Marie Antoinette. At the novel's end, we learn that the ruby ring was a royal gift of favor and had in fact been the pawned jewel enabling Sally to run away to Bourton.[11]

As the novel's erotic locus, the young Sally Seton decapitates flowers, walks naked down Bourton's halls, and is desired by both the young Clarissa and the young Hugh Whitbread. Both of these attachments—Clarissa's homosexual crush and Hugh's outburst of heterosexual passion in the smoking-room—are clearly not "respectable," are "unofficial." Further, Sally is herself a direct heir to the "not respectable" through her French ancestry and family lore of an illicit relationship with a queen. The evidence of this tie is, of course, the ring through which Woolf creates a tantalizing mesh of family and fiction, history and romance, truth and rumor, queens and jewels, monarchs and favorites, illicit couplings and sanctioned unions, all of which fall short, for one reason or another, of her own ruby "vision" of "official" love.

An important lesson in *Mrs. Dalloway* is that beauty and beautiful objects—especially jewelry—exist behind glass (Septimus reflects that "beauty was behind a pane of glass"), beyond reach, or hidden away. Clarissa admires, but does not buy, jewelry; she does not wear Richard's bracelet; Hugh does not buy the Spanish necklace. Opposing the visible social sign of the engagement ring, romantic relationships and personal identity come to be represented as jewels—a pearl or diamond—that are lost in the grass or hidden away and unapprehended by others: "And [Clarissa] felt that she had been given a present, wrapped up, and told just to keep it, not to look at it—a diamond, something infinitely precious, wrapped up, which, as they walked (up and down, up and down), she uncovered, or the radiance burnt through, the revelation, the religious feeling!"[12]

In contrast to Clarissa's musings on lost or concealed gems, Sally takes her real ruby ring and puts it to use for practical, not romantic, ends: to gain power over her own life. Although there is no question that Clarissa has an enduring crush on Sally, the young Sally pawns her ring "to stay at [or "come to"] Bourton" and to come to "them," not to go to Clarissa and to see her: "Oh yes, Sally remembered; she had it still, a ruby ring which Marie Antoinette had given her great-grandfather. She never had a penny to her name in those days. . . . But going to Bourton had meant so much to her—had kept her sane, she believed, so unhappy had she been at home." For Sally, the goal is not so much communion with Clarissa as escape from her family.[13] The means to her escape is a family heirloom that, like the other jewelry in the novel (metaphoric and real), never actually appears—it spends time "behind glass" at the pawnbroker's. Unlike the characters in *Night and Day* who cannot figure out the ruby ring's owner, shy away from its social significance, and fail to fulfill its romantic symbolism, Sally asserts her ownership, uses the intrinsic value of her ring, and functions in the novel, from beginning to end and in contrast to Clarissa, as an empowered woman. We know of Sally's husband and sons, but she appears at Clarissa's party as an independent personality from Clarissa's past inhabiting an independent present. To exaggerate Sally's independence would be a mistake, but the character was obviously important to Woolf, given that she takes on Woolf's own ancestry and is a vehicle for rewriting the history of Woolf's ruby ring (presumably sold more than a decade earlier) so that the ring liberates its owner and yet, in the end, is back in her possession. It is also important to remember that, of all the key characters in *Mrs. Dalloway,* Sally appears to be the least unhappy and the most fulfilled.

The totemic, but subverted, social power of the ruby ring in *Night and Day* that makes it "too hot to handle," as well as the eclipse of the ruby ring's historic past in *Mrs. Dalloway* by its value in pawn, are ambiguous statements—signaling an ambiguity Woolf develops elsewhere in her fiction. In *Orlando,* for example, the rubyless ring in the family crypt is, in one sense, a symbol of loss and corruption; in another sense, the ruby that has "rolled in a corner" is still a ruby while "crimson velvet turns to dust," and it is still bright while "the eye which was so lustrous, shines no more." In the earlier *Jacob's Room,* however, the perfect world of the store window appears to be the only place where the ruby can "live," where the color remains true: "Nothing is to be won from the shops, and Heaven knows it would be better to sit at home than haunt the plate-glass windows in the hope of lifting the shining green, the glowing ruby, out of them alive." In *The Years,* Woolf "destroys" a ruby: "With one blast," the March wind "blew out colour—even a Rembrandt in the National Gallery, even a solid ruby in a Bond Street window: one blast and they were gone." Later in the novel, the spectacle of the glowing ruby in a jewelry store window is crudely imitated in a "bright crowded street; here stained ruby with the light from picture palaces." Still, the nighttime street is full of people window-shopping and seeking genuine jewels, behind glass.[14]

But in *To the Lighthouse* there had been no question about the genuineness and permanence of the ruby. For Mrs. Ramsay it becomes a touchstone of incorruptibility and eternity: "there is a coherence in things, a stability; something, she meant, is immune from change, and shines out (she glanced at the window with its ripple of reflected lights) in the face of the flowing, the fleeting, the spectral, like a ruby."[15] This passage suggests a different reading of the passage from *Jacob's Room.* Perhaps those unworthy or incapable of wearing the ruby or dealing with its symbolism have "no hope" of obtaining it from the jeweler's window and "living up" to its significance. In this reading, the power of the stone has a discernible effect on those who have the proper presence for wearing it.

Several women who wear rubies in Woolf's writings are described, like Elizabeth in "Reading," as shriveled with age yet invested with masculine attributes of power—modern equivalents of the peacock's feathers and the "stiff brocade." In *The Voyage Out*, Mrs. Parry, perhaps the earliest "Elizabethan" character in Woolf's fiction, is described as an "insolent old harridan" who amuses herself while her husband is objectified as another gem in a collection: "poor Mr. Parry, who was understood to be shut up downstairs with cases full of gems."[16] In short, these bejeweled and "rubied" female characters are witchlike, and, as witches were thought to age prematurely from the occult power they used, so too in Woolf these powerful women show the marks of their age and experience.

In *The Years*, for example, Lady Lasswade's dinner party, which is given a curious "metallic" setting, provides a context for Aunt Warburton, another harridan-like woman whose marginal status is indicated by her approval of disobedience ("She liked boys who got into trouble") while she nevertheless displays a "rough" Elizabethan appearance: "She had a wedge-shaped yellow face with an occasional bristle on her chin; she was over eighty; but she sat as if she were riding a hunter, Kitty thought, glancing at her hands. They were coarse hands, with big finger-joints; red and white sparks flashed from her rings as she moved them." Further, Aunt Warburton is not the only Elizabethan icon in this novel. As if to demonstrate that there is little room between the aged, powerful, sexually rapacious, but undesirable crone and the more positive figure of the mature, sexually desirable woman, Woolf also gives us Eleanor Pargiter. In the chapter in which she visits her brother Morris at his wife's family estate, Eleanor observes her aging body while putting on her ruby pendant: "She twisted her thick hair, with the grey strand in it, rapidly into a coil; hung the jewel, a red blob like congealed raspberry jam with a gold seed in the centre, round her neck; and gave one glance at the woman who had been for fifty-five years so familiar that she no longer saw her—Eleanor Pargiter. That she was getting old was obvious; there were wrinkles across her forehead; hollows and creases where the flesh used to be firm."[17]

But the novel in which these complicated, contradictory images of the Virgin Queen had already come together most powerfully is, not surprisingly, *Orlando*. Elizabeth's entry there has much in common with Woolf's earlier portrait of the queen in "Reading," but it introduces an element of aggressive, female sexuality to be developed later in the novel:

> Such was his [Orlando's] shyness that he saw no more of her than her ringed hand in water; but it was enough. It was a memorable

hand; a thin hand with long fingers always curling as if round orb or sceptre; a nervous, crabbed, sickly hand; a commanding hand; a hand that had only to raise itself for a head to fall; a hand, he guessed, attached to an old body that smelt like a cupboard in which furs are kept in camphor; which body was yet caparisoned in all sorts of brocades and gems. . . . All this he felt as the great rings flashed in the water. [18]

As in "Reading," Woolf connects the queen's heavily ringed hands with her unwashed and aged body. The explicit male persona assigned to the queen in the essay merges with other qualities, however, to present a multilayered Elizabethan image of female sexual power.

In *Orlando,* Woolf aligns a predatory sexuality with the queen's very real, very public, sovereign power. Both of these aspects of Elizabeth's persona are registered in Orlando's olfactory memories of preoedipal sense perceptions— first felt as he kneels before the queen in the public space of the banquet hall and then verified when the queen pulls him into her bed. The image of Orlando as sexual prey "caught" in a private, secret, and sexual place by a "fur-bearing" queen whose body reminds him of a secret, sexual, and maternal space is superseded, however, by an expression of male sexual release as the skyrocket explodes and dyes the queen's face a passionate red: "'This,' she breathed, 'is my victory!'—even as a rocket roared up and dyed her cheeks scarlet."[19]

It would be easy to conflate the queen's sexual aggressiveness in this passage with her other "masculine" behavior and "maleness" as depicted by Woolf. The ravenous, bone-gnawing, "peacock" queen of "Reading," the snuff-sniffing queen who had but to raise a hand "for a head to fall" or who finds victory in forcing Orlando into her embrace, appropriates the popular image of Elizabeth's father Henry VIII—fittingly, since the historical Elizabeth may have boasted in the Armada Speech of 1588 of having "the body of a weak and feeble woman, but the heart and stomach of a king—and of a king of England too."[20] The Elizabeth of *Orlando,* however, also bears witness to a distinctly feminist, distinctly personal cluster of associations: complicating the image of the queen as crone is an alternative, much more positive (I cannot but see all of Woolf's images of the queen as positive) image that begins to suggest the depth of Woolf's personal identification with her.[21]

This depiction of Elizabeth pays detailed attention to her person—specifically her hands—as part of a narrowing process that takes the reader away from the Elizabeth of both official and factual history to a tightly focused ahistorical Woolfian perspective. In Woolf's review of Mumby's book, Elizabeth, processing through the London streets, is a blur of gold and stones. In "Reading," the mature queen walks on a terrace, but then the scene changes to an interior where the last detail is the queen's ruby-ringed hands at a banquet table. This narrowing of perspective, the moving away from the public to an interior setting and then to a "close-up" of the private Elizabeth, continues in *Orlando* where Orlando kneels before the queen at a banquet table and is at eye level with her jeweled hands. This limited view of the queen—this nonpublic, nontraditional, and, most important, nonmale historical perspective—"perhaps, accounts for [Orlando's] seeing nothing more likely to be of use to a historian."[22]

It was the patriarchal historical perspective that Woolf was most concerned with rejecting and revising as she modeled her own image of Elizabeth as a personification of female power. In "Waxworks at the Abbey," an essay published in the same year as *Orlando*, Woolf rejects the official voice and procedures of the tour guide and finds herself "in a very small chamber alone with Queen Elizabeth." Here, as in "Reading" and as in Orlando's first encounter with the queen, the last and most focused details are on the queen's hands: "The orb and the sceptre are held in the long thin hands of an artist, as if the fingers thrilled at the touch of them." As complement and contrast to the Duke of Wellington's top hat (suggestively described as "tall as a chimney, as straight as a ramrod"), the wax funeral figure of Elizabeth dominates the essay and, with the duke's top hat, concludes it as a real presence that silences crowds and "beckons" visitors to the Abbey, especially visitors willing to break rules and enter locked rooms before visiting hours.[23]

The essay also helps establish why the figure of Elizabeth came to dominate Woolf's concept of female power, particularly sovereign power. Two of her female successors are mentioned: Mary II and Anne. These monarchs, however, clearly do not measure up to Woolf's needs. Mary II was part of "an amiable pair of monarchs, bazaar-opening, hospital-inspecting, modern," a description that erases the historical Mary II, a shrewd, subtle ruler who died too soon, and invokes the "bazaar-opening" consort of George V in *Mrs. Dalloway*. Further,

Anne, in Woolf's view queen "only by accident," "fondles her orb in her lap with plump womanly hands that should have held a baby there." Although this description of Anne in maternal and wifely roles is poignant, suggestive of Woolf's own ambiguity about children and marriage, Anne clearly is no match for the "immensely intellectual, suffering and tyrannical" artist Woolf sees in Elizabeth's wax figure.[24]

And, crucially in this preview of the larger, more detailed depiction of Elizabeth in *Orlando,* Woolf describes the queen as possessing "the long thin hands of an artist"—an artist of power. By so characterizing Elizabeth, Woolf empowers herself as a female artist, and, as a female artist manipulating the image of a powerful historical figure, she appropriates and redirects the patriarchal power of the historians and biographers formerly in charge of the queen's reputation and image. On a personal level, Woolf's manipulation of Elizabeth bears directly on her friendly rivalry with Lytton Strachey, whose *Elizabeth and Essex,* published in the same year as *Orlando,* Woolf found "feeble," "shallow," and disappointing. But the larger context is, of course, the continuity of her interest in Elizabeth throughout her career and the consistent details of her Elizabethan icon as aligned against the patriarchal historical perspective. Indeed, Woolf's harshest response to official Elizabethan biography, albeit in a specific reference to a description of Mary Queen of Scots at her execution, came after *Orlando* in a 1934 diary entry regarding J. E. Neale's *Queen Elizabeth* (1934): "pretending to impartiality," she complains, the book "emphasises the double chin & the wig of Mary at the critical moment: a fig for impartial & learned historians! All men are liars."[25]

Woolf's most sustained response to "all men" as "liars" in the telling of history is *Between the Acts.*[26] Along with attempting much else, she continued in her last novel to weave real and metaphorical jewelry and gems into the narrative. Like *The Waves* it begins with a ring image as words become for Isa "two rings, perfect rings that floated them" (5). *Between the Acts* ends with Mr. Oliver's meditation on "the scurry and the scuffle, the rouge and the rings" (204). Giles, like the young Richard Dalloway in *The Voyage Out,* wears a red signet ring that "looked redder, for the flesh next it whitened as he gripped the arm of his chair" (60). Like *Jacob's Room* and *To the Lighthouse, Between the Acts* includes a lost brooch, and, as in *Night and Day,* an engagement ring is fumbled when the pageant character Eleanor hides the would-be public emblem of

Edgar's intentions. As in *Orlando,* there is an effective but inaccurate reference to the riches brought to Elizabeth by her ships (here *"[c]argoes of diamonds"* [84]).[27] And there are the personal references that pair *Between the Acts* with *Orlando.* The latter has been described by Sackville-West's son as "the longest and most charming love letter in literature," in which Sackville-West is the hero. Mitchell Leaska suggests that *Between the Acts* is a private, coded "letter of farewell" from Woolf to Sackville-West, where, one could add, Sackville-West becomes the novel's "antiheroine." Mrs. Manresa's rubies, red fingernails, and red lips, together with her passion and her extravagance, recall one of Woolf's last diary entries about Sackville-West: "She has grown opulent & bold & red— tomatoe coloured, & paints her fingers & lips which need no paint."[28]

As Woolf's response to "lying" male historians, *Between the Acts* is not so much reinvented history or a "new" history as an argument *"[d]rawn from our island history"* (76). It is a scenic, elliptic (literally full of ellipses), and literary gloss on men's "lies," but a gloss that, for all its inventiveness and reinvention, is still predicated on the "lies" themselves. For example, a portrait of a real Elizabethan hangs above an Oliver staircase; Mrs. Swithin's favorite reading is (Woolf's parody of) H. G. Wells's 1920 *Outline of History* (8); the Oliver library is filled with traditional history and science (19–20); and the section on Pointz Hall in "Figgis's Guide Book (1833)" (52) is still accurate. Further, the histori-cally informed reader of the novel is told that not every English soul reflects "the anguish of a Queen or the heroism of King Harry" (16); Mrs. Manresa counts off the British ruling dynasties at the pageant's beginning (81–82); and all the members of the audience for Miss La Trobe's production have a sense of historical order reinforced by the printed program. Still, *Between the Acts* is mostly historical revision, and at the heart of this revision is Woolf's most elaborate and detailed exposition of the Elizabethan icon. It is a Woolfian historicism that defines Elizabeth's role both in the pageantry of "male" history and in the world of Pointz Hall on the eve of war.[29]

In fact, the novel offers us no less than three Elizabeths: the pageant's fake Elizabeth, Eliza Clark; the bejeweled, regal Elizabeth, Mrs. Manresa; and the artist as ruler, Miss La Trobe. In Miss La Trobe's pageant, Elizabeth is the first and only real historical personage. All the other characters are allegorical or fictional, and all of English history before Elizabeth is personified by either a female allegorical figure or a chorus. Thus, the first true English voice can be read as not Chaucer's, but that of England's first successful female monarch.[30] Moreover, in implicit recognition of the layers of patriarchal history that are embedded in the queen's authorized image (Woolf here manages to get the pearls right), that image is both celebrated and caricatured by Eliza Clark:

> From behind the bushes issued Queen Elizabeth—Eliza Clark, licensed to sell tobacco. Could she be Mrs. Clark of the village shop? She was splendidly made up. Her head, pearl-hung, rose from a vast ruff. Shiny satins draped her. Sixpenny brooches glared like cats' eyes and tigers' eyes; pearls looked down; her cape was made of cloth of silver—in fact swabs used to scour saucepans. She looked the age in person. (83)

Eliza Clark as Elizabeth rules over a pageant that includes *"[c]argoes of diamonds"* and bushels of diamonds and rubies, and thus she is aligned with Woolf's earlier portraits, but this particular interpretation of male history and traditional iconography is Woolf's mockery of "lying" men as she alters the focus of their rituals ("'Why leave out the British Army?'" [157]). Woolf further appears to mock herself as she ostensibly turns the figure of "Waxworks at the Abbey" and the beginning of *Orlando* into a spokeswoman for kitchen products and a dime-store fashion jewelry department.[31]

Yet there are real rubies in *Between the Acts*, and they belong to Woolf's last Elizabethan icon: the "over-sexed, over-dressed" (41), and powdered Mrs. Manresa. Like Sally Seton in *Mrs. Dalloway*, she is the happiest and perhaps the most materially successful character in *Between the Acts*. Like Elizabeth of *Orlando*, she is fond of "half-men" (73) (William Dodge) and, like Aunt Warburton in *The Years*, of young men (Giles). As with all of Woolf's characterizations of female power discussed in this essay, Mrs. Manresa has a connection with rubies: "Also it was said her diamonds and rubies had been dug out of the earth with his own hands by a 'husband' who was not Ralph Manresa." Mrs. Manresa's rubies appear only briefly in the novel, but her hands are full of rings under her gloves, and her ruby-red fingernails become the most unforgettable element of Woolf's "close-up" (as in her characterization of Elizabeth and, later, of Aunt Warburton) on Mrs. Manresa's hands: "Her hat, her rings, her finger nails red as roses, smooth as shells, were there for all to see" (39).[32]

Although Mrs. Manresa turns up a "ploughboy" in the cherry stone game played at luncheon (50), she is undoubtedly a queen. She arrives at Pointz Hall in a "great silver-plated car . . . with the initials R. M. twisted so as to look at a distance like a coronet" (46). The initials stand for the absent Ralph Manresa, but they could also stand for "Regina Manresa," a title Mrs. Manresa quickly appropriates from the play as she edges out the "Great Eliza": "'Bravo! Bravo!' she cried. 'There's life in the old dog yet!' And she trolloped out the words of the song with an abandonment which, if vulgar, was a great help to the Elizabethan age. For the ruff had become unpinned and Great Eliza had forgotten her lines. But the audience laughed so loud that it did not matter" (85).[33]

Shortly after this "edging out" of Eliza Clark, Mrs. Manresa is called a queen: "Mrs. Manresa applauded loudly. Somehow she was the Queen; and he (Giles) was the surly hero" (93). She crowns herself: "I am the Queen, he my hero, my sulky hero" (107). Even so, the Elizabethan play-within-a-play does not contain a queen or a hero. The only references that fit are to Elizabeth/Eliza Clark and the boy-prince (Ferdinando) in the play's play. Elizabeth/Eliza Clark and Mrs. Manresa are both spectators of the antics of men who are or become demasculinized. In the play, Ferdinando is dependent on an old woman for recognition of his "princehood" (91). In the novel, Giles Oliver is possessed ("my hero") and gradually infantilized (man to youth to boy). First "surly," then "sulky," Giles is finally Mrs. Manresa's "little boy" and, ironically, "her surly hero" (177).

Yet, despite these similarities, despite the ironic inversion of their joint relation to the historical Elizabeth, Eliza Clark as Elizabeth and Mrs. Manresa as Elizabeth differ in one crucial respect. The latter is not just a spectator of a play-within-a-play, an imitation of an imitation (a bad actor bungling an interpretation of a legend); not just a cleverly contrived spectacle of British consumerism (the scouring-pad costume). As a character in the novel (as opposed to the pageant), Mrs. Manresa is an unapologetic, public embodiment of power—an individualized, sexual, but nevertheless female power. As in *Orlando* Woolf used the historical Elizabeth's progressions as the basis for the opening scene, so in *Between the Acts* she returns to the theme of a royal progression and casts Mrs. Manresa as Pointz Hall's queenly visitor. But the narrowing focus that gradually attends Woolf's malleable images of Elizabeth is here reversed: Mrs. Manresa's Elizabethan persona is a very public expression of female sexual power aligned with the novel's preoccupation with "savagery" and, I would argue, only tangentially related to Woolf's pacifist or socialist agendas. Mrs. Manresa serves, along with Miss La Trobe, an intensely personal, intensely feminist, and intensely aesthetic agenda: to tie together Woolf's concept of queenly power with the creative power of the female artist.[34]

Between the Acts is full of artists. Mrs. Manresa, known as a reasonably accomplished singer, sings impromptu (85, 96). William Dodge is called an artist by Mrs. Manresa (38), is known for his beautiful handwriting (61), and throughout the novel displays a keen appreciation of art and poetry. Isa writes poetry in secret, shares a family background of art and poetry with William, and considers herself his "semblable" (207). Less obvious are the connections between Mrs. Manresa and the only professional artist in the novel: Miss La Trobe. Both women are known only by surnames and honorifics. Both are positive and blatant sexual beings—Mrs. Manresa in her heterosexual dalliances and Miss La Trobe in her homosexual relationships. Without question, Mrs. Manresa is the bejeweled queen of the novel at her sexual and social peak; Miss La Trobe lacks the outward marks of an Elizabethan icon. Yet she is characterized as possessing power associated in Woolf with the Elizabethan icon as crone: "Ah, but she was not merely a twitcher of individual strings; she was one who seethes wandering bodies and floating voices in a cauldron, and makes rise up from its amorphous mass a re-created world. Her moment was on her—her glory" (153).

Miss La Trobe's moment of "glory" is also Elizabeth's moment of "victory" in *Orlando*. Her "re-created world" is also the re-ordered world of couples in *Night and Day*. It is the re-vised world of Woolf's own ancestry in *Mrs. Dalloway*. It is the re-told world of British history in "Reading," "Waxworks at the Abbey," *Orlando*, and the *Between the Acts* pageant. Of course, Miss La Trobe's glory is momentary, a specific, unpreserved, unrepeatable performance presented to an ambivalent audience. Her rubies are not real, and at the novel's end she is left to wallow in the "mud" of words without meaning (212). Woolf is not, however, placing Mrs. Manresa and her rubies in opposition to Miss La Trobe and her muddy, meaningless words. For all their differences as Elizabeth types, they are not queens in conflict; moreover, they are characters in a novel full of scenes of potential conflict that never play themselves out. The "long thin hands of the artist" in *Between the Acts* do not attempt to wrest the sceptre from the "long thin [bejeweled] hands of the artist" as queen.

Rather than an iconoclasm, *Between the Acts* presents a revelation of "icon-maker" to the icon as Artist La Trobe ends her pageant with mirrors and Regina Manresa takes advantage of the stagecraft: "All evaded or shaded themselves— save Mrs. Manresa who, facing herself in the glass, used it as a glass; had out her mirror; powdered her nose; and moved one curl, disturbed by the breeze, to its place" (186). In her last gesture as a redefiner of the historical Elizabeth, Woolf ends not with a refutation of "all men" as "liars" but with a reification of power as artistry that is female, homoerotic, and personal in a character who is female, heteroerotic, and public. In her last exposition of the Elizabethan icon, Woolf ends with an acclamation: "Long live the Queen!"

❧ Notes

1. Roy C. Strong, *Gloriana: The Portraits of Queen Elizabeth I* (London: Thames and Hudson, 1987), 32, 36. In *Of Chastity and Power: Elizabethan Literature and the Unmarried Queen* (New York: Routledge, 1989), 62–67, Philippa Berry places Strong's work, including his earlier *Cult of Elizabeth: Elizabethan Portraiture and Pageantry* (1977), at the end of a scholarly tradition begun by E. C. Wilson in *England's Eliza* (1966) and continued and expanded by Frances Yates in *Astraea: The Imperial Theme in the Sixteenth Century* (1975). Berry values all this scholarship but finds Yates responsible for "bequeath[ing] many of her erroneous assumptions to later generations of critics" (67). Berry's concerns focus on earlier critics', especially Yates's, "blind[ness] to the ideological and political problems inherent in the rule of an unmarried female monarch" (67). Thus, she finds "the Elizabethan icon" far more controversial than does Yates or Strong, but an icon nevertheless. For an analysis of Elizabeth I's virginity, its power, and its problems, see Berry's study.

2. Alex Zwerdling, *Virginia Woolf and the Real World* (Berkeley: University of California Press, 1986), 115; Virginia Woolf, *Orlando: A Biography* (1928; reprint, New York: Harcourt Brace Jovanovich [Harvest], 1973), 239–40, 47, 140; Woolf, *The Diary of Virginia Woolf*, edited by Anne Olivier Bell and Andrew McNeillie, 5 vols. (New York: Harcourt Brace Jovanovich, 1977–84), 3:157, 162.

3. Ruby references in *Orlando* are at 30, 300–301; the snuff-taking is at 100. See also *The Oxford English Dictionary*, 2d ed., s. v. "snuff." In "Elizabethan Tobacco," in *New World Encounters*, edited by Stephen Greenblatt (Berkeley: University of California Press, 1993), 272–312, Jeffrey Knapp notes a 1588 declaration prohibiting priests from using tobacco before mass (293), and he refers to a 1650 anecdote of a wager between

Elizabeth and Walter Raleigh about the amount of smoke in a pound of tobacco (283), but his thorough analysis makes no reference to the queen's ever using tobacco.

4. The complexity of Woolf's performance as literary historian has been steadily gaining critical attention. See, for example, Melba Cuddy-Keane, "Virginia Woolf and the Varieties of Historicist Experience," in *Virginia Woolf and the Essay*, edited by Beth Carole Rosenberg and Jeanne Dubino (New York: St. Martin's, 1997), 59–77; and Gillian Beer, "Virginia Woolf and Prehistory," in *Virginia Woolf: The Common Ground* (Ann Arbor: University of Michigan Press, 1996), 6–28.

5. Beer, 8.

6. Woolf, *"The Girlhood of Queen Elizabeth"* (1909), a review of Frank A. Mumby's book of the same name (Boston: Houghton Mifflin, 1909), in *The Essays of Virginia Woolf,* 4 (of 6) vols. to date, edited by Andrew McNeillie (London: Hogarth Press, 1986–94), 1:319–24, 323. Cf. Il Schifanoya's letter, dated 23 January 1559, in Mumby, *The Girlhood of Queen Elizabeth,* 298–310; the quoted passage is at 299. The fifteen-year-old Woolf had received as birthday present from her brother Thoby Stephen a copy of Mandell Creighton's *Queen Elizabeth* [1896; rev. ed., 1899] (New York: Longmans, Green, 1927); see Woolf, *The Letters of Virginia Woolf,* edited by Nigel Nicolson and Joanne Trautmann, 6 vols. (New York: Harcourt Brace Jovanovich, 1975–80), 1:3 (26 January 1897).

7. Horace Walpole, Lord Orford, *Anecdotes of Painting in England* (1761; reprint, World Library of Standard Works, London: Ward, Lock, and Co., 1879), 150; Woolf, "Reading" (1919), in *Essays,* 3:141–61, 145–46.

8. Mumby, 300. For descriptions of Elizabeth's hands, see Strong, 18–19; Creighton, 282; and Anne Somerset, *Elizabeth I* (New York: Knopf, 1991), 360. On Elizabeth's dress, see Janet Arnold's magnificent *Queen Elizabeth's Wardrobe Unlock'd* (Leeds, Eng.: W. S. Maney, 1988).

Regarding primary documentation of Elizabeth, Woolf could have researched the historical materials, but there is no indication that she did so. In 1932 she wrote Helen McAfee of the *Yale Review* that "to write anything of interest about Elizabeth one would have to make a far more serious study of the time than I have leisure for" (*Letters,* 5:20).

Had she researched the question, she could have found that the Coronation Portrait clearly depicts three jeweled rings, one of which presumably "wedded" her to England. In *The Heart and Stomach of a King: Elizabeth I and the Politics of Sex and Power* (Philadelphia: University of Pennsylvania Press, 1994), Carole Levin cites William Camden's famous, though suspect, version of Elizabeth's 1558 speech to Parliament (41–42). Camden writes of Elizabeth's showing "the ring of gold" while reminding Parliament of "this my wedlocke and marriage with my kingdome" (quoted at 41). And in another portrait that should have been familiar to Woolf, the Rainbow Portrait, the queen wears a ruby heart on her left sleeve; see Mary C. Erler, "Sir John Davies and the Rainbow Portrait of Queen Elizabeth," *Modern Philology* 84 (1987): 364.

Notable also is a ruby-and-diamond ring that figures in Lytton Strachey's *Elizabeth and Essex: A Tragic History* (New York: Harcourt, Brace, 1928). This ring was put forth as evidence in the notorious case of Dr. Lopez, the queen's physician convicted of treason. Strachey finds "baseless" the accusation that Lopez as an agent of Philip of Spain planned to poison the queen (83). But, there was the ring. It had come from Spain as a token to one of the many spies at work in England (87). The queen remembered the ring, and, after Lopez and others had been executed, "[s]he slipped it—who knows with what ironical commiseration?—on to her finger; and there it stayed till her death" (92). Though, according to legend, this ring never left the queen's hand, it is absent from the representations of her.

9. Woolf, "A Sketch of the Past," in *Moments of Being,* edited by Jeanne Schulkind [1976], 2d ed. (New York: Harcourt Brace Jovanovich [Harvest], 1985), 64–159, 105. Stella Duckworth's engagement ring (lost before the wedding) seems to have been an opal; see Woolf, *A Passionate Apprentice: The Early Journals, 1897–1909,* edited by Mitchell A. Leaska (New York: Harcourt Brace Jovanovich, 1990), 67. Vanessa Bell's ring was "a very pretty old French ring"; shortly before her affair with Roger Fry, it too was lost; see Frances Spalding, *Vanessa Bell* (New Haven, Conn.: Ticknor and Fields, 1983), 96. *Cymbeline,* in *The Norton Shakespeare,* edited by Stephen Greenblatt, Walter Cohen, Jean E. Howard, and Katharine Eisaman Maus (New York: Norton, 1997), 2.2.17. (In "Rewriting Family Ties: Woolf's Renaissance Romance," chap. 6 of this volume, Diana E. Henderson discusses *Cymbeline* as a crucial intertext to *Mrs. Dalloway. — Ed.*)

10. Woolf, *Night and Day* (1919; reprint, New York: Harcourt Brace Jovanovich [Harvest], 1973), 147, 421–23, 495. The ruby engagement ring in *Night and Day* was not typical for the period. When a plentiful supply of diamonds was discovered in South Africa in the late 1860s, diamonds had become favored, especially after the turn of the century. See Diana Scarisbrick, *Rings: Symbols of Wealth, Power, and Affection* (New York: Harry N. Abrams, 1993), 194; see also George Frederick Kunz, *Rings for the Finger* (1917; reprint, New York: Dover, 1973), 227.

11. Woolf, *Mrs. Dalloway* (1925; reprint, with a foreword by Maureen Howard, New York: Harcourt Brace [Harvest], 1990), 33, 188. For more of Woolf's interpretation of her French ancestry, see *Letters,* 3:163 (5 February 1925), 295 (9 May 1928). In *Virginia Woolf: A Biography,* 2 vols. (New York: Harcourt Brace Jovanovich, 1972), 1:14, Quentin Bell traces Woolf's lineage to Versailles. In Woolf's writings, Marie Antoinette stands in obverse to Elizabeth. Elizabeth was a powerful, long-lived, successful monarch in her own right who shrewdly combined her love for jewels and dress into her image as ruler. Marie Antoinette was a powerless, doomed consort and an

unwitting participant in a scandal involving jewelry—the "Necklace Affair." As a separate project, I am researching this issue as well as Woolf's interest generally in Marie Antoinette.

12. Woolf, *Mrs. Dalloway*, 87, 35–36.

13. Ibid., 33, 188.

14. Woolf, *Orlando*, 71; Woolf, *Jacob's Room* (1922; reprint, New York: Harcourt Brace Jovanovich [Harvest], 1978), 115. Woolf's conceit of a "blown" or "blown away" ruby may originate in Ruskin: "Whenever [the poppy] is seen . . . always it is a flame, and warms the wind like a blown ruby." "The Flower," chap. 4 of *Proserpina*, in *Love's Meinie and Proserpina*, in *The Works of John Ruskin* (New York: Longmans, Green, 1906), 25:249–65, 258. Woolf, *The Years* (1937; reprint, New York: Harcourt, Brace, and World [Harvest], 1969), 146, 333.

15. Woolf, *To the Lighthouse* (1927; reprint, with a foreword by Eudora Welty, New York: Harcourt Brace Jovanovich [Harvest], 1989), 105.

16. Woolf, *The Voyage Out* (1915; reprint, New York: Harcourt, Brace, and World [Harvest], 1968), 203.

17. Woolf, *The Years*, 248, 258, 198.

18. Woolf, *Orlando*, 22.

19. Ibid., 25.

20. Carole Levin takes Elizabeth's famous utterance as the title of her analysis of Elizabeth's politics, *The Heart and Stomach of a King*. Though questioning whether Elizabeth actually spoke these words, which were first attributed to her in the seventeenth century (206 n. 56), Levin cites several authorities who conclude that the speech can reasonably be accepted as Elizabeth's. Her chapter 6, "Elizabeth as King and Queen," focuses on Elizabeth's ability to use the medieval doctrine of the king's two bodies to personal advantage.

21. This merger of masculine and feminine behavior in Elizabeth—or this concept of a queen regnant as a "king in drag"—is exploited by Sally Potter in the casting of Quentin Crisp as Elizabeth in her 1993 film adaptation of Woolf's *Orlando*.

22. Woolf, *Orlando*, 22.

23. Woolf, "Waxworks at the Abbey" (1928), in *Granite and Rainbow*, edited by Leonard Woolf (1958; reprint, New York: Harcourt Brace Jovanovich [Harvest], 1975), 216–18, and in *Essays*, 4:540–42. Andrew McNeillie states that the wax funeral effigy, "probably not the original," dates from 1760. *Essays*, 4:542 n. 2.

24. "Waxworks at the Abbey," in *Granite and Rainbow*, 217, and in *Essays*, 4:541; *Mrs. Dalloway*, 16–17.

Woolf's concept of Anne does not improve in *The Years*, where the queen's statue serves as nothing more than a traffic marker in the street and, metonymically, as a marker in history (226–27). In chapter 4 of this volume, "The Memory Palace of Virginia Woolf," Anne E. Fernald has more to say about Woolf's use of London landmarks; there is an undeniable connection between Woolf's denigration of Edith Cavell's statue (336) and her treatment of Anne's statue. In *Between the Acts* (1941; reprint, New York: Harcourt Brace Jovanovich [Harvest], 1970), the allegorical figure of Reason is mistaken for Anne (123). Thus, in "Waxworks" and in both novels, Anne appears as a prop for patriarchal history, not as a queen regnant.

25. Q. Bell, *Virginia Woolf,* 2:79 n. 163; Woolf, *Diary,* 4:201 (14 February 1934). Neale's book was sent to Woolf for review, but the diary offers no further information.

26. Woolf, *Between the Acts* (1941; reprint, New York: Harcourt Brace Jovanovich [Harvest], 1970). Subsequent references included parenthetically in the text are to this edition.

27. The *"[c]argoes of diamonds"* (*Between the Acts,* 84) are not historically correct; diamonds were not discovered in the New World (Brazil) until the eighteenth century.

28. Nigel Nicolson, *Portrait of a Marriage* (New York: Athenaeum, 1973), 202. Mitchell Leaska, in his edition of Woolf's Pointz Hall: *The Earlier and Later Typescripts of* Between the Acts (New York: University Publications, 1983), 315–16. Woolf, *Between the Acts,* 5, 204, 60; *Diary,* 4:226 (17 July 1934).

29. Beer argues for "a spatial landscape, not a linear sequence" in the novel (20), but the historical consciousness of the audience, as well as that reflected in the pageant itself, is "linear." Even when Woolf, according to Beer, "amalgamates" Wells (21), she preserves a sense of historical linearity, even developmental or progressive.

30. See, however, Barbara Apstein, "Chaucer, Virginia Woolf, and *Between the Acts,*" *Woolf Studies Annual* 2 (1996): 117–33, for a perceptive reading of Mrs. Manresa as a descendant of the Wife of Bath (129–30).

31. My comments on Eliza Clark as Elizabeth are an extension of my earlier comments on the Pointz Hall pageant as a spectacle of consumerism in "What Miss Kilman's Petticoat Means: Virginia Woolf, Shopping, and Spectacle," *Modern Fiction Studies* 38 (1992): 211–14.

32. Later, "thin Ralph Manresa," absent but connected with precious stones like Mr. Parry of *The Voyage Out,* is the source of "rubies dug up . . . in his ragamuffin days" (202). That Mrs. Manresa's rubies are procured by a "husband" would, on the surface, support the claim that her power derives from her marriages. But she, like Sally Seton in *Mrs. Dalloway,* has an undeniable power of personality that far exceeds her marital status. Ralph Manresa, like "Mr. Seton" and Mr. Parry, is an attenuated appendage to his wife; indeed, the confusion about her husbands suggests that they are interchangeable, unimportant.

33. Eliza Clark's "play acting" as Elizabeth parallels Mrs. Swithin's impassioned remark to Miss La Trobe that she "could have played . . . Cleopatra!" (153). Beer, 22, connects Mrs. Swithin's remark about Cleopatra with the fecund Nile to encompass all of natural history: a Wellsian pastiche of primordial ooze and amphibians. The emphasis here should be on the word "played," meaning "to perform or act" (Mrs.

Clark and Mrs. Swithin as actresses, not queens), not, as Beer claims, on "human being[s] . . . unchanging, standing in for each other across the centuries" (8).

34. My analysis of Mrs. Manresa is directly opposed, for example, to James English's characterization of her as being trained in "properly feminine behavior" or as being a "docile participant in patriarchal constructions of femininity," in "Broken English: Disarticulated Community in *Between the Acts*," chap. 3 of *Comic Transactions: Literature, Humor, and the Politics of Community in Twentieth-Century Britain* (Ithaca, N.Y.: Cornell University Press, 1994), 107, 120. Mrs. Manresa's behavior is clearly that of an aggressive, self-confident individual who defies the conventions of proper feminine behavior. Furthermore, English's reading of "patriarchal violence" in Mrs. Manresa's "lipstick and blood-red nails" (108) is questionable. Manresa's actions are not violent; along with her repeated, public face-powdering (133, 178, 186), they are unconventional.

4

The Memory Palace of Virginia Woolf

~ Anne E. Fernald

The room Virginia Woolf desires in *A Room of One's Own* (1929) is a study, a private place apart from the demands of family life and the reminders of injustices toward women. But the room where her narrator spends the most time is the Reading Room of the British Library. This room and what it symbolizes—the patriarchally endorsed canon, the breadth of human knowledge—enrages and frustrates her, but it also excites her admiration and inspires her argument. Virginia Woolf's depiction of the Reading Room participates in, and marks a significant departure from, a history of the connection between memory and the library spanning from Simonides of Ceos in the fifth century B.C.E. to Freud, Borges, and Eco in our own time. For the library, especially the national library, is print culture's embodiment of the imaginary memory palaces of the Renaissance. This essay examines Woolf's depiction of the relationship between memory and the library. It focuses on three historical moments: the sixteenth century, when Renaissance neoplatonists gave philosophical importance to the art of memory as a system for organizing human knowledge; the nineteenth century, when the rise of print culture and the fascination with system made it possible to build an actual memory palace in the shape of a national library; and the early twentieth century, when critics, Woolf early among them, began to notice that all of our memories, social and individual, are constructions and, as such, are open to analysis.

In the classical world, the *ars memoriae* referred to memory as one of the five parts of Ciceronian rhetoric; in the Renaissance, the art expanded far beyond the boundaries of rhetoric to promise a master key to all knowledge. Since the development of printing, and now computers, we have become far less dependent on individual powers of memory. We can scarcely imagine the time before printing when memory was counted among the liberal arts. Fortunately, Frances Yates documents the former stature of this lost art in her still influential 1966 book *The Art of Memory.* Those who practiced the art of memory memorized not by rote, but by constructing elaborate and personal imaginary architectures. These mnemonists profited from the observation that, in passing a familiar landmark, we often remember what we were thinking the last time we passed it. Thus they memorized a spacious room, a cathedral, or a street scene, and then deliberately "placed," in order, the elements of a speech or a list they need to remember.[1] This way, a person could retrieve his or her speech in its correct order by taking an imaginary walk through a "memory palace." With the increasing availability of books, the art of memory gradually changed from a mental exercise into one that most often takes form in print, for, as Mary Carruthers astutely notes, "the symbolic representations that we call writing are no more than cues or triggers" for memory.[2] Instead of memory palaces, people came not only to rely on but also to believe in libraries.

From ancient to medieval times, the architectural mnemonic flourished as both method and metaphor; words and ideas could be organized by placing them in a memory palace, and the mind was often analogized (most notably in Augustine) to a storehouse. In the Renaissance, thinkers saw potential for comprehending all knowledge—not just a speech or even a few books—in the organized and trained memory. This expanded interest in memory was most closely linked to the projects of the neoplatonists, whose belief in ideal forms lent spiritual urgency to their quest for system. Thus, Nicolas of Cusa (1401–64) published a series of meditations on "symbols that convey divine mysteries." The neoplatonist syncretism of Marsilio Ficino (1433–99) continued Nicolas's intellectual project of reconciling Plato and Plotinus with the Bible, of developing a hermeneutic so that "Plato could be read in a manner analogous to the fourfold meanings of medieval biblical commentary."[3] Pico della Mirandola (1463–94) took this effort even further, turning to the cabala for additional wisdom. Nicolas, Ficino, and Pico paved the way for the sixteenth-century mnemonists Giordano Bruno and Giulio Camillo, who shifted the focus from knowledge to memory, the container and organizer of knowledge, and envisioned a memory palace vast enough to hold all knowledge. The mnemonists' debt to the neoplatonists marks only part of an intellectual genealogy. In fact, Nicolas himself was influenced by the medieval mnemonist Raymond Lull (1235–1316). However odd the art of memory may seem to us now, it was central to Western intellectual life for centuries.

Memory palaces have two major components: the architecture, which is generally systematic and familiar, and the images contained therein, generally striking, violent, and idiosyncratic. Whereas the Renaissance art of memory depends on an individual's ability to build a memory palace in the mind, Virginia Woolf shows us how the British Library presents itself *as* a mind. In turning the metaphor of memory-as-palace inside out, Woolf displays the contents of the mind for our admiration as well as our scrutiny. Elaborate memory images find their parallel in such emblematic figures as Judith Shakespeare and Mrs. Brown. Woolf's criticism of the art of memory emerges with the turn to architecture, especially with her observation that the British Library operates as a culturewide memory image, not an individual one. In "The Art of Memory Reconceived," Patrick Hutton argues that if we see the art of memory as a way to make "paradigms of cultural understanding," we begin to see "the larger significance of this topic."[4] For Hutton, Freud's search for the origins of memory and forgetting share something with the Renaissance magus.[5] Woolf's ambivalence toward Freud's totalizing metaphors is well documented. Yet holding her work in juxtaposition with that of the Renaissance mnemonists sharpens the distinction between her ability to create new images and her consistent commitment to questioning cultural myths, totalizing schemes, and the way that memory images reinforce them. As Hutton traces it, the history of the art of memory demonstrates our intense impulse toward system and may even suggest something about the deep structure of our minds. Woolf has to deal with the systematizing obsession that was part of the Renaissance art, but, in rejecting the systematic, she revives the personal element of the art of memory. Whereas the Renaissance mnemonists would have understood the image as mainly a tool to assist what for them was the higher faculty—memory—her romantically informed move is to understand and emphasize the image itself as the product of an individual imagination.

When memory images enter the culture—in habits of mind, books, standardized education, or architecture—they become part of the collective memory. Maurice Halbwachs was the first to distinguish what we now call collective memory, and Pierre Nora's multivolume project connects the collective memory of France to places by way of a term—*lieux de mémoire*—he derived from his reading of Yates.[6] Like Yates and Carruthers, Halbwachs and Nora are naming and identifying as an object of study a phenomenon that has gone on for centuries.

In their recent study of social memory, an idea deeply indebted to Halbwachs's study of collective memory, James Fentress and Chris Wickham discuss the methodological problems associated with studying the collective memory of women: "it is notoriously difficult even to tape-record women, remembering in the presence of their husbands: most men interrupt, devalue their wives' memories, take over the interview, tell their own stories instead, or even, most bizarrely, themselves recount their wives' life stories."[7] Thus, the idea of social memory, already a difficult one to document, may in fact conflict with or even obscure the memories of women. That is, social memory may vary along class, race, religious, and gender lines, variations that often put it in tension with official, national memory. Sociologists are just now finding methods to recover women's memories. Woolf sought—in *A Room of One's Own* and elsewhere—to destroy those officially endorsed "collective" memories, and their cues, which interfere with women's ability to think for themselves. In creating her own memory images, Woolf emphasizes the idiosyncratic, personal, and flexible over the static official memories prompted by public architecture. She profits from the tension between the official and the individual, and in doing so she attempts to create, if not recapture, a social memory of and for women.

Woolf is original in basing her criticism of artificial memory on feminist principles. Yet, as we might expect from the complexity of her writing elsewhere, her engagement with the art of memory is not only oppositional. Her descriptions of memory, the mind, and the library all draw upon metaphors with ancient sources; her arguments often depend on lively fictions (Professor von X., Mrs. Brown, Mary Carmichael's novel, the kitchen table when you're not there) that, like Renaissance memory images, are memorable precisely because they are composite and caricature. In each of these cases, however, she uses the techniques of the art of memory—creating vivid, dramatic, allegorical images to stand for complex ideas—to destroy patriarchal images.

In fact, one of her funniest memory images attacks the very notion of ideal forms while linking idealism to that most patriarchal of patriarchs, Mr. Ramsay: Lily Briscoe's image of the kitchen table when no one is there, which "now she always saw, when she thought of Mr. Ramsay's work. . . . It lodged now in the fork of a pear tree."[8] Mocking the philosophic idealism that was central to the Cambridge education of her male friends (and had been more gently spoofed in the opening pages of E. M. Forster's *The Longest Journey*), Woolf replaces it with her own version of the real: a real that is disorganized and comically concrete and, in consequence, both irreverent and memorable. This real contains a critique of knowledge, but one that thoroughly refuses the role of critique as counterargument. Instead, it offers itself up as self-deprecating satire consistent with Lily's nascent feminism: Silly me, a table in a pear tree! Woolf's account asks us to observe the distances separating Lily's confusion, Woolf's own critique, and Andrew's good-natured but bafflingly concrete explanation: "'Think of a kitchen table then,' he told her, 'when you're not there.'"[9] In *The Longest Journey*, Forster uses a cow for the same purpose and teases that the cow "seemed to make things easier";[10] Woolf shows us just how little help that cow or kitchen table is and, by extension, creates a memory image of the preposterousness of ideal forms themselves.

As these examples from Woolf and Forster demonstrate, memory cues flourish everywhere. The streets of any capital town function as reminders of the nation's history. From very early on, the mental process of using architecture as the basis of an artificial memory system got reversed, and people began to design buildings with a mnemonic function. In Renaissance England and France, stately homes—including, notably, Montaigne's tower and the home of Francis Bacon's father, Nicholas—were sometimes "decorated with *sententiae* as well as with emblems and *imprese* so that a visitor to such a room felt as if he had entered an emblem book."[11] This footnote in the history of interior design emphasizes the way in which the essay—a genre that Montaigne and Bacon originated—itself functions as a storehouse or memory palace. In Woolf's own time, E. M. Forster marks the vitality, intelligence, and unconventionality of his characters the Emersons in part by the wardrobe in their front hall on which "the hand of an amateur had painted this inscription: 'Mistrust all enterprises that require new clothes,'"[12] a slight misquotation from that other great American essayist, Thoreau. In each of these cases, historical and fictional, whether we are referring to essays, wardrobes, or rooms, the quotations and inscriptions are personal, even private. Public architecture, by contrast, carries inscriptions that serve an entirely different and often conflicting purpose: the assertion of cultural and political authority over a citizenry.

While government buildings and cathedrals may be decorated with images and symbols of power and faith, cultural institutions adorn themselves with the names and portraits of great artists, soldiers, and politicians. Since memory has so long been described as a storehouse, it makes sense that, among such public buildings, libraries themselves are particularly apt to be decorated with names, murals, or statues. In their decoration and, more basically, in the grandeur of their design, libraries are confident monuments to what a culture knows and treasures.

In figuring the British Library as a mind, Woolf articulates one of the great ambitions of a library: to keep knowledge beyond any individual mind's ability. The library is a vexed site for Virginia Woolf. Certainly there is nothing ambiguous in her narrator's anger at being kept out of the library at "Oxbridge" in *A Room of One's Own:* she curses it.[13] Nor is she indefinite in *Three Guineas* (1938): "Do not have museums and libraries with chained books and first editions under glass cases."[14] But other libraries, especially private ones, are remembered fondly, as in *Between the Acts* (1941), as well as in the essays "Reading" (1919), "How Should One Read a Book?" (1926), and "Leslie Stephen" (1932).[15] In "The Lives of the Obscure" (1925), the prospect of "rescuing" neglected books from the closed stacks of a library is imbued with romance. In "The Leaning Tower" (1940), a librarian's request to be notified of defective books gets transformed into a credo of the common reader's responsibility, "England's way of saying: 'If I lend you books, I expect you to make yourselves critics.'"[16]

In *A Room of One's Own,* much of the narrator's anger at being kept out of one library, or frustration during research at another, stems from the suspicion that the library may contain the "truth," that after a morning's reading she shall have "transferred the truth to my notebook."[17] But in her second feminist pamphlet, *Three Guineas,* the object of Woolf's satire has shifted from an amused and gentle look at the predicament of the intimidated female student, still hoping for enlightenment, to a straightforward attack on the guardians of knowledge who treat books as treasured captives. As central as books are to Virginia Woolf, she finds something obnoxious in the institution of the library.

As the West moved from a memory culture to a print culture, the mnemonist was replaced by the bibliographer and the librarian. In his essay on seventeenth- and eighteenth-century bibliographic catalogs, Roger Chartier notes that, from the beginning, bibliographers fantasized about a complete library—a dream that has only grown, from the library at Alexandria, whose burning remains the sorrow of librarians and book-lovers, to Borges's fantasy of "The Library of Babel." At the same time, these librarians have known the achievement of completeness to be impossible. "Even for those who held that a library must be encyclopedic," Chartier notes, "selection was an absolute necessity."[18] And yet the great national libraries of the West—the Library of Congress, the Bibliothèque Nationale, the British Library—boast not of their selectivity, but of their completeness (an ambition shared with the creators of the great memory palaces, Giordano Bruno and Giulio Camillo). Libraries, as national shrines, become "actual memory palaces, constructed of imposing architecture and adorned with aesthetically pleasing icons and artifacts designed to evoke memories of a heroic or glorious past and to imprint them vividly on the minds of visitors."[19]

When later twentieth-century writers recognized the ambition of completeness as impossible, they did so on terms distinct from Woolf, whose predicament is always about gender. Thus, for example, Borges's library of Babel is obscure, impossible to navigate, and absurdly complete. Meanwhile, Michel Foucault confirms the centrality of reading even as he, too, suggests that knowledge may lie "dormant": "The imaginary now resides between the book and the lamp. The fantastic is no longer a property of the heart, nor is it found among the incongruities of nature; it evolves from the accuracy of knowledge, and its treasures lie dormant in documents."[20] But, again, we must contrast Foucault's and Borges's celebrations of textuality with Woolf's resistance. Gender creates an obstacle between Woolf and the text; at times she looks with fond nostalgia on those readers who do not experience the obstacle;

at times, it is anger; ultimately, the obstacle itself becomes a source of inspiration, interest, and insight into the problems of believing in the value of knowledge. For Virginia Woolf, the failure of the British Library's designers to "leave room for an Eliot or a Brontë"[21] remains a constant reminder of what the library has left out: the lives and works of women.

In 1857, the round Reading Room of the British Library opened to great public acclaim, chiefly, it seems, expressed as national pride at the vast size of the dome itself—a feat of industrial-age ironwork. The schematic diagram of the contents of the room reprinted in the 1924 *Guide to the Use of the Reading Room* (fig. A) looks a lot like Yates's sketch of Giordano Bruno's memory system (fig. B) or the memory theater of Giulio Camillo (fig. C). And for a moment it would seem that Victorian engineering and bibliography combine to fulfill the dreams of these late sixteenth-century mnemonists. If these Renaissance thinkers dreamed of a system for organizing and remembering human thought, what better culmination of that dream than its embodiment in the very architecture of a great national library?

In proposing this system of wheels within wheels, which Yates's diagram commits to paper, Bruno maps the images of the classical art of memory onto the combinatory wheels of Raymond Lull's art of memory.[22] In her descriptions of Bruno's ambitions, his sense that these magic images comprised a worthy store of "secret" knowledge, Yates continually admits that Bruno's project is "extremely difficult for a modern to recapture."[23] The design of the Reading Room offers a less distant example of a related impulse. The appeal of the circular room, like that of Bruno's wheels, is not mysterious: the circle is both ordered and without beginning or end. The reader enters the room flanked by atlases on the right and maps of the British Isles on the left, implicitly equating orientation in the library with the work of surveyors and explorers. At the center sits the superintendent at a raised desk: the library as panopticon. The "History" section presents a transparent narrative of the official history of Britain: from "Ancient History," the reference works progress to Scotland, Ireland, and Wales, to culminate in "State Papers" and "British History," finally winding down with two sections of "Foreign History" surrounding (to avoid contamination?) a section on France. Theological works stand at the far end of the room as if to guard the entrance to the North Library, where the library's most rare and valuable books are kept. In spite of the logic of this arrangement, the designers

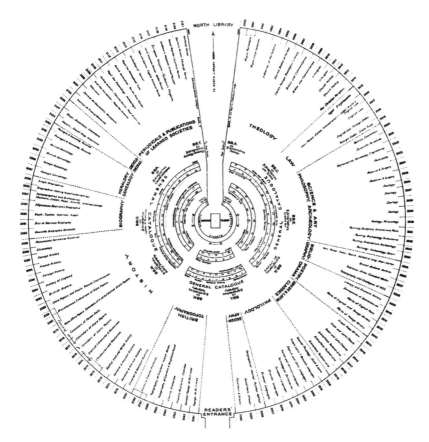

Fig. A. Floor plan of the Round Reading Room, British Library. By permission of The British Library. From *A Guide to the Use of the Reading Room*, published by the British Museum, 1924.

of the library plainly had no intention for us to seek knowledge from imagined combinations derived from revolving the general catalog clockwise; it is of no significance that the topography catalog rotated ninety degrees would be opposite heraldry. This kind of fancy comes of spending too much time with the Renaissance mnemonists. Yet a faith in the potential significance of this sort of correspondence is precisely what inspires Bruno and Camillo to pass their time in the design of memory systems.

The designers of the Reading Room failed to appreciate what Woolf continually emphasizes: that in fastening onto the systematic principle of the

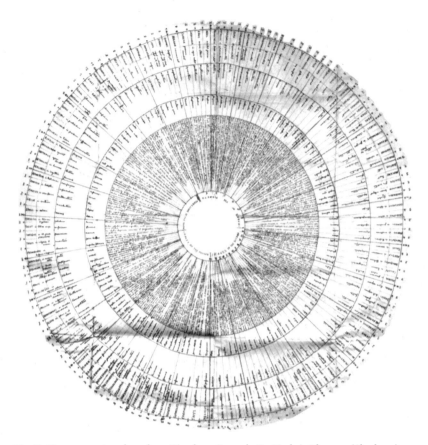

Fig. B. Memory system based on Giordano Bruno's *De Umbris Idearum* (Shadows), Paris, 1582. By permission of the University of Chicago Press. From Frances A. Yates, *The Art of Memory*, published by the University of Chicago Press, 1966. © The Estate of Frances A. Yates, 1966.

architectural mnemonic, the Victorians lost sight of the importance of the personal. The memory palace through which the reader walks is not her own, but someone else's. Simply by its existence, the Reading Room influences the imagination of its readers: an influence that is precisely the ambition of the national library.

The size and promise of completeness of the library was great, but the difficulty of settling on a scheme to decorate it was the first clear crack in the Victorian plan for the British Library as an embodiment of the Renaissance

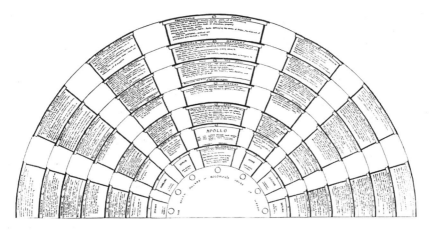

Fig. C. Yates's diagram of the Memory Theater of Giulio Camillo based on *L'Idea Del Theatro*. By Permission of the University of Chicago Press. From Frances A. Yates, *The Art of Memory*, published by the University of Chicago Press, 1966. © The Estate of Frances A. Yates, 1966.

memory palace. Although several artists proposed schemes for decorating the dome of the British Library Reading Room with allegorical statues and paintings, the dome was left plain for decades. Finally, in 1907, a more modest scheme was adopted and "the names of nineteen British writers were painted on the panels,"[24] only to be left to fade and disappear. The names, which, according to J. Mordaunt Crook, "evoked some controversy at the time,"[25] were Chaucer, Caxton, Tindale, Spenser, Shakespeare, Bacon, Milton, Locke, Addison, Swift, Pope, Gibbon, Wordsworth, Scott, Byron, Carlyle, Macaulay, Tennyson, and Browning.[26]

When John Burnet oversaw the 1907 redecoration, he may have struggled over the choice of some of these nineteen names, but it is unlikely that he foresaw the attitude Virginia Woolf would take to his choices just sixteen years later:

> Miss Julia Hedge, the feminist, waited for her books. They did not come. She wetted her pen. She looked about her. Her eye was caught by the final letters in Lord Macaulay's name. And she read them all round the dome—the names of great men which remind us—"Oh damn," said Julia Hedge, "why didn't they leave room for an Eliot or a Brontë?"[27]

This is more than just a moment of distracted study; it is more, even, than a moment of criticism of the canon, though it is both of those things. Sitting in the Reading Room, waiting for her books, Julia Hedge falls into the automatic thoughts that are precisely what such rooms mean to inspire: "the names of great men which remind us . . ." But Woolf's character interrupts that involuntary thought with another concern: those men's names remind her not of the greatness of English literature but of the immensity of the feminist project before her. How long must she work and wait until a woman's name joins that uninterrupted band?

And with that intrusion of a personal thought, we return to Frances Yates. As she is careful to explain, the art of memory was not nearly so orderly as the form of the dome, the wheels within wheels, or the theater would lead one to believe:

> Very singular is the art of this invisible art of memory. It reflects ancient architecture but in an unclassical spirit, concentrating its choice on irregular places and avoiding symmetrical orders. It is full of human imagery of a very personal kind; we mark the tenth place with a face like that of our friend Decimus; we see a number of our acquaintances standing in a row; we visualize a sick man like the man himself, or if we did not know him, like someone we do know. These human figures are active and dramatic, strikingly beautiful or grotesque. . . . They appear to be completely amoral, their function being solely to give an emotional impetus to memory by their personal idiosyncrasy or their strangeness.[28]

Here, we begin to grasp the tension within the Renaissance art of memory: it combines a strong impulse toward system (which would seem to call for symmetry and regularity) with an acknowledgment that each individual must construct his or her own memory, that each image must be striking and evocative, not just for the culture at large, but for the rememberer himself or herself. Thus, as Yates says, "if we did not know" the sick man we are meant to remember, we visualize him "like someone we do know."

In contrast to the art of memory, the design of the Reading Room is distinctly classical. In decorating the Reading Room, in the selection of which authors would be honored, the Victorians significantly distorted one of the purposes of the Renaissance art. A band of names does nothing to help the patron distinguish a Chaucer from a Caxton, an Addison from a Shakespeare. Thus, in her refusal to succumb to the automatic prompts for memory of the Reading Room, Woolf's Julia Hedge is closer than the room's designers to the Renaissance spirit of transforming a familiar room into a personal memory palace, one full "of human imagery of a very personal kind." She knows she is meant to be reminded of the institutionally endorsed English writers, but the impersonal band of names reminds her of her desire to resist the power of collective memory and continue her feminist work.

But whereas medieval mnemonists are eager to remember the Bible and Cicero, and whereas Renaissance mnemonists conjure up "all that the mind can conceive and all that is hidden in the soul,"[29] Woolf creates anti-images that aim to liberate women's imaginations from official memory without constructing an equally imposing replacement. Once we understand why she resists remembering and memorializing on a national scale, we may be better able to see what, if anything, she proposes as a replacement. Since Giordano Bruno proposes, as the first memory image of Saturn, "a man with a stag's head on a dragon, with an owl which is eating a snake in his right hand,"[30] a simple mark on the wall hardly seems a fitting parallel. Yet what Woolf makes of that mark in her 1917 story "The Mark on The Wall" says much about the effects of historical context on these two powerful imaginations. The story, written against the backdrop of World War I, begins with the narrator shaking off a childishly militaristic "automatic fancy" "of red knights riding up the side of [a] black rock"[31] triggered by the fire in the grate. When she sees the mark, new to the narrator and as yet free of significance, she is relieved to be free of the automatic fancy. Such fancies, always irritating to Woolf's characters,[32] indicate the potential of artificial memory: our minds are attracted to and retain elaborate images. But whereas automatic fancies emerge from the collective memory, artificial memory images are the conscious constructions of an individual.

The artificial memory is an art, a subject of study, a method by which ideas can be retrieved swiftly and in any order; Woolf's meditation on the mark suggests something of the power of concentration that the art of memory requires. But her ultimate refusal to give the mark significance emphasizes her distance not only from the Renaissance mnemonists but, further, from any universalizing or generalizing turn of mind. Woolf's resistance to institutional memory, to culturally endorsed memory, is integral to her resistance to all patriarchal structures, here especially the war machine. In "The Mark on the Wall," she demonstrates how deeply habits of mind are affected by culture and how fierce a woman must be to resist patriarchy. "Generalizations," she writes, "are very worthless. The military sound of the word is enough."[33]

Instead, the mark permits the mind to wander freely, and even the antiquarians, who are, in her imagination (and from her reading), "retired colonels," have given up their fealty to Whitaker's Almanack and the Table of Precedency and feel "agreeably philosophic in accumulating evidence on both sides." Their wives, meanwhile, busy with the details of housekeeping, "have every reason for keeping that great question of the camp or the tomb in perpetual suspension." Because the mark is, in the end, a snail, it will move, though its presence there once, now recorded in the story, will always inspire the memory of the thoughts surrounding it. But what are those thoughts? "I can't remember a thing,"[34] says the narrator, refusing summary. The narrator's refusal, together with the colonels' and their wives' acceptance of ambiguity, emphasizes how far the mark is from a memory image: it stands for too many different things.

Just after the narrator asserts that she cannot remember, someone enters and reveals that the mark is just a snail, thus doubly destroying the mark's potential as a memory image. For the snail, as Woolf presents it, is both too real and too mundane to symbolize a single idea. In either case, "The Mark on the Wall" dramatizes a pacifist's wartime desire to obliterate memory, to reject a world in which memorials are necessary. The story is an antimemorial and the mark, a sign of interpretive possibility, a memory image for the impossibility of fixing meaning.

As we have already seen, as early as *Jacob's Room* (1922)—her third novel but the first published by her own press—Woolf was critical of the canon of British writers painted around the dome of the Reading Room. There, however, in her fantasia of the library, emptied out of its patrons for the day, she had offered a different vision, distinct from the feminist project of canon critique and instead focused on the romance of reading:

The books were now replaced. A few letters of the alphabet were sprinkled round the dome. Closely stood together in a ring round the dome were Plato, Aristotle, Sophocles, and Shakespeare; the literatures of Rome, Greece, China, India, Persia. One leaf of poetry was pressed flat against another leaf, one burnished letter laid smooth against another in a density of meaning, a conglomeration of loveliness.[35]

It takes a moment for the letters to resolve themselves into names, and when they do, it becomes apparent that only one among them—Shakespeare— matches what was really painted around the dome. Instead of depicting the library as a national treasure, Woolf makes it a global one, one even more playful than Forster's image of all British novelists "as seated together in a . . . sort of British Museum reading-room."[36] Although the three writers she joins with Shakespeare are all ancient Greeks, her list of the literatures represented is broad. More important, she makes the library disorganized in its decoration and, implicitly, its catalog. The letters are "sprinkled round the dome" like stars. So, instead of the roughly chronological, orderly progression of names that she would have seen when she visited the library, Woolf depicts the letters scattered about, becoming legible as names as a group of stars can be read as Orion or the Seven Sisters: with a little imagination and a squint of the eye.

In contrast to the pompous language of the library catalog that would surface in *A Room of One's Own,* where women are subdivided according to "Condition in the Middle Ages of, / Habits in the Fiji Islands of, / Worshipped as goddesses by," here, at night, once the books are replaced, Woolf imagines only poetry. What is beautiful here, as with the mark on the wall, is the moment just before things make sense. Fixing meaning to name the great authors of the English tradition, or the stars themselves, spoils the moment and limits the imagination. In *Mrs. Dalloway* (1925), old Joseph and Peter Walsh interrupt Clarissa and Sally's kiss by naming the stars, for which Clarissa hates them: "She heard the names of the stars. 'Oh this horror!' she said to herself."[37]

Woolf includes scenes of the British Library in both *Jacob's Room* and *A Room of One's Own.* Although the feminism of the latter text is more explicit, both books resist the institutional power of the library while confessing a reluctant attraction for the vast dome full of books. For the purpose of this argument, the differences between the earlier novel and the subsequent feminist essay are less important than the continuity of Woolf's metaphor of the mind for the library and her troubled resistance to its ambition to completeness, its omission of women. For Woolf the domed room symbolizes the false promise of patriarchal education; she uses it as a memory image dedicated to destroying the complacent acceptance of the all-male canon of English literature. At the same time, she attempts to recuperate a less dominating image of the library through which to celebrate her own love of books and the intellectual freedom she finds in reading.

In *Jacob's Room* Woolf invokes the idea of the library as a mind, turning the ancient metaphor of memory as a storehouse inside out: "There is in the British Museum an enormous mind. Consider that Plato is there cheek by jowl with Aristotle; and Shakespeare with Marlowe. This great mind is hoarded beyond the power of any single mind to possess it." In this vision, selection between Plato and Aristotle, Shakespeare and Marlowe, is unnecessary; reconciliation is complete. Woolf accomplishes the dream of the Renaissance mnemonists, but through imagination, not system. The silence of nightfall rids the library of its human actors, who bring with them the "little grunts of satisfaction" of winning arguments. We are left with "a conglomeration of loveliness." [38] And in other texts, Woolf's images of the library or the book as treasure house or storeroom are even less organized—especially when she considers the Elizabethans: "Now we are in the presence of sublime imagination; now rambling through one of the finest lumber rooms in the world—a chamber stuffed from floor to ceiling with ivory, old iron, broken pots, urns, unicorns' horns, and magic glasses full of emerald lights and blue mystery." [39] This lovingly chaotic description shows Woolf's debt to the romantic Renaissance of Michelet. It rebels against Mary Carruthers's sensible observation that "[m]emory without conscious design is like an uncatalogued library, a contradiction in terms" but resonates with Nicholson Baker's celebration of accidental finds in his 1994 elegy for the card catalog, "Discards." [40]

The Reading Room episodes of *A Room of One's Own* and *Jacob's Room* emphasize a feminist's dissatisfaction with the dome's interior. *Jacob's Room* also registers another objection, this one from the outside. Here, as noted above, the dome of the library (the central architectural feature of the British Museum) is depicted—for the first time—as a mind:

> Stone lies solid over the British Museum, as bone lies cool over the visions and heat of the brain. Only here the brain is Plato's brain and Shakespeare's. . . . Meanwhile, Plato continues his dialogue; in spite of the rain; in spite of the cab whistles; in spite of the woman in the mews behind Great Ormond Street who has come home drunk and cries all night long, "Let me in! Let me in!"[41]

The cold and forbidding skull of the museum encloses brains: those of Shakespeare and Plato. Woolf contrasts the cool decorum of the external architecture with her enthusiasm for the energy and genius it contains. From an exterior perspective, the cold and forbidding dome (one of London's "leaden domes"[42]) refuses to disclose the mysteries and wisdom it contains. Woolf revisits this contrast in "Abbeys and Cathedrals" (1931), where the neoclassical Saint Paul's— "mountainous, immense, greyer, colder, quieter"—is like the outside of the library, while the gothic riot of Westminster Abbey resembles the library's contents: "Everybody in this brilliant assembly has a mind and a will of his own. The Abbey is shot with high-pitched voices; its peace is broken by emphatic gestures and characteristic attitudes. Not an inch of its walls but speaks and claims and illustrates."[43]

Only those who have been inside the library, we are reminded in *Jacob's Room,* know what lies there; and even they can see that there is something a bit strange, if not ridiculous, in Plato's continuing his dialogue "in spite of the rain." That is, readers see scholarly work both as noble and continuous and as irrelevant and disconnected—here, after two millennia, and in Bloomsbury! Plato is still at work. The dialogue is unaffected by the weather, a London rain, so different from the sunny cliffs and plane trees of Greece. Nor is it affected by the whistles of cab drivers, whose "good-natured" humor Woolf contrasts with the "cruelty" of the Greeks.[44] Finally, it cannot hear the cry of a drunk woman on the street, "Let me in! Let me in!"

And with that, Woolf sets out on a feminist analysis of the library that continues through the voice of "Miss Julia Hedge, the feminist" in *Jacob's Room,* in *A Room of One's Own,* and in later books. "And what was London doing?" her narrator asks at the end of *A Room of One's Own.* "Nobody, it seemed, was reading *Antony and Cleopatra.* London was wholly indifferent."[45] This scene advances to become the setting for the man and woman getting into the taxi, which, in turn, introduces her now famous meditation on androgyny. In *Jacob's Room,* published seven years earlier, the ambiguity is more compact: the drunk woman there is at first part of everyday street theater. But she also represents the voice of the women who have been locked out of the libraries—the Outsiders with whom Woolf was to ally herself later in *Three Guineas,* the unheeded cry of frustration before the unseeing brain of the great cultural mind. That does sound dramatic, but there is no other way to describe it. However quickly Woolf's wit or her lyricism may return after such moments, the woman crying "Let me in!"—like the woman singing "ee um fah um so" in *Mrs. Dalloway* or the Cockney singers' "Etho passo tanno hai" at the end of *The Years*—remains;[46] their presence acts as an underground chorus, both present and unintelligible, a distant echo of the suppressed voices of women. Woolf depicts in fiction the problem that the scholars James Fentress and Chris Wickham lament in sociological terms: how are we to recover the distinct social memory of women?

Once the problem of access to the library has been surmounted, new problems develop. In *A Room of One's Own,* Woolf adopts a pointedly anti-academic strategy for expressing the distance between the library and women readers: "The British Museum was another department of the factory. The swing-doors swung open; and there one stood under the vast dome, as if one were a thought in the huge bald forehead which is so splendidly encircled by a band of famous names."[47] Although the band of names is still splendid, the library has been demoted to part of the factory of London. This industrial image drains the space of any of the special claims for the intellectual that persisted in *Jacob's Room.* And, even though the dome is still a mind, it is now a bald—and thus definitely male—mind, and the narrator finds herself just one insignificant thought inside.

The desks in the Reading Room are arranged like spokes in a wheel; the librarians sit at a raised desk in the center; catalogs and reference materials are shelved around the outer wall. So, when Woolf describes the way in which "many hundreds of the living sat at the spokes of a cart-wheel copying from printed books into manuscript books; now and then rising to consult the catalogue; regaining their places stealthily, while from time to time a silent man replenished their compartments," she is describing the room fancifully but accurately. When her narrator becomes distracted and frustrated by her research into the question of women and poverty, her doodle is inspired by the room itself: "What could be the reason, then, of this curious disparity, I wondered, drawing cart-wheels on the slips of paper provided by the British taxpayer for other purposes." Later she makes another doodle, this one of Professor von X., which introduces the idea of anger into the argument.[48]

What interests me about these doodles is that both are images of the memory: the reading room, with its radial symmetry, resembles Renaissance memory diagrams and represents a fantasy of an organized and complete mind. Once again, it would seem that the combination of the dome—so like a mind—and the cartwheel floor-plan—so legible, so organized—embodies the dream of a memory palace. Woolf's use of these two images as her distracted narrator's doodles must arouse our suspicion as to their adequacy. She returns to the cartwheel doodle in *The Years* as a sign of Eleanor Pargiter's boredom: "Mr. Pickford spoke. She drew more spokes; blackened them."[49] Thus, by means of a pun, Eleanor cancels out a dull speech. His words suffer a double demotion, first from a speech to a mere spoke in a wheel, then, in an ambiguous move, she blackens the spoke, emphasizing and obscuring it. In Woolf's own doodles in the manuscript of *The Pargiters,* which resemble Eleanor's, we can see resemblances to a web, an image she preferred.[50] In *A Room of One's Own,* the doodles quickly (and far less ambiguously) become a small but violent expression of resistance: "It is only human nature, I reflected, and began drawing cart-wheels and circles over the angry professor's face till he looked like a burning bush or a flaming comet—anyhow, an apparition without human semblance or significance."[51] Thus, she obliterates the image of the library as a man's mind by drawing the image of the mind as an organized and complete system on top of it. In place of these two unsatisfactory images, she offers a third image, at once mystical and angry, of thought as inspiration, divine, unpredictable, and, most important, illegible, "without human semblance or significance." Woolf replaces two images of the memory with a new sign of the imagination, and though we can read, in her language, allusions to biblical and astronomical wonders, she deliberately confuses their significance, making a definitive or systematic reading impossible.

Bruno and Camillo created a system that was personal. In honoring the memory, they honored their age's most valued aspect of the mind. It may be worth remembering the point with which Mary Carruthers begins her study of memory: "When we think of our highest creative power, we think invariably of the imagination."[52] As we have seen, such was not always the case, and certainly not in the Renaissance, when the imagination was put to the service of a trained and systematic memory. The Victorians continued the development of the system while neglecting all of the art of memory that was personal and idiosyncratic. When they designed and executed plans for the British Library Reading Room, they honored system and memory at the expense of the individual. In criticizing and rejecting the systematic and emphasizing the personal, Virginia Woolf honors an esteem for the imagination she inherits from Romanticism. This emphasis, in turn, reconnects the memory of the Renaissance (both their memory and our memory of it) to the modernist imagination. Furthermore, Woolf's modernist memory—her continuation of a long-standing metaphor for the mind and her instinct for the power of images—enables us to see the imagination central to the creation of the striking and strange images that populate Renaissance memory palaces.

The Renaissance art of memory declined in the seventeenth century with the fall of neoplatonic idealism and the rise of print culture. The art of memory's decline was further hastened by the rise of scientific empiricism and, what is more interesting for its relevance to Woolf, the Puritans. Puritans cast suspicion on all arts of memory, especially in their cabalistic forms. They much preferred the dialectical method of Peter Ramus (which owed much to Raymond Lull),[53] for it "was emotionally aseptic. Memorizing lines of Ovid through logical disposition would help to sterilize the disturbing affects aroused by the Ovidian images."[54] And so, in discrediting the vivid images of Bruno and Camillo, the Ramists achieved an "inner iconoclasm" that demoted the imagination.[55]

We began with Woolf's criticism of the embodiment of the architectural mnemonic in the actual architecture of the British Library; we end, then, with a puzzle. Certainly Virginia Woolf was no Puritan, and she would never be accused of demoting the imagination. As we have seen, her images, though they may be replacing the patriarchal images of her predecessors, are created according to similar imaginative principles. But her destructive doodle of the burning bush, along with another one of her memory images, that of Milton's bogey,[56] suggests iconoclasm: "my aunt's legacy unveiled the sky to me, and substituted for the large and imposing figure of a gentleman, which Milton recommended for my perpetual adoration, a view of the open sky."[57] Here, Woolf makes England's greatest Puritan writer—and the author of *Eikonoklastes*—into the author of an image so powerful she must destroy it in order to think for herself. When Woolf looks at the sky, she wants to be asked to remember not Milton, or Milton's God ("a gentleman"), but just the sky. And in the process, she makes a memory image of equal or greater power: that of the domineering and unimaginative patriarch, unsympathetic to the interests of women. But the desire to rid the sky of Milton's bogey does not make Woolf a strict iconoclast. In fact, in creating Milton's bogey, she revises our interpretation of a heretofore unquestioned image—something she does throughout the texts we have been examining here. In this case, her move contributed to the feminist rebellion against the dominance of Milton.[58] Once again, we see that the problem, for Woolf, is not with the image but with its power and its origin. The complication is that her claim that she wants a view of the open sky is not always compatible with her ambition to show us *her* sky.

In the sixteenth century, Bruno and Camillo carefully guarded their memory systems, saving them for presentation to the king of France: in doing so, they betrayed their awareness that others did not understand their grand projects, while expressing a grand confidence in the power of those projects. Although her audience is not the king but all women and her aim is not universalizing, Woolf, too, is torn between the intuition that, in order to work, such memory images must be personal, and the desire to be known as the author if not of a memory palace then certainly of a series of memory images. The kitchen table lodged in a pear tree, the mark on the wall, the disorganized library, and Milton's bogey work as memory images because they are asymmetrical, idiosyncratic, personal, and strange. Unlike the Renaissance memory images, however, these images were never meant to be part of a systematic record of human knowledge. Instead, each functions as an indictment of the human impulse toward the universal, ideal, or general.

I have focused here on those architectural memory systems that mapped vivid images onto a series of vast rooms; the mnemonist Johannes Romberch, among others, made use of entire abbeys or even a city, with "sets of objects to be memorized in the courtyard, library, and chapel of the abbey."[59] In

Bruno's dialogue in defense of Copernicus, a major piece of evidence in the Inquisition against him (he was burned at the stake in 1600), he includes a narrative of a frustrating, muddy, and circuitous walk through London with Fulke Greville to a dinner party at Philip Sidney's house. As Bruno knew, to defend Copernican astronomy was to take a great intellectual risk—one he paid for with his life. In *The Ash Wednesday Supper,* he uses a walk through the unsafe streets of a provincial capital to signify the intellectual obstacles before him.[60] Each muddy street and wrong turn makes Bruno and his companion later to a dinner at which he will be able to discuss the new astronomy with like-minded men. These difficulties in arriving at the beginning of the conversation dramatize the intellectual barriers between new ideas and their acceptance. *The Ash Wednesday Supper* is not a memory treatise, but in the walk through London Bruno uses some of the metaphoric strategies of the architectural mnemonic to make his point. The greater freedom represented by these looser memory schemes resembles Woolf's own placement of memory images in her texts. Such mnemonic walks also remind us how frequently she linked reading to walking, urging her readers to trespass on the private ground of literature.[61]

In her ambition to unseat public memory images, Woolf succeeded; her readers learn to be suspicious of individual buildings and the messages they intend to impart: "Walk through the Admiralty Arch (I had reached that monument), or any other avenue given up to trophies and cannon, and reflect upon the kind of glory celebrated there." Instead of succumbing to automatic thoughts of glory, Woolf forces us to think about what "kind of glory" is being put forward for our admiration. She has transformed London for her readers. The chimes of Big Ben are "first a warning, musical; then the hour, irrevocable"; the Elephant and Castle is the site of Judith Shakespeare's unmarked grave; the statue of Nurse Edith Cavell "always reminds me of an advertisement of sanitary towels"; and Whitehall is the place where "if one is a woman one is often surprised by a sudden splitting off of consciousness . . . when from being the natural inheritor of civilisation, she becomes, on the contrary, outside of it, alien and critical."[62] Thus, without changing London, Virginia Woolf has succeeded in changing our memory of it. If in doing so she has replaced Milton's bogey with her own, she has also taught us how to destroy it.

Notes

1. See Frances A. Yates, *The Art of Memory* (1966; reprint, London: Pimlico, 1992), 18; James Fentress and Chris Wickham, *Social Memory* (Oxford: Blackwell, 1992), 8–15. For an excellent account of Yates, see Patrick H. Hutton, "The Art of Memory Reconceived: From Rhetoric to Psychoanalysis," *Journal of the History of Ideas* 48 (1987): 373–76.

2. Mary Carruthers, *The Book of Memory: A Study of Memory in Medieval Culture* (Cambridge: Cambridge University Press, 1990), 31.

3. William Kerrigan and Gordon Braden, *The Idea of the Renaissance* (Baltimore: Johns Hopkins University Press, 1989), 83–84, 103. See also Yates, 187.

4. Hutton, 372.

5. Ibid., 386.

6. Maurice Halbwachs, *On Collective Memory,* edited and translated by Lewis A. Coser (Chicago: University of Chicago Press, 1992); Pierre Nora, "Between Memory and History: *Les Lieux de Mémoire,*" translated by Marc Roudebush, *Representations* 26 (1989): 7–25. Nora attributes both the inspiration for the term and his use of the *topos* to his reading of Yates. For an important complementary view of social memory, one focused more on ritual and body-memories than on buildings and texts, see Paul Connerton, *How Societies Remember* (Cambridge: Cambridge University Press, 1989).

7. Fentress and Wickham, 140.

8. Virginia Woolf, *To the Lighthouse* (1927; reprint, with a foreword by Eudora Welty, New York: Harcourt Brace Jovanovich [Harvest], 1989), 23.

9. Ibid.

10. E. M. Forster, *The Longest Journey* (1907; reprint, New York: Vintage, 1962), 2.

11. William E. Engel, "Mnemonic Criticism and Renaissance Literature: A Manifesto," *Connotations* 1 (1991): 12–13; see also Elizabeth McCutcheon, ed. and trans., "Sir Nicholas Bacon's Great House *Sententiae,*" *English Literary Renaissance Supplements* 3 (1977). For more on Woolf's relationship to Montaigne and her and Leonard's visit to his inscription-filled tower, see Nicola Luckhurst, "'To quote my quotation from Montaigne,'" chap. 2 of this volume.

12. E. M. Forster, *A Room with a View* (1908; reprint, New York: Vintage, n.d.), 144.

13. Woolf, *A Room of One's Own* (1929; reprint, with a foreword by Mary Gordon, New York: Harcourt Brace Jovanovich [Harvest], 1989), 8.

14. Woolf, *Three Guineas* (1938; reprint, New York: Harcourt Brace Jovanovich [Harvest], 1966), 33.

15. Woolf, *Between the Acts* (1941; reprint, New York: Harcourt Brace Jovanovich [Harvest], 1970); Woolf, "Reading" (1919), in *The Essays of Virginia Woolf,* 4 (of 6)

vols. to date, edited by Andrew McNeillie (London: Hogarth Press, 1986–94) 3:141–61; Woolf, "How Should One Read a Book?" (1926), revised version in *The Second Common Reader* [1932], edited by Andrew McNeillie (New York: Harcourt Brace Jovanovich [Harvest], 1986), 258–70; and Woolf, "Leslie Stephen" (1932), in *The Captain's Death Bed and Other Essays*, edited by Leonard Woolf (1950; reprint, New York: Harcourt Brace Jovanovich [Harvest], 1978), 69–75.

16. Woolf, "The Lives of the Obscure," three essays published in 1923, 1924, and 1925, combined and revised in *The Common Reader: First Series*, edited by Andrew McNeillie (New York: Harcourt Brace Jovanovich [Harvest], 1984), 106–33; Woolf, "The Leaning Tower" (1940), in *The Moment and Other Essays*, edited by Leonard Woolf (1947; reprint, New York: Harcourt Brace Jovanovich [Harvest], 1975), 128–54, 153.

17. Woolf, *A Room of One's Own*, 26.

18. Roger Chartier, *The Order of Books* (Stanford, Calif.: Stanford University Press, 1994), 63. Jorge Luis Borges, "The Library of Babel," in *Labyrinths: Selected Stories and Other Writings*, edited by Donald A. Yates and James E. Irby (New York: New Directions, 1964), 51–58.

19. Hutton, 386.

20. Michel Foucault, "Fantasia of the Library" (1967), in *Language, Counter-Memory, Practice: Selected Essays and Interviews*, edited by Donald F. Bouchard, translated by Donald F. Bouchard and Sherry Simon (Ithaca, N.Y.: Cornell University Press, 1977), 87–109, 90.

21. Woolf, *Jacob's Room* (1922; reprint, New York: Harcourt Brace Jovanovich [Harvest], 1978), 106.

22. Yates, 208–9.

23. Ibid., 212.

24. J. Mordaunt Crook, *The British Museum* (New York: Praeger, 1972), 190; see also P. R. Harris, *The Reading Room* (London: British Museum, 1979).

25. Crook, 190.

26. Ibid., 191. Interestingly, more recent visitors to the room insist that they remember quite different names there inscribed, but Judith Harrison of the British Library assures me that Crook's and Harris's accounts are accurate. E-mail message to the author, 2 July 1997.

27. Woolf, *Jacob's Room*, 106.

28. Yates, 32.

29. Ibid., 161.

30. Translated and quoted in Yates, 211. See also Giordano Bruno, *De Umbris Idearum* [1582], edited by Rita Sturlese (Firenze: Leo S. Olschki, 1991), 159: "Prima Saturni imago: homo cervini vultus super dracomem habens bubonem in dextra qui serpentem deglutit."

31. Woolf, "The Mark on the Wall" (1917), in *The Complete Shorter Fiction of Vir-*

ginia Woolf, edited by Susan Dick [1985], 2d ed. (New York: Harcourt Brace [Harvest], 1989), 83–89, 83.

32. As we see not only here and in Miss Julia Hedge's "Oh damn," but also in Mrs. Ramsay's "We are in the hands of the Lord." Woolf, *To the Lighthouse,* 63.

33. Woolf, "The Mark on the Wall," in *Complete Shorter Fiction,* 86.

34. Ibid., 87, 89.

35. Woolf, *Jacob's Room,* 107–8.

36. E. M. Forster, *Aspects of the Novel* (New York: Harcourt, Brace, 1927), 9.

37. Woolf, *A Room of One's Own,* 28; *Mrs. Dalloway* (1925; reprint, with a foreword by Maureen Howard, New York: Harcourt Brace [Harvest], 1990), 36.

38. Woolf, *Jacob's Room,* 108; Woolf, *A Room of One's Own,* 28; Woolf, *Jacob's Room,* 108.

39. Woolf, "The Elizabethan Lumber Room," in *The Common Reader,* 39–47, 47.

40. See Sally Greene, "Michelet, Woolf, and the Idea of the Renaissance," chap. 1 of this volume. Carruthers, 33; Nicholson Baker, *The Size of Thoughts* (New York: Vintage, 1996), 125–81.

41. Woolf, *Jacob's Room,* 109.

42. Woolf, *The Years* (1937; reprint, New York: Harcourt, Brace, and World [Harvest], 1969), 62.

43. Woolf, "Abbeys and Cathedrals" (1932), in *The London Scene* (New York: Random House, 1975), 30–36, 31, 34.

44. Woolf, "On Not Knowing Greek," in *The Common Reader,* 23–38, 25.

45. Woolf, *A Room of One's Own,* 95.

46. Woolf, *Mrs. Dalloway,* 80–81; Woolf, *The Years,* 429–30.

47. Woolf, *A Room of One's Own,* 26.

48. Woolf, *Jacob's Room,* 105; Woolf, *A Room of One's Own,* 27, 31.

49. Woolf, *The Years,* 176.

50. Woolf, The Pargiters: *The Novel-Essay Portion of* The Years, edited by Mitchell A. Leaska (1977; reprint, New York: Harcourt Brace Jovanovich [Harvest], 1978), 39 and passim.

51. Woolf, *A Room of One's Own,* 32.

52. Carruthers, 1.

53. Yates, 228–38; Hutton, 376.

54. Yates, 267.

55. Ibid., 231.

56. Woolf, *A Room of One's Own,* 114.

57. Ibid., 39.

58. In fact, Woolf's understanding of Milton was quite complicated. See Lisa Low, "'Listen and save': Woolf's Allusion to *Comus* in Her Revolutionary First Novel," chap. 5 of this volume.

59. Yates, 116.

60. Giordano Bruno, *The Ash Wednesday Supper,* edited and translated by Edward A. Gosselin and Lawrence S. Lerner (Hamden, Conn.: Archon Books, 1977), 109–27.

61. For further discussion of Woolf's habitual linkages between writing and walking, see Rachel Bowlby, "Walking, Women, and Writing: Virginia Woolf as *Flâneuse,*" chap. 1 of *Still Crazy after All These Years: Women, Writing, and Psychoanalysis* (New York: Routledge, 1992).

62. Woolf, *A Room of One's Own,* 38; Woolf, *Mrs. Dalloway,* 4; Woolf, *A Room of One's Own,* 48; Woolf, *The Years,* 336; Woolf, *A Room of One's Own,* 97.

Rewriting the
Renaissance

5

"Listen and save"

Woolf's Allusion to Comus in Her Revolutionary First Novel

Lisa Low

*I*n the final chapters of her first novel, *The Voyage Out* (1915), Virginia Woolf's heroine, Rachel Vinrace, slides into a coma carrying the words of Milton's *Comus* with her. Shortly thereafter, she dies. In classic readings of this allusion, Milton is said to "kill" Rachel off in a book about books. *The Voyage Out* is thus read as a *feminist* metatext, one that seeks to rewrite the bourgeois novel's violent marriage plot—a plot that has historically trapped, even "raped" women, denying them full humanity in their status as wives and mothers.[1] Milton is often read as the baleful originator of this plot and thus as the source of female oppression under modern Western capitalism.[2] Having demanded in *Paradise Lost* that women submit to their husband's authority, having sentimentalized the private sphere and so locked early modern women into the asphyxiating domesticity that accompanies emergent capitalism, and, most important, having founded in *Paradise Lost* the bourgeois novel with its woman-constricting and all-pervasive marriage plot—Milton is read as the father of modern female doom. According to this reading, if things are to

William Blake, "Sabrina Disenchanting the Lady," from *Comus: A Mask with Eight Illustrations by William Blake*, edited from the edition of 1645 and the autographed manuscript, with a preface by Darrell Figgis. Published for the Julian Editions by Ernest Benn Ltd., 1926. A copy of this limited edition is in the library of Leonard and Virginia Woolf, now in the possession of Washington State University, Pullman. Reproduction courtesy of the Museum of Fine Arts, Boston; gift of Mrs. John L. Gardner and George N. Black.

improve for women, the father, the master discourse-writer of Western patriarchy, must be slain. So, in her first novel (in which the young Woolf is said to
take her first clumsy steps toward rewriting female history), Woolf takes on
Milton in the form of her allusion to *Comus,* a work, like *The Voyage Out,*
about the sexual violation of a female heroine. In plotting Milton as her first
heroine's murderer, she provides a revolutionary revisioning of the woman's
place in Western society and, by implication at least, herself emerges as a
master discourse-writer of feminism. According to this reading, in writing
Milton out of the picture Woolf exposes and deconstructs the soul of the
patriarchy he establishes in *Paradise Lost.*

But such a reading can only be sustained at the expense of *Comus*'s plot.
Even a brief look at *Comus* will show that the protagonist of Milton's masque,
despite her being born in 1634 in an age when women were expected to be
chaste, silent, and obedient, is no shrinking violet, no sensitive plant who
cannot face her enemies.[3] On the contrary, she is a powerful and speaking
heroine who resists her suitor and slays her enemies single-handedly. In fact,
despite Milton's reputation as a misogynist, female readers have historically
turned to *Comus* to find a model not of female subservience but of female
self-reliance.[4] In this essay I will argue that not only does *Comus* not represent
the patriarchal plot that Christine Froula and Louise DeSalvo have claimed,[5]
but, further, Woolf must go as far back as Milton's *Comus*—before, that is, the
fall into the eighteenth- and nineteenth-century novel with its woman-
strangling marriage plots—to find an alternative in which the heroine is not
diminished but made mighty by being permitted her solitary integrity outside
marriage.[6] More particularly I will argue that Woolf's allusion to *Comus* in *The
Voyage Out* is a masterstroke revealing the centrally important theme of sexual
violation otherwise partially veiled within the text.

Comus tells the story of an unnamed "Lady" who finds herself alone at
night in the woods. Approached by Comus, an evil orgiast, she is persuaded to
go with him in search of her brothers. The masque's second half discovers the
Lady trapped in Comus's palace, with Comus trying to force her to drink from
his glass. Significantly, the Lady's brothers botch a rescue attempt, and only
Sabrina, a motherless nymph who has drowned herself to avoid rape, can save
her. The masque's dominant theme is mental chastity, but it is suffused with an
atmosphere of sexual innuendo. One feels intensely the sordidness of the Lady's

encounter with Comus, especially when Milton describes the chair to which the Lady is stuck as "[s]mear'd with gums of glutinous heat" (line 917), gums that insinuate ejaculation—probably on the part of the disgusting Comus.[7]

Woolf's first novel also tells a tale of sexual violation. In *The Voyage Out*, Rachel Vinrace, a twenty-four-year-old virgin, "voyages out," with her shipping magnate father and her aunt and uncle, on a ship to an island in South America. Rachel, whose mother died (like Woolf's own mother) when she was a child, has been raised in typically Victorian fashion by maiden aunts. They have protected her virginity above all else, telling her nothing about sex. Though a brilliant pianist, Rachel is intellectually and emotionally a sort of *tabula rasa* on which the world can imprint itself, which is exactly what happens in the course of the novel. On the boat Rachel meets the Dalloways, an impressive parliamentarian and his wife. After she is kissed unexpectedly by Richard Dalloway, Rachel comes under the solicitous protection of her aunt, Helen Ambrose, who gains permission from Rachel's bullying father to escort her to Santa Marina, where the bulk of the novel takes place.[8] On Santa Marina Rachel becomes engaged to a young and sympathetic novelist, Terence Hewet. But before their marriage can be consummated, Rachel falls ill with a mysterious fever and dies.

Dalloway's kiss is usually read as important, but certainly not as central to the novel. Thomas Caramagno argues, for example, that the sexually protected Rachel is neurotically overreactive to what, for most women, would be the harmless imposition of an innocent, perhaps even fatherly kiss.[9] I argue to the contrary that Dalloway's kiss is the central event in a novel about sexual violence.

The kiss occurs early (in only the fifth of twenty-seven chapters), but it is a disturbing and, indeed, fatal experience for Rachel. Both drawn to the kiss and horrified by it, she suffers a nightmare afterward. In the nightmare she is trapped in a vault with a repulsive dwarf who squats "on the floor gibbering, with long nails" (77). The vault walls are damp, oozing fluids that collect in drops and slide to the floor. This dream motif as well as its theme of sexual repulsion recurs in Rachel's death scene. As Rachel's fiancé reads to her from *Comus*, her head begins to ache and she slips gradually into a coma, taking images from *Comus* with her. Picturing bestiality in nightmarishly distorted visions, Rachel listens to the echo of Terence's voice as he enunciates words from the masque. The bed Rachel lies on becomes a watery grave, like the boat she rode on to the island in the sea where she will die and like the river Severn in which *Comus*'s suicidal but chaste savior, Sabrina, lives "under the . . . wave" (line 861).

Significantly, the dwarf appearing in Rachel's nightmares recalls both the bestiality of Comus and his crew and Woolf's own description of early molestation. When she was "very small," Gerald Duckworth felt her "private parts" in front of a looking glass. Afterward Woolf had a nightmare in which she "was looking [at herself] in a glass when a horrible face—the face of an animal—suddenly showed over [her] shoulder."[10] Both *Comus* and *The Voyage Out* are knitted up, in other words, with the important theme of sexual molestation in Woolf's life.

The single most important point to be made in connection with *Comus* and *The Voyage Out* is that they are both narratives about sexual violation. In both stories a virgin voyages out surrounded by well-wishers; but when she is left alone, she is accosted by a disingenuous male figure who exploits her virginity and leaves her to her fate. The principal difference between the two texts is that, although Milton's heroine survives and is even strengthened by the encounter, Woolf's heroine—who does not share the confident male subjectivity of Milton's Lady—dies because of it.

The rape story is more obvious in *Comus* than it is in *The Voyage Out*, and indeed, my claim that *The Voyage Out* is about sexual violation may take some skeptical readers by surprise. Dalloway, after all, only kisses Rachel. But to minimize the kiss is both to misunderstand the Victorian and patriarchal contexts that govern the novel and to collaborate with Helen Ambrose in a view that fails (or refuses) to acknowledge the psychological impact of sexual aggression against women. Rachel is not just Rachel but everywoman in this clearly feminist text. Her education in sexual violence is systematic within a culture that raises women to be sexually paralyzed, even as it preys upon female sexuality. Far from being harmless, Dalloway's kiss signifies the sexual abuse Woolf herself suffered but cannot tell. Indeed, the central event in a novel about sexual violence, the kiss symbolizes the violence against women that is constitutive of the patriarchy. That the kiss is followed by a nightmare, that it recalls the sexual abuse Woolf suffered as a child, and that it is recapitulated in hallucinogenic detail in the closing chapters of *The Voyage Out*—together provide incontrovertible evidence of sexual violence as a *cause* in Rachel's death.

In "The Daughter's Seduction: Sexual Violence and Literary History," Froula argues convincingly that the inability to tell the story of sexual violation denies women subjectivity. Reading canonical scripts drawn from Homer to Freud as rape scripts, Froula argues that literature serves as a training manual for young male and female readers alike and that it plays a *violent* role in the construction of female destiny. Female silence is "an effect of repression, not of absence," for literary culture, like "real life," endorses rape, even as it suppresses the woman's need to tell its story. The inability to tell the story of rape produces female silence, and female silence produces absence, the lack of female subjectivity under the patriarchy. But if literature has played its role in silencing, it can also play an equivalent role in liberating women. Indeed, Froula uses Woolf's prophecy in *A Room of One's Own* that the "woman's freedom to tell [and know] her stories . . . would come . . . once she is no longer the dependent daughter, wife, and servant" to argue that, once daughters begin to tell the story of rape—as, for example, Maya Angelou and Alice Walker in novels such as *I Know Why the Caged Bird Sings* and *The Color Purple* have more recently told it—they will begin to be free.[11]

Woolf's Victorian context prevents the story of rape from being obvious in *The Voyage Out*. Buried beneath a stolen kiss in chapter 5, but connected to nightmares that return to Rachel at her death, the violence plot that drives *The Voyage Out* is hard to see, as if Woolf herself, writing her first novel in her late twenties, was not yet free to speak the unspeakable; or as if she only dimly foresaw what Froula, writing from a postmodernist perspective, sees clearly: the significance of rape in patriarchal self-maintenance.[12] This is the "true" meaning of Woolf's allusion to *Comus* at the end of her revolutionary first novel: like the story the tongueless and mutilated Philomela tells her sister in her tapestry, *Comus* reveals the rape story buried in Woolf's narrative. Woolf thus makes Milton essential not only to the emergence of feminism, but also to female subjectivity, even as she makes *Comus* a string to help the female reader find a path by which to escape from the deadly labyrinth and into the light of psychological freedom.

Catherine Belsey has argued that *Comus* is "about rape" but that unusual about Milton's masque is the perspective it takes on that act. Whereas conventional male-authored plots take apparent delight in depicting what Annette Cafarelli calls the "suicidal asthenia" of heroines, *Comus* resists "the implications of its own plot," as Belsey puts it, for the Lady, far from shrinking from Comus in terror, is defiant and articulate.[13] Although the bare outline of *Comus* suggests that the Lady springs from and anticipates a long and still popular misogynist tradition of imperiled but helpless Paulines, in fact, the Lady remains majestically self-possessed throughout her ordeal, as if invested with Godlike power, sustaining an unmovably fierce self-reliance and imperturbable calm more typical of Milton's Christ than of his Eve. Wise beyond her years, the Lady is more than a match for her assailant, saying to him with "sacred vehemence" (line 795) as he presses close, "Thou canst not touch the freedom of my mind" (line 663). Similarly, although Comus might in another context be portrayed as a smooth-talking hero, a swashbuckling cavalier spouting carpe diem poetry, Milton satirizes him: instead of maintaining easy mastery of his prey, Comus recoils astonished after his encounter with the Lady, his manly power drained. "She fables not" (line 800), he says, and is silenced. The Lady's brothers are satirized as well. Instead of saving a sister in need, they are ineffectual and stoogelike, botching the job, and it is only the mothering, defiantly not male-identified Sabrina, brought back from the dead, who can save the Lady. In each of these plot elements, a supposedly misogynist Milton seems to provide less a justification for than a critique of the patriarchy.

The principal theme of *Comus* is chastity, but importantly by chastity Milton means not the patriarchal injunction that women must remain virgins, but rather a mental state available to men and women alike, best defined as the sanctity or integrity of self, the ability, requiring enormous moral strength and self-possession, to remain "clad in complete steel" (line 421), unpracticed in evil despite a rapacious world. If Comus is the incarnation of evil, forefather to feminist-inspired gothic villains and to imperialistic predators alike—amoral, licentious, domineering, and revolting—the Lady remains unintimidated by him. She defies her adversary, deftly exposing the greed that underlies Comus's feigned solicitude and the corrupt culture he exemplifies. When Comus offers to take the Lady to a cottage, the Lady criticizes luxury, saying that "honest offer'd courtesy" is "sooner found in lowly sheds" than in "tap'stry Halls / And Courts of Princes" where it "is most *pretended*" (lines 322–26, emphasis mine). When Comus argues that beauty should be used, not hoarded, the Lady responds with a proto-Marxist speech that demonstrates her awareness of the connections between sexual and economic exploitation:

        If every just man that now pines with want
        Had but a moderate and beseeming share
        Of that which lewdly-pamper'd Luxury
        Now heaps upon some few with vast excess,
        Nature's full blessings would be well dispens't
        In unsuperfluous even proportion.

                                        (lines 768–73)

Self-possessed and powerful, sublimely aware of injustice, the Lady is politically heroic: positioned in a desperate situation, her defense is for herself and also for the poor and for the natural world with whom she sympathizes and among whom she is condemned.

    Comus has been, but should not be, confused with *Paradise Lost*. A number of critics have described *Paradise Lost* as the first novel, most recently Mary Nyquist. For Nyquist, in its idealization of marriage and its privatization of the female as man's subordinate within the domestic sphere, *Paradise Lost* provides a philosophical foundation not only for emergent capitalism but for the principal themes and structures of the eighteenth-century novel as well. But *Comus* hardly anticipates the marriage plot; in fact, if anything, *Comus* does what it can to steer culture away from the marriage plot (about to descend on early modern women like an avalanche), both by its preference for solitude over marriage and by its analysis of the violence that subtends marriage. Indeed, in its contempt for exploitation and cruelty, its indictment of rape, and its suggestion that only a community of women can save women,[14] *Comus* tells a story that is as yet not fully decipherable by a culture such as ours, still characterized by class structures in which the other is dominated; by the amoral accumulation of capital for the few on the backs of the many; by the exploitation of nature for excessive use by the wealthy; and by indifference to, or even encouragement of, the violence that makes such hierarchical arrangements possible. Like *The Voyage Out*, in other words, *Comus* imagines human history that has not yet come to pass.

    For her part, Woolf's heroine shows little of the fortitude of Milton's Lady. Rachel resists oppression, even preferring, like the motherless Sabrina, to die to avoid it, but she is ultimately crushed by her assailant, unable to hold herself aloof and steely against the dehumanization that would annihilate her. Most emphatically, unlike the Lady, Rachel dies.

The underlying cause of Rachel's mysterious death can be found not only in chapter 25 (where Rachel dies meditating on phrases from Milton's masque) but also much earlier, in chapter 5, where Woolf stages her version of the masque, one in which the assaulted Lady is unsuccessful in resisting her captor. Though twenty-two chapters remain to be played out, in a sense Rachel's life is over after chapter 5 with the sexual initiation that comes in the form of Richard Dalloway's kiss. The kiss, reintroduced in chapter 25 when Rachel lies on her deathbed, foreshadows Rachel's death months later, on the eve of her marriage, and implicates a culture in which male sexual violence cuts women's lives short.

Richard Dalloway is an elegant man whose power and well-connectedness are implied by his ability to board Rachel's father's ship, the Euphrosyne, without a pass or prior arrangement.[15] Though Rachel feels humiliated by Dalloway, for "her face was not the face she wanted, and in all probability never would be" (41), Dalloway considers himself superior to the other passengers on board ship, with the exception of Rachel's father, Willoughby Vinrace, a shipping magnate with whom, since "'[h]e knows Sutton and all that set,'" Dalloway, educated at Cambridge and Oxford, thinks he shall have something in common. Dalloway is a patriarch, an imperialist, and an antifeminist. With his "chest slowly curv[ing] beneath his waistcoat," he imagines his son becoming "'a leader of men,'" at the head of a fleet of English ships. Like his wife, he thinks sentimentally of "'all we've done'" for "'the people in India and Africa'" and reviews with pride the English "conservative policy" that "gradually enclosed . . . enormous chunks of the habitable globe" (50–51). To Dalloway "'the English seem, on the whole, whiter than most men, their records cleaner'" (64). Though idealizing them, he considers women, like Indians and Africans, inferior. He never permits his wife "'to talk politics'" (65), believing that "'no woman has . . . the political instinct'" (67). He is against equal rights for the sexes, saying with conviction, "'[M]ay I be in my grave before a woman has the right to vote in England!'" (43).

Rachel is intimidated by Dalloway. Indeed, the difference between Rachel and her would-be mentor, the Lady of *Comus,* is most pronounced in the Lady's self-possession. Whereas the Lady is articulate, even brilliant, in outwitting and undermining her adversary, whereas powerful lines such as "Fool, do not boast" (line 662) come to her unbidden, Rachel is tentative and un-selfconfident. The naive Rachel is amazed that "a man like [Dalloway] should be willing to talk to her" (56); indeed, talking to "a man of such worth and authority" makes her "heart beat" (65). Nevertheless, in an early conversation with Dalloway, the feminist-in-embryo Rachel braves a tentative criticism of the empire. Unconvinced by Dalloway's utilitarianism, she raises the image of an isolated widow in her private lodgings in Leeds whose cupboards may be well stocked by the empire but whose spiritual life, whose "soul," remains unengaged (66). But Rachel's critique, unlike the Lady's, stalls.

Shortly after the arrival of the Dalloways, a storm swells up and sickens almost everyone on board. Rachel and Mr. Dalloway, among the only well, bump into each other on the windy deck, and when Dalloway comes to Rachel's cabin to talk, the encounter that follows enacts a sexual violation that echoes *Comus.* When Dalloway speaks sanctimoniously of the great opportunities open to the young in their time, Rachel reminds him that she is a woman. Sentimentally and hypocritically, he tells her that to be a young woman is to have "'the whole world at her feet.'" To the contrary, Rachel is about to have "the whole world" yanked out from under her. When the ship lurches, Dalloway takes "her in his arms and kisse[s] her," holding her "tightly" and "passionately," enough so that she feels "the hardness of his body and the roughness of his cheek printed upon hers" (76).

If at first Rachel feels exalted by the kiss, by dinner she is uncomfortable, "as if she and Richard had seen something together which is hidden in ordinary life, so that they did not like to look at each other" (77). At dinner, the now explicitly serpent-like Dalloway "*slid* his eyes over her uneasily once, and never looked at her again" (77, emphasis mine). Rachel's sexual initiation results that night in a nightmare that suggests prior molestation, likely at the hands of her father, Willoughby Vinrace.[16] After a horrifying dream involving bestiality, one that recalls scenes of molestation from Woolf's childhood, Rachel wakes in sweating terror and locks her door but continues to feel pursued by revolting presences: "A voice moaned for her; eyes desired her. All night long barbarian men harrassed [*sic*] the ship; they came scuffling down the passages, and stopped to snuffle at her door" (77). On the following day the Dalloways leave, Richard without so much as saying good-bye. When Rachel tells her Aunt Helen of the incident, Helen betrays her, dismissing Rachel's fears and expecting that she enjoyed the kiss: "'I'm rather jealous,'" she says, "'that Mr. Dalloway kissed you and didn't kiss me'" (81).

The Voyage Out, like *Comus,* is most radical in its exposure of the violence that subtends the marriage plot. For Froula, Dalloway's kiss represents Rachel's "violent abduction into male culture." It teaches Rachel that "her [proper] place is in the underworld" and that she is a sexually vulnerable object whose enclosure by the patriarchy will be enforced.[17] By kissing her, Dalloway pulls the world out from under Rachel's feet, leaving her to fall into an endlessly deepening pit of self-loathing, confusion, sexual guilt, and, most important, fear of the men (now all of them powerful because all of them threatening) who dominate and surround her. Dalloway's is the "kiss of death." Though partly enjoyed since it seems to speak of love, something that understandably exhilarates Rachel, by its unexpectedness, its violence, and its dismissiveness the kiss forces Rachel from innocence into experience, from trust to betrayed trust, with the suddenness of a needle yanked across the grooved surface of a record. The somewhat sublime melody Rachel has been hearing is replaced with cacophonous and inassimilable sounds of grotesque and horrible connotation, and her education, now descended into the sexual that Woolf decries as the destiny of the female under the patriarchy, is complete. The *bildung* sinks, here sordidly, into violation, and Rachel's nightmarish death is foreshadowed. Her life and education cut short, her tragic ending already set in motion, Rachel has become a heroine without a future, and, in many ways, the novel is over.

After the encounter with Dalloway, Rachel's aunt escorts her to Santa Marina, where she meets and becomes engaged to Terence Hewet. Hereafter, the novel is concerned with Rachel and Terence's courtship and the possibility of their establishing an androgynous marriage. Though Terence is in some ways the best of men, kind and sympathetic to Rachel, he becomes increasingly oppressive after they are engaged. Sometimes staring at Terence dispassionately, even with disgust, Rachel is constantly torn between her desire to marry him (as young lovers are supposed to do) and her stronger desire for celibacy, a life that will allow her freedom to play piano, read, and daydream. As the marriage nears, Rachel becomes increasingly reluctant and confused. Indeed, horrified at the thought of her engagement party, Rachel says, "'I'd rather have my right hand sawn in pieces'" than go (308).

At the head of the novel's climactic twenty-fifth chapter, Rachel becomes mortally ill, a reversal of marriage expectations accompanied by the novel's second, this time more explicit and extended, allusion to *Comus*. The complex allusion is difficult to decipher, for it is woven, like a musical theme, throughout the text's most critical chapter. In a sense, the lines from *Comus* sing Lady Rachel to her death.

Rachel's mysterious illness sets in on the day set for their engagement party. As she sits in the garden courtyard, nauseated and feverish, Terence says he will read to her. After trying several authors, Terence settles at last on Milton (specifically, *Comus*), for only Milton, the now patriarchally tainted Terence claims, can stand up to the heat. Since "the words of Milton had substance and shape," Terence says, "it was not necessary to understand what he was saying" (326). But Terence's "reading" of Milton—a patriarchal (and patronizing?) one that prefers form and ceremony to content—is totally different from Rachel's. For Rachel, who hears a different Milton than Terence does, one that might save her, or at least, one to which she wishes to listen especially carefully, Milton's words are curiously "laden with meaning" (326). Significantly, Woolf selects lines from the end of the masque, where the brothers have proved incapable of saving their sister and Sabrina, the "Virgin pure" (line 826) who drowned herself to avoid rape, is called upon to save the Lady. "There is a gentle nymph not far from hence," Hewet reads,

> That with moist curb sways the smooth Severn stream.
> Sabrina is her name, a virgin pure;
> Whilom she was the daughter of Locrine,
> That had the sceptre from his father Brute.

For the motherless and unsaveable Rachel, a confused heroine vaguely formulating a feminism that does not yet exist, the words are painful to listen to, and her mind goes off on "curious trains of thought suggested by [harsh-sounding] words such as 'curb' [the curbing of women?] and 'Locrine' and 'Brute.'" In the intermediate state between sense and nonsense that fever and revolutions inspire, words mean "different things from what they usually meant" to Rachel (326–27). (We can speculate that the brutal-sounding, Anglo-Saxon words "curb" and "Locrine" and especially "Brute"—which recalls *Brut*, the series of British chronicle histories tracing the Roman Brutus's colonization of England—suggest the exclusion of women and the violence of the patriarchy to Rachel, even as the soothing words "Sabrina" and "stream" lure her to the matriarchy she desires.) This difference of meaning, this sliding slantwise across language, suggests the rewriting of history that Woolf attempts through Rachel. It also suggests a different reading of Milton from the standard one, for Sabrina, on whose name and presence Rachel fixates, is the saving matriarch Rachel/Woolf does not have, the mother to whom Rachel, on her deathbed to avoid rape, is about to go. As Rachel's headache intensifies, Terence continues, this time reading the very lines that call Sabrina from the river:

> Sabrina fair,
>> Listen where thou art sitting
> Under the glassy, cool, translucent wave,
>> In twisted braids of lilies knitting
> The loose train of thy amber dropping hair,
> Listen for dear honour's sake,
>> Goddess of the silver lake,
>> Listen and save!
>
> (327)

Exactly at this point, perhaps because she is in despair of being listened to or saved, Rachel's head begins to ache unbearably, and she says that she will go inside. Over the next few days, as she sinks gradually into the coma that leads to her death, Rachel's "chief occupation during the day [is] to try to remember how the lines [from *Comus*] went." Her mind recites:

> Under the glassy, cool, translucent wave,
>> In twisted braids of lilies knitting
> The loose train of thy amber dropping hair;

but "the effort" to call on Sabrina "worried her because the adjectives persisted in getting into the wrong places" (329). Rachel concentrates on Sabrina, the lost mother she wishes would save her, but her perception of her inability to get the adjectives in the right places signals her doom. For this "real life" woman born of a novel, trying alone to invent a feminism not yet there, there is no masque-born Sabrina to listen to her voice and no masque-born Sabrina to come from the waves to save her. Writing and rewriting her script, looking for a lost mother and a nonexistent female community, Rachel remains unable to bring about the feminist conditions that would ensure her salvation.

As days pass, fever, headaches, chills, and delirium further distort Rachel's ordinary world: the walls curve and Rachel's bed swims, seemingly cast out to sea. The window cord dragging across the floor frightens her, as if there were some animal in the room, and when Helen comes in with the doctor, again in an image that recalls the bestiality of Comus, the first thing the sexually nauseated Rachel notices about him is that he has very hairy hands. By the second day of her illness, Rachel is "completely cut off, and unable to communicate with the rest of the world" (330). The "glassy, cool, translucent wave [is] almost visible before her, curling up at the end of the bed" (329). She longs for it, as if, like Sabrina, by "commend[ing] her fair innocence to the flood" (line 831), she could disappear. Feverish, suicidal, Rachel longs to descend at last into the alien but maternal world of the sea where women—the Sabrinas who do not yet belong to, who cannot yet live safely in this world—survive, half alive, half dead, not yet ready to be born.

After a week Rachel looks "as though she were entirely concentrated upon the effort of keeping alive." Her cheeks are "sunken and flushed" like the dead. When Terence kisses her "she only saw an old woman slicing a man's head off with a knife" and murmurs, "[T]here it falls!" (339). On the fourth day Rachel goes underwater completely, falling

> into a deep pool of sticky [semen-like?] water, which eventually closed over her head. She saw nothing and heard nothing but a faint booming sound, which was the sound of the sea rolling over her head. While all her tormentors thought that she was dead, she was not dead, but curled up at the bottom of the sea. There she lay, sometimes seeing darkness, sometimes light, while every now and then some one turned her over at the bottom of the sea. (341)

If she has, at least in her feverish imagination, joined Sabrina, no water nymphs have reached out to save her, holding "up their pearled wrists" (line 834) to take her in, and none has borne her "straight to aged *Nereus'* Hall" (line 835), where she might have been revived and transformed, immortalized as a goddess who would henceforth save maidens in distress. Days later Rachel, having made it only to the threshold of feminism, is dead.[18]

Rachel's death is considered mysterious by most critics, even unfathomable. Although it is possible that she contracted a fever on her journey with Terence up the Amazon River, most critics have read Rachel's death as a self-willed and, for Woolf, a symbolic one, carrying on its back Woolf's perhaps somewhat clumsy attempt as feminist novelist to escape the "marriage plot" originating (some have argued) in *Paradise Lost* and invoked repeatedly in the bourgeois novel of the eighteenth and nineteenth centuries. But it is not only the marriage plot but also its sexual violence that causes Rachel's death, and it is not Milton, but the culture of violence *Comus* stands against, that Woolf condemns. For Woolf, Milton is not, as he is too reductively for mainstream feminist criticism, the enemy. Rather, he is a radical forebear whose works, if they in some ways perpetuate the patriarchy, in other ways give guidance to women looking for a way out of a Minos-like labyrinth.

The difference between the heroines of *Comus* and *The Voyage Out* lies ultimately in their male and female subjectivity. Woolf's heroine is born into a Victorian world that silences because it sexualizes women. The revolutionary heroine of Milton's *Comus,* on the other hand, is born into an England on the fiery verge of Civil War, and she is invested with the power and revolutionary self-confidence of newfound male speech and male subjectivity. Milton's Lady is unassailably powerful because she incorporates the privileged subjecthood of Milton himself: she shares the position of strength in speaking that even a revolutionary outsider like Milton occupies by being a man. Instead of internalizing the violence of her assailant, she denounces him, speaking in a mighty voice that, charged with the revolutionary fervor of the English Civil War, Woolf dimly foresaw as one that could prepare the way for feminism. Unlike the Lady, Woolf's heroine shares the underprivileged female subjecthood, the fatal vulnerability, the tongueless silences, of Woolf herself. She is Woolf's portrayal of a real woman for whom rape is rape and death is death. If Milton's heroine navigates the Siren-lined straits and wandering rocks of female terror, even as she calls upon and is saved by the lost-mother Sabrina, Woolf's heroine dies unable to be strong and articulate in self-defense. For her, in contrast to the Lady, there is no freedom of mind that Dalloway can not touch. Having been touched by Dalloway, Rachel folds like a flower and dies.

Woolf's revolutionary first novel lays a foundation for contemporary novels like *The Color Purple* and *I Know Why the Caged Bird Sings* that are more free to tell the story of rape. Not entirely successfully, *The Voyage Out* attempts to reveal the secret that underlies patriarchal culture—the primal sexual abuse (especially the incest) that silences women, curtailing their lives, killing them before they are born into the *bildung,* making sure that they are submissive and that, their mouths covered, they never tell their tales. In this sense, though Rachel Vinrace dies, she has the power to heal women readers. For male and female readers alike, the Sabrina-like Rachel can help "unlock / The clasping charm and thaw the numbing spell" (lines 852–53). She can help unfreeze, in other words, the paralyzing sexual terror of daughters to come who wander in the perilous flood of patriarchy.

T. S. Eliot argues in his essay "The Metaphysical Poets" that following Milton English literature suffered a dissociation of sensibility, a falling off from its ability to synthesize thought and feeling simultaneously, and that, had not Milton been there to block the progress of English literature, literature would have continued to flourish in the Elizabethan mode. In certain respects, we can read *The Voyage Out* as Woolf's version of "The Metaphysical Poets." *Comus* represents for Woolf not the patriarchal narrative par excellence as Froula claims, but an earlier alternative to the marriage plot that has reigned over female readers from the novel's inception at least until Woolf's time. *Comus* presents a strong, not sentimentalized, woman, one who, significantly, chooses in some sense not to marry.

If Rachel Vinrace cannot follow the path of Milton's intellectually chaste and revolutionary heroine, if she does not yet have the fierce strength to say with the Lady, "thou canst not touch the freedom of my mind" (line 663), if Rachel is unsuccessful in calling upon Sabrina, the mythological woman/ nymph under the wave who has killed herself to avoid rape—it is because not Milton but the tradition Milton's text militates against has educated Rachel in servitude and dependence. *Comus*'s protagonist does not succumb to but rather successfully resists male coercion and molestation, even as she is saved, ultimately, not by a man but by a woman. *Comus* thus represents not the epitome of the patriarchal plot against women and women artists but rather its more attractive alternative: female self-reliance (what Woolf would later call "mental chastity"),[19] including the self-reliance of a woman-saving-woman community. If the allusion to *Comus* comes too late in *The Voyage Out* to save Rachel Vinrace's life, it nevertheless offers a paradigm that both Woolf herself and future novelists like Angelou and Walker can convert and fruitfully employ. In the Lady of *Comus* Woolf saw a model not of what woman is, but of what woman might be, and in its mournful tale of Sabrina she saw a sighting, on Milton's part, of a matriarchy to come. Like Rachel, Woolf listens to Milton so that she might be saved by him. In the end Woolf's allusion to *Comus* in *The Voyage Out* points not to the entrapment of women in marriage, but to the as-yet-unwritten plot of female liberty that Froula and DuPlessis would have us believe would have been Rachel's had she not died on the threshold of modernism.

⤳ Notes

I would like to thank Sally Greene, John Shawcross, Michael Chappell, and members of the Feminist Research Group at Pace University (in particular, Martha Driver, Mark Hussey, Karla Jay, Sid Ray, Walter Srebnick, and Jean Fagan Yellin) for helpful readings of this essay.

1. See Rachel Blau DuPlessis, "'Amor Vin—': Modifications of Romance in Woolf," in *Virginia Woolf: A Collection of Critical Essays,* edited by Margaret Homans (Englewood Cliffs, N.J.: Prentice Hall, 1993), 115–35; Christine Froula, "Out of the Chrysalis: Female Initiation and Female Authority in Virginia Woolf's *The Voyage Out*," in *Virginia Woolf: A Collection of Critical Essays,* 136–61; Louise A. DeSalvo, *Virginia Woolf's First Voyage* (Totowa, N.J.: Rowman and Littlefield, 1980); Louise A. DeSalvo, "A Portrait of the *Puttana* as a Middle-Aged Woolf Scholar," in *Between Women: Biographers, Novelists, Critics, Teachers, and Artists Write about Their Work on Women,* edited by Carol Ascher, Louise A. DeSalvo, and Sara Ruddick (Boston: Beacon Press, 1984), 35–53; and especially Louise A. DeSalvo, "Virginia, Virginius, Virginity," in *Faith of a (Woman) Writer,* edited by Alice Kessler-Harris and William McBrien (Westport, Conn.: Greenwood, 1988), 179–89. Froula and DeSalvo argue specifically that Milton—the father, through *Paradise Lost* and *Comus,* of the patriarchal "chastity and then marriage" plot against women—causes Rachel's death.

2. In Froula's interpretation, "Milton's words are fatal to Rachel, not because no nymph arrives to save her but because they represent a tradition in which bound,

endangered 'ladies,' drowned nymphs, and the marriage plot with its tightwoven construction of female sexuality as virginity, domesticity, and maternity, figure woman's 'destiny.'" "Out of the Chrysalis," 157. See also DeSalvo, "Virginia, Virginius, Virginity," esp. 181–82, 187.

3. Suzanne Hull, *Chaste, Silent, and Obedient: English Books for Women, 1475–1640* (San Marino, Calif.: Huntington Library, 1982).

4. See Annette Wheeler Cafarelli, "How Theories of Romanticism Exclude Women: Radcliffe, Milton, and the Legitimation of the Gothic Novel," in *Milton, the Metaphysicals, and Romanticism*, edited by Lisa Low and Anthony John Harding (Cambridge: Cambridge University Press, 1994), esp. 94–96.

5. See notes 1 and 2 above.

6. There is a fairly long literary history of women's pursuit of chastity as an alternative to marriage. See Theodora A. Jankowski's "'The Scorne of Savage People': Virginity as 'Forbidden Sexuality' in John Lyly's *Love's Metamorphosis*," in *Renaissance Drama* (1993), esp. 132. For a Victorian corollary, see Karla Jay, "The Religion of Love," in *The Amazon and the Page* (Bloomington: Indiana University Press, 1988), 81–95. That Woolf reaches all the way back to *Comus* to find an alternative to marriage may signify the masque's historical position as immediately prior to the emergence of the eighteenth- and nineteenth-century novel, which it is the business of *The Voyage Out* to untangle.

7. All quotations from *Comus* ("A Mask Presented at Ludlow Castle, 1634"), cited parenthetically in the text by line number, are taken from *John Milton: Complete Poems and Major Prose*, edited by Merritt Y. Hughes (Upper Saddle River, N.J.: Prentice Hall, 1957).

8. Rachel's aunt, Helen Ambrose, suspects Willoughby Vinrace "of nameless atrocities with regard to his daughter, as indeed she had always suspected him of bullying his wife." Virginia Woolf, *The Voyage Out* (1915; reprint, New York: Harcourt, Brace, and World [Harvest], 1968), 24. Subsequent parenthetical references in the text are to this edition. In "'Nameless Atrocities' and the Name of the Father: Literary Allusion and Incest in Virginia Woolf's *The Voyage Out*," *Woolf Studies Annual* 1 (1995): 26–46, Lisa Tyler has argued convincingly that Rachel was sexually molested by her father.

9. Thomas Caramagno, *The Flight of the Mind: Virginia Woolf's Art and Manic-Depressive Illness* (Berkeley: University of California Press, 1992). See esp. 158ff.

10. Woolf, "A Sketch of the Past," in *Moments of Being*, edited by Jeanne Schulkind [1976], 2d ed. (New York: Harcourt Brace Jovanovich [Harvest], 1985), 69.

11. In "The Daughter's Seduction: Sexual Violence and Literary History," in *Feminist Theory in Practice and Process*, edited by Micheline R. Malson et al. (Chicago: University of Chicago Press, 1989), 139–62; the quotes are at 140.

12. In the marginal notes to a draft of *The Voyage Out*, Woolf writes that she will use either Keats's "Ode to a Nightingale" or "the poems of Milton" [specifically, as it turns out, *Comus*] as the poetry that sings Rachel to her death. DeSalvo, *First Voyage*,

9. Keats's "Nightingale" ode is significant, since it also suggests Philomena's story of rape. Jane Marcus has argued that the myth of Philomela can serve as a metaphor for many of Woolf's performances, including, in *A Room of One's Own,* the narrator's telling of the silenced story of Judith Shakespeare; see J. Marcus, "Taking the Bull by the Udders," chap. 7 of *Virginia Woolf and the Languages of Patriarchy* (Bloomington: Indiana University Press, 1987), esp. 142–45.

13. Catherine Belsey, *John Milton: Language, Gender, Power* (Oxford: Blackwell, 1988), 47; Cafarelli, 99. See also John Shawcross, *John Milton: The Self and the World* (Lexington: University Press of Kentucky, 1993), chap. 3, for further psychological analysis of Milton's chaste—somewhat feminine, somewhat fussy?—deportment and its effect on *Comus.*

14. For Christopher Kendrick, in "Milton and Sexuality: A Symptomatic Reading of *Comus,*" in *Re-Membering Milton: Essays on the Texts and Traditions,* edited by Mary Nyquist and Margaret W. Ferguson (New York: Methuen, 1988), 43–73, Sabrina's "rescue suggests that the mother must not be written out of existence" (51). Tyler, 37, also finds it significant that Sabrina, a mother-figure, saves the Lady, since the matriarchal has been silenced historically.

15. Woolf's ship's name might allude to Milton's "L'Allegro," lines 11–12: "But come thou Goddess fair and free, / In Heav'n yclep't *Euphrosyne.*" Whereas "L'Allegro's" Euphrosyne signifies innocent mirth, the satyrs in *Comus* practice a darker mirth, sin.

16. Caramagno, 158ff.

17. Froula, "Out of the Chrysalis," 146.

18. As Rachel becomes more and more ill, her uncle paces back and forth outside, reciting lines from Milton's ode "On the Morning of Christ's Nativity":

> Peor and Baalim
> Forsake their Temples dim,
> With that twice batter'd God of Palestine
> And mooned Astharoth—
>
> (lines 197–200)

"The sound of these words"—thrummed out like a deadly march—is "strangely discomforting" to Terence, "but they had to be borne" (351). The words are fitting, for Milton's ode celebrates the birth of Christ and the death of the pagan gods. The poem celebrates a new dispensation, when justice will reign. Rachel, too, stands on the threshold of a world about to be born: not this time the still patriarchal world of Christian orthodoxy, but the matriarchal world of feminism.

19. Woolf, *Three Guineas* (1938; reprint, New York: Harcourt Brace Jovanovich [Harvest], 1966), 82.

6

Rewriting Family Ties

Woolf's Renaissance Romance

Diana E. Henderson

> We must then have a theory as to what this influence is.
> But let us always remember—influences are infinitely
> numerous; writers are infinitely sensitive; each writer has a
> different sensibility. That is why literature is always
> changing, like the weather, like clouds in the sky. . . . We
> can only hope therefore to single out the most obvious
> influences that have formed writers into groups. Yet there
> are groups. Books descend from books as families descend
> from families.
>
> —Virginia Woolf, "The Leaning Tower"

*T*he dirge from *Cymbeline* echoes in Virginia Woolf's modern London, encouraging both Clarissa Dalloway and Septimus Smith to "[f]ear no more the heat o' the sun"—nor the daylight structures of a British empire upon which the sun never sets. Woolf's reiteration of the allusion recalls more of *Cymbeline* than just the lyrics to its pastoral dirge. The dynamic transformation of *Cymbeline*'s romance tropes and structures serves as an allegory both for Woolf's transformation of Clarissa Dalloway into the narrative fulcrum of her innovative representation of female experience and for her own establishment of literary and personal authority as a woman writer. The earlier story "Mrs. Dalloway in Bond Street" primarily satirized the class insularity and superficiality of its protagonist as an embodiment of society ladies whom Woolf knew; the novel complicates that image by interspersing romance elements of a remembered, recovered past for Clarissa as well as adding a dying male double.[1]

As is true of the heroine Imogen in *Cymbeline*, Clarissa journeys through a symbolic death to rediscover at last her lost "siblings." In Shakespeare's play, "Fear no more" is chanted over Imogen's apparently dead but only drugged body by the men whom the audience knows to be her brothers. Although Imogen's ultimate reunion with those blood brothers displaces her as royal heir, she celebrates it. Restoration of the male line of inheritance removes the impediment to her marriage with the commoner Posthumus Leonatus; that marriage is always her primary concern. By contrast, the return of Clarissa's long "lost" sibling surrogates (her youthful loves Peter Walsh and Sally Seton) challenges the centrality of the conventional marriage plot that led Clarissa away from those friends to become Mrs. Richard Dalloway.[2] Despite *Cymbeline*'s self-conscious ironies about representation and its attentiveness to the paradoxes inherent in mystifying aristocratic blood, the play nevertheless melds several aspects of the romance genre compatible in the Renaissance: the love-and-marriage plot and the ancient motif of lost and recovered siblings, linked as familial concerns; the subordination of individuated characterization to formal or thematic patterns; and (to some extent subsuming these particulars) a vision of a providential cosmos in which certain social relations are privileged as natural as well as conventional.[3] *Mrs. Dalloway* draws on Shakespeare in order to combine similar elements (which Shakespeare after all had himself adapted from narrative fiction) but more clearly ironizes the relationships among them and the naturalness of each. Within Woolf's narrative, the formal perspective of Shakespearean romance serves as a means of muting the more oppressive aspects of both blood and marital ties for Clarissa. For Woolf, whose beloved older brother died in 1906, the romance tropes seem to distance her from the difficulties of writing about the death of an actual sibling (her connection with Clarissa, who has lost a sister before the action of the novel begins). At the same time, her creative adaptation of romance conventions allows her to assert her complex identity as a woman writer. This mixed claim of writerly inheritance and innovation remains interwoven with Woolf's sense of familial identity, differentiating her position from Clarissa's and, more important, from the post-Renaissance tradition of masculine authorial singularity.

Woolf's rewriting of the romance trope of sibling recovery as metaphorical befits an author who constructs her own family romance out of literary history. Despite her attention to and veneration for a female tradition "thinking back through our mothers," and despite a specific debt in this novel to *Jane Eyre,* she represents herself not as Austen's or the Brontës' daughter but as Shakespeare's younger sister.[4] In so doing, she replaces the vexatious nineteenth-century "parents" whose realist conventions of characterization and narrative she deplored; she turns instead to a recovered Renaissance amenable to her symbolic, poetic sensibility yet requiring her twentieth-century perspective to render female subjectivity in a more satisfactory fashion. As part of her construction of a congenial ancestry, Woolf also traces the genealogy of the sociopolitical structures she wishes to criticize most forcefully in *Mrs. Dalloway* back to the Enlightenment rather than to her more esteemed Renaissance. Patriarchal empire-building is allegorically personified by Sir William Bradshaw (whose gods of Proportion and Conversion spur Septimus to suicide) and, in an ironic gender twist, the emigration-obsessed, military-minded Lady Bruton (who, Peter Walsh observes approvingly, "derived from the eighteenth century").[5]

Woolf repeatedly structures her work to make the present moment the one of feminine completion, the omega to Shakespeare's alpha male: in *Orlando* and *A Room of One's Own,* as well as within the romance logic of *Mrs. Dalloway.* As part of *A Room of One's Own* she revises an untitled story about women's erasure from history originally set in the fifteenth century, publishing instead the fiction of Judith Shakespeare's doom;[6] the temporal shift more conveniently shapes history to present Woolf herself as the female fulfillment (not just any surrogate sister) of Shakespeare. Despite her slyly hesitant peroration to *A Room of One's Own* and her assertions elsewhere that the female Shakespeare had not yet arrived, her fictions often belie such tentativeness. They also show, however, that her literary self-positioning is a fully conscious construction, neither a natural nor an inevitable inheritance.

In Woolf's first recorded writerly response to Shakespeare, a letter composed at age nineteen to her admired older brother Thoby, the two levels of her concern with "sibling rivalries" converge in her reading of *Cymbeline:* her authorial claim to criticize and appreciate Shakespeare as a brother-craftsman intersects with her claim to an intuitive understanding despite her status as an outsider, denied her actual brother's access to formal education. Virginia Stephen tentatively interrogates both the interpretive ability and the masculine prerogative of her university-educated, analytical brother. She announces that she "read Cymbeline just to see if there mightnt be more in the great William than I supposed," and she does indeed find it, in the poetry, though she feels "a little oppressed by his—greatness I suppose. I shall want a lecture when I see you; to clear up some points about the Plays. I mean about the characters. . . . I find them beyond me—Is this my feminine weakness in the upper region? . . . Of course they talk divinely. I have spotted the best lines in the play—almost in any play I should think."[7] As Christine Froula observes, the letter as a whole

> acts out a covert sibling rivalry. . . . thrilling to Shakespeare's "best" lines, she paints herself his true inheritor. . . . the Shakespeare she makes her own is . . . associated with male cultural privilege, yet not inseparable from it—on the contrary, admitting of appropriation by the daughter-writer, even from her position outside the line of succession.[8]

Inverting Imogen's journey in *Cymbeline* from being her father's sole heir to the status of politically marginalized but contented sibling, Virginia Stephen first defers to her esteemed brother but gradually comes to assert her own perception. And in fact she was fated to outlive Thoby, ultimately becoming the Stephen family's primary bearer of the word. Thoby's premature death of course devastated Virginia, and his absent presence informs many of her works, from the obvious elegy of *Jacob's Room* to the fallen hero Percival in *The Waves.* But in *Mrs. Dalloway,* a turn to romance provides a more oblique mode of remembrance, one that allows Woolf to transmute some of the pain of personal loss into a poetic narrative of female survival.

Thus, on a biographical level as well as a characterological one, it seems particularly apt that *Cymbeline* should haunt the Woolf novel in which the shadow-double to the titular character is a doomed, Shakespeare-loving young man. As Woolf reveals explicitly in her preface to the 1928 edition, Septimus died that Clarissa might live: "in the first version Septimus, who later is intended to be her double, had no existence; . . . Mrs. Dalloway was originally to kill herself, or perhaps merely to die at the end of the party."[9] Septimus's narrative trajectory concludes with the surviving woman reciting words from the dirge that he recalled just before his death, words "originally" sung by Imogen's brothers over her seemingly dead body; the novel's scene of gendered inversion could hardly avoid evoking for its author the memory of Thoby, by then Woolf's own dead sibling. And indeed, Thoby's specter returns explicitly in a diary entry for 15 August 1924, as she approached her "last lap" in composing *Mrs. Dalloway*.

Woolf recalls him when contemplating the greater understanding of poetry she has acquired over the years: "When I was twenty, in spite of Thoby who used to be so pressing and exacting, I could not for the life of me read Shakespeare for pleasure; . . . [whereas] It is poetry that I want now—long poems."[10] Either she is forgetting that her youthful letter to Thoby hinged precisely upon her poetic appreciation, or she is revealing just how much her earlier perception had been crafted to please him. As a mature writer, she has come to see herself encompassing and longing for the poetic tradition that had once seemed, if not entirely masculine and alien, at least a source of anxiety for Virginia Stephen. Her authority has come in part through the act of fiction-making, using a surrogate "brother," Shakespeare, to help her craft a story in which the death of an actual sibling (Clarissa's sister) recedes into the background; familial bonds and losses are played out through less personal sorrows, such as Clarissa's feelings for Septimus, the young man she never meets. Without collapsing the obvious differences between Woolf and her female protagonist in *Mrs. Dalloway,* one may remark that both come to terms with loss and exclusion through an act of cultural collaboration that requires identification with and lamentation for a young man whose elective affinity is with Shakespeare. Under the sign of romance, death brings renewed life, and inheritance from the male brings female authority.

For all the sympathy and androgyny Woolf applauds in Shakespeare, he remains a father figure in his comic solutions.[11] In the final act of *Cymbeline,* he restores a male British monarchic line along with a happily motherless family (sons returned, wicked stepmother dead) and celebrates a marriage in which Imogen remains subordinate and faithful even after "dis-covered" of her emblematic disguise as the servant Fidele. The rediscovery of Cymbeline's two lost sons licenses Imogen's secret marriage to her commoner-love Posthumus as an exchange for sacrificing her entitlement to sovereignty—a power in which she never expressed interest.[12] Given the ideological import of the last act, it is not surprising that (despite her recognition of its beautiful lines, quoted in the letter to Thoby) Woolf turns instead to Shakespeare's pastoral interlude for her quoted refrain.

In act 3 of *Cymbeline*, Imogen dons the disguise of a pageboy after Posthumus's servant Pisanio reveals to her that his master, misled by Iachimo's claims to have lain with her, has commissioned her murder. Posthumus's ravings about "the woman's part" (2.5.20, 22)—and specifically, inheritance from the female—have thus forced Imogen to discard its trappings in favor of a boy's (an unsettling of gender within the fiction, always implicit in "her" theatrical representation by a boy actor but now made doubly significant). In the magical way of pastoral romance, s/he is driven by hunger to enter the very cave that houses her long-lost brothers. Without knowing their relationship, the siblings become deeply devoted. Seeming to have died from a drug Pisanio gave her, the pageboy Imogen/Fidele becomes the corpse over which her brothers chant the dirge whose first words return repeatedly in Woolf's novel:

Guiderius.   Fear no more the heat o' th' sun,
Nor the furious winter's rages.
Thou thy worldly task hast done,
Home art gone and ta'en thy wages.
Golden lads and girls all must,
As chimney-sweepers, come to dust.

Arviragus.   Fear no more the frown o' th' great,
Thou art past the tyrant's stroke.
Care no more to clothe and eat,
To thee the reed is as the oak.
The sceptre, learning, physic, must
All follow this and come to dust.

(*Cymbeline* 4.2.259–70)

Although attention appropriately has been paid to Imogen's gender blurring and to her resurrection following this scene, the dirge itself focuses not on the specificity of Imogen but on the universal leveling of death; since the brothers do not know their own, much less their addressee's, direct relation to the "sceptre" they mention, the piece makes sense for them primarily as a lyrical moment bringing peace. For the audience it also serves as such; yet while moving beyond narrative specificity, it can simultaneously appeal to our greater awareness of the play's multiple layering of identity and its issues of governance. Akin to Woolf's desire to supplant individuation with "views" and interconnectedness in her creation of characters, Shakespeare's song works by self-consciously stepping back from the plot even as it elaborates upon its themes, obliquely justifying the play's own disregard for mimetic plausibility through a meditation on last things.[13]

As if to reiterate the point as farce, directly after the dirge the boys bring on the headless corpse of the "truly" dead Cloten (wearing Posthumus's clothes), laying him beside Imogen. Setting the stage for her mistaken horror upon awaking next to "Posthumus," the moments after the dirge further emblematize not only the erasure of difference in death but also the arbitrariness of the physical signifiers of social status and of identity itself. This layering of fictions and truths ultimately recalls us to the level of performance, to the recognition that all death is a fiction onstage: in this regard, even the doltish Cloten and our heroine Imogen could be subject to confusion—another motivation for differentiating "his" body through its beheading. Yet as Imogen's mistaking of the headless corpse to be Posthumus makes obvious, to clarify one difference is to blur another.[14] What remains clear is that all "come to dust."

The terms of the dirge's meditation on last things, though not specifically linked to Imogen as a character, remain specific in another sense: in their emphasis on material disintegration. The words draw attention not to the traditional Christian consolation of an afterlife but rather to obliteration, the silver lining of which is the erasure of class and hierarchical social power. In this respect, the dirge might seem less elegiac than nihilistic.[15] But the dramatic ironies of this scene preclude the audience's resting with this lyric reading alone. Within the fiction, the brothers who recite the dirge are in truth those great ones whose frowns—the second stanza suggests—may soon induce fears; their putative father has already suffered from "the tyrant's stroke." What might seem a facile or self-destructive dismissal of social distinctions were the brothers to realize their own elite status here becomes a reminder of the sheer arbitrariness and whimsical shifting of British royal power, whether lost or gained. Furthermore, we are told that the song was "originally" sung to mourn the actual death of the boys' seeming mother, whereas now their singing laments (what they cannot know is) the seeming death of their actual sister. In other words, even within *Cymbeline* the dirge functions as an allusion demonstrating that verbal repetition is never simply that. What the boys intend as a simple gesture of homage (like "mother," like "brother") signifies the complexities of blood and inheritance, the performance context involving an inversion as well as a quotation. Until one comes to dust, the bonds of family and state remain powerful if elusive, even deceptive, constructs. Here they shape the significance of the lyrics, making them into an "interlude" rather than the last words of a last rite. Nor can the performers know and control all the meanings of "their" words.

The first time Clarissa Dalloway recites the dirge, she is thinking of those who suffered in the Great War (she sees the words in a book displayed in a shop window during her morning errands). The last time, she thinks specifically of Septimus Smith: the young war veteran who has died, his name unknown to her. The dirge in fact echoes in both their thoughts during their respective final scenes, creating a narrative connection between the society lady and her less privileged "double." Clarissa cannot doff her social position as she would her hat, and many critics have therefore read her attempts to sympathize with the young men whom war has destroyed as a failure, an object of satire.[16] Yet the context of the scene in *Cymbeline* recalls the complexities always attendant upon interpretation; at the very least, Clarissa has sensitively heard lines appropriate to her endeavor to cross class as well as gender boundaries. Moreover, the link with this romance underscores the generic choices Woolf makes in rethinking the novel form, choices that prevent the characters from having unqualified agency or control over their actions' import. In both Shakespearean romance and Woolf's novel, order comes—if it comes—through the mysterious threads stretched between figures, figures who (sometimes) gain momentary access to a symbolic system more potent than that of the individual.

Or so a reading of romance would have it. In both play and novel, however, the specifics of gender and social status do not disappear; indeed they constitute another reason why *Cymbeline* of all Shakespeare's romances is the one appropriate for Woolf's revision in *Mrs. Dalloway.* For Shakespeare remains true to the history play convention of naming the play after its sovereign, even as the narrative of this romance centers on a woman who has made her own marital choice. To the extent that the play should thus be known as *Cymbeline,* it is because it locates the love-and-marriage and sibling recovery plots within a larger struggle between political states whose hierarchies also come under scrutiny. Kneejerk identification with a British nation fighting Roman domination is subverted by association with its most animated spokespeople, the wicked queen and her imbecilic son Cloten; Cymbeline's bad judgment in relying on corrupt courtiers and his second wife undermines his sovereign authority and has caused his family's disintegration.

The extremity of corruption that transpires under the auspices of nationalism, patriarchy, and aristocratic privilege is precisely what requires *Cymbeline's* turn to the conjurations of romance in order to find a social and familial solution. Among the many "miraculous" discoveries and reversals of the final act, perhaps the most unexpected is Cymbeline's decision to undo the consequences of his military victory over Rome, agreeing to free his prisoners and pay the tribute that had occasioned violence. The romance *topos* of forgiveness after suffering displaces—without logically resolving—the complex power struggles over sovereignty.

Like *Cymbeline,* Woolf's novel hovers between the logics of romance and historically specific satire.[17] It tries to expose the particular social structures that limit the lives of women and nonelite men, associating oppression with the workings of empire and patriarchy. At the same time, excursions into a myth-inflected landscape (in Peter Walsh's dream of the solitary traveler, or the ancient woman singing her song of love by the Tube station) qualify that focus on the particular ills of 1923 Britain. It is in the treatment of social inequities explicitly linked with the material of Shakespearean romance—woman's place in marriage, erotic possessiveness, and the analogy between state and domestic tyranny—that the two generic impulses effectively combine in a specific yet generalizable critique of Britain's dominant ideology.

Woolf shifts tone and vantage to comment on those who do or would tyrannize; this strategy becomes especially notable when the narrative perspective dissociates from that of any particular character or group of characters.

Thus we learn of Lady Bradshaw's slowly "going under" (like an etherized patient), her sense of identity obliterated by her doctor-husband's "reasonable" dominance. Explicitly linking this domestic tyranny with the Enlightenment thinking that undergirds British colonialism, Woolf's description of Lady Bradshaw's submission serves as a foil to the stories of both Septimus and Clarissa: submitting to Bradshaw whereas Septimus refuses, Lady Bradshaw loses the potential for a life or a narrative presence independent of her husband. She is reduced to a cautionary tale, a reminder of the ideology that threatens to reduce all wives to appendages—a subordination that Peter and Sally fear has also transformed Clarissa into a mindless society hostess. They are indeed correct in surmising that she has replaced her youthful radical politics with kneejerk support for her husband's political views; now consciously indifferent to world affairs, she has diverted her intense love of "life" into diversion itself, hosting parties.

But Clarissa has only partially succumbed, and the Bradshaw model helps explain why: Clarissa's marital choice of mild, independence-allowing Richard Dalloway. Lacking the force of personality that leads others in that culture to preach and convert, Dalloway allows Clarissa that which he cannot understand, allows her to retain her tenacious hold on her own notions of "life." Septimus leaps to his death rather than allow the doctors control over his body; Richard encourages Clarissa's recovery from influenza and heart damage by allowing her the private bedroom she prefers. Her movement beyond symbolic death, and Septimus's resurrection in her thoughts, are possible in part because of her class privilege, in part because Richard does not fully inhabit the dominant position of husband that the social order approves (a choice that in turn may have limited his political career, as Lady Bruton laments). The satirical representation of the Bradshaws, then, contrasts with the romantic compromise that allows Clarissa to survive.

The remembered death of Clarissa's own blood sibling, Sylvia Parry, also epitomizes the use of romance mingled with satire in a way analogous to *Cymbeline*'s. That is, romance serves to temper (or dilute, depending on one's investment in a political critique) the gendered commentary on the corruption of the given order, the thoughtless inheritance of the English powers-that-be. Sylvia's death is recalled only obliquely, through the memory of Peter Walsh— who thereby accounts for Clarissa's fatalistic view of the cosmos (117–18).[18]

Thoroughly transmuted into a gendered allegory with the temporal remoteness and symbolic consequence characteristic of romance, the death of Clarissa's sister provides a distanced though parallel case to Septimus's suicide. Both are victims of violent daylight forces, those phallic pillars of society associated with an insensitive patriarchy. Whereas Septimus reluctantly leaps to his death (impaled on iron fence spikes) to avoid capture by the doctors, Sylvia is struck down by a falling tree, the responsibility for which accident Peter Walsh attributes entirely to the carelessness of Clarissa's father, old Justin Parry: the family patriarch.

The traumatizing loss of this venerated older sister (Woolf's stepsister Stella Duckworth, as well as Thoby, comes to mind here) is supplanted in Clarissa's memories of adolescence by her passionate love for a surrogate sister, Sally Seton, and by her vexed but formative relationship with Peter. Surrogate siblings, in Clarissa's case, allowed her to begin to integrate sexuality with friendship, albeit imperfectly and temporarily. Moreover, they encouraged her to make radical new intellectual and political affiliations, breaking from blood and class allegiances. And the desire for distance from blood ties persists. Even when as an adult she is brought back to political conservatism by her husband, Clarissa still wishes she could have resisted inviting her more distant relative, Ellie Henderson, to her party; it is Peter Walsh rather than Clarissa who attends to her aging Aunt Parry. Clarissa's desire for distance resists both the fatalism of birth and the inevitability of death. It is an act at least akin to Woolf's own veiling in her representations of lost siblings—through class difference, in Septimus's case; through mediated narrative, in Sylvia's case; through the mode of romance, in which relations and social positions become symbolically laden and formalized.

The use of Shakespeare's Renaissance romance even provides Woolf with a model for miraculous restorations at the close; Clarissa's party not only brings figures from her Bourton youth to mingle with many of the novel's London characters but also allows her "discovery" of a dead spiritual brother, Septimus—and, crucially, the return of those two dearest living friends.[19] With Peter and Sally, she finally acknowledges, "(more even than with Richard) she shared her past. . . . A part of this Sally must always be; Peter must always be" (182). Putting her husband in parentheses as the past flows into a willed perpetual present, the reunion of this triad from Clarissa's young adulthood constitutes the novel's final event, altering the hierarchical balance between sibling and marital love that resolved Shakespeare's play so differently.

As the cases of the Bradshaws and Sylvia Parry demonstrate, the deployment of romance motifs does not erase anger at the forces that oppress and destroy. Indeed, in her final thoughts Clarissa also decides that hatred is more useful than love at her stage of life. Nevertheless, her hatred of "tyranny" is not easily interpreted as a feminist recognition that women must turn from self-loathing to social action; nor, arguably, is Woolf's. In this respect, *Mrs. Dalloway* not only represents but also participates in a more conservative social order than do several of Woolf's subsequent writings. Despite her explicit desire to avoid anger, the narrator of *A Room of One's Own* curses an Oxbridge beadle and savagely cartoons a misogynous professor. By contrast, Clarissa's most intense hatred is directed at Miss Kilman, who has suffered from both anti-German "patriotism" and the limitations of a rigid class and gender hierarchy. While it is arguable whether Woolf sees the dynamic of blaming the victim at work in her unappealing portrait of Miss Kilman, Clarissa certainly does not recognize her hatred as symptomatic but rather considers it personality-driven, viewing Kilman both as an unpleasant rival for her daughter's affection and as a would-be tyrant like Bradshaw.

Nor does Woolf's representation of Kilman encourage us to read Clarissa's response simply as an object of satire or delusion.[20] As in the case of her linkage with Septimus, Mrs. Dalloway's class differences and limitations remain obvious, yet the narrative's presentation of Kilman at least partially endorses Clarissa's perception. To claim Woolf's representation of Kilman as part of a progressive politics, one must emphasize the author's recognition of the systemic consequences of gender inequities and her refusal to essentialize behavior by fitting all members of a class or gender into a politically congenial grid; the alternative is to acknowledge that both Clarissa and Woolf make judgments founded on what they would consider aesthetic and personal grounds that cannot wholly be discounted as epiphenomena of oppressive social structures. *Mrs. Dalloway,* as much as *Cymbeline,* collaborates with its culture's categorizations: not those categories that subordinate groups of people because of gender or birth (though class remains a thorny issue), but rather those categories that value personal identity and behavior as involving something more important than social construction. Despite the criticism of certain social inequities in each work, beauty and kindness, of appearance and of behavior, remain virtues presented in some measure as if transcendent of the possessor's social position.

And in this regard, it is telling that the dirge from *Cymbeline* is not the only line of Shakespeare's to echo through the pages of Woolf's novel. The other repeated quotation concerns a moment of unconventional transcendent love, also extending the novel's concern with possessive desire and its social as well as emotional consequences. The line is from *Othello*, a play related to *Cymbeline* most directly by its similar emphasis on a husband's deluded sexual jealousy, provoked by an artful Italian villain. "If it were now to die, / 'Twere now to be most happy," says Othello as he is reunited in Cyprus with his new bride. Though many scholars interpret this statement as a death wish, the situation is more complex, and indeed the words are spoken at a nearly miraculous moment of celebration that life can afford such "perfect happiness." So Woolf herself cited the line in her diary about the time she was completing *Mrs. Dalloway,* to describe the joyous moments in her own unconventional marriage to Leonard:

> But L. and I were too too happy, as they say; if it were now to die etc. Nobody shall say of me that I have not known perfect happiness, but few could put their finger on the moment, or say what made it. Even I myself, stirring occasionally in the pool of content, could only say But this is all I want; could not think of anything better; and had only my half superstitious feeling at the Gods who must when they have created happiness, grudge it. Not if you get it in unexpected ways, though.[21]

On the one hand, Woolf's words share a kinship with the cosmic skepticism Peter Walsh attributes to Clarissa, imagining the sorts of grudging classical gods whom Shakespeare transmutes into (ultimately) providential figures in his romances—as, for example, the gruff Jupiter who chastises the Leonati in *Cymbeline*'s masque/dream vision, allowing unexpected happiness to Posthumus and Imogen but only after great suffering. But in contrast to Woolf's location of Othello-like moments of great joy within her marriage, her fiction uses the Shakespearean citation to describe an even less socially acceptable form of romance. It is Clarissa's passionate love for Sally Seton, potentially as challenging to typical representations of romance in the novel as was the interracial marriage of Othello and Desdemona to Elizabethan dramatic conventions: "she could remember going cold with excitement. . . . feeling as she crossed the hall 'if it were now to die 'twere now to be most happy.' That was her feeling—Othello's feeling, and she felt it, she was convinced, as strongly as Shakespeare meant Othello to feel it, all because she was coming down to dinner in a white frock to meet Sally Seton!" (34–35).

Along with the poetic imagery of "an illumination, a match burning in a crocus" (32), the line makes more explicit those same-sex desires that Mrs. Dalloway herself acknowledges but shies away from. It gives the relationship with Sally an intensity as charged as was Peter Walsh's passionate, possessive, and thwarted love for Clarissa at the same time in their lives.[22] Thus the youthful friends become overdetermined figures of both "true love" and sibling-like affinity, mediating between the marital romance plot and the familial. Both relationships remain distinct from the milder, appreciative affection between the Dalloways—the marriage Clarissa chose in order to sustain her independence, her "virginal" sense of self, but also the relationship through which she is further interpellated into the privileged, sterile society of Westminster.[23]

Mrs. Dalloway does see the compromise she has made in having distanced herself from Sally and Peter. She remembers the "purity, the integrity, of her feeling for Sally. It was not like one's feeling for a man." But she in part rationalizes its sacrifice by locating it within a particular, irrecoverable stage of life: "it had a quality which could only exist between women, between women just grown up. It . . . sprang from a sense of being in league together, a presentiment of something that was bound to part them (they spoke of marriage always as a catastrophe)" (34). For their female friendship, Clarissa's marriage to Dalloway is indeed a catastrophe, not dramatic yet as heartbreaking in its way as that same event had been for Peter Walsh. It is the cost of the normative female developmental plot.[24] But the passion of the youth, the love Clarissa tries to embalm in the past, is not so easily entombed—not for Clarissa, and certainly not for Peter Walsh.

Even Peter, whom she never loved so passionately as she loved Sally, arouses feelings that challenge Clarissa's decision to become Mrs. Dalloway, allowing her past to haunt and ultimately revivify her present. At midday when he barges into her quiet hour of mending, she imagines that their marriage would have been the stuff of a five-act drama. In part because such drama had been written already (by Shakespeare), it need not be lived to be understood: "Take me with you, Clarissa thought impulsively, as if he were starting directly upon some great voyage; and then, next moment, it was as if the five acts of a play that had been very exciting and moving were now over and she had lived a lifetime in them and had run away, had lived with Peter, and it was now over" (47). What Clarissa need not live is the romance material that Woolf wants to reconceive, to revive in a way that does not subdue female subjectivity.[25] The solution would not be to return to the old bourgeois one-and-only-love and marriage plot, as both Clarissa and Peter realize at later moments in the novel; but the problem of how to reintegrate intensity of emotion and a social practice remains, not to be solved simply through the intentional actions of these represented characters.

For them to find resolution would be for Woolf to erase the social critique of the Dalloway world too absolutely, to empty the novel of its satiric power. It would remove the blinders and restrictions created by class and gender ideologies, which limit even the more thoughtful characters. And it would also blunt Woolf's interwoven insight about nationalist ideologies: Britain's imperial projects carry an ideological force shaping even those who rationally would resist their logic, and from which there is no escape through particular personal relationships. The contradictory attitudes of reforming, domineering Peter Walsh toward his participation in the colonization of India most richly represent this latter mental bind. Clarissa's collaboration with social conventions (choosing heterosexual marriage to the most unexceptionable man while recognizing and enshrining other loves) conveys the matching domestic dilemma.

Nevertheless, though they do not find answers, the characters are allowed to recognize their dilemmas and are ultimately given moments of romancelike, even mystical, connection. Clarissa is shown struggling with the taint of her choices when she repeats Othello's line again, as she thinks about Septimus Smith's death, during her party:

> They went on living (she would have to go back; the rooms were still crowded; people kept on coming). They (all day she had been thinking of Bourton, of Peter, of Sally), they would grow old. A

thing there was that mattered; a thing, wreathed about with chatter, defaced, obscured in her own life, let drop every day in corruption, lies, chatter. This he had preserved. Death was defiance. Death was an attempt to communicate; people feeling the impossibility of reaching the centre which, mystically, evaded them; closeness drew apart; rapture faded, one was alone. There was an embrace in death.

But this young man who had killed himself—had he plunged holding his treasure? "If it were now to die, 'twere now to be most happy," she had said to herself once, coming down in white. (184)

Read satirically, her "use" of Septimus Smith to sustain her own spirit replicates the nation's recent use of many such naively patriotic young clerks in the war—destroying them to sustain an idealized image of English duty and nationhood.[26] But read under the aegis of romance, it also signals a reawakening of sorts for Clarissa, if only to the recognition of her moral bankruptcy in sustaining a status quo that squelches passion and compromises integrity. Thus meditation leads Mrs. Dalloway both back to Sally and forward to overt criticism of Sir William Bradshaw. Earlier she had reluctantly left Sally and Peter because she felt she "must" go to the Bradshaws, "whom she disliked" (182), thus subordinating her own affections and bonds again to sustain the most superficial of definitions of "polite" society. Now she correctly imagines and identifies with the response of Bradshaw's victim: "forcing your soul, that was it—if this young man had gone to him, and Sir William had impressed him, like that, with his power, might he not then have said (indeed she felt it now), Life is made intolerable; they make life intolerable, men like that?" (184-85). Finally, this associative process leads her back to *Cymbeline*. Through authorial "magic," she repeats the line that Septimus was thinking in his last moments before leaping to his death:

> The young man had killed himself; but she did not pity him; with the clock striking the hour, one, two, three, she did not pity him, with all this going on. There! the old lady had put out her light! the whole house was dark now with this going on, she repeated, and the words came to her, Fear no more the heat of the sun. She must go back to them. But what an extraordinary night! She felt some-

how very like him—the young man who had killed himself. She felt glad that he had done it; thrown it away. The clock was striking. The leaden circles dissolved in the air. He made her feel the beauty; made her feel the fun. But she must go back. She must assemble. She must find Sally and Peter. And she came in from the little room. (186)

With this passage, the last in the book from Clarissa's perspective, she also enters the room to find Sally and Peter. Thus (even as she can be regarded as trivializing his death and her recognition by speaking of "fun") she carries a version of Septimus and the past into the present, into the fictional moment at which the book will end when represented from Peter's perspective. And as Woolf again cites the dirge, she now deploys its elegiac ironies—sung for a seemingly dead man, it leads to the resurrection of that figure as female survivor—to signal its allegorical power. Already Woolf has presented one return from the dead during the party, having had Peter Walsh believe Clarissa's Aunt Parry to have died and then presenting her otherwise: "For Miss Helena Parry was not dead: Miss Parry was alive. She was past eighty" (178). Embracing but also subsuming Clarissa in a romance pattern of rebirth after suffering, these motifs undo linear temporality in a book whose working title was "The Hours"; they signal the allegorical complexity of any narrative conclusion for Clarissa or the social milieu she animates.[27] The charged citations from Shakespeare again reinforce the double-edged perspective Woolf brings to the representation of Clarissa Dalloway as female survivor and social collaborator.

What one chooses to adapt from Shakespeare's text is ultimately that which serves the interpreter. Woolf says as much, using Septimus's response to *Antony and Cleopatra* as her example. Before the war when Septimus first came to London, the experience "made him anxious to improve himself, made him fall in love with Miss Isabel Pole, lecturing in the Waterloo Road upon Shakespeare"; it had been she who "reflected how she might give him a taste of *Antony and Cleopatra* and the rest; lent him books; wrote him scraps of letters; and lit in him such a fire as burns only once in a lifetime, without heat, flickering a red gold flame infinitely ethereal and insubstantial over Miss Pole; *Antony and Cleopatra*; and the Waterloo Road" (85). But the same cluster of associations also leads Septimus to war and his destruction, as he "went to France to save an England which consisted almost entirely of Shakespeare's plays and Miss Isabel Pole in a green dress [matching the color of Clarissa's party dress] walking in a square" (86). The education that began as a romanticized way out of the anonymity and uniformity of being born into a certain class and being absorbed into the city's masses of clerks (Woolf's narration presents Septimus as one of the "many millions of young men called Smith" whom "London has swallowed up" [84]) becomes another means of interpellation into the machinery of empire. For Woolf too, resistant to educational institutions yet eager to be respected as part of a great British literary tradition, the comparable risks inherent in her own "collaboration" with Shakespeare would not have been invisible.

After the war, Septimus "opened Shakespeare once more. That boy's business of the intoxication of language—*Antony and Cleopatra*—had shrivelled utterly. How Shakespeare loathed humanity—the putting on of clothes, the getting of children"; even "[l]ove between man and woman was repulsive to Shakespeare. The business of copulation was filth to him before the end" (88–89). Obviously Septimus "discovers" in Shakespeare exactly what his own situation brings to the reading. The aftershock of the Great War overshadows the pleasurable warmth of nature's sun; indeed, the sun itself has been refigured by that symbolic system, proclaimed never to set upon the British Empire. Septimus's interpretation of Shakespeare is correspondingly transformed. Moreover, he feels disgust at the idea of others reading without sharing his sensibility: one of his most painful thoughts, for him exemplary of human cruelty and horror, is the image of his constraining doctor "Holmes reading Shakespeare" (140). On the verge of parodying her own novelistic obsession with Shakespearean romance, Woolf presents the attempt to commune with or claim a particular authority from the Bard as a sign of possessive madness.[28]

Septimus's illness is characterized by his writings of "how the dead sing behind rhododendron bushes; odes to Time; conversations with Shakespeare" along with "messages from the dead" (147–48). In one regard, it seems as if Septimus is trapped in late Shakespeare—or Woolf's version thereof. His sense of affinity contributes to his dysfunctionality, even as *Cymbeline*'s words echo consolation in his final hours:

> Fear no more, says the heart in the body; fear no more.
>
> He was not afraid. At every moment Nature signified by some laughing hint like that gold spot which went round the wall—there, there, there—her determination to show, by brandishing her plumes, shaking her tresses, flinging her mantle this way and that, beautifully, always beautifully, and standing close up to breathe through her hollowed hands Shakespeare's words, her meaning. (139–40)

Within this desperate search for authorial meaning in the world, the figure of the Bard becomes, for shell-shocked Septimus as for his female creator, both an alternative source of British authority and a fluid construct destined to reflect his interpreter's needs, perhaps illusory but ultimately keeping the imperial patriarchs at bay.

To seek the "meaning," the clarity of an answer, in Woolf's echoing of Shakespeare may be, if not a madness as extreme as Septimus's, at least as delusive as is his proclamation of "the" meaning of *Antony and Cleopatra*. In each case, changes wrought upon the interpreter by time and history become enmeshed with the "original" words. What does become more apparent after attending to this intertextual play is a fuller sense of Woolf's narrative logic in revivifying the past and reformulating the present at Clarissa's party. Perhaps softening though certainly not erasing the novel's satiric stabs at the British imperial project, the borrowings from *Cymbeline* suggest as well the redemptive possibilities in reconceiving female experience outside the traditional plots premised on aristocratic blood ties or the bourgeois equation of love and marriage. They imply the importance of recovering that which conventionally must be displaced or discarded in a search for "maturity" and social stability. Shakespeare's play provides Woolf with a model worth revising to account for gendered experience differently, subordinating Shakespeare's interest in sexual jealousy while exploiting the analogical systems of thought that encourage us to see parallelism between domestic and imperial domination. Rewriting romance in *Mrs. Dalloway* becomes Woolf's means of collaboration with, rather than simple rejection or inversion of, the Shakespearean literary tradition; it is her means of revivifying the Renaissance as herself.

Notes

The scholarship on Woolf has become too compendious for anyone to acknowledge all that is of value or influence; I have cited essays primarily to clarify where my reading diverges from or complements related essays. Among the most important discussions of the connections between *Cymbeline* and *Mrs. Dalloway*, see Reuben Brower, "Something Central Which Permeated: 'Mrs. Dalloway,'" in *Virginia Woolf*, edited by Harold Bloom (New York: Chelsea House, 1986), 7–8, 13–14; Alice Fox, *Virginia Woolf and the Literature of the English Renaissance* (Oxford: Clarendon Press, 1990), 117–18; Jean M. Wyatt, "*Mrs. Dalloway*: Literary Allusion as Structural Metaphor," *PMLA* 88 (1973): 440, 442; David Dowling, *Mrs. Dalloway: Mapping Streams of Consciousness* (Boston: Twayne, 1991), 62–63, 92; and Mark Hussey, *The Singing of the Real World* (Columbus: Ohio State University Press, 1986). Fox, *Virginia Woolf*, also notes allusions to *Cymbeline* in *Jacob's Room* and *Between the Acts* (117, 154). On Woolf's link with the romances, see generally Avrom Fleishman, *Virginia Woolf: A Critical Reading* (Baltimore: Johns Hopkins University Press, 1975); Maria DiBattista, *Virginia Woolf's Major Novels: The Fables of Anon* (New Haven, Conn.: Yale University Press, 1980); and Brower. More generally, Alex Zwerdling, *Virginia Woolf and the Real World* (Berkeley: University of California Press, 1986), observes that the model for Woolf's interest in verbal economy "was not a novelist at all but Shakespeare" (19).

1. Woolf was thinking of Kitty Maxie and Lady Ottoline Morrell most specifically: "I want to bring in the despicableness of people like Ott [Morrell]. I want to give the slipperiness of the soul. I have been too tolerant often. The truth is people scarcely care for each other. They have this insane instinct for life. But they never become attached to anything outside themselves." *The Diary of Virginia Woolf*, edited by Anne Olivier Bell and Andrew McNeillie, 5 vols. (New York: Harcourt Brace Jovanovich, 1977–84), 2:244 (4 June 1923). This early attitude matches the representation of the Dalloways in Woolf's first novel, *The Voyage Out*; but as *Mrs. Dalloway* developed, Woolf's "tolerance" again emerged to temper their representation (for example, the type of sexual advances Richard made there are transferred to the character of Hugh Whitbread in *Mrs. Dalloway*; see Beverly Ann Schlack, *Continuing Presences: Virginia Woolf's Use of Literary Allusion* [University Park: Pennsylvania State University Press, 1979], 6–7). She instead worried about making Clarissa too "glittery" and sterile a figure; hence the additions. On the re-creation of Mrs. Dalloway, see also Fleishman, *Virginia Woolf*, 78; and Lucio Ruotolo, "*Mrs. Dalloway*: The Unguarded Moment," in *Virginia Woolf: Revaluation and Continuity*, edited by Ralph Freedman (Berkeley: University of California Press, 1980), 141–45. (Richard Dalloway's behavior in *The Voyage Out* is taken up at greater length in Lisa Low's "'Listen and save': Woolf's Allusion to *Comus* in Her Revolutionary First Novel," chap. 4 of this volume. —*Ed.*)

2. On the limitations of the marriage plot as the central developmental narrative for females in fiction, see especially Elizabeth Abel, "Narrative Structure(s) and Female Development: The Case of *Mrs. Dalloway,*" in *Virginia Woolf,* edited by Harold Bloom (New York: Chelsea House, 1986); and Carolyn G. Heilbrun, *Writing a Woman's Life* (New York: Norton, 1988).

3. Shakespeare's narrative sources included the tale *Frederycke of Jennen* as well as the *Decameron,* but he was also influenced more generally by the neochivalric romances and hybrids so popular in his day; for more on these relationships, see my forthcoming essay coauthored with James Siemon, "Shakespeare's Reading: Reading Vernacular Literature," in *A Companion to Shakespeare,* edited by David Scott Kastan (Oxford: Blackwell).

The bibliography on Renaissance conventions of romance and Shakespeare's late plays is as compendiously daunting as that on Woolf, and again I can list here only some of the works most useful to me. Regarding *Cymbeline* and the question of genre, see E. C. Pettet, *Shakespeare and the Romance Tradition* (London: Staples Press, 1949): 56, 161–85; Hallett Smith, *Shakespeare's Romances* (San Marino, Calif.: Huntington Library, 1972), 7–19, 162–89; Nosworthy's introduction to William Shakespeare, *Cymbeline,* edited by J. M. Nosworthy (1955; reprint, New York: Routledge [Arden], 1996); Barbara Mowat, *The Dramaturgy of Shakespeare's Romances* (Athens: University of Georgia Press, 1976); Diana T. Childress, "Are Shakespeare's Late Plays Really Romances?" in *Shakespeare's Late Plays: Essays in Honor of Charles Crow,* edited by Richard C. Tobias and Paul G. Zolbrod (Athens: Ohio University Press, 1974), 48–52; the introduction to George M. Logan and Gordon Teskey's coedited collection, *Unfolded Tales: Essays on Renaissance Romance* (Ithaca, N.Y.: Cornell University Press, 1989). On the family (in) romance, see the essays by Richard P. Wheeler, C. L. Barber, Meredith Skura, and Coppélia Kahn in *Representing Shakespeare: New Psychoanalytic Essays,* edited by Murray M. Schwartz and Coppélia Kahn (Baltimore: Johns Hopkins University Press, 1980); Carol Thomas Neely, *Broken Nuptials in Shakespeare's Plays* (New Haven, Conn.: Yale University Press, 1985); 166–209; and Janet Adelman, *Suffocating Mothers: Fantasies of Maternal Origins in Shakespeare's Plays, "Hamlet" to "The Tempest"* (New York: Routledge, 1992): 193–238. On Jacobean topical references and historicity, see David Moore Bergeron, *Shakespeare's Romances and the Royal Family* (Lawrence: University Press of Kansas, 1985); Leah S. Marcus, *Puzzling Shakespeare: Local Reading and Its Discontents* (Berkeley: University of California Press, 1988), 106–59; Patricia Parker, "Romance and Empire: Anachronistic *Cymbeline,*" in Logan and Tesky, *Unfolded Tales,* 189–207; Jodi Mikalachki, "The Masculine Romance of Roman Britain: *Cymbeline* and Early Modern English Nationalism," *Shakespeare Quarterly* 46 (1995): 301–22; and Jean Howard, introduction to *Cymbeline,* in *The Norton Shakespeare,* edited by Stephen Greenblatt, Walter Cohen, Jean E. Howard, and Katharine Eisaman Maus (New York: Norton, 1997): 2955–64. Subsequent citations from *Cymbel-*

ine refer to this Norton edition, although I retain the First Folio spellings of the characters' names. Parenthetical references in the text and the notes are to act, scene, and line.

4. *Jane Eyre* in fact provided Woolf with an intermediary text, in which (precisely as in *Cymbeline*) the exhausted heroine collapses, alone and starving, at the threshold of unknown relatives, a crucial step leading to her recovery of social position and a marriage for love along with new/old family ties. I discuss this doubled inheritance in a longer essay in progress.

Beth C. Schwartz, in "Thinking Back through Our Mothers: Woolf Reads Shakespeare," *ELH* 58 (1991): 721–46, argues that Woolf sees Shakespeare himself as a "Mother" rather than a paternal figure; but, as my comments about her gendered revisions of his conclusions (among other evidence) make clear, Woolf does not so absolutely erase the complexity of her predecessor's masculinity. The fraternal substitution more aptly captures Woolf's ability to negotiate between two stances toward Shakespeare, claiming a less oppressive kinship while acknowledging the masculine gaps that in part license her addition of another authorial perspective.

5. Virginia Woolf, *Mrs. Dalloway* (1925; reprint, with a foreword by Maureen Howard, New York: Harcourt Brace [Harvest], 1990), 173. Subsequent parenthetical references in the text are to this edition.

6. See Louise A. DeSalvo, "Shakespeare's 'Other' Sister," in *New Feminist Essays on Virginia Woolf,* edited by Jane Marcus (Lincoln: University of Nebraska Press, 1981, 61–81); DeSalvo unearthed and analyzes this unpublished story.

7. Woolf, quoted in Christine Froula, "Virginia Woolf as Shakespeare's Sister: Chapters in a Woman Writer's Autobiography," in *Women's Re-Visions of Shakespeare,* edited by Marianne Novy (Urbana: University of Illinois Press, 1990), 124. The lines include Posthumus's famed simile, "Hang there like fruit, my soul, / Till the tree die" (5.6.263–64).

8. Froula, "Virginia Woolf as Shakespeare's Sister," 125.

9. Woolf, introduction to *Mrs. Dalloway* (New York: Modern Library, 1928), vi.

10. Woolf, *Diary,* 2:310 (15 August 1924).

11. In *A Room of One's Own* (1929; reprint, with a foreword by Mary Gordon, New York: Harcourt Brace Jovanovich [Harvest], 1989), 82, Woolf remarks on the dearth of female friendships in Shakespeare; it is particularly apt that the novel's conclusion brings back Clarissa's female friend and beloved, Sally Seton, even though the encounter between them is presented briefly and in a mediated fashion. This is not to say that Woolf's characterization is in fact true of late Shakespeare, merely that she so perceived the work and thus the need for a corrective in which "Chloe loves Olivia." It may nevertheless be worth noting with Carol Neely in *Broken Nuptials,* 182, that "unlike other chaste heroines [in late Shakespeare] . . . Imogen has no female friend and double"—perhaps another reason her story appealed as one in particular need of revision.

12. See especially Imogen's comments at 1.7.1–9; 3.4.130–36; 3.7.48–51; and 5.5.374–79. On the absence of mothers in the romances, see Adelman; Neely, *Broken Nuptials*, 171ff.; and more generally in Shakespeare, see Lynda E. Boose's influential early essay, "The Father and the Bride in Shakespeare," *PMLA* 97 (1982), esp. 325–27. Boose further observes that in the romances, "the shattered human world, through obsessive reenactments of broken rituals, strives to recapture what has been lost and thus to reconnect itself with the sacred world of its origins" (338). Woolf revises the gendered and familial dimensions of this attempt to recapture what has been lost.

13. Woolf's essays "Modern Fiction" and "Mr. Bennett and Mrs. Brown" famously discuss her desire to reconceive characterization, as do many of her diary comments. See, e.g., *Diary*, 2:265 (5 September 1923): "Characters are to be merely views: personality must be avoided at all costs." Frank D. McConnell, in "'Death among the Apple Trees': *The Waves* and the World of Things," in *Virginia Woolf*, edited by Harold Bloom (New York: Chelsea House, 1986), notes the "sublime and self-sufficient *un*-humanity which finds articulation in the dirge from *Cymbeline*" as "an important 'hidden theme' for both *Mrs. Dalloway* and *The Waves*" (63).

14. A fuller reading of this remarkable scene would confront its abrupt tonal shifts and obsessive attention to bodies as dubious signs; here I can only suggest its interpretive complexities. See the works listed in note 3 above.

15. Harold Bloom, in *Virginia Woolf* (New York: Chelsea House, 1986), levels this accusation of nihilism at *Mrs. Dalloway* as well, before qualifying the comment in his acknowledgment of Woolf's writerly craft as a positive value of sorts (2). The mood certainly accords with that of both Mrs. Dalloway and Mrs. Ramsay in some of their key moments of solitude.

16. See Deborah Guth, "'What a Lark! What a Plunge!': Fiction as Self-Evasion in *Mrs. Dalloway*," *Modern Language Review* 84 (1989): 21ff., for an even stronger criticism of Woolf as colluding with Clarissa's bad faith; though I will comment below on certain forms of societal collaboration shared by character and author, such a judgmental reading seems to me to discount the dilemmas each confronts. Wyatt, "*Mrs. Dalloway*," 443; and Gillian Beer, in "The Body of the People: *Mrs. Dalloway* and *The Waves*" (1987), in *Virginia Woolf: The Common Ground* (Ann Arbor: University of Michigan Press, 1996), 48–73, 54–55, provide more nuanced interpretations.

17. My reading obviously counters the premise of Fleishman, in *A Critical Reading*, that *Mrs. Dalloway* lacks "the mixture of genres which was to enrich her later fiction" (69). Here I also diverge from Brower, who emphasizes connection with *The Winter's Tale*.

18. Dowling sees a potential link between Sylvia's death and the prophecy in *Cymbeline* involving a cedar's revival; he asks whether Septimus might be "the diseased branch, lopped off for the sake of Britain's health?" (63). If so, the point must be deeply ironic, since Septimus has become "diseased" precisely by serving Britain in

battle; the implicit antinationalism of this critique goes well beyond anything in Shakespeare, as if to satirize Cymbeline's presentation of the princes as natural warriors as well.

19. These two arrive unexpectedly during Clarissa's day—Sally's appearance at the party without a formal invitation in particular adding to the magical quality of the scene. Edward Mendelson, in "The Death of Mrs. Dalloway: Two Readings," in *Textual Analysis: Some Readers Reading,* edited by Mary Anne Caws (New York: Modern Language Association Publications, 1986), 273–79, remarks on the book's break with realistic chronology in its final pages, as well as the unplanned arrival of Peter and Sally (perhaps exaggerating the problems of reading these in terms of novelistic conventions); a reading that acknowledges the generic influence of Renaissance romance accounts for both dimensions of the conclusion.

20. Emily Jensen's romanticized reading of homosexual love, in "Clarissa Dalloway's Respectable Suicide," in *Virginia Woolf: A Feminist Slant,* edited by Jane Marcus (Lincoln: University of Nebraska Press, 1983), leads her to venerate Miss Kilman's "power . . . to love women" (175), but this hardly captures the tone of Woolf's representation: greedily wolfing down eclairs in a way that leads Elizabeth to flee, desperately praying for relief in the Abbey, Kilman is portrayed as a pathetic when not fearsome creature. See Wyatt, "*Mrs. Dalloway,*" for an antithetical reading of Clarissa's laughter at Kilman as the triumph of "the comic spirit of civilized society" (447). Abel, 263, adds that Kilman's desires to "grasp" and "clasp" Elizabeth parody the line from *Othello* that Clarissa applies to her love of Sally (see my discussion below).

21. Shakespeare, *Othello,* in *The Norton Shakespeare,* 2.1.186–87; Woolf, *Diary,* 3:8–9 (8 April 1925).

22. Fox, *Virginia Woolf,* stresses the echo of *Othello* here as a sign of "sisterhood" (116) rather than sexuality; clearly the moment involves both. Jensen, however, goes too far in making repressed homosexual feelings the key to Septimus's death and the reason Clarissa's London life should be viewed as a "punishment" (162). As a result, she also reads Septimus's postwar reading of *Antony and Cleopatra* as if it were both accurate and Woolf's own (164); see my concluding discussion of that passage below.

23. My use of interpellation draws upon the analysis of ideology by Althusser, adapted by Teresa de Lauretis (among others) to address questions of gender specifically; see the introduction to her *Technologies of Gender* (Bloomington: Indiana University Press, 1987).

24. See Abel, 246ff., for a psychoanalytic feminist reading of the novel, discussed in relation to such norms.

25. As Brower notes, Walsh is an "interrupter" and a "destroyer" (13–14), though he too experiences "life"; I see a broader parallelism between the figures of Walsh and Posthumus. Woolf gives Peter a major narrative role and energizing force in

Clarissa's life, without allowing him to dominate or marry her. It is here that the recent film adaptation directed by Marleen Gorris, with screenplay by Eileen Atkins, reveals itself as far more conventional than Woolf's novel: while admirably capturing Clarissa's love for Sally and Peter's heartbreak, the film repeatedly implies that Clarissa's "fear" kept her from marrying Peter, whom she loved more than Richard, and presents Septimus's suicide as impetus for her to seek and dance with Peter, specifically. That is, it still implies that the lost alternative was another heterosexual marriage plot. Nevertheless, the final still of the film aptly returns to the trio of Peter, Sally, and Clarissa on the lawn at Bourton—the less conventional lost possibility (and, according to Gorris, her own directorial addition; personal conversation following the London Film Festival screening, 14 November 1997).

26. See Dowling, 304.

27. J. Hillis Miller, in "*Mrs. Dalloway:* Repetition as the Raising of the Dead," in *Virginia Woolf,* edited by Harold Bloom (New York: Chelsea House, 1986), regards the novel's "climax" not as the party but as Clarissa's moment of withdrawal; he makes a rather cavalier linkage between Septimus's death and Woolf's own, further remarking that Clarissa's "obsession" with *Cymbeline* "indicates her half-conscious awareness that in spite of her love of life she will reach peace and escape from suffering only in death" (185–89, 187). Romanticization of suicide here mars an otherwise powerful reading, which does ultimately acknowledge that Clarissa is resurrected for the reader. I would add that the romance trope of sibling recovery informs the final scene's rhetorical movement to the present tense ("It is Clarissa" [194]), reviving a link between Clarissa and her past within the novel as well as for the reader. One may note that Sally has in fact gotten up, preparing to leave a "moment" before Peter becomes conscious of Clarissa's return; nevertheless, the narrative links the three figures in the final paragraphs, and it remains suitably ambiguous whether the "moment" is long enough to have allowed the now portly Lady Rosseter to reach Richard to say her farewells. For Clarissa certainly, "Sally and Peter" remain the unit to which she is planning to return, and the book seems to confirm that intention in its close.

28. Whereas Fox, in *Virginia Woolf,* stresses Septimus's postwar reading as "a badly distorted view" (132), my point is stronger: that Woolf's presentation shows the interested, distorting effect of all readings, not merely the unpleasant ones.

7
~

Circe Resartus

To the Lighthouse *and William Browne of Tavistock's* Circe and Ulysses *Masque*

~ Kelly Anspaugh

𝐼n her 1979 study *Continuing Presences: Virginia Woolf's Use of Literary Allusion*, Beverly Ann Schlack elucidates the presence and function of John Milton's masque *Comus* in Virginia Woolf's first novel, *The Voyage Out*. Woolf's echoes of Milton's text, argues Schlack, are not merely incidental or local; rather the novelist "recreates and enlarges the reverberations of her chosen allusion so masterfully that *Comus* makes itself felt on all levels—setting, plot, structure, characterization, theme are all deepened by its presence."[1] Such systematic and organic allusion is characteristic of Woolf's high modernist technique, or what Avrom Fleishman has identified as the "encyclopedic style: the network of allusion that stands as the dominant mode in modern British literature."[2] In employing this style Woolf resembles her contemporary James Joyce, whose systematic incorporation of correspondences to Homer's *Odyssey* in the text of *Ulysses* is perhaps the best-known example of modernist intertextuality.

Here I will argue that, just as Woolf employed Milton's *Comus* as a hypotext for her first novel, so she employs another and earlier Renaissance text,

Engraving by Mark Severin, from the Golden Cockerel Press edition of
Circe and Ulysses (1954). By permission of Associated University Presses.

William Browne of Tavistock's *Circe and Ulysses: The Inner Temple Masque* (1614), in *To the Lighthouse* (1927). Woolf's use of Browne's masque is, as was her use of Milton's, extensive and systematic; it informs her text on the level of character, imagery, theme—even genre. Before turning to an analysis of the presence and function of Browne's masque in Woolf's novel, however, let us first briefly consider Browne and his little-known *Circe* in historical context.

Of the man William Browne, as is the case with so many Renaissance figures, relatively little is known. He was born at Tavistock in 1591 into a good knightly family. After attending Oxford he became, in 1611, a member of the Inner Temple, one of the four inns of court, which institutions at the time were less training camps for would-be lawyers than finishing schools for rich young gentlemen. The inns were also a breeding ground for poets, as one commentator observes: "between Wyatt and Surrey and the appearance of Spenser and Sidney, all the poets, in fact almost all writers of any value, were connected with the inns of court . . . they were the literary center of England."[3] Browne actually came at the tail end of this distinguished poetic line, *Britannia's Pastorals* (1613–16) (his best-known and best-loved work, the first book of which he produced before the tender age of twenty) being "the last poetic work of any consequence written by a resident member [of the Inner Temple] before the Civil War"—that is, before the Puritans ruined all the fun.[4] In 1624 he returned to Oxford and received permission to be created master of arts, and in the public register of the university he is characterized as *"vir omni humana literarum et bonarum artium cognitione instructus."* The short entry on Browne in the *Dictionary of National Biography* concludes as follows:

> Like his friend Michael Drayton, whom he resembled in many respects, Browne possessed a gentleness and simplicity of character which secured him the affection and admiration of his contemporaries. Prince tells us that "he had a great mind in a little body." Whether this description is to be taken merely as a flower of speech, or whether the poet was of short stature, it would be difficult to determine.[5]

As for *Circe and Ulysses,* its editor Gwyn Jones thinks it Browne's best piece of writing and rates it "among the very best masques in English."[6] The text is

certainly unusual, given that most Renaissance masques, as they exist in manuscript, are little more than records of stage direction enlivened with snatches of
poetry. Such spareness is understandable if it is indeed the case that the masque,
as its most famous designer Inigo Jones insisted, is "nothing else but pictures
with Light and Motion"—ephemeral spectacle.[7] While reading Browne's *Circe*,
though, one gets the distinct impression that the author wrote it down with the
intention that it be read—in other words, he anticipated his fond admirer Ben
Jonson in looking upon the masque not as mere spectacle but as literature.
Jonson, in fact, in his dedicatory verse for *Britannia's Pastorals* praises the preco-
cious Browne precisely for his readability: "But I have seen thy Worke, and I know
thee: / And, if thou list thy selfe, what thou canst bee. / For, though but early in
these paths thou tread, / I finde thee write most worthy to be read."[8] Another
careful reader of Browne was John Milton, whose handwriting appears in the
margins of a copy of the first edition of *Britannia's Pastorals* and whose masque
Comus, some scholars have argued, owes a good deal to *Circe and Ulysses*.[9]

Browne's Yuletide offering (the date given for its presentation in Jones's
1954 edition is 13 January 1614) is a short text, requiring but twenty minutes to
read. It features an epigraph from Ovid's *Ad Pisonem*: "*non semper Gnosius
arcus / Destinat, exempto sed laxat cornua nervo.*"[10] Jones renders this passage
into English, "Nor for ever does the Cretan aim his bow, but, its string freed,
he relaxes its horns," and interprets it in context: "Calpurnius is praised for
knowing that a grave-browed eloquence is not pleasing on all occasions" (35).
So Browne signals his audience that the work to follow is likely to appeal to
those who know how to loosen up, as befits the season. And the makeup of
that audience? This is made clear in a prefatory address "TO THE HONORABLE
SOCIETY OF THE INNER TEMPLE":

> Gentlemen, I give you but your owne: if you refuse to foster it I
> knowe not who will. By your meanes it may live. . . . What is good
> in it that is yours, what bad myne, what indifferent both, and that
> will suffice, since it was done to please our selves in private, by him
> that is, All yours, W. Browne. (5)

Browne's masque was unusual, then, in that it was written not for presentation
before king and court (as were most masques of the time), but instead for

private, fraternal delectation. This exclusivity may have allowed Browne a certain license in regard to subject matter and language. In short, this one was for the boys.

The masque is divided into three scenes. The setting is the isle of "Æœa," demesne of the witch Circe, daughter of Apollo. As the masque gets under way we are greeted by two "Syrens," who, in accordance with the best classical precedent ("Hyginus and Servius"), have "their upper parts like women to the navell and the rest likc a hen" (7). One of these begins a song, this "beinge as lascivious proper to them" to attract the wandering Ulysses and his mates:

> Steere hither, steere, your winged Pines
>> All beaten Mariners:
> Here lye loves undiscovered Mines,
>> A prey to passengers:
> Perfumes farre sweeter then the best
> Which make the Phœnix urne and nest:
>> Feare not your ships,
> Nor any to oppose you save our lips;
>> But come on shore,
> Where no joy dyes till love hath gotten more.
>
> (7–8)

At this point the song is rudely interrupted by "Triton" ("a minor sea-god cast in the shape of a merman; the son of Poseidon and Amphitrite"),[11] who warns the siren away from seducing Ulysses, for whom his mistress, the Titaness Tethys, has other plans. The siren replies that she will obey only the bidding of her mistress, the all-powerful Circe. Triton peevishly withdraws, and the siren continues her song:

> For swellinge waves, our pantinge brestes
>> Where never stormes arise
> Exchange; and be a while our guestes:
>> For starres, gaze on our eyes.
> The compasse, love shall hourely singe,
> And as he goes aboute the ringe,

> We will not misse
> To telle each pointe he nameth with a kisse.
>   *Chorus:*
> Then come on shore,
> Where no joye dyes till love hath gotten more.
>
> (10–11)

At this Circe makes her appearance, "quaintly attyr'd, her haire loose aboute her shoulders, an Anadem of flowers on her head, with a wand in her hand" (11), and announces that she has prevailed, that Ulysses and his mates are safe asleep in her bower of bliss, whither she withdraws. End of scene 1.

As the second scene opens, Circe employs the magical root moly to awaken Ulysses from his charmed sleep. The Greek hero is terrified of her and her intentions: "But may I aske (greate Circe) whereto tendes / Thy never failinge hand? Shall we be free? / Or must thyne anger crush my mates and mee?" To this Circe responds, "Neyther, Laertes sonne. With winges of love / To thee and none but thee, my actions move." The sorceress explains that she has been acting in the office of Ulysses' guardian angel throughout his adventures, "This for Ulisses love hath Circe done," and now intends to keep him by her forever and forever in bliss (17).

Then enters the first "Antimasque," a collection of grotesque characters— "beinge such," Browne tells us, "as by Circe were supposed to have beene transformed" (19)—a motley crew consisting of an ass and some wolves and baboons and a hog. These dance an antic dance, sing a silly song, then are scattered by the woodsman. When Circe asks Ulysses how he liked the spectacle, he, thinking the dancers were his men transmogrified, complains of Circe's cruelty: "Most abjecte basenesse hath enthrald that breste / Which laughes at men by misery oppreste" (23).

In response to this reproach Circe offers an *apologia*—a speech that is clearly the center and climax of Browne's text and so worth quoting at length:

> In this, as Lyllies or the new falne snowe
> Is Circe spotlesse yet. What though the bowe
> Which Iris bendes appeareth to each sight
> In various hewes and colours infinite?

The learned knowe that in it selfe is free,
And light and shade make that varietye.
Thinges farre off seene seeme not the same they are,
Fame is not ever Truth's discoverer;
For still where envy meeteth a reporte
Ill she makes worse, and what is good come shorte.
In whatso'ere this land hath passive beene,
Or she that here 'ore other raigneth queene,
Let wise Ulisses judge. Some I confesse
That tow'rds this Isle not longe since did addresse
Their stretched oares, no sooner landed were,
But (carelesse of themselves) they heere and there
Fed on strange fruites, invenominge their bloodes,
And now like monsters range about the woods.
If those thy mates were yet is Circe free,
For their misfortunes have not byrth from mee.

(23–24)

Circe claims to have been the victim of bad press, as it were. She is not a wicked witch, as envious Fame reports, but a good one. All she wants, really, is to love Ulysses and be loved by him. And if some men who came to her island were transformed into animals, well, that was their own fault, the fruits of their selfish recklessness. Ulysses is won over by this eloquent defense: "Æœa's queene, and great Hyperions pride, / Pardon misdoubtes; and we are satisfi'de" (24). Thus forgiven, Circe rewards her love with a second antimasque, a dance of sea-green Nymphes and Nereides—a much more genteel spectacle than the first anti-masque. The second scene ends with Circe voluntarily surrendering her magical wand to Ulysses, in order that he might wake his sleeping men with it.

So we move to the third scene, the "revels" or general dance that tradition-ally concludes the masque. Ulysses' men, the "maskers," pair off with "the ladyes" to the following strains:

Choose now amonge this fairest number,
Upon whose brestes love would for ever slumber:
Choose not amisse since you may where you wylle,

> Or blame your selves for choosing ylle.
> Then doe not leave though ofte the musicke closes,
> Till lillyes in their cheekes be turn'd to roses.
>
> (31)

After a good deal of stepping to "the old measures," the masque closes with a chastisement of Time—that ancient enemy of all festivity—and a ringing endorsement of hedonism:

> ⌐   Who but Tyme so hasty were
>   To fly away and leave you here?
>   Here where delight
>   Might well allure
>   A very Stoicke from this night
>   To turne an Epicure.
>   But since he calles away; and TIME will soone repente,
>   He staid not longer here, but ran to be more idly spente.
>
> (33)

That Browne's masque was meant as a Yuletide romp is clear; it is good, not-too-clean fun. In the first antimasque the boar, Grillus, is driven from the hall: "O let there be no staye / In his waye, / To hinder the Boare from his kinde" (22)—a pun working here, certainly, on "boar," the author bidding all bores and killjoys, those who might be offended by his good-humored entertainment, be gone and good riddance. Browne is careful at the opening of his masque to cite a number of classical sources for the tale he will tell, including especially Homer and Virgil (7), thus apparently borrowing from these august predecessors poetic authority. What he does in the body of the text, however, is to turn these "grave-browed" precursors on their heads and rewrite their epic narratives. Let us consider some of Browne's revisions of Homer's *Odyssey,* for example.

In Homer's narrative Circe is a lewd and dangerous woman, a very wicked witch. She does indeed work her "foul magic" to transform Odysseus' men into swine and has every intention of similarly casting him into abjection.[12] Browne's Circe, on the other hand, is an allegory of love, who is closer in character to

Homer's Calypso or Nausicaa than to his Circe—and whose magic is decidedly white. Whereas in Homer the sirens are hideous female monsters about whose deadly deceptive song the conquered Circe warns Odysseus in advance, in Browne's masque these creatures are transformed into the docile and devoted (literally henlike) handmaidens of Circe, and their song brings, not pain and death, but everlasting joy. In Homer Odysseus receives the magic root moly from the hand of Hermes, this as an antidote to Circe's "numbing drops of night and evil" (174); in Browne it is Circe who employs moly to awaken Ulysses from the gentle sleep she has lovingly induced. In Homer's version Odysseus must employ threats of violence to wrest power from Circe: "without a word, I drew my sharpened sword / and in one bound held it against her throat" (175); in Browne, when Ulysses accepts as true Circe's claim to innocence, she voluntarily relinquishes her wand as a gesture of good faith. Finally, whereas in Homer's tale Odysseus takes his leave of Circe to continue his *nostos,* there is at the end of Browne's masque no sign of Ulysses' imminent departure for home—and who can blame him?

It is too easy to dismiss all of this crafty inversion and textual transformation as just so much funny business (although it is funny—as humorous in its way as Joyce's transformation of Homer's "wily Odysseus" into a less-than-wily Dublin ad canvasser). Browne's text cries out to be read as allegory, and though numerous possibilities suggest themselves (political allegory, religious allegory), one interpretation in particular recommends itself: *feminist* allegory. In this reading the figure of Circe stands for Everywoman, and as such she is, like Eve, blamed by male observers (Homer, for example) for all the evil in the world. Browne's project is to revise or rehabilitate this figure and thereby expose the traditional, patriarchal view of Woman as a lie. If only men would treat women with respect, as Browne's Ulysses does his Circe, then (Browne appears to be suggesting) we could enter a Golden Age of Love. "Then come on shore, / Where no joye dyes till love hath gotten more."

One can imagine that such an interpretation of Browne's masque would be particularly intriguing to the feminist author of *A Room of One's Own,* with its much-abused Renaissance heroine, Ms. Judith Shakespeare. And it is with this feminist-allegorical interpretation in mind that I now turn to an analysis of Woolf's allusions to Browne in a text published just a few years prior to *A Room of One's Own.*

Near the conclusion of "The Window," first book of *To the Lighthouse*, Mrs. Ramsay joins her husband in the drawing room, hoping for a quiet moment alone with him at the end of a hectic day. She finds him preoccupied—immersed in an anxious rereading of Scott's *The Antiquary*—so resumes knitting the stocking she plans to give to the son of the lighthouse keeper. Then, recalling with pleasure the recitation of a lyric poem at dinner, she picks up and begins to leaf through a poetry anthology:

> And she opened the book and began reading here and there at random, and as she did so she felt that she was climbing backwards, upwards, shoving her way up under petals that curved over her, so that she only knew this is white, or this is red. She did not know at first what the words meant at all.
>
> *Steer, hither steer your winged pines, all beaten Mariners*
> she read and turned the page, swinging herself, zigzagging this way and that, from one line to another as from one branch to another, from one red and white flower to another, until a little sound roused her—her husband slapping his thighs.[13]

The line from the anthology cited is, of course, the first (slightly modified) of the siren song that begins Browne's masque. It is the only direct quotation of Browne in Woolf's novel. The most extensive commentary on this intertext to date—although only a page or so long—has been offered by Alice Fox in *Virginia Woolf and the English Renaissance* (1990). Fox reproduces in full the sirens' song and observes that it "deliberately suppresses the sirens' motive of destruction, and would perhaps have attracted Woolf by its elimination of the misogyny implicit in Homer's tale. Instead it celebrates in two lovely verses the joys to be found on the sirens' island home."[14] She goes on to note that the song "is quite appropriate for Mrs Ramsay. If the lighthouse to which she hoped James might sail has any meaning for her, it is as the place of restful love following whatever difficulties life may bring him."[15]

Fox's reading of the function of Browne's song in Woolf's novel is excellent as far as it goes. I do not think it goes far enough, however, in that the critic never ventures to suggest that Woolf's knowledge of Browne's masque may extend beyond that possessed by her character Mrs. Ramsay's—that is, beyond a stanza or two gleaned from an anthology. Is it just a coincidence that Mrs. Ramsay's reading is represented as an ascension through what could only be described as a bower of bliss, full of red and white flowers? Browne's Circe, after all, resides on a shaded hilltop "Where everlastinge Springe with sylver showres / Sweet roses doth encrease to grace our bowres, / Where lavish Flora prodigall in pride / Spendes what might well enrich all earth beside" (12). And is it coincidence that the action of the remainder of Woolf's first book consists of Mrs. Ramsay's winning over of Mr. Ramsay, her solely beaten Mariner (who, despite his self-identification with Cowper's abject "Castaway" in the first book, will lead a successful expedition to the lighthouse at novel's end), bewitching and mastering him with love? The closing words of "The Window":

> A heartless woman he called her; she never told him that she loved him. But it was not so—it was not so. . . . Then, knowing that he was watching her, instead of saying anything she turned, holding her stocking, and looked at him. And as she looked at him she began to smile, for though she had not said a word, he knew, of course he knew, that she loved him. He could not deny it. . . .
>
> "Yes, you were right. It's going to be wet tomorrow. You won't be able to go." And she looked at him smiling. For she had triumphed again. She had not said it: yet he knew. (123–24)

There are differences here, of course: whereas Browne's Circe wins over Ulysses with eloquent words (her *apologia*), Mrs. Ramsay wins over her husband with an eloquent gaze. Nevertheless, the basic situations and their resolutions are the same. In both cases, the female has been maligned, falsely accused of heartlessness (again, Browne's Ulysses to his Circe: "Most abjecte basenesse hath enthralled that breste / Which laughs at men by misery oppreste"). In both cases, the female concedes the male mastery (Circe by handing Ulysses her wand; Mrs. Ramsay by acknowledging the accuracy of Mr. Ramsay's weather forecast) only *after* having won the day—that is, after having won the male's love and devotion—and thereby establishing true mastery.

If Woolf had indeed read Browne's masque in its entirety, one might expect resonances of that larger text in the immediate vicinity of its sole explicit citation. But what of elsewhere in Woolf's novel? Say, earlier in "The

Window"? Or in the middle book, "Time Passes," or in the third and concluding book, "The Lighthouse"? Are there traces of Browne's masque there? Any
echoes in Woolf's characters, images, or themes?

Let us consider for a moment the enigmatic character of Mr. Carmichael,
who, as J. Hillis Miller has pointed out, is unusual among Mrs. Ramsay's guests
in that not once in the course of Woolf's narrative is his stream of consciousness represented, so we never get to know him intimately as we do, say, Mr.
Ramsay or Charles Tansley.[16] One critic has suggested that this character is
modeled upon that famous English opium-eater, Thomas De Quincey, whom
Woolf was reading at the time of writing her novel; another has responded
that, no, the character is a fictional representation of a certain "Mr. Wollstone-
holme," a friend of Leslie Stephen, who had been a brilliant academic but had
ruined his life with a bad marriage.[17] It appears to me likely that both of these
critics are correct, for Woolf's characters are inevitably overdetermined, com-
posites of a number of originals from her life and from her reading. In fact, I
think room must be made for one other source for the character of Mr.
Carmichael: Browne's figure of Triton.

Recall that Triton makes a cameo appearance in the first scene of Browne's
masque, pops up to interrupt the sirens' song, to warn them away from tempt-
ing Ulysses. He is clearly presented, then, as a potential foe to Circe, in the
service of those immortals who wish to foil her plans for "trapping" the hapless
mariners. In Woolf's novel Mr. Carmichael is presented as a potential antago-
nist to the Circe correspondent, Mrs. Ramsay. In the third book of the novel,
Lily Briscoe recalls that Mr. Carmichael was always "trying to avoid Mrs.
Ramsay whom for some reason he did not much like. . . . It was perhaps her
masterfulness, her positiveness, something matter-of-fact in her. She was so
direct" (195). All of these, of course, are qualities of Circe. Mrs. Ramsay gives
Mr. Carmichael every attention, often asks what she can do for him, but is met
with coldness:

> the sense she had now when Mr. Carmichael shuffled past, just nod-
> ding to her question, with a book beneath his arm, in his yellow
> slippers, that she was suspected; and that all this desire of hers to
> give, to help, was vanity. . . . she did not feel merely snubbed back
> in her instinct, but made aware of the pettiness of some part of her,

and of human relations, how flawed they are, how despicable, how
self-seeking, at their best. (41–42)

Mr. Carmichael's indifference to Mrs. Ramsay (some critics have suggested that
he is homosexual and consequently does not respond to the siren song of Mrs.
Ramsay's beauty) she interprets as a reproach, and she reacts in much the way
Browne's Circe reacts to the accusation that she is self-seeking and out to
destroy Ulysses.

The imagery of other passages in Woolf's novel also suggests an
identification of Augustus Carmichael with Browne's Triton. In the dinner
scene of "The Window," Mrs. Ramsay admires her daughter Rose's centerpiece:
"What had she done with it, Mrs. Ramsay wondered, for Rose's arrangement
of the grapes and pears, of the horny pink-lined shell, of the bananas, made
her think of a trophy fetched from the bottom of the sea, of Neptune's banquet" (97). Triton was a son of Neptune and associated with conch shells
(Woolf's "horny pink-lined shell"?), since he used one of them "as a trumpet
in order to calm the stormy seas."[18] If Mr. Carmichael is an avatar of Triton,
then, we would expect him to also be attracted to this centerpiece, and so he
is: "she [Mrs. Ramsay] saw that Augustus too feasted his eyes on the same plate
of fruit, plunged in, broke off a bloom there, a tassel here, and returned, after
feasting, to his hive. That was his way of looking, different from hers. But
looking together united them" (97). The dinner scene culminates in a "moment of being" (Woolf's term) wherein a "community of feeling with other
people" (113) is achieved and antagonisms between individuals are ironed out.
It is fitting that in this scene Mrs. Ramsay and Mr. Carmichael are reconciled,
become one in their enjoyment of the object of beauty, and also fitting that at
the conclusion of the scene it is Mr. Carmichael who takes the lead in paying
tribute to his hostess:

Augustus Carmichael had risen and, holding his table napkin so
that it looked like a long white robe he stood chanting:
To see the Kings go riding by
Over lawn and daisy lea
With their palm leaves and cedar sheaves,
   Luriana, Lurilee,

and as she passed him, he turned slightly towards her repeating the last words:

Luriana, Lurilee

And bowed to her as if he did her homage. Without knowing why, she felt that he liked her better than he had ever done before; and with a feeling of relief and gratitude she returned his bow and passed through the door which he held open for her. (111)

Although there is no reconciliation between Triton and Circe in Browne's text, the intersubjective harmony that characterizes the conclusion of Woolf's dinner scene is paralleled in the third scene of the masque by the revels wherein all antagonisms are banished and universal love is the order of the day.

Woolf's novel is built upon repetition. The above scene from "The Window" finds an echo in the very conclusion of the novel, where once again Mr. Carmichael plays an important role. Lily Briscoe is looking out toward the lighthouse, thinking of Mr. Ramsay there:

"He has landed," she said aloud. "It is finished." Then, surging up, puffing slightly, old Mr. Carmichael stood beside her, looking like an old pagan god, shaggy, with weeds in his hair and the trident (it was only a French novel) in his hand. . . . He stood there as if he were spreading his hands over all the weakness and suffering of mankind; she thought he was surveying, tolerantly and compassionately, their final destiny. Now he has crowned the occasion, she thought, when his hand slowly fell, as if she had seen him let fall from his great height a wreath of violets and asphodels which, fluttering slowly, lay at length upon the earth. (208)

Critic John Ferguson has noted that no one has satisfactorily explained why this "apparently minor character is transfigured in the penultimate paragraph of Woolf's novel."[19] Here I want to venture an explanation: Mr. Carmichael's "transfiguration" is the result of Woolf's making explicit her character's heretofore subtextual identification with Browne's immortal Triton. How else to explain the comparison with a shaggy sea god? How else account for the comparison of the novel he holds to a trident? ("[Triton] also carried a trident, like his father Poseidon.")[20] "One feels," writes Ferguson, "as the mortals in Greek myth or in the Bible must have felt when the unknown visitor suddenly dropped his masque and blazed before them—a god or an angel."[21] This, I argue, in a manner of speaking is precisely what happens: Woolf's character blazes forth as Browne's Triton.

Or not precisely Browne's Triton. Through blowing in his conch shell, Triton calms the seas, and legend has it that when Jason and the Argonauts lost their way, Triton "showed them the direction to take in order to find the sea again."[22] Here Mr. Carmichael is represented as a benevolent demigod ("He remained benignant, calm—if one chose to think it, sublime" [180]), watching over Mr. Ramsay and his children on their expedition to the lighthouse, blessing particularly Mr. Ramsay in his Homeric *nostos*, his homecoming, and helping him achieve his destiny (in springing onto the rock [207] Mr. Ramsay reaches "R" [34]). Mr. Carmichael also in a sense helps Mrs. Ramsay achieve her destiny, for the "violets and asphodels" that Lily imagines falling from his hands were earlier associated with Mrs. Ramsay ("[w]ith stars in her eyes and veils in her hair, with cyclamen and wild violets" [14]; "The Graces assembling seemed to have joined hands in meadows of asphodel to compose that face" [29]). My argument here, in short, is that Woolf is not only drawing upon Browne for assistance in the creation of character, but also following his example as a revisionary artist. Woolf is perhaps most like Browne, ironically enough, when she *revises* Browne, transforms his truculent Triton into a sort of guardian angel, just as Browne had transformed Homer's wicked witch into a good one.

And what of Browne's witch? Is it forcing things to say that the character of Mrs. Ramsay, which we well know is based primarily upon Woolf's mother, Julia Stephen, owes a little something to Browne's Circe? Consider that Mrs. Ramsay is all-but-queen of her Isle of Skye (at one point she is even associated, in Charles Tansley's vision, with Queen Victoria [14]), just as Circe rules over the island Æœa. That those around Mrs. Ramsay perceive her as having Circean powers over them is also clear. "There was something frightening about her," Lily Briscoe thinks. "She was irresistible. . . . She put a spell on them all" (101). As is also the case with Circe, Mrs. Ramsay's special powers are envied, make her enemies, as she herself recognizes: "a woman had once accused her of 'robbing her of her daughter's affections'. . . . Wishing to dominate, wishing to interfere, making people do what she wished—that was the charge against her, and she thought it most unjust" (57). Is this not the same charge made against Circe, who also feels it is unjust? And by the end of both texts the reader is compelled to agree with the heroines that they have been wronged.

All Browne's Circe really wants, once again, is to bring people together so that they can love one another. This, also, is Mrs. Ramsay's aim. And just as Circe achieves her goal in the revels ("Choose now amonge this fairest number, / Upon whose brestes love would for ever slumber"), so Woolf's heroine brings her guests to loving harmony in the dinner scene: "Some change at once went through them all, as if this had really happened, and they were all conscious of making a party together in a hollow, on an island; had their common cause against that fluidity out there" (97). If Circe's great enemy is Time ("Who but Tyme so hasty were / To fly away and leave you here?"), so is Mrs. Ramsay's, and by the end of their respective stories we are left with the impression that our good witches have gotten the best of this shared foe. "And if it lay in Circe's power," Browne's Chorus chants to the prancing couples, "Your blisse might so persever, / That those you choose but for an hower / You should enjoy for ever" (33). As for Mrs. Ramsay, Lily Briscoe, looking back, testifies to her triumph over time:

> Mrs. Ramsay bringing them together; Mrs. Ramsay saying, "Life stand still here"; Mrs. Ramsay making of the moment something permanent . . . this was of the nature of a revelation. In the midst of chaos there was shape; this eternal passing and flowing (she looked at the clouds going and the leaves shaking) was struck into stability. Life stand still here, Mrs. Ramsay said. (161)

It appears to me that Woolf, drawing upon Browne's text to create certain aspects of Mrs. Ramsay, in places conflates the characters of Circe and her sirens—which would be logical, given that Browne's sirens are, after all, simply Circe's mouthpieces (their song is her song). Browne's sirens represent the Eternal Feminine, or more precisely femininity as a lure to men—a counter to masculine thought, a distraction from masculine pursuits. Recall the second stanza of their song:

> For starres, gaze on our eyes
> The compasse, love shall hourly singe,
> And as he goes aboute the ringe,
>   We will not misse
> To telle each pointe he nameth with a kisse.
>
>   (10–11)

Charles Tansley is self-seduced by his romantic vision of Mrs. Ramsay "[w]ith stars in her eyes and wind in her hair" (14); and Mrs. Ramsay is herself aware of the siren power of stars: "And looking up, she saw above the thin trees the first pulse of the full-throbbing star, and wanted to make her husband look at it" (71). Men are creatures of time, live in time—are always consulting their watches. Mr. Ramsay does so, for example, at the dinner table, in the course of a discussion of square roots. Mrs. Ramsay reacts: "What did it all mean? To this day she had no notion. A square root? What was that? Her sons knew. She leant on them. . . . she let it uphold her and sustain her, this admirable fabric of the masculine intelligence" (105-6). Mrs. Ramsay's daughter Cam, in exhibiting an ignorance of applied science as well as a dependence on masculine virtue, is clearly her mother's daughter. In the third book of the novel she and her brother accompany their father on an expedition to the lighthouse; while en route her father begins to tease her:

> Didn't she know the points of the compass? he asked. Didn't she know the North from the South? Did she really think they lived right out there? . . . "Tell me—which is East, which is West?" he said, half laughing at her, half scolding her, for he could not understand the state of mind of any one, not absolutely imbecile, who did not know the points of the compass. Yet she did not know. . . . He thought, women are always like that; the vagueness of their minds is hopeless; it was a thing he had never been able to understand; but so it was. It had been so with her—his wife. . . . But he had been wrong to be angry with her; moreover, did he not rather like this vagueness in women? It was part of their extraordinary charm. (167)

Both Mrs. Ramsay and her daughter, then, share with Browne's sirens an ignorance of science and its instruments; yet this ignorance, while at times annoying to men, also acts as a powerful lure for them, as they perceive it as a sign of sexual difference. Whereas Mr. Ramsay is interested in the literal compass, his wife and daughter, like Browne's Circe and her sirens, are concerned only with "the compass of the soul" (128), which is accessed through love. "Tell me," the Eternal Masculine inquires of the Eternal Feminine, "which is East, which is West?" The Eternal Feminine, confident of its allure, boldly answers: "We will not misse / To telle each pointe [you] nameth with a kisse" (11).

In "The Window" Mrs. Ramsay is the central character; in "The Lighthouse" it is Lily Briscoe who becomes the focus, and consequently the character to whom most traces of Browne's masque attach. Because Lily is so different from Mrs. Ramsay—a less conventional, less traditionally feminine woman—we would expect the allusions that attach to her to be different. For example, whereas an association of Mrs. Ramsay with Browne's sirens is appropriate—at least in certain moments and contexts (Mrs. Ramsay being, after all, that "happier Helen of our days," and like Helen irresistible to men)—it would be altogether inappropriate for Lily to be so associated, there being nothing at all siren-like about her ("With her little Chinese eyes and her puckered-up face," thinks Mrs. Ramsay, "she would never marry" [17]). It is instead Circe's *apologia,* that character's most self-assertive and so least feminine gesture (least feminine, that is, according to traditional definitions of femininity), that most clearly informs Lily's character and thought. Recall the opening lines of Circe's speech, wherein she defends herself against the charge that she had turned men into beasts:

> In this, as lyllies or the new falne snowe,
> Is Circe spotlesse yet. What though the bowe
> Which Iris bendes appeareth to each sight
> In various hewes and colours infinite?
> The learned knowe that in it selfe is free,
> And light and shade make that varietye.
> Thinges farre off seene seeme not the same they are,
> Fame is not ever Truth's discoverer;

> For still where envy meeteth a reporte
> Ill she makes worse, and what is good come shorte.
>
> (23)

I think it not unlikely that the contrasting metaphors of the lily and the rose that run throughout Browne's text ("Then doe not leave though ofte the musicke closes, / Till lillyes in their cheeks be turn'd to roses"—that is, until the conventional comic ending of marriage has been achieved), if they did not determine, at least to a certain degree influenced Woolf's choice of character names Lily Briscoe and Rose Ramsay.[23] For Lily is indeed virginal, and, despite Mrs. Ramsay's wishes to the contrary, her flower will never turn rose. Lily is married to her art, and it is particularly in Woolf's representation of Lily's art, of her artistic sensibility and vision, that echoes of Circe's *apologia* can be heard.

We detect in Circe's speech a metaphor based upon the idea—a relatively new idea in the Renaissance—of perspective: "What though the bowe / Which Iris bendes appeareth to each sight / In various hewes and colours infinite? / The learned knowe that in it selfe is free, / And light and shade make that varietye." Science teaches us that the rainbow is in itself colorless, that its color is a matter of perspective: of the position of the perceiver relative to the angle of light passing through water. And so it is in men's lives—this is Circe's message, Browne's trope—in their perception of each other. Your view of someone, of whether the person is good or evil, depends upon your perspective, your angle of vision. "Things farre off seene," continues Circe, offering another signifier, "seeme not the same they are." Then the signified: "Fame [that is, rumor, hearsay] is not ever Truth's discoverer." Thus Browne offers in his masque a philosophy of what might be termed "ethical perspectivism," a rather optimistic philosophy (appropriately enough, given his comic aims) that suggests that our perception of evil in another being is often erroneous, the result of a lack of proper perspective. (Browne's metaphor might have been particularly striking and effective for his contemporary audience, who, while listening to Circe's lines, could have been contemplating his stage setting: "a sea being done in perspective on one side of the cliffe" [7]).

Lily Briscoe, as a painter, is comfortable with the idea of perspective. She is also aware of its power as a metaphor for ethical relations. In "The Window,"

William Bankes questions her abstract representation of Mrs. Ramsay reading to her son as a "triangular purple shape," wonders if it might be deemed irreverent. Lily responds that, in modern painting, "[a] mother and child might be reduced to a shadow without irreverence. A light here required a shadow there" (52–53). "The learned knowe," Circe tells us, that "light and shade make that varietye." That Lily can be numbered among the learned—that her artistic instinct is a good one here—we learn later on in "The Window," in the passage where Mrs. Ramsay, alone, thinks of herself, her true self, as "a wedge-shaped core of darkness" (62). Lily clearly possesses the perspective necessary to represent Mrs. Ramsay as Mrs. Ramsay sees herself—a perspective that William Bankes lacks.

"Things farre off seene seeme not the same they are," Circe cautions us. "So much depends then," observes Lily—considering her painting, considering at the same time Mr. Ramsay—"so much depends, she thought, upon distance: whether people are near us or far from us; for her feeling for Mr. Ramsay changed as he sailed further and further across the bay" (191). Circe's insight and Lily's are identical, and Lily is not alone among the book's characters in possessing it. Cam, sailing to the lighthouse with her father, looks back at their house: "The shore seemed refined, far away, unreal. Already the little distance they had sailed had put them far from it and given it the changed look, the composed look, of something receding in which one has no longer any part" (166). "Distance" here is a matter not only of space but of time as well. The characters of the third book are separated from Mrs. Ramsay by a distance of ten years, and not only they, but also Mrs. Ramsay herself, have been "much changed" (to use Mr. Ramsay's expression) by the passage of time. Seeing becomes difficult indeed. "One wanted fifty pairs of eyes to see with, she [Lily] reflected. Fifty pairs of eyes were not enough to get round that one woman with, she thought" (198).

Note that in the above passage, although it occurs late in Woolf's third book, Lily is speaking as if Mrs. Ramsay survives, as if she still needs all those eyes to see the woman. This is appropriate, for, although much changed, Mrs. Ramsay endures. Her daughter glimpses her for a moment on her way to the lighthouse:

> They don't feel a thing there, Cam thought, looking at the
> shore. . . . Her hand cut a trail in the sea, as her mind made the
> green swirls and streaks into patterns and, numbed and shrouded,

wandered in imagination in that underworld of waters where the pearls stuck in clusters to white sprays, where in the green light a change came over one's entire mind and one's body shone half transparent enveloped in a green cloak. (182–83)

We detect echo upon echo in this passage: an echo of a passage from "The Window"—a prophetic one, it turns out—wherein Mrs. Ramsay imagines herself a weary sailor, half in love with easeful death, thinking how, "had the ship sunk, he would have whirled round and round and found rest on the floor of the sea" (84); an echo here as well of Ariel's song from *The Tempest:* "Full fathom five thy father lies; / Of his bones are coral made; / Those are pearls that were his eyes; / Nothing of him that doth fade / But doth suffer a sea-change / Into something rich and strange."[24] The "green cloak" Cam sees here is an echo of Mrs. Ramsay's green shawl from "The Window," the same shawl she had used to wrap the boar's skull to hide if from Cam, to comfort her daughter. So, although having undergone a "sea-change," Mrs. Ramsay endures in the vision of her daughter.

And Mrs. Ramsay endures as well in Lily Briscoe's artistic vision. The whole of Woolf's third book, I argue, is necromantic: it is the record of Lily's attempt to overcome Time by raising Mrs. Ramsay from the dead—Lily's struggle reflecting Mrs. Ramsay's struggle in "The Window" to overcome Time and chaos through establishing intersubjective harmony. And Lily, like Mrs. Ramsay—after a number of false starts, a number of agonizing setbacks—is ultimately successful in her attempt:

> "Mrs. Ramsay! Mrs. Ramsay!" she cried, feeling the old horror come back—to want and want and not to have. Could she inflict that still? And then, quietly, as if she refrained, that too became part of ordinary experience, was on a level with the chair, with the table. Mrs. Ramsay—it was part of her perfect goodness—sat there quite simply, in the chair, flicked her needles to and fro, knitted her reddish-brown stocking, cast her shadow on the step. There she sat. (202)

Overcoming time, then, is simply a matter of acquiring the correct perspective. That insight is the essence of Circe's vision and of Lily's ultimate "vision"

(209)—which two visions resolve in the final (intertextual) analysis, I argue, into the same vision.

We have seen above how Browne's text informs Woolf's on the level of character, plot, setting, imagery, and theme. But what of genre? It was Woolf herself who declared this category problematic: "I am making up 'To the Lighthouse'—the sea is to be heard all through it. I have an idea that I will invent a new name for my books to supplant 'novel.' A new by Virginia Woolf. But what? Elegy?"[25] Elegy makes sense, of course, given that the text's two main characters are based upon Woolf's dead parents and that the time and setting of the narrative reflects a world passed away. Yet here I want to suggest that Woolf's reading of masques in general and Browne's masque in particular may have influenced her choices concerning the overall structure and character— that is, the genre—of her text.

Typically the masque falls into two parts: the masque proper and the antimasque (also at times referred to as the "ante-masque" because it usually precedes the main entertainment). The antimasque is usually boisterous and chaotic, performed by low, sometimes grotesque characters. It was introduced (reportedly by Ben Jonson in his 1609 *Masque of Queens*) to provide a contrast to the order of the masque proper—the latter functioning to cure, as it were, the disease of the former, to establish harmony where before there was dis-cord.[26] The antimasque was often chased off stage by a figure of great authority, such as a god or, in court masques, a royal personage (sometimes, in Jonson's masques, the king himself). The masque typically ends with the "revels" or general dance, in which the audience is invited to join, thus transforming what had up to that point been spectacle into ritual.[27]

We see that Browne's masque is a variation on this basic plan. Rather than being dualistic in structure, his masque is essentially tripartite. He begins with a sort of exposition wherein he sets the scene, establishes characters and motives. Then he introduces the antimasque, the antic dance of men transmogrified. The disorder this antimasque represents is dispelled, not simply by the figure of the woodsman (who is, after all, another low character), but in effect by Circe's well-ordered *apologia,* which prepares the stage for the third part of the masque: a second, more genteel antimasque followed by the closing revels.

Woolf's text is also tripartite, and the three parts function in much the way the three parts of Browne's masque do. "The Window" sets and orders the scene, introduces characters and their relationships. The focal character, of course, is Mrs. Ramsay, which would make sense according to the logic of textual correspondence, since Circe—Mrs. Ramsay's metaleptic echo—is the focus of the first part of Browne's masque. And just as Circe is portrayed as the prime authority and ordering principle in Browne's text, so Mrs. Ramsay fulfills the same role in Woolf's.

We would expect, then, the second part of Woolf's text to somehow echo the antimasque that—typically—threatens Browne's masque world with disorder. And this is indeed the case. Whereas the first and third books of Woolf's novel each represent the orderly passage of a few hours in a single day, "Time Passes" telescopes the chaotic passage of ten years, during which span the world portrayed in "The Window" is thrown into violent disarray. Time, the arch-enemy of both heroines (Browne's and Woolf's), has served up the disaster of World War I and cut off the lives of Mrs. Ramsay, her son Andrew, and her daughter Prue. Time is out of joint, so the world is "out of harmony":

> There was the silent apparition of an ashen-coloured ship for instance, come, gone; there was a purplish stain upon the bland surface of the sea as if something had boiled and bled, invisibly, beneath. This intrusion into a scene calculated to stir the most sublime reflections and lead to the most comfortable conclusions stayed their pacing. (133–34)

An "intrusion into a scene calculated to stir the most sublime reflections" could well stand as a definition of the antimasque, which intrudes upon the masque proper, denies easy answers, delays "comfortable conclusions."

If "Time Passes" is indeed a sort of antimasque, we would expect the sudden entrance of grotesque characters performing antic measures, and this is precisely what we get:

> Only through the rusty hinges and swollen sea-moistened woodwork certain airs, detached from the body of the wind (the house was ramshackle after all) crept round corners and ventured indoors. Almost one might imagine them, as they entered the drawing-room questioning and wondering, toying with the flap of hanging

> wall-paper, asking, would it hang much longer, when would it fall?
> Then smoothly brushing the walls, they passed on musingly as if
> asking the red and yellow roses on the wall-paper whether they
> would fade, and questioning (gently, for there was time at their dis-
> posal) the torn letters in the waste-paper basket, the flowers, the
> books, all of which were now open to them and asking, Were they
> allies? Were they enemies? How long would they endure? (126)

Whereas Browne's antimasque characters are human beings transmogrified (in
accordance with the Homeric hypotext), Woolf's are inhuman forces personified—yet equally grotesque and clearly, as are Browne's creatures, in the
service of Entropy: "the trifling airs, nibbling, the clammy breaths, fumbling,
seemed to have triumphed. The saucepan had rusted and the mat decayed"
(137). And just as Browne introduces into his antimasque a grotesque character
in the service of Circe and (thus) Order—that is, the Woodsman, who chases
off the beastmen—so Woolf offers up her own serviceable grotesque, previously under the authority of Mrs. Ramsay:

> As she lurched (for she rolled like a ship at sea) and leered (for
> her eyes fell on nothing directly, but with a sidelong glance that
> deprecated the scorn and anger of the world—she was witless, she
> knew it), as she clutched the banisters and hauled herself upstairs
> and rolled from room to room, she sang. . . . [A] sound issued
> from her lips . . . like the voice of witlessness, humour, persistency
> itself, trodden down but springing up again, so that as she lurched,
> dusting, wiping, she seemed to say how it was one long sorrow and
> trouble. (130)

So Mrs. McNab seems to embody the melancholy humor, not only of the
underclass, but also of the antimasque itself: "there was a force working; something not highly conscious; something that leered, something that lurched;
something not inspired to go about its work with dignified ritual or solemn
chanting" (139). Here the line between the antimasque world, the world of
"leering" and "lurching," and the masque world, the world of "dignified ritual"

and "solemn chanting," is clearly drawn. Note as well that when "high" characters from parts one and three of Woolf's text are explicitly named in the body of "Time Passes," this naming is put in brackets ("[A shell exploded. Twenty or thirty young men were blown up in France, among them Andrew Ramsay, whose death, mercifully, was instantaneous]" [133])—thus preserving the discrete nature of masque and antimasque realms.[28]

Because Mrs. McNab is a part of the antimasque world, she does not in herself possess the power or authority to overcome the disorder the antimasque represents. (Woolf's narrator acknowledges this limitation: "What power could now prevent the fertility, the insensibility of nature? Mrs. McNab's dream of a lady, of a child, of a plate of milk soup?" [138]). If Time is indeed out of joint, it is left to the artist, Lily Briscoe, to set it right. Above I have suggested that in Browne's masque it is Circe, more than the Woodsman, who chases the antimasque from the stage—who reestablishes order through her orderly *apologia;* I have also suggested that Lily is the prime correspondent for Circe in the last book of Woolf's novel. It follows, then, that Lily's act of painting corresponds to Circe's artful rhetoric as an ordering device. At the beginning of the third book, Lily is struggling to establish some sense of order, to make sense of the blooming buzzing confusion of the postwar, post–Mrs. Ramsay world:

> What does it mean then, what can it all mean? Lily Briscoe
> asked herself. . . . What does it mean?—a catchword that was,
> caught up from some book, fitting her thought loosely, for she
> could not, this first morning with the Ramsays, contract her feel-
> ings, could only make a phrase resound to cover the blankness of
> her mind until these vapours had shrunk. For really, what did she
> feel, come back after all these years and Mrs. Ramsay dead? Noth-
> ing, nothing—nothing that she could express at all. (145)

The remainder of Woolf's third book, I would argue, is a record of Lily's attempt to overcome this initial impotence and paralysis, to use her art to dispel the chaos that Time has wrought (in "Time Passes"), and to reestablish—perhaps one should say resurrect, bring back from the dead—order. If a masque generally ends with revels—an orderly set of dances in which all present, including spectators, are involved—so Woolf's novel ends with a sort of general dance, all the characters (and perhaps even the reader?) moving together toward the same end, which is universal love. Recall John Ferguson's characterization of Woolf's penultimate paragraph, where the enigmatic Mr. Carmichael joins Lily on the lawn: "One feels, reading this passage, as the mortals in Greek myth or in the Bible must have felt when the unknown visitor suddenly dropped his masque and blazed before them—a god or an angel."[29] Ferguson's comparison is perhaps revealing of Woolf's reliance upon the masque form, for it is in the closing revels, quite often, that the masks worn by the performers are discarded—a signal of transition from spectacle to ritual, from exclusion to inclusion.

What I have attempted to establish is that Woolf, in making up *To the Lighthouse,* was drawing upon not simply a fragment of Browne's masque (as Fox's reading suggests) but the whole of it. Given that there is none of the usual evidence that Woolf read the masque in its entirety (no mention of it in reading notebooks, in letters or diaries), one would be justified in questioning whether that reading ever actually took place, especially considering the relative obscurity of the work in question. The fact is, however, that Browne's masque was more readily available to Woolf than it is to most readers today: two editions were published in London in the nineteenth century.[30] Woolf's good friend Lytton Strachey, a Renaissance scholar, undoubtedly knew the masque and may well have recommended it to her. Furthermore, as Fox notes, Woolf was not afraid "of lesser known [Renaissance] figures and works."[31] The obscurity of Browne's masque, in fact, may have appealed to her, allowed her to congratulate herself on being among the small and exclusive company of *Circe* readers.[32]

Which company contained as well a poet far less obscure than Browne: John Milton. I mentioned above that scholars have suggested that Milton's *Comus* owes something to Browne's *Circe;*[33] I made reference as well to Beverly Ann Schlack's reading of Woolf's first novel, *The Voyage Out*—in which novel, Schlack demonstrates, Woolf has incorporated a set of allusions to *Comus.* One might suggest the possibility, therefore, that Woolf approached Browne's masque *through* Milton's masque—in other words read Browne's masque as hypotext to Milton's hypertext. Given Woolf's interest in intertextual relationships, her conviction that "books continue each other, in spite of our habit of judging them separately," this conclusion appears to me not at all unlikely.[34]

That one could read Milton's *Comus* as a *reaction against and revision of* Browne's *Circe* is something that, as far as I have been able to ascertain, no scholar has yet suggested. Yet the heroine of Milton's masque is, after all, Chastity, whereas the heroine of Browne's masque is Charity, or more exactly sexual charity—the song of the sirens is described in Browne's stage directions as "beinge as lascivious proper to them" (7), and Circe's self-sworn task is to transform, not men into beasts, but "lillyes" into "roses." Milton's Lady, a "virgin pure," is heroic precisely to the degree that she struggles to and succeeds in keeping her lily from being so transformed. Whereas the closing revels of Browne's masque celebrate sexual union, the closing dance of Milton's masque celebrates virginity—the dancers exhorted "*To triumph in victorious dance / O'er sensual Folly and Intemperance.*"[35] If one reads Milton's masque as a reaction to Browne's, Browne himself emerges as a possible model for the character Comus (who is, interestingly enough, the offspring of Circe, as Milton is careful to note).[36] Recall the valedictory song of Browne's masque, in which Circe's world is depicted as a paradise "where delight / Might well allure / A very Stoicke from this night / To turne an Epicure." Milton's Comus, in attempting to seduce the "virgin pure," cries out: "O foolishnes of men! that lend their ears / To those budge doctors of the *Stoic* Fur, / And fetch their precepts from the *Cynic* Tub, / Praising the lean and sallow Abstinence."[37] Milton's masque, then, can be construed as a Puritan reaction against Browne's Epicureanism, as well as a backslap for Browne's banishment of the Puritanical boars/boors of the antimasque ("O let there be no staye / In his waye, / To hinder Boare from his kinde").

That Woolf was acutely aware of Milton's exhortation to chastity in *Comus* is evident from her allusive use of that masque in *The Voyage Out*. Rachel Vinrace is faced with a decision: should she surrender herself to Terence Hewet—allow him to make her lily blush, as it were—or reject his offer of marriage? Schlack rightly asserts that "*Comus* is an allusive restatement of Rachel's dilemma: marriage to Hewet would put her virtue in jeopardy."[38] Rachel remains true to her hypotextual model, Milton's chaste Lady, even unto death. She dies a virgin.

In *To the Lighthouse* Lily Briscoe may be seen as an avatar of both Milton's Lady and Rachel Vinrace in that she is also a "virgin pure" to the end. The difference, of course, is the end: not death for Lily but "vision." And part of the substance of Lily's vision, I would argue, is the insight that lilies and roses need not be mutually exclusive, that we can and should accept both virginity and chastity as legitimate life choices. In her reading reverie of "The Window" Mrs. Ramsay imagines herself at first ascending through red flowers and then through white flowers ("she only knew this is white, or this is red"); this distinction, however, quickly breaks down: "she read and turned the page, swinging herself, zigzagging this way and that, from one line to another as from . . . *one red and white flower* to another" (119, emphasis added). In Charles Tansley's pastoral-elegiac vision of Mrs. Ramsay, she appears decked "with cyclamen and wild violets" (14)—the flower of the cyclamen being red or white or red *and w*hite. This fusion of colors suggests a momentary coming together of separate visions and perhaps otherwise antagonistic personalities, as in the dinner scene ("Augustus too feasted his eyes. . . . That was his way of looking, different from hers. But looking together united them"). So in her allusive technique Woolf brings together the antagonistic vision of Milton (the white lily) and Browne (the red rose), establishes harmony between them, unites them in her own artistic envisioning. Her textual practice, like her ethical belief, can be summed up in the unofficial Bloomsbury motto (coined by Forster): "only connect."

The metaphor of harmony, important to Woolf, is especially prominent in her description of intertextual relations. "I am reading six books at once," she wrote to a friend, "the only way of reading: since, as you will agree, one book is only a single unaccompanied note, and to get the full sound, one needs ten others at the same time."[39] What is true of Woolf's reading is also true of her writing. She needed to bring in the others, the literary precursors, to get the full sound. Browne it was particularly important to bring in, primarily because, I argue, of his humane (protofeminist?) rehabilitation of the figure of Circe. That was a crucial note indeed. Browne, Woolf surely felt, despite his distance from her in time, would have understood both Mrs. Ramsay and Lily, would have appreciated both the red of the rose and the white of the lily. He would have known it was only a matter of connecting the two, of bringing them into harmony. Then all dance.

⌒ Notes

1. Beverly Ann Schlack, *Continuing Presences: Virginia Woolf's Use of Literary Allusion* (University Park: Pennsylvania State University Press, 1979), 27. (For another consideration of Woolf's response to Milton, see Lisa Low, "'Listen and save': Woolf's Allusion to *Comus* in Her Revolutionary First Novel," chap. 5 of this volume.—*Ed.*)

2. Avrom Fleishman, "Virginia Woolf: Tradition and Modernity" in *Forms of Modern British Fiction*, edited by Alan Warren Friedman (Austin: University of Texas Press, 1975), 134.

3. F. J. Finkelpearl, cited in Wilfred R. Prest, *The Inns of Court under Elizabeth I and the Early Stuarts: 1590-1640* (Totowa, N.J.: Rowman and Littlefield, 1972), 155.

4. Ibid., 156.

5. *Dictionary of National Biography*, ed. Leslie Stephen and Sidney Lee, vol. 3 (Oxford: Oxford University Press, 1921-22), s.v. "Browne, William," at 75.

6. Gwyn Jones, "William Browne and the English Masque," in William Browne, *Circe and Ulysses: The Inner Temple Masque*, edited by Gwyn Jones ([London]: Golden Cockerel Press, 1954), 39-61, 57.

7. Cited in Stephen Orgel, *The Jonsonian Masque* (Cambridge, Mass.: Harvard University Press, 1965), 3.

8. Cited in Jones, in Browne, 59.

9. *Dictionary of National Biography*, 73-74. Some question exists as to whether Browne's masque was ever performed. A. Wigfall Green, in his 1931 study *The Inns of Court and Early English Drama* (1931; reprint, New York: Benjamin Blom, 1965), comments that "[t]his masque, one of the most poetic in the language, was so popular that guests climbed on the outer window sills to get glimpses of the entertainment" (116). The author of the entry on Browne in the *DNB*, however, reasons that "[a]s the books of the Inner Temple contain no mention of any expenses incurred by the performance, it is probable that the arrangements for the representation of the masque were at the last moment countermanded" (73).

10. Browne, *Circe and Ulysses*, edited by Gwyn Jones ([London]: Golden Cockerel Press, 1954), 4. Subsequent references included parenthetically in the text are to this edition.

11. Michael Grant and John Hazed, *Gods and Mortals in Classical Mythology* (Springfield, Mass.: G. and C. Merriam, 1973), 408.

12. Homer, *The Odyssey*, translated by Robert Fitzgerald (Garden City, N.Y.: Doubleday, 1963), 173. Subsequent references included parenthetically in the text are to this edition.

13. Virginia Woolf, *To the Lighthouse* (1927; reprint, with a foreword by Eudora Welty, New York: Harcourt Brace Jovanovich [Harvest], 1989), 119. Subsequent parenthetical references in the text are to this edition.

14. Alice Fox, *Virginia Woolf and the Literature of the English Renaissance* (Oxford: Clarendon Press, 1990), 45.

15. Ibid. Woolf's citation of Browne has also been noted by Avrom Fleishman (in *Virginia Woolf: A Critical Reading* [Baltimore: Johns Hopkins University Press, 1975], 106) and by Jean M. Wyatt (in "The Celebration of Eros: Greek Concepts of Love and Beauty in *To the Lighthouse*," *Philosophy and Literature* 2 [1978]: 164), although neither gives it more than a passing exegetical glance.

16. J. Hillis Miller, "Mr. Carmichael and Lily Briscoe: The Rhythm of Creativity in *To the Lighthouse*," in *Modernism Reconsidered*, edited by Robert Kiely (Cambridge, Mass.: Harvard University Press, 1983), 171.

17. John Ferguson, "A Sea Change: Thomas De Quincey and Mr. Carmichael in *To the Lighthouse*," *Journal of Modern Literature* 14 (1987): 45–63; Ellen Tremper, "'The Earth of Our Earliest Life': Mr. Carmichael in *To the Lighthouse*," *Journal of Modern Literature* 19 (1994): 163–71.

18. Grant and Hazed, 408.

19. J. Ferguson, 46.

20. Grant and Hazed, 408. Anne Hoffman has argued, without naming a possible hypotext, that Mr. Carmichael is an allusive shadow of Poseidon, "tamer of waves, and as such [is] the appropriate figure to preside over a novel which tackles the waters." "Demeter and Poseidon: Fusion and Distance in *To the Lighthouse*," *Studies in the Novel* 16 (1984): 184. I think it altogether probable that there are aspects of Poseidon in Mr. Carmichael and Demeter in Mrs. Ramsay, given that, once again, Woolf's characters—particularly Mrs. Ramsay—are invariably overdetermined in respect to sources.

21. J. Ferguson, 58.

22. Grant and Hazed, 408.

23. Woolf's text is again overdetermined: in naming these characters she also undoubtedly had in mind Shakespeare's sonnet 98, "From you have I been absent in the spring," cited in "The Window" (181), which contains the same contrasting metaphors: "Nor did I wonder at the lily's white, / Nor praise the deep vermilion in the rose." Not only does Woolf's text echo earlier texts, but, in addition, her many hypotexts speak to and echo each other.

24. William Shakespeare, *The Tempest*, in *The Norton Shakespeare*, edited by Stephen Greenblatt, Walter Cohen, Jean E. Howard, and Katharine Eisaman Maus (New York: Norton, 1997), 1.2.400–406.

25. Woolf, *The Diary of Virginia Woolf*, edited by Anne Olivier Bell and Andrew McNeillie, 5 vols. (New York: Harcourt Brace Jovanovich, 1977–84), 3:34 (27 June 1925).

26. Orgel, 72–73, 80, 93.

27. Ibid., 6–7.

28. Jerzy Limon, in his *Masque of Stuart Culture* (Toronto: Associated University

Presses, 1990), has commented on this absolute separation of realms in respect to character interaction: "[T]he antimasque characters cannot really communicate with the characters of the masque proper: they are usually scared or chased away by the appearance of the latter, and consequently the chaos or the evil of the antimasque is brought to order or otherwise neutralized."

29. J. Ferguson, 58.

30. See the second volume of William Carew Hazlitt, ed., *The Whole Works of William Browne, of Tavistock, and of the Inner Temple* (London: Whittingham and Wilkins, 1868–69); and Arthur Henry Bullen, ed., *The Poems of William Browne of Tavistock* (London: Lawrence and Bullen; New York: Scribner, 1894).

31. Fox, *Virginia Woolf*, 19.

32. An even better example of Woolf's allusion to obscure texts: the recitation in "The Window" of Charles Elton's lyric "Luriana Lurile," which was first published in its entirety in 1945. Elizabeth Boyd, "Luriana Lurilee," *Notes and Queries* (1963): 380. At the time *To the Lighthouse* appeared, only a handful of people had ever heard the poem recited.

33. Whether Browne's masque did indeed influence Milton in the composition of *Comus* is also a point of contention. Green observes that "*Ulysses and Circe* [sic] has so many attributes in common with *Comus* that it seems to have inspired Milton. Its influence upon other masques of the seventeenth century was unquestionably considerable" (116–17). The author of the Browne entry in the *DNB,* however, chides another commentator for suggesting this connection "with little show of plausibility" (73).

34. Woolf, *A Room of One's Own* (1929; reprint, with a foreword by Mary Gordon, New York: Harcourt Brace Jovanovich [Harvest], 1989), 80.

35. John Milton, "A Mask Presented at Ludlow Castle, 1634"*(Comus),* in *John Milton: Complete Poems and Major Prose,* edited by Merritt Y. Hughes, (Upper Saddle River, N.J.: Prentice Hall, 1957), lines 974–75.

36. Ibid., line 153.

37. Ibid., lines 706–9.

38. Schlack, 21.

39. Woolf to Saxon Sidney-Turner, 12 August 1928, *The Letters of Virginia Woolf,* edited by Nigel Nicolson and Joanne Trautmann, 6 vols. (New York: Harcourt Brace Jovanovich, 1975–80), 3:516.

8

Laura at the Crossroads

A Room of One's Own *and the Elizabethan Sonnet*

 Rebecca Laroche

*W*hy discuss the Elizabethan sonnet along with *A Room of One's Own?* Such a form would seem to represent everything that work—Virginia Woolf's genre-defying series of feminist meditations—is not. In other works, as Alice Fox has shown, Woolf does explicitly engage with the Elizabethan love sonnet. In *Night and Day,* for example, William Rodney recites Philip Sidney's "With how sad steps, O Moon! Thou climb'st the skies!" while walking with Katharine by the Thames. Fox also cites Woolf's "slight mockery" of Orlando's sonnets to Clorinda and company as "registering a modern reaction to the outdated conventions of the Elizabethan love sonnet." Fox goes on to refer to sonnets in *To the Lighthouse, Mrs. Dalloway, Between the Acts,* and *The Waves,* almost every major work in Woolf's corpus. But nowhere does she refer to *A Room of One's Own* and the Elizabethan sonnet in one sentence.[1]

And this omission is in some ways logical. *A Room of One's Own* (1929), in fact, presents an overtly anti-Petrarchan position, one that undoes decorous convention and defies formal strictures as well as challenges objectifying gender binaries. Indeed, given what Rachel Bowlby describes in her consideration of this work as Woolf's "disturbance of conventional generic boundaries" with regard to the realist novel and the essay, we can see her lyrical prose as disrupting poetic convention as well.[2] But as we will see, Woolf's work engages with both Petrarchan and anti-Petrarchan poetics, or what Heather Dubrow calls Petrarchism and its "counterdiscourses," the latter of which exist throughout Renaissance love poetry because of the prevalence of the former.[3] That is, Woolf does not invoke the conventions of the Elizabethan sonnet only to dismiss them and keep them at the margins. The sonnet is too dominant a presence in early twentieth-century letters for her to accomplish its marginalization merely through virtual neglect, though such would be a telling neglect.

Building upon Ilona Bell's contention that love poetry of the English Renaissance "cannot be a-Petrarchan,"[4] I argue that works on literary history— particularly those touching on the English Renaissance—of which *A Room of One's Own* is certainly an example, cannot wholly omit a discussion of the sonnet and its conventions. The love sonnet is there, in the poetry and criticism she mentions and in the metaphors she uses; it is just that, as late twentieth-century readers, we have to look closely to find it. Woolf faces the sonnet practice, in all its abstraction of women, and seeks to undo it by giving body and voice to women in her own text. She does so by reading the tradition differently. Along with articulating the restrictive practices of a tradition, she sets out upon a further feminist task: to find, as such critics as Dubrow, Bell, and Barbara Estrin have more recently found, "the self-conscious woman" in "male-authored texts."[5] By occupying, inverting, and subverting the sonnet tradition, *A Room of One's Own* opens literary history to new and female voices.

∽ Chained Up, Locked Out: Interrogating the Sonnet

After twenty years of research projects and anthologies concentrating on women writers in the Renaissance (many of which respond to Woolf's *Room*), we know that women in Italy, France, and England participated in the sonnet tradition. But at the time *A Room of One's Own* was written, the principal sonnet scholarship was that of Sidney Lee. Lee's anthology *Elizabethan Sonnets* was first published as part of the English Garner series (1877–90), a set of books that Woolf often consulted. His *Life of William Shakespeare* (1898), which includes an extensive discussion of the sonnet "vogue," Woolf mentions in *A Room of One's Own* and elsewhere.[6] Lee, who would assist Leslie Stephen with the *Dictionary of National Biography* and inherit the task from him, established "the supremacy of Petrarch."[7] His work channels most every sonnet sequence into a very specific line that runs from Italian to French models, to Wyatt and to Drayton, a line that has come to be known as the "sonnet tradition."

Let us dwell for a moment on Lee's assessment of this tradition in *A Life of William Shakespeare,* since that is the work Woolf engages directly in *A Room of One's Own.* The first work he cites in an appendix entitled "The Vogue of the Elizabethan Sonnet" is Tottel's *Songes and Sonnetes* of 1557. With Thomas Wyatt and the Earl of Surrey, Lee begins his litany: Thomas Watson, Philip Sidney, Samuel Daniel, Henry Constable, Bartholomew Griffin, Barnabe Barnes, Giles Fletcher, Thomas Lodge, Michael Drayton, William Percy, Richard Barnfield, Edmund Spenser, a certain "E. C., Esq.," John Davies, Richard Linche, Thomas Campion, William Smith, Robert Tofte, William Alexander, Fulke Greville, William Drummond, John Davies of Hereford, and William Browne.[8] Lee intersperses among these names those of French and Italian influences (none female) and those of English writers of individual sonnets (again, all male). Only in the short "bibliographical note on the sonnet in France 1550–1600" do we find the names of women: Louise Labé, Les Dames des Roches, Anne de Marquets, all authors of "minor collections," according to Lee.[9] But during the age of Elizabeth, "when every other man, it seemed, was capable of song or sonnet," there is not a woman to be found. According to Lee, the sonnet vogue had died by 1610, before Mary Wroth, the first Englishwoman to publish an extended love sequence, had even lifted her pen. In the English sonnet tradition, therefore, it *seems* that "no woman wrote a word."[10]

We can see how Woolf's perception of Renaissance women as silent and restricted was to develop. We can also see the influence of this perception as it appears in 1980s feminist criticism of the sonnet. Of this silence Nancy Vickers writes, challenging lyric assumptions (at the same time alluding to Woolf): "bodies fetishized by a poetic voice logically do not have a voice of their own."[11] The active and verbose lover-poet sees his verse as an attempt to overcome the barrier separating his beloved from him, be that barrier the fortress of Christian chastity, the barricades of a jealous husband, or, as in the later poems of the forebear of the tradition—Petrarch—the insurmountable death of the beloved. If the lover cannot literally overcome these barriers, he momentarily and imaginatively conquers them through fantasy and memory. The origins of feminist perceptions of the sonnet tradition, including Woolf's, are easy to trace.

In *A Room of One's Own,* which reads literary history for silenced female voices, I perceive a composite figure made up of the female beloved, the woman writer, and the female scholar. Woolf's narrator engages with the position of the female beloved in the sonnet paradigm in order to show how that paradigm is representative of a larger literary history. The way the sonnet comes to represent this history in Woolf's work may be examined through the analogy she makes between the woman writer, who is restricted by censorious voices, and the female scholar, who is not allowed free rein in research, both of whom she aligns with the female beloved confined by the objectifying conventions of the Elizabethan love sonnet. In establishing this identification, the critic Woolf is able to examine literary history from within it—and in turn she begins to reread that history.

In order to illuminate the narrative that I see uniting the woman scholar, the writer, and the beloved, I will work backward from one of *A Room of One's Own*'s most wonderfully copious (in the Renaissance sense of "generative") and infinitely slippery passages. The passage in question combines the trials of the woman writer and the female scholar while alluding not to a sonnet, but to a Renaissance work that comments upon the sonnet tradition: Milton's *Comus*.

Toward the end of chapter 4, Woolf in effect fuses the three female voices by having a voice of the recent past, using words from the distant past, speak as if for the present. At this point in the essay, her narrator discusses the "discouragement and criticism" (76) directed against women writers and artists of the eighteenth and nineteenth centuries. After describing the trials and triumphs of Jane Austen and Emily Brontë, the narrator interjects,

> One must have been something of a firebrand to say to oneself, Oh, but they can't buy literature too. Literature is open to everybody. I refuse to allow you, Beadle though you are, to turn me off the grass. Lock up your libraries if you like; but there is no gate, no lock, no bolt that you can set upon the freedom of my mind. (75-76)

This voice of one who "must have been" does not defy her own critics, however. Instead, in the mind the narrator imagines for her, this "firebrand" addresses a stand-in, the beadle, who had earlier turned the narrator off the grass and locked up the university gates (6, 13). Her protest also refers to a moment in the first chapter when another "kindly gentleman" (8) had not allowed the narrator to enter one of the "famous" libraries to see the manuscript of Milton's "Lycidas." In a kind of metaphysical conundrum, the forbidding beadle, the "kindly gentleman," and the censorious critic become one in the mind that is at once the narrator's and the woman writer's. The projection into the recent past of a voice that speaks about the present elides the distinction between the pre-twentieth-century woman writer and the contemporary female scholar.

This fusion intensifies as female literary critic united with woman writer joins voices with the female beloved, a voice that surfaces through the allusion to *Comus*. In the passage above, the phrasing "freedom of my mind" and the predicament of imprisonment call up the moment when Milton's Lady, who has been confined to a chair through a spell, defies the magician Comus's power over her:[12]

Comus.   Your nerves are all chain'd up in Alabaster,
             And you a statue; or as *Daphne* was,
             Root-bound, that fled *Apollo*.

Lady.   Fool, do not boast,
             Thou canst not touch the freedom of my mind
             With all thy charms, although this corporal rind
             Thou hast immancl'd.[13]

Sally Greene discusses the "sense of empowerment" garnered from Milton's words here. Of course, as Greene recognizes, this empowerment is tentative and complicated, as is Woolf's larger relationship to Milton, a subject taken up by Lisa Low earlier in this volume and elsewhere.[14] But here I am more interested in how Woolf uses Milton's words to create a set of analogies linking the beloved, the writer, and the scholar.

The Lady endures a physical restriction that is importantly linked to lyric poetry, specifically to the objectification of the beloved. First, by making the

Lady a type of "root-bound" Daphne transformed into a laurel tree, Comus turns her into his muse and himself into a type of the poet Apollo, an import-ant mythical paradigm for the sonneteer, particularly Petrarch himself, who praises his Laura as a laurel tree. For example, in poem 263, Petrarch cries, "Arbor vittoriosa triunfale, / onor d'imperadori et di poeti: / quanti m'ài fatto dì dogliosi et lieti / in questa breve mia vita mortale!" [Victorious triumphal tree, the honor of emperors and of poets, how many days you have made sorrowful and glad for me in this brief mortal life].[15] The next stanza begins "Vera Donna [true lady]," blurring the distinction between tree and beloved. The Elizabethans pick up this mythology for themselves, as when Edmund Spenser writes in his *Amoretti,*

> Proud Daphne, scorning Phoebus' lovely fire,
> On the Thessalian shore from him did fly:
> For which the gods, in their revengeful ire,
> Did her transform into a laurel-tree.
>   Then fly no more, fair Love, from Phoebus' chase,
>   But in your breast his leaf and love embrace.[16]

Then in having Comus say that the Lady is "chain'd up in Alabaster" and call her a "statue," Milton draws not only on the Pygmalion myth (finding another type for the artist obsessed with a female object) and other Ovidian myths that figure individuals turning to stone or beloveds who are "like stat-ues," but also on Petrarchan convention, which consistently compares the beloved's skin to alabaster or other smooth stone.[17] Sidney's Astrophil com-pares "Stella's face" to a "front . . . of alabaster pure"; Daniel, after likening himself to Pygmalion, speaks of his beloved's "marble breast"; Linche describes the "alabaster" neck of his Diella.[18] Woolf demonstrates an awareness of this convention, as well as the other clichés of sonnet-writing, in her 1932 essay on Donne: "That great ideal, built up by a score of eloquent pens, still burns bright in our eyes. Her body was of alabaster, her legs of ivory; her hair was golden wire and her teeth pearls from the Orient."[19]

In using Petrarchan counterdiscourses found in Milton's masque, Woolf gives women writers and scholars a path of resistance. Similar to Milton's Lady, who is successful in overcoming her "immancl'd" body, Woolf's speaker, whether she is the imagined woman writer or the fictionalized woman scholar, denies the existence of any "bolts" upon her mind and thus overcomes material restrictions, the economic confinement of not having five hundred pounds and a room of one's own. Woolf gives background to these restrictions when, earlier in *A Room of One's Own*, she exposes the conditions surrounding Petrarchan objectification. The narrator quotes a fragment from G. M. Trevelyan's history that describes how "the daughter who refused to marry the gentleman of her parent's choice" in the Renaissance was "liable to be locked up, beaten and flung about the room" (42) and thus finds a literalization of the metaphoric confinement, of being "chain'd up in Alabaster," found in poetic convention. The later allusion to *Comus*, which dramatizes the terms of Petrarchan logic, takes the next step of exposing the likeness of restrictions placed upon the Petrarchan lady, the female writer, and the female scholar.

Implicit in the nexus of confined beloved, discouraged writer, and thwarted scholar, therefore, is an analogy between Woman as object of poetry and Woman as object of scholarship. This analogy occurs structurally in Woolf's *Room* in the similarities between its second and third chapters. In the second chapter, the narrator experiences the effect of an ossified scholarly tradition in the British Museum (a figure Anne E. Fernald elucidates elsewhere in this volume).[20] There she confronts an unfathomable number of books "written about women in the course of one year" (26). These books, covering topics ranging from Woman, the "[w]eaker muscles of" to Woman, "Shakespeare's opinions of," are written by men (28–29). With all of this compiled "evidence," Virginia Woolf's W. (her abbreviation for Woman) becomes as elusive as Shakespeare's W. H. Her narrative persona can no more know the essence of Woman than describe the mind of Petrarch's Laura, Drayton's Idea, or Daniel's Ideal.

What Rachel Bowlby writes of the experience in the second chapter can also be said of the third: "It is as if there is a continuous and never completed effort on the part of man to keep woman in the place assigned to her by him: outside the precincts of representational power, defined, bounded, in a proliferation of heterogeneous characteristics."[21] Indeed, the third chapter gives evidence of the "continuity" of this "effort." When Woolf's persona begins this chapter describing how Woman, although "all but absent from history," "pervades poetry from cover to cover" (43), she finally makes explicit a connection between scholarship and poetry on women. The "proliferation" (to use Bowlby's word) of sonnet sequences during the reign of Elizabeth, when "every other man, it seemed, was capable of song or sonnet," taken together with the mountain of studies claiming to know something about Woman in Woolf's British Museum, registers the perceived realities: that women are "pervasive" in history only as its objects, are "all but absent" as active participants.

Although this analogy of the female beloved and the female scholar and writer identifies the way Woolf's text conveys a certain "bound"-ness experienced by women, it does not wholly illuminate her depiction of the female scholar/writer's "outside"-ness—a subject to which I now turn. Though her narrator identifies with the Renaissance daughter, who is "locked up, beaten and flung about the room," and with Milton's Lady, who is "immancl'd" by the poet's representational powers, the narrator's condition is one of being not "locked up" but rather *locked out*. Not simply imprisoned by the male scholar within the confines of his definitions of her, she is also deprived of any say in her self-definition. Woolf articulates this exclusion as early as *Jacob's Room* (1922), in which a drunken woman cries "Let me in!" at the doors of the impassive British Museum and thus tries to make her way into her own construction, frustrated, as Fernald so eloquently puts it, by "the unseeing brain of the great cultural mind."[22] *A Room of One's Own* goes on to illuminate the slippage between inside and outside, desired and desirer, from the perspective of one who is both within and without. The positioning of the allusion to Milton, therefore, destabilizes the very analogy between female beloved and female scholar/writer that it implies. Aligning someone who is locked out with the Petrarchan beloved, who is usually "chain'd up in alabaster," undoes the binary correspondences between lover and beloved, outside and inside, male and female, central to the sonnet tradition.

In the opening moments of *A Room of One's Own*, we find that frustrated access, a conventional dilemma of the Petarchan lover desiring to consummate his love, is transferred onto a woman. The Oxbridge beadle does not allow the unescorted visitor into the "famous library" to see manuscripts of Milton's "Lycidas." This library "where the treasure is kept" (7) is enclosed by "[g]ate after gate," where "innumerable keys" fit into "well-oiled locks" (13). Woolf's description of the library "with all its treasures safe locked within its breast" (8), moreover, brilliantly emphasizes the library sanctum's affiliation with its contents. As a consequence, the male scholar's proximity to these manuscripts, in his own mind, implies a chaste relation to the poet. He claims virtually to inhabit the poet's mind, whereas he designates the female scholar, in her attempt to cross the library threshold, a threat to the purity of that space.

And that space comes to represent the exclusive, constructed space of literary history itself. In Woolf's depiction of the library, the enclosed "beloved" is pointedly a male poet, the library simply a facade for a "homosocially desirous" literary scholarship and the history it encloses.[23] The male-centered world of literary study excludes the female reader: it is like a fortress. Three times removed from the poet Edward King, who is honored by Milton in "Lycidas," whose manuscript is studied and described by Lamb and in turn harbored in the library regulated by the "kindly gentleman," Woolf's persona cannot get near the poetic center of literary history. Indeed, her proposed entrance challenges the core of this enclosed economy.

∾ A "lack of tradition": An Alternative Beloved

But Woolf does not have her narrator storm the library walls or give in to her restriction. Rather she takes her cue from the "counterdiscourses" found in and around the sonnet tradition and attempts to find an alternative. In the overt discourse of Petrarchism, many sonneteers, beginning with Petrarch (who writes from the death of his Laura), write an ideal beloved out of the "actual" beloved's absence. We can see examples of this practice in writers as diverse as Lodge, who tells his Phillis, "thy want doth wound me"; Griffin, who claims "Thus absent, presence; present, absence maketh"; and Shakespeare, who in sonnet 61 is kept awake by the "image" of his absent beloved. All conjure up the image of their beloveds despite their absences.[24] For the most part (Shakespeare's of course being the exception), these moments of absence and idealized imaginings contribute to the perception of Petrarchism's objectifying stance.

One of the sonneteers for whom this absence is most generative and conflicted, however, is Philip Sidney, and through an analysis of his sonnet 88 I hope to outline the strategy that allows Woolf to construct her alternative. In this poem, Stella (as in many other poems) is absent from court, and Astrophil finds himself tempted by the "brave array" and sexual promises of another court woman.

> Out! TRAITOR ABSENCE! Darest thou counsel me
>   From my dear Captainess to run away?
>   Because, in brave array, here marcheth she
> That to win me, oft shows a present pay.
>   Is faith so weak, or is such force in thee?
> When sun is hid, can stars such beams display?
> Cannot heaven's food, once felt, keep stomachs free
> From base desire, on earthly cates to prey?

Then in the sestet, Astrophil performs the typical Petrarchan maneuver of turning to "inward sight" and finds there his ideal, Stella:

> Tush! ABSENCE! while thy mists eclipse that light,
> My orphan sense flies to the inward sight;
> Where memory sets forth the beams of love.
>   That where before heart loved and eyes did see;
> In heart both sight and love both coupled be.
> United powers make each the stronger prove.[25]

But because of the *presence* of the other woman, the reader (like Astrophil) cannot wholly believe in the ideal, abstracted vision of the sestet. In the presence of his "base desire" and of the actual Renaissance woman, there exists the potential for dismantling that "typical figure of Elizabethan love poetry," as Woolf articulates it in her essay on Donne, that "great ideal" of alabaster and gold wire.[26]

Through the alternative presented by Donne, in fact, many feminist critics, beginning with Woolf, start to question the Elizabethan lyric tradition.[27] Barbara Estrin, for example, complicates the debate between those critics who see Donne's poetry as misogynistic and those who believe it to be protofeminist. Much as Woolf sees Milton's Lady's willful defiance as a means of resistance, Estrin finds a counterdiscourse in Donne's "The Dreame," in which the poet has an erotic vision of his beloved only to wake and find the woman at his side: "If, like most Petrarchan women, she is the 'god of his idolatry,' the image of perfection he worships," Estrin writes, "in this poem she is both a statue that moves and the Pygmalion that wills the movement." Not exactly protofeminist, these moments that invoke a Petrarchan paradigm at the same time that they resist that paradigm provide a means of escaping its restrictions. In "The Dreame," Estrin goes on to write, "the woman emerges poet and poem."[28] Through this kind of imagining of a woman who is present, who is physical and willful, Woolf finds the model for her biography of Judith Shakespeare.

And with Judith Shakespeare, Woolf makes up for what is lacking in literary history. She ends the first chapter of *A Room of One's Own* thinking of "the effect of tradition and of the lack of tradition upon the mind of a writer" (24). Something besides a shadowing presence in Woolf's essay, "tradition" is also an absence, an absence that is a condition for a different kind of presence. Both suggesting and countering the withdrawal of the chaste beloved that leads the Renaissance poet to inventive fantasy and memory, the historical lack of a woman of Shakespeare's influence—and the consequent shortage of a female tradition—brings Woolf to speculative flights, to what Rachel Bowlby calls "an openness to kinds of thinking ruled out by pedantic discipline."[29] The name of these speculative flights is Judith Shakespeare. Through these flights, through the freedom of her mind, Woolf's narrator is able to overcome the barriers that a "lack of tradition" presents, just as Judith Shakespeare herself defies objectifying social conventions.

Woolf imagines a mind "adventurous," "imaginative," thwarted, and, as a result, filled with "heat and violence" (47, 48). Unable to express herself through the venues of publication that men enjoy, she cries out in another way: she kills herself. This is not the beloved, although she is beloved. She is not the "typical figure of Elizabethan love poetry" described in Woolf's essay on Donne, whose "emotions were simple, as befitted her person." She is more akin to the alternative Woolf sees Donne presenting: "She was brown but she was also fair; she was solitary but also sociable; she was rustic yet also fond of city life; she was sceptical yet devout, emotional but reserved—in short she was as various and complex as Donne himself."[30] Judith Shakespeare exists as an anti-Petrarchan beloved, who, like Milton's Lady, defies her imprisonment. Like Trevelyan's Renaissance woman, she is "locked up" and "beaten" because "[s]he cried out that marriage was hateful to her" (49). She opposes an enforced chastity and confinement when she "let[s] herself down by a rope" from this locked room. But while she can get out by the window, she still cannot get in by the stage door. Ridiculed and rejected, in her death she comes to represent all women who face overwhelming obstacles. But through the perpetuation of her memory, Judith Shakespeare can live in all stages of literary history, filling in for its absences and offering the hope that, in future generations, restrictions of gender may be overcome.

But Shakespeare's sister does not literally exist. We are told that we will not find her in the pages of Sidney Lee's *A Life of William Shakespeare,* and here we come full circle. In a literary history of lack, literary biography necessarily differs from that which had come into fashion by the end of the nineteenth century. Lee's *Life* dutifully reproduces the physical "remains," the signatures and portraits, of Shakespeare. Yet Woolf mentions Lee's work in the final paragraph of her *Room* not for its thoroughness, but for the kind of life it does not include: "I told you in the course of this paper that Shakespeare had a sister; but do not look for her in Sir Sidney Lee's life of the poet. She died young—alas, she never wrote a word" (113). One of the few scholarly works Woolf specifically names in her essay, Lee's biography serves as the sort of book that, by definition, *A Room of One's Own* cannot be. Whereas Virginia Woolf's stance requires the speculative, Lee's *Life* is all manuscripts and solidity, a solidity Woolf describes in her essay on "the new biography" as "granite-like."[31] As he describes his project, his "exhaustive and well-arranged statement of the facts of Shakespeare's career" aims to "reduce conjecture to the smallest dimensions consistent with coherence."[32] In "reducing conjecture," Lee also proposes to put an end to certain critical debates—including the W. H. controversy—and to curtail the search for the beloved young man and the vexing dark woman. Lee means to accomplish this final blow to an endless debate by "exhaustively" studying the Renaissance sonnet and defining the tradition. His purpose in including two chapters and, as we have noted, an appendix on the sonnet tradition was to contextualize Shakespeare's sonnets in literary history and thus to refute any notion that they may be autobiographical, that they may communicate an episode in Shakespeare's life. Lee fixes on what is present rather than what is absent.

Shakespeare's biography is ground oft-trodden and overextended. Earlier in *A Room of One's Own,* Woolf quite humorously summarizes Shakespeare's life:

> Shakespeare himself went, very probably—his mother was an heiress—to the grammar school, where he may have learnt Latin—Ovid, Virgil and Horace—and the elements of grammar and logic.

He was, it is well known, a wild boy who poached rabbits, perhaps shot a deer, and had, rather sooner than he should have done, to marry a woman in the neighbourhood, who bore him a child rather quicker than was right. That escapade sent him to seek his fortune in London. He had, it seemed, a taste for the theatre; he began by holding horses at the stage door. Very soon he got work in the theatre, became a successful actor, and lived at the hub of the universe, meeting everybody, knowing everybody, practising his art on the boards, exercising his wits in the streets, and even getting access to the palace of the queen. Meanwhile . . . (46–47)

This summary gives a phrase or a sentence to subjects that are "coherently" and "exhaustively" covered in Lee's thick volume, appearing under such subheadings as "Shakespeare's learning," "The poet's marriage," "Birth of a daughter," "Poaching at Charlecote." Contrasting with Lee's verbose biography of the bard is the brief fictional biography of Judith Shakespeare, Shakespeare's "gifted sister," who was "as agog to see the world as he was. But she was not sent to school." This biography is what follows Woolf's "Meanwhile" and begins with the phrase "let us suppose" (49). Woolf's essay necessitates what Lee's study reacts against: the speculative, the female. Unlike Lee's *Life*, which is intent on "reducing conjecture" (which had run rampant in the W. H. debates), Woolf's *Room* is necessarily conjectural; her subject Judith Shakespeare "never wrote a word." In raising Judith Shakespeare, she creates a fiction out of an absence and formulates an airy "life" against the often too-solid biographies of Shakespeare. Lee's "piles . . . of such hard facts . . . worthy of all our respect"[33] come at a moment when a certain literary history is well established and solidifying, while the "scarcity of facts" (44) about Elizabethan women dictates that subtle speculation must forego "solidity."

Furthermore, in embodying the person who is absent—whether from Lee's biography or from literary history—Judith Shakespeare in some way becomes an alternative beloved. Outside the famous library, Woolf's narrator had been put in the position of desiring access to the male poet; now the woman scholar desires her own beloved. By including Judith Shakespeare within her *Room*, Woolf creates a female potential that both has a history and will continue beyond the space of the lecture on that history. "[F]or great poets do not die," Woolf writes; "they need only the opportunity to walk among us in the flesh" (113). Judith Shakespeare is no abstraction, no Woman with a capital "W," no "Idea," no "Laura." Neither is "her body of alabaster, her legs of ivory; her hair . . . golden wire," nor "her teeth pearls from the Orient."[34] Beloved and celebrated in Woolf's pages, she is "as various and complex" as Woolf herself.[35]

∽ Why the Sonnet?

In this essay I have tried to show how Woolf does more with the presence of the sonnet than expose oppressive conventions and play with the stanzaic sense of "room" found, for example, in the line from Donne's "Canonization," "We'll build in sonnets pretty rooms."[36] I have attempted to demonstrate how Woolf describes, through the sonnet tradition, her own personal relation, as a woman in a particular economic situation, to a larger literary history. One last example of Woolf's engagement with the form provides the conclusive "couplet" to this analysis and shows the potential of using the sonnet to suggest ways to open literary scholarship.

The essay "Why?" first published in 1934 in the journal *Lysistrata*,[37] comments, almost allegorically, upon issues raised earlier in *A Room of One's Own*. At the end of this short essay, which questions (among other things) the merits of academic lecturing, Woolf visits a female friend who is a publisher's reader. Upon Woolf's entry, the friend breathes a tragic sigh, tells a story of a writer who "once . . . cared about English literature," and then violently rejects a book-length study of the English sonnet by throwing it across the room and, as a result, breaks into "fragments" "a teapot that had belonged to her grandmother" (233–34). The juxtaposition of these objects, the all-too-solid "'three hundred pages on the evolution of the Elizabethan sonnet'" (233) (perhaps a descendant of Lee's *Elizabethan Sonnets*), and the shards of a matrilineal inheritance, points to the two types of work accomplished by this friend. First, in rejecting the "unfortunate work" on the sonnet, Woolf's friend defies a practice "bound in the end to be the death and burial of English literature" (233–34). This moment is not merely an aggression against the sonnet per se, as Alice Fox implies;[38] rather, it is a resistance to those practices that ossify the sonnet tradition, that make the literary body's spinal cord into bone. For the publisher's reader, sonnet scholarship, which is so commonplace that Woolf finds no need to describe its stifling dullness, thus becomes a synecdoche for a more general literary scholarship. If the sonnet tradition is defined and redefined in the same manner, it becomes lifeless, static. In rejecting this scholarship, the reader indicates a need for something new. But when she does so, she inadvertently shatters—because of the weight of scholarly tradition—something much more fragile. The second type of work she performs is recuperative: The reader, with the help of the writer Virginia Woolf, collects the pieces of the teapot (and with it her matrilineal inheritance) and continues the work of breathing new life into literature.

Looking back through this allegorical lens, through this moment of rejecting conventional sonnet criticism and turning to the grandmother's broken teapot, we discover a new view of *A Room of One's Own*. As the essay "Why?" describes it, literary scholarship had developed its own set of conventions, which were being purveyed by lecturers on, and teachers of, English. Woolf's essay, based on lectures to women at Newnham and Girton Colleges, had thrown out these conventions. Not only did Woolf's meditations defy the fixed "I" of the lecture format, but they also looked for new voices, women's voices. In examining the early centuries of English literary history (when the sonnet was at its most popular), Woolf's narrative persona found only remnants written by and about the historical women of that time. She then began to make sense of the fragments that remained. We may consider *A Room of One's Own*, both university lectures and printed volume,[39] as an alternative to the system of education—of taking courses and exams in English literature—that Woolf's friend, the publisher's reader, determines to be the root cause of that deadening three-hundred-page manuscript. Unlike this system, which teaches a tomb-like "English literature," Woolf's *Room* both topples a literary tradition and picks up the fragments of a female inheritance.

A Room of One's Own ends with a promised resurrection: that one who had been "buried at some cross-roads" (48) might again "walk among us" (113). Judith Shakespeare's rebirth may not, however, be the only one that issues from Woolf's *Room*. "Why?" concludes with the threatened "death and burial of literature," a threat Woolf had articulated six years previously in a passage we have seen before: "Oh, but they can't buy literature too. Literature is open to everybody. I refuse to allow you, Beadle though you are, to turn me off the grass. Lock up your libraries if you like; but there is no gate, no lock, no bolt that you can set upon the freedom of my mind" (75–76). In revisiting this passage, we recognize that Woolf has enacted yet another slippage. The woman writer, who speaks with the same voice as the female scholar and the female beloved, also shows some affinity with literature itself: the threat at the beginning of this passage is aimed at all of literature, not only at the woman. It is literature that is "open," that cannot be bought or "locked up." Woolf frees literature from its manacles and lets the poet "down by a rope" from an ivory fortress. Her method of scholarship presents an alternative to the "death and burial of literature."

For the life and love of literature, Woolf seeks to undefine the sonnet and, in doing so, makes *A Room of One's Own*.[40] When the sonneteer meets Judith Shakespeare, we discover that—just as Woman is not inherently "[w]eaker in moral sense" than Man (28)—the sonnet is not inherently about "solidified" gender positions, exclusive systems, and chasms dividing outside and inside. Anticipating the feminist sonnet criticism of the past twenty years, Woolf proposes a feminism that, instead of throwing out the sonnet form (and with it the Western literary tradition), looks to introduce female potential into a literary history that, if it stays self-enclosed, may die from lack of oxygen. Woolf understands the sonnet to be flexible, slippery, and negotiable. And she shows us that it is only if the definition of literature is allowed to remain as flexible that Judith Shakespeare will "walk among us in the flesh."

∼ Notes

1. See Alice Fox, *Virginia Woolf and the Literature of the English Renaissance* (Oxford: Clarendon Press, 1990), 75–77, 75. Woolf, *Night and Day* (1919; reprint, New York: Harcourt Brace Jovanovich [Harvest], 1973), 67 (Rodney recites sonnet 31 of *Astrophil and Stella*). Later in the novel, with obvious knowledge of the textual debates surrounding Shakespeare's sonnets, Woolf playfully has Mrs. Hilbury speculate that Anne Hathaway wrote them (305).

2. Rachel Bowlby, "The Trained Mind," chap. 2 of *Virginia Woolf: Feminist Destinations* (Oxford: Blackwell, 1988),17–48, 35.

3. Heather Dubrow, *Echoes of Desire: English Petrarchism and Its Counterdiscourses* (Ithaca, N.Y.: Cornell University Press, 1995).

4. Ilona Bell, "Milton's Dialogue with Petrarch," *Milton Studies* 28 (1992): 109, quoted in Dubrow, 7.

5. Barbara Estrin, *Laura: Uncovering Gender and Genre in Wyatt, Donne, and Marvell* (Durham, N.C.: Duke University Press, 1994), 15. See also Dubrow; and Ilona Bell, "The Role of the Lady in Donne's *Songs and Sonnets,*" *Studies in English Literature 1500–1900* 23 (1983): 113–30.

6. Sidney Lee, ed., *Elizabethan Sonnets*, 2 vols. [1877–90], rev. ed. (Westminster: Archibald Constable, 1904). Alice Fox, in *Virginia Woolf,* points out that Edward Arber's *English Garner* was a favorite work of Woolf's: "So frequently did [she] read these volumes that she eventually had to repair and rebind the set, and she even prepared her own index to works she especially enjoyed" (159). Sidney Lee, *A Life of William Shakespeare* (London: Macmillan, 1898). See Woolf's reference to the *Life* in "The New Biography" (1927), in *Granite and Rainbow,* edited by Leonard Woolf (1958; reprint, New York: Harcourt Brace Jovanovich [Harvest], 1975), 149–56. There she writes, "Truth being thus efficacious and supreme, we can only explain the fact that Sir Sidney's life of Shakespeare is dull . . . by supposing that though [it is] stuffed with truth, he failed to choose those truths which transmit personality" (149–50).

7. S. Lee, *Elizabethan Sonnets,* 1:ix. See S. Schoenbaum, *Shakespeare's Lives* [1970], rev. ed. (New York: Oxford University Press, 1991), 367–74, for an extended discussion of Lee's work with the *Dictionary of National Biography.*

8. For a discussion of Woolf's engagement with one work by William Browne, see Kelly Anspaugh, "Circe Resartus: *To the Lighthouse* and William Browne of Tavistock's *Circe and Ulysses* Masque," chap. 7 of this volume. —*Ed.*

9. S. Lee, *William Shakespeare,* app. 9, 427–41; app. 10, 442–45.

10. Woolf, *A Room of One's Own* (1929; reprint, with a foreword by Mary Gordon, New York: Harcourt Brace Jovanovich [Harvest], 1989), 41. Subsequent references included parenthetically in the text are to this edition.

11. Nancy Vickers, "Diana Described: Scattered Woman and Scattered Rhyme," *Critical Inquiry* 8 (1981): 277.

12. Juliet Dusinberre also notes this allusion in *Virginia Woolf's Renaissance: Woman Reader or Common Reader?* (Iowa City: University of Iowa Press, 1997), 14, simply stating that the allusion "gives Woolf's protest its intellectual roots in the period she loved the best."

13. "A Mask Presented at Ludlow Castle, 1634" *(Comus),* in *John Milton: Complete Poems and Major Prose,* edited by Merritt Y. Hughes (Upper Saddle River, N.J.: Prentice Hall, 1957), lines 660–65.

14. Sally Greene, "Reading into Writing: The Courtly Wit of *A Room of One's Own,*" chap. 2 of "Reading Woolf Reading the Renaissance: Tracing an Elizabethan Modern's Search for Peace" (Ann Arbor, Mich.: Dissertation Abstracts International, 1996), 92–179, 157–58. Lisa Low, "'Listen and save': Woolf's Allusion to *Comus* in Her

Revolutionary First Novel," chap. 5 of this volume. For another example of Low's work, see "'Two Figures in Dense Violet Night': Virginia Woolf, John Milton, and the Epic Vision of Marriage," *Woolf Studies Annual* 1 (1995): 68–88. See also I. Bell, "Milton's Dialogue with Petrarch," for a different approach to similar questions.

15. *Petrarch's Lyric Poems,* translated by Robert Durling (Cambridge, Mass.: Harvard University Press, 1976), poem 263, lines 1–4.

16. Edmund Spenser, *Amoretti,* sonnet 28, in S. Lee, *Elizabethan Sonnets,* 2:230.

17. See Ovid, *The Metamorphoses,* translated by Mary M. Innes (London: Penguin, 1955), on the myths of Niobe, Medusa, Aglauros, and Ino, for examples of women being turned to stone; Narcissus, Hermaphroditus, and Andromeda, among others, are likened to statues.

18. Philip Sidney, *Astrophel and Stella,* sonnet 9, in S. Lee, *Elizabethan Sonnets,* 1:15. (Lee reproduces the 1591 spelling Astrophil.) Samuel Daniel, *Delia,* sonnet 7, ibid., 1:92. Richard Linche, *Diella,* sonnet 3, ibid., 2:302.

19. Woolf, "Donne after Three Centuries," in *The Second Common Reader* [1932], edited by Andrew McNeillie (New York: Harcourt Brace Jovanovich [Harvest], 1986), 24–39, 29.

20. Anne E. Fernald, "The Memory Palace of Virginia Woolf," chap. 4 of this volume.

21. Bowlby, "The Trained Mind," in *Feminist Destinations,* 22.

22. Woolf, *Jacob's Room* (1922; reprint, New York: Harcourt Brace Jovanovich [Harvest], 1978), 109. Fernald, chap. 4 of this volume.

23. Eve Kosofsky Sedgwick, *Between Men: English Literature and Male Homosocial Desire* (New York: Columbia University Press, 1985), 1–20.

24. Thomas Lodge, *Phillis,* sonnet 25, in S. Lee, *Elizabethan Sonnets,* 2:14; Bartholomew Griffin, *Fidessa,* sonnet 18, ibid., 2:274; William Shakespeare, sonnet 61, in Shakespeare, *The Sonnets,* edited by G. Blakemore Evans (Cambridge: Cambridge University Press [New Cambridge Shakespeare], 1996), 63.

25. Sidney, *Astrophil and Stella,* sonnet 88, in S. Lee, *Elizabethan Sonnets,* 1:55.

26. Woolf, "Donne after Three Centuries," in *The Second Common Reader,* 29.

27. Woolf's questioning of gender roles through her reading of Donne is further taken up in chap. 9 of this volume, Diane F. Gillespie's "Through Woolf's 'I's': Donne and *The Waves.*"—Ed.

28. Estrin, 181, 192.

29. Bowlby, "The Trained Mind," in *Feminist Destinations,* 37. I have also drawn my conception of "speculative flights" from fruitful conversations with Paul Fry. Though I admit that these speculations may have a Paterian tinge to them, as Perry Meisel would argue (*The Absent Father: Virginia Woolf and Walter Pater* [New Haven, Conn.: Yale University Press, 1980]), I contend that these flights have some sonnet in them as well.

30. Woolf, "Donne after Three Centuries," in *The Second Common Reader,* 29.

31. Woolf, "The New Biography," in *Granite and Rainbow* (1975), 149.

32. S. Lee, preface to *William Shakespeare,* vi.

33. Woolf, "The New Biography," in *Granite and Rainbow* (1975), 149.

34. Woolf, "Donne after Three Centuries," in *The Second Common Reader,* 29.

35. Ibid. Ilona Bell, to similar effect, quotes "Donne after Three Centuries" in her own essay on Donne, "The Role of the Lady," 128.

36. Donne is punning, of course: *stanza* is Italian for "room." See Michael Spiller, *The Development of the Sonnet: An Introduction* (New York: Routledge, 1992), esp. 26; and Michael Spiller, *The Sonnet Sequence: A Study of Its Strategies* (New York: Twayne, 1997), for discussions of the flexible "space" of the sonnet.

37. Woolf, "Why?" (1934), in *The Death of the Moth and Other Essays,* edited by Leonard Woolf (1942; reprint, New York: Harcourt Brace Jovanovich [Harvest], 1974), 227–34. Subsequent references included parenthetically in the text are to this edition.

38. Fox, *Virginia Woolf,* 75.

39. S. P. Rosenbaum has edited and published the manuscript versions as *Women and Fiction: The Manuscript Versions of* A Room of One's Own (Oxford: Blackwell, 1992).

40. Cf. Harold Bloom, "Feminism as the Love of Reading," *Raritan* 14, no. 2 (1994): 29–42. Bloom examines *A Room of One's Own* and *Orlando* for evidence of Woolf's "extraordinary love for and defense of reading" (29), though he avoids the most overtly feminist moments in *A Room of One's Own.*

9

Through Woolf's "I's"
Donne and The Waves

❧ Diane F. Gillespie

I did mean that in some vague way we are the same person, and not separate people. The six characters [in *The Waves*] were supposed to be one. I'm getting old myself—I shall be fifty next year; and I come to feel more and more how difficult it is to collect oneself into one Virginia.

—Virginia Woolf to G. L. Dickinson, 27 October 1931

"[I]t is not one life that I look back upon; I am not one person; I am many people; I do not altogether know who I am—Jinny, Susan, Neville, Rhoda, or Louis: or how to distinguish my life from theirs."

—Bernard in *The Waves*, 1931

That, finally, is one of the reasons why we still seek out Donne. . . . we cannot see how so many different qualities meet together in one man.

—Woolf, "Donne after Three Centuries," 1932

[T]hough we know what Donne thought of Lady Bedford, we have not the slightest inkling what Lady Bedford thought of Donne.

—Woolf, "Dorothy Osborne's *Letters*," 1928, 1932

If we love things long sought, *Age* is a thing
Which we are fifty yeares in compassing.

—John Donne, elegy 9, "The Autumnall"

$\mathcal{F}$rom the perspectives of different stages in her life, Virginia Woolf explores the related questions of what constitutes a self and what gives life meaning. She challenges the questions themselves by communicating the complex fluidity of people who, in spite of the often restricting roles into which they are socialized, elude categories, hierarchies, and labels. Her recognition of the simultaneous existence of multiple facets of the self emerges out of *Orlando* (1928), with greater emphases on both the way human identity is constructed not just over an individual lifetime but over cultural and human history, and the way this creation called a "self" is embedded in, and encompasses, a community of such selves—all ultimately dissolved in the repetitive cycles of the natural world. In these contexts, we can read Woolf's "playpoem" *The Waves* (1931) with an essay never to my knowledge associated with it, "Donne after Three Centuries," written for *The Second Common Reader* (1932).[1] Both appeared at a pivotal point in her life, around the time when, turning fifty, she felt increasingly "how difficult it is to collect oneself into one Virginia."[2] Both appeared at the end of her most innovative period in prose fiction and, in literary criticism, a productive period during which she established herself professionally. Then, in her fifties, as Carolyn Heilbrun says, Woolf found herself sufficiently free, confident, and indifferent to criticism to express her "submerged gaiety" as well as her anger at the patriarchy. Then, as Juliet Dusinberre says, she was able to articulate "what she was doing in her critical writing," which was to "reach out to a new audience, not common readers but women readers," in order to establish an "alternative literary history along the female line."[3] Although *The Waves* may have had as much impact on "Donne after Three Centuries" as her earlier reading of Donne had on *The Waves*, both Woolf's essay and her nuanced and much discussed "playpoem" reflect the preoccupations of this turning point in her life. *The Waves* can be read, therefore, at least on one of many possible levels, as Woolf's mixture of identification with, and re-visioning of, the complexities of Donne's life and the diversities of his writing for her own use in prose fiction.

Necessary to a reading of *The Waves* together with "Donne after Three Centuries" is an understanding of Woolf's growing knowledge of Donne within a contemporary cultural context preceded by her father, then dominated by her university-educated male friends. In the essay itself, the culmination of her increasing interest, she not only demonstrates the complexities of

John Donne, from an engraving accompanying his *Poems* in the editions of 1635, 1639, 1649, 1650, and 1654, as reproduced in Herbert J. C. Grierson's 1912 edition, *The Poems of John Donne*. Courtesy Alden Library, Ohio University.

Donne's life and mind that parallel her own but also shifts the focus to the aristocratic women who were his patrons, addressed in his poetry but tantalizingly silent themselves. *The Waves* reflects similar preoccupations. In it Woolf deconstructs the aristocracy within which Donne struggled for preferment, writes her own secular *Divine Poems*, feminizes Donne's cosmology, and, incorporating Donne-like imagery, gives voices to some of the kinds of people, historically marginalized and silent, addressed in his poems.

Woolf was well aware of the revival of interest in Donne during the early decades of her century. The foundation had been laid, in part, by Edmund Gosse's 1899 *Life and Letters of John Donne: Dean of St. Paul's,* to which Woolf's father responded with an essay. Leslie Stephen is "attracted as much as repelled" by Donne's poetry; curious about "the man himself" idealized by Izaak Walton and presented more realistically by Gosse; but certain that Donne was a man "not with one strong will," as Gosse describes him, "but with many conflicting wills." Her father's interest in Donne may be behind the earliest echo of his poetry in Woolf's work. In "Reminiscences," a memoir begun in 1908, her image of emotions stretching like "the finest goldbeater's skin, over immense tracts of substance" recalls the expansion of two lovers' souls "[l]ike gold to ayery thinesse beate" in Donne's "A Valediction: Forbidding Mourning."[4] Woolf very likely tested her own evolving reading of Donne against her father's, then against those of her university-educated male friends.

The appearance of Herbert J. C. Grierson's edition of *The Poems of John Donne* in 1912 sparked the enthusiasm of her contemporaries. Virginia and Leonard Woolf were married on 10 August of that year, and in November Lytton Strachey wrote to Virginia that perhaps their "great-great-grandchildren" will reevaluate the Victorians just as "we have discovered the charm of Donne, who seemed intolerable to the 18th century."[5] Leonard, not Virginia, was the one, however, reading Donne's poems in December 1912;[6] and Lytton Strachey, Desmond MacCarthy, and, in particular, T. S. Eliot were the ones who subsequently responded to Donne in print. Although Strachey applauds Donne's "[n]aturalistic reaction against the conventional classicism of the Renaissance" and MacCarthy notes Donne's penchant for "the rough touch of actual fact," most influential was "The Metaphysical Poets" (1921), T. S. Eliot's famous review of Grierson's edition, *Metaphysical Lyrics and Poems of the Seventeenth Century.* Eliot blames Milton and Dryden for aggravating the "dis-

sociation of sensibility" that replaced the unity of intellect and passion characteristic of Donne and the other metaphysicals.[7]

Woolf's early novels suggest that, as a young woman, she was conscious of
moving among university-educated men who—whether they accepted or chal-
lenged individual writers and genres—confidently proclaimed their views of
English literature. Her young female characters, "daughters of educated men"
somewhat like Woolf herself, must negotiate from the outside, if they are
successful, some rapprochement between their own readings and preferences
and those of the differently socialized sons of the patriarchy.[8] Appropriately, in
Woolf's first novel, *The Voyage Out* (1915), an intellectual named St. John Hirst,
who resembles the learned Lytton Strachey, finds "little to be said for the
moderns" (Ibsen, Meredith) whom Rachel Vinrace prefers. He wonders if she
has read, among other writers, Donne. St. John, who is curious about the
potential "enlightenment of women," pays Rachel the compliment, one might
argue, of assuming that she can understand a difficult writer; or perhaps, as
when he gives her Gibbon to read, he wishes to test her capacities. Enlisted by
Helen Ambrose to educate the innocent Rachel Vinrace in "the facts of life,"
St. John Hirst also might think Donne's candor appropriate.[9] Rachel's ultimate
inability to find her own voice as a reader of both books and life—one
sufficiently critical of preconceptions and capable of finding meaning for herself—is perhaps one reason why she does not survive.[10]

Similarly, in *Jacob's Room,* the university-educated Jacob—based in part, like
Percival in *The Waves,* on Woolf's Cambridge-educated brother Thoby Stephen
—rejects Sandra Wentworth Williams's preference for Chekhov and gives her
Donne's poems with the "savage" passages marked.[11] In neither *The Voyage Out*
nor *Jacob's Room* does Woolf offer a reason beyond "savagery" for her male
characters' preference of Donne over Ibsen, Meredith, or Chekhov. The word
"savage," however, hints at the egotism of Donne's youthful masculine readers,
and, in a draft of "Donne after Three Centuries," Woolf attributes the "savagery"
of Donne's satires to his youth.[12] One can imagine that Jacob, as a young man,
read Donne's poems selectively, identifying with the rebellious, candid "I"s of his
poems: their energetic satires, their relatively frank appropriations, from a masculine perspective, of women. The examination of more contemporary social
problems, including the confining roles of women, characteristic of later male
writers such as an Ibsen or a Chekhov would have required more self-awareness.

Perhaps because Woolf's references to Donne, culminating in her essay on him, represent a stage in her life and a perspective different from those of her male friends, the extent and nature of her dialogue with him has long gone unrecognized.[13] Yet Donne is certainly among the many literary ancestors who, as she says in "A Letter to a Young Poet" (1932), "sometimes move your pen a little to the right or to the left."[14] She took much longer to work out her responses than MacCarthy, Strachey, and Eliot, who were in their early thirties when they published their conclusions.[15] Although Woolf did not write any essay on Donne during her preparation of *The Common Reader,* before 1925 she had already thought of putting one "into the mouth of Mary Bickley, an obscure woman 1845. her diary," and she had taken several pages of notes on Grierson's 1912 edition of Donne's poems.[16] She was then in her late thirties and early forties, less prone to identify so readily with the naturalism, the rough facts, the youthful savagery, even the unity of opposites that attracted various of her male peers. She was more likely to look not just at one binary, but at multiple contradictions within the complex and fluid trajectory of his whole life and work, and to think of doing so in diary form, from the perspective of a woman reader.

During the years between Woolf's initial note-taking and some later research in about 1931—this time related directly to the preparation of "Donne after Three Centuries"—editions of his writings accumulated in her library, and allusions and references appear in her work.[17] In her diaries and review-essays, she tests Donne's qualities against those of other writers, finding in him the intellect of Meredith and Rupert Brooke as well as the changing emotions of Chaucer and Dickens.[18] In an initial attempt to account for what Strachey calls "the rise in Donne" in the "stock market of literature," Woolf concludes that her "only interest as a writer lies . . . in some queer individuality" of the kind found in "Peacock, for example: Borrow; Donne. . . . People with this gift go on sounding long after the melodious vigorous music is banal." Her isolation of Donne's "queer individuality" anticipates her later comment in "Donne after Three Centuries" that he takes his readers into his own unique world: "All other views are sharply cut off."[19] Although this ability of the artist to create a world apart was one of the tests Woolf and her friends applied to both writing and painting, she had expressed concern in *A Room of One's Own* (1929) that the repetitive, individualistic, masculine "I" that indicates "such freedom of mind, such liberty of person, such confidence in himself" could obliterate everything else.[20]

Yet the reiteration of "I" can have the opposite effect. As Ruth Porritt points out, the frequency with which the characters in *The Waves,* both male and female, say "I" calls attention to itself to such a degree that the unity of the self is "radically cast into doubt."[21] These "I"-sayers, who self-consciously attempt to define themselves in the face of ultimate dissolution and the relentless cycles of nature, also expose the desperation and the fragility of their attempts, and the overlapping of their vocabularies and perceptions blurs the lines among them. Perhaps these are reasons why—in spite of Woolf's contrast of Donne to Shakespeare, whose "grudges and spites and antipathies are hidden from us" and whose writing therefore does not "remind us of the writer"—she is able to identify to some degree with him. In any case, she does not charge Donne with the limitations of less self-conscious role players like Galsworthy or Kipling.[22] Her sense of Donne's powerful individuality is thus tempered in her essay by the degree to which she sees his "I's" as "eyes," multiple subject positions from which he views the world.

One "I" whom Woolf detects is that of the solitary thinker finding words for his meditations. With a reference to Donne at the end of "Notes on an Elizabethan Play" (1925), she anticipates her emphasis in "Poetry, Fiction, and the Future" (1927; later published as "The Narrow Bridge of Art") and in *The Waves* on the mind's "soliloquy in solitude." She remarks that, after an immersion in the energetic public world of Elizabethan drama, the mind "steals off to muse in solitude; to think, not to act; to comment, not to share; to explore its own darkness, not the bright-lit-up surfaces of others." At these times, one's thoughts turn "to Donne, to Montaigne, to Sir Thomas Browne, to the keepers of the keys of solitude."[23] Not only when we are in love, therefore, do we find apt words in Donne, but also, she says elsewhere, when we are isolated and ill, when we react more with our senses than with our reason. Then, we "creep beneath some obscure poem by Mallarmé or Donne . . . , and the words . . . ripple like leaves, and chequer us with light and shadow, and then, if at last we grasp the meaning, it is all the richer for having travelled slowly up with all the bloom upon its wings."[24] Linking Donne with writers as different as Peacock, Montaigne, and Mallarmé, Woolf suggests not only Donne's complex individuality but also, as a reader, her own variety of tastes and overriding preoccupation with the resonances and capabilities of words.

As a working journalist and common reader, Woolf does not treat Donne as a coterie poet, whose acknowledged verbal intricacies are accessible in her century only to an educated few. In a draft of "Donne after Three Centuries," she stresses that "the continued lives of poets must depend largely upon the interest of the unlearned and the amateur." So, earlier (1920), she approves the inclusion of some of his sermons in a prose anthology. In another review-essay (1924), she sketches a scene in which his colloquial lines are mistaken for an embarrassing personal confession as a woman in an adjacent room recites the opening lines of "Love's Growth" from a popular collection called *The Week End Book*. There eight of Donne's poems appear, along with poems by Shakespeare, Shelley, Keats, and Emerson, among assorted "games and songs and recipes" and (quoting Milton's "L'Allegro") "quips and cranks."[25] During the same year, Woolf presents Donne to the broad readership of *Vogue*, not as one of the "keepers of the keys of solitude" but more conventionally as "a poet, whose love of women was all stuck about with briars; who railed and cursed; was fierce and tender; passionate and obscene. In the very obscurity of his mind," she continues, "there is something that intrigues us on; his rage scorches but sets on fire; and in the thickest of his thorn bushes are glimpses of the highest heavens, and ecstasies and pure and windless calms." Then, possibly alluding to the engravings in Grierson's edition, she concludes, "Whether as a young man gazing from narrow Chinese eyes upon a world that half allures, half disgusts him, or with his flesh dried on his cheek bones, wrapped in his winding sheet, excruciated, dead in St Paul's, one cannot help but love John Donne."[26]

"Virginia Woolf declared that no woman could read Donne without falling in love with him," Juliet Dusinberre writes, referring to the *Vogue* essay. Influenced by her projected audience, however, Woolf's multiplication of opposites strikes me as more ambiguous, closer, in fact, to her father's attraction/repulsion. "Ya gotta love 'im," we might say in our contemporary vernacular, implying that we do so unwillingly, in spite of his faults. Her use of "obscene," for instance, complicates Dusinberre's assertion that Woolf found poems like elegy 19 ("Going to Bed") "wonderfully liberating."[27] True, Woolf wrote in her pre-1925 notebook,

      Going to bed: a sensual one, about a woman's getting naked
      License my roaving hands, & let them go
      O my America! my new-found-land,
      My kingdom, . . .[28]

She left out line 26, however, in which the "roaving hands" go "Before, behind, between, above, below." Liberating on one level Donne must have been to those questioning the prudish reticences of a Victorian upbringing.[29] Nevertheless, Woolf's discomfort with what she had told T. S. Eliot in 1922 were the "virile . . . he-goat" aspects of James Joyce's *Ulysses* leads one to suspect that she also may have found lines like this one of Donne's less pleasantly erotic than uncomfortably graphic, even, with the geographical imagery, imperialistic and invasive.[30]

Having already demonstrated considerable knowledge, Woolf continued her note-taking for "Donne After Three Centuries" while she waited for *The Waves* to appear, which it did in October 1931.[31] Her reactions to the project were mixed. In September 1931 she is happy, "writing easily & interestedly at Donne of a morning, & poems all about me." Lytton Strachey, however, died on 22 January 1932. On 3 February she still notes in her diary her great interest in Donne. By the next day, however, she is "going through the stages of Lytton's death," pondering its meaning, feeling (in part because of the cremation with no ceremony) a lack of closure.[32] Her enthusiasm for her work on Donne is dampened. By 5 and 8 February she is "toiling over Donnes poetry . . . with antlike assiduity." "I am aghast at the futility of life—Lytton gone, and nobody minding," she writes. "I've been writing about Donne . . . and wondering what use it is."[33] Strachey's enthusiasm for Donne may have been on her mind, along with the impossibility of any dialogue with him when "Donne after Three Centuries" would be published in *The Second Common Reader* late in 1932. Woolf, who had turned fifty early that year, had just been looking at the aging of the speakers in *The Waves*—one of whom (Neville) resembles Strachey, one Eliot (Louis), one to some degree MacCarthy (Bernard), with Thoby Stephen (Percival) in the background.[34] So her meditations on the life and accomplishments of John Donne are woven among her thoughts on her own life and that of her fictional speakers and friends, and they anticipate her later memoir pieces and her work on the life of the equally complex and mercurial Roger Fry.

Although *The Waves* was published prior to "Donne after Three Centuries," it seems appropriate to discuss the essay first, as a culmination of references to Donne and the complexities of his mind in Woolf's journalism. The relationship between essay and "playpoem" is not so much one of influence as of affinity with Woolf's own mature perceptions, as I have said, and both texts reflect and develop, in different ways, her earlier interest in Donne. Woolf's first concern in "Donne after Three Centuries" is the "quality the words of Donne possess" that lets us "still hear them distinctly today" when so many others are silent. What first "arrests" the reader, she decides—quoting from "Love's Deitie," "The Broken Heart," "A Lecture upon the Shadow," and "The Relique"—is "the explosion with which he bursts into speech," immediately engaging the senses, "surprising and subjugating" the reader.[35] Although Desmond MacCarthy, for one, precedes her in quoting Donne's poems to indicate their spoken quality, and although Woolf had already privileged the intimacy and immediacy of oral expression in the "dramatic soliloquies" of *The Waves*, Dusinberre rightly observes that "[f]or Virginia Woolf Donne is not read, but heard."[36] Observing the development of Donne's audible individuality through a highly condensed version of his life and work, Woolf eliminates much from even her cryptic notes on Gosse's biography and focuses upon what her own multiple "I's" detect, his many "strange contraries" (25).[37]

Woolf re-creates the youthful Donne of the *Satyres* and the *Elegies* as a product of his society and its aesthetic values—not through conformity but through rebellion against them. As a poet he is a "nonconformist," she declares, who, a bit like Browning and Meredith later, willfully refuses to adopt "the current usage" (25–26). So she elsewhere identifies herself and her sister Vanessa as young "[e]xplorers and revolutionists," trapped in an upper-middle-class environment that was, for women and artists, "about fifty years too old for us."[38] When she describes Donne's mind, unlike that of Spenser, Sidney, or Marlowe, as one "which struggles to express" not "the broader aspect of things" but "each shock exactly as it impinges upon his tight-stretched senses" (26–27), the words parallel her comments on the "shock of emotion" conveyed to the common viewer by Vanessa Bell's tight-stretched, nonrepresentational, postimpressionist canvases as well as Bernard's "shock of emotion" in *The Waves*.[39]

Like the intense and mercurial poet himself, the women of Donne's love poems, Woolf says, are human beings of great variety and complexity (28–29).

Prone to seeing "each spot and wrinkle which defaced the fair outline" (28), though, Donne is also able to perceive a spiritual level—to rise above, if only momentarily, the physical "Hee and Shee" ("The Undertaking") and to achieve a higher unity (30–31). Woolf had already noted in reviewing an experimental novel of her own day, Dorothy Richardson's *The Tunnel* (1919), that the traditional "'him and her' [plots] are cut out."[40] Like Richardson, and like Woolf herself (most recently in *The Waves*), Donne transforms the standard treatment of relationships between men and women and "snatches the intensity," captures the fleeting transcendent moment (32).

As in *A Room of One's Own*, Woolf is interested in "Donne after Three Centuries" in a writer's "circumstances." Donne "had married secretly; he was a father; he was . . . a very poor yet a very ambitious man, living in a damp little house at Mitcham with a family of small children." Their crying disrupted his work (32), although, as she says in "Dorothy Osborne's *Letters*," a woman writer of a similar social class "was impeded also by her belief that writing was an act unbefitting her sex."[41] Her interest in this facet of an older Donne, husband and father, precipitates an examination of the literary marketplace and of audience, in this case the "sanctuary" Donne found in the homes of "great ladies" and "rich men" (32).

Up to this point in her account of Donne's life and work, Woolf is able to respond as a twentieth-century writer of prose fiction: "We may claim to be akin to Donne in our readiness to admit contrasts, in our desire for openness, in that psychological intricacy which the novelists have taught us with their slow, subtle, and analytic prose" (32–33). Now, however, she has to shift gears. In this new aristocratic context, she says, Donne seems no longer the "harsh satirist" or the "imperious lover" who refuses to conform. As a dependent hoping for favors, he is instead "servile and obsequious," subdued (like Woolf's Victorian Orlando) by "the spirit of the age" (32).

Showing an awareness of the rhetorical limitations borne by Renaissance courtier poets, Woolf takes the opportunity to suggest an alternative history of literature through her focus on the role of women in the patronage system of Donne's time and on the complex and inverted gender relationship between aristocratic female patron and dependent male poet. Lady Bedford, she writes in her reading notebook, "must have had a good head, to understand; perhaps liked him to show off—anyhow a curious relation between them." The poems to "Ly.

Bedford-Herbert," Woolf concludes, "were not mere exercises," as were those written about the deceased Elizabeth Drury to please her father. In those to his female patron(s), Donne is "a man—complex passionate, personal—divided. This leaks in. This is to be detected."[42] This sense of Donne's conflicted, though rhetorically submerged, engagement intrigues Woolf, although she does not pursue her speculations in the essay.[43] There she ponders these "noble ladies" who "live only in the reflection, or in the distortion," of Donne's poems (33). Lacking their own poems and diaries, Woolf characterizes the female patrons of Donne's day through an example she does have, that of Lady Anne Clifford, in whose chapel Donne had preached and for whose published diary Vita Sackville-West had written an introduction. Though "busied with all the cares of wealth and property," Woolf writes, Lady Anne "still read good English books [Spenser, Sidney, Chaucer] as naturally as she ate good beef and mutton." She "felt it incumbent on her to respect the men of low birth and no fortune who could write" such works, and she nailed "words from great writers" to her walls (34).

With this example in mind, Woolf returns not to Lady Bedford the woman and Donne the man, but to their social roles. She suggests that his "relation to the Countess of Bedford was very different from any that could exist between a poet and a countess at the present time." In an exchange both "distant and ceremonious," her position "inspired reverence apart from her personality," and her rewards to "her Laureate" "inspired humility." When Donne calls the countess "God's Masterpiece," therefore, it is a case of "Poetry saluting Rank." Donne's ambition and the formulaic writing task, which might have "killed many poets," only stimulate another side of his "many-faceted brain." He writes subtle, learned, ingenious flattery that not only gives "intoxicating pleasure" to what must have been "a very clever woman" but also indicates, should the verses be "handed round among statesmen and men of affairs," that the poet is capable, not just of poetry, but of his real goal, "office and responsibility" (35).

Woolf concludes that, because of the multiple facets of Donne's brain and the "acuteness and ardour of his intellect," he met the challenge of this period in his life and found much "to write about when the season of love is over." Instead of satirizing some courtier or analyzing his own love for a particular woman, he turned "from the personal to the impersonal" and thus freed his imagination for "An Anatomie of the World" and "Of the Progresse of the Soule," "flights of extravagant exaggeration" quite unrelated to the person or occasion about which he supposedly writes (36). In "Poetry, Fiction, and the Future," often discussed with *The Waves,* Woolf had projected a book that would borrow from both poetry and drama to give "the outline rather than the detail," that would "give not only or mainly people's relations to each other and their activities together . . . , but . . . the relation of the mind to general ideas and its soliloquy in solitude." In short it would give, not just "that queer conglomeration of incongruous things—the modern mind,"[44] but also, as she says of Donne's mature work, the impersonal. In a comparable season of her life, Woolf too, through the "acuteness and ardour" of mind she attributes to Donne, "survived the perils of middle age" (36) and found much to write about.

The last stage of Donne's life, as dean of Saint Paul's, Woolf represents as one in which his voice continues complex and contradictory even though the patron is "replaced by a Prince still more virtuous and still more remote" (37):

> Just as his love poetry at its most sensual will suddenly reveal the desire for a transcendent unity "beyond the Hee and Shee," and his most reverential letters to great ladies will suddenly become love poems addressed by an amorous man to a woman of flesh and blood, so these last divine poems are poems of climbing and falling, of incongruous clamours and solemnities, as if the church door opened on the uproar of the street. (38)[45]

No simple resolutions are possible with such a complex and imposing man, who is yet "always consciously and conspicuously himself." That, Woolf says, is why we continue to read him, because "we cannot see how so many different qualities meet together in one man," because he is "more imperious, more inscrutable than any [figure] of his time" (39). A literary biography in miniature, Woolf's construction of Donne in her own equally complex, mature image ponders his relationships with influential and intelligent women patrons and finds his distinctive personality—in all of its multiplicity and curiosity—to be the continuity in the different stages of his work.

We know, Woolf writes in "Dorothy Osborne's *Letters,*" "what Donne thought of Lady Bedford," but "we have not the slightest inkling what Lady Bedford thought of Donne." Even if she could have "explained for what reasons Donne seemed to her strange," she left no such description.[46] When Woolf wrote her essay on Donne, women's perspectives on the patronage system of his era were largely missing.[47] Speculating from her own professional position, however, she doubts that "the Bedfords and the Drurys and the Herberts were worse influences than the libraries and the newspaper proprietors who fill the office of patron nowadays" (33). In "The Patron and the Crocus" (1924), she had already listed the "bewildering variety" of patrons faced by contemporary writers like herself: "the daily Press, the weekly Press, the monthly Press; the English public and the American public; the best-seller public and the worst-seller public; the high-brow public and the red-blood public." Because knowing one's audience is knowing "how to write," finding the right patron "is one of the tests and trials of authorship," one, she implies, not easily passed.[48] Nevertheless, by the early twentieth century, Woolf found herself in a situation considerably more fluid and open-ended than that of either Donne or his aristocratic female patrons. Indeed, she sat on both sides of the patronage fence and maneuvered, especially in her journalism, among many of the patrons she lists. At the same time, as publisher at the Hogarth Press, which she and Leonard had founded in 1917, and as a reviewer of books, she also played the role of patron, influencing what was printed and how it was received. In both roles, Woolf reveals her thorough awareness of literary power structures.

Missing from Woolf's list in "The Patron and the Crocus," however, is the aristocracy, still very much a part of British society three hundred years after Donne lived. There were, in her experience, aristocratic women who wished they were writers or artists, or who wished to raise their status by being associated with creative people.[49] The Hogarth Press not only freed Woolf from editors' demands but also put her and Leonard in a position to publish books by members of the aristocracy, notably by Vita Sackville-West. These, in turn, made considerable money for the press. Although Vita's "opulence & freedom" intrigued Virginia, she did not admire Vita's writing.[50] And although, as Woolf's lover and the inspiration for *Orlando,* Sackville-West is celebrated with some of the amorousness Woolf suspects may be submerged in Donne's poetic salutes to rank, she also punishes her increasingly estranged lover in that text by appropriating her life and describing some of its painful episodes.[51] Who is the patron, who the patronized writer here?

In *The Waves,* the recurring image of the unknown female—referred to as the "lady" who "sits between the two long windows, writing" at a walled country house called Elvedon[52]—parallels the noble ladies, reputedly "poets of merit," reflected or distorted in Donne's poems.[53] This writer, as "lady," evokes the aristocracy. Occasionally referring to her as "woman" (241) and even "women" (255), however, Woolf democratically broadens her identity. Still, because she does not give us access to this female writer's soliloquies any more than Donne gives us Lady Bedford's, we know neither what the woman writes nor how she perceives the world. Perhaps, as Clare Hanson suggests, the gender of the woman is less important than the "voyeurism and the breaking of a taboo" represented by the scene in which the children see her.[54] In this connection, the woman writing recalls a passage in Woolf's "The Pastons and Chaucer" (1925): "Thus the little Pastons would see their mother writing or dictating page after page, hour after hour, long long letters, but to interrupt a parent who writes so laboriously of such important matters would have been a sin."[55] In *The Waves,* more fatally, the writer may be the author who, if disturbed, will end the speakers' lives. Because Bernard and Susan may be imagining her, however, she is also "a creation of the characters she creates."[56] In either case, just as Mrs. Ramsay, who "sitting there writing under the rock resolved everything into simplicity,"[57] so the recurring image of the lady/woman writing in *The Waves* becomes a "fixity" (241) that is "symbolic" of something "outside our own predicament" (248). She suggests a timeless necessity, among women as much as among men: uninterrupted privacy in which to create meaning through words.

Besides their association with the "lady," if she is one, writing at Elvedon, Woolf's speakers in *The Waves* have a somewhat more direct contact with the upper classes, one that provides a link with Donne and the Renaissance and at the same time deconstructs the social hierarchy in which he struggled for social and financial success. Elvedon, as Bernard and Susan trespass there, or imagine doing so, is a privileged rural setting. Yet as middle-aged adults, violating no taboo, they invade its equivalent in Hampton Court. After Percival's death, Bernard regrets having refused an invitation to accompany Percival there (158). Rhoda, trying to "recover beauty, and impose order upon my raked, my dishevelled soul" after Percival dies, considers visiting its formal gardens (161). Just as the friends have gathered at a London restaurant to see Percival off to India, so, long after his death, they gather again for dinner, but this time on the outskirts of London at an inn at Hampton Court.

The setting is appropriate for reasons other than the associations with

Percival. With two of the five original Tudor quadrangles remaining, along with a third built by Christopher Wren for William III, Hampton Court was a site visited by Virginia Woolf and her own friends, as well as by characters in several of her novels, as she explores human intimacy and the human life cycle in a context redolent with British history.[58] In an early journal entry (5 July 1903), she and her companions "strolled through the quadrangles," untouched by restoration and thus conducive to uncomplimentary visions of "Charles & Nell Gwynn idling there with voluptuous Court ladies lounging after them." Diffi-cult as it is to imagine the rooms as they were in past ages, still, she writes, "wits & beauties without end have past [sic] through these rooms."[59] Although she does not mention any by name, Donne was among them. Woolf, as well as her six speakers in *The Waves*, thus walk where he and his fellow courtiers did more than three hundred years earlier as frequenters of the court of James I's wife, Anne of Denmark, whose chief residences were Somerset House and Hampton Court. Socializing there, and making and breaking alliances and reputations in games of wit, would have been Donne's patron Lucy, Countess of Bedford, one of Queen Anne's favorites, as well as Donne and "other favor seekers."[60]

While working on *The Waves* in October of 1930, Woolf in a different mood took a break to ward off a headache and visited Hampton Court. She simply notes in her diary, with an echo of *Macbeth*, "My misery at the sere & yellow leaves, & the ships coming in & I not there & I not there—drove me to take a day off."[61] Her impressions on this site of converging historical mo-ments, revolving as they do around realizations of aging and loss, emerge in the Hampton Court dinner scene in *The Waves*. A loosely knit and long-asso-ciated group like Woolf's Bloomsbury friends, the six speakers gather among "the red chimneys, the square battlements." There Neville thinks of himself and his friends as "middle-aged, loads are on us. . . . What have you made of life, we ask, and I?" since that previous gathering prior to Percival's going to India when "we could have been anything" (211, 214).

Woolf had noted with mixed emotions in 1903 the incongruity of ordinary people moving among the aristocratic rooms representing the history of En-gland.[62] Now her ordinary characters' individual histories and their references to English history in the context of Hampton Court undermine the import-ance of both. The male speakers travel in their imaginations through time and space and dismantle the social ladder of which they are parts. Bernard recalls that "a King, riding, fell over a molehill here" (227), echoing Neville's earlier musings on Percival's fatal fall in India (151). Percival, whose name links him to the political and religious hierarchies of the Arthurian past, is schooled in "regimentation and militarism" and epitomizes the potential leader within a contemporary imperialist regime.[63] Now the detail that occurs to the middle-aged Bernard in the Hampton Court setting is one that renders the historical power structures impotent and kings fragile, interchangeable human beings:

> But how strange it seems to set against the whirling abysses of infinite space a little figure with a golden teapot on his head. . . . Our English past—one inch of light. . . . It is a trick of the mind— to put Kings on their thrones, one following another, with crowns on their heads. . . . Our lives too stream away, down the unlighted avenues, past the strip of time, unidentified. (227)

From the vantage point of infinite space and time, the three hundred years of English history and human life—called to mind by the title of Woolf's essay on Donne and by Hampton Court, as well as by the soliloquies of the friends who currently walk there—dwindle and flicker out. Neville reduces the historical aristocrats of Hampton Court to their costumes: "Three hundred years now seem more than a moment vanished. . . . King William mounts his horse wearing a wig, and the court ladies sweep the turf with their embroidered panniers" (227–28). Louis thinks of the "many dead, boys and girls, grown men and women, who have wandered here, under one king or another" (228, 230). So Bernard turns from this home of historic kings and courtiers to watch "the lights coming out in the bedrooms of small shopkeepers on the other side of the river" and to wonder how successful the day of ordinary people has been and whether they will have enough to survive (233).

Woolf justifiably might have expected some of her readers to know that Hampton Court was also the site of the Hampton Court Conference—convened by James I in 1604 as an attempt to mediate between the high- and low-church factions and resulting in the Authorized Version of the Bible (1611). The period during which this translation was in preparation overlapped the crucial years in Donne's life prior to 1615 when, at age 43, he was ordained in the Church of England. Although the dating is a matter of some debate, it remains possible that Donne, born Roman Catholic in an era of persecution, may have written some of his Holy Sonnets during this period.[64] *The Waves* is in a sense Woolf's secular *Divine Poems*. Born into a publicly agnostic family, she wrote *The Waves* in part to embody, if not so radical a departure from her upbringing perhaps as Donne's, what she calls "the mystical side of this solitude; how it is not oneself but something in the universe that one's left with. . . . a fin passing far out,"[65] an epiphanic image appearing in the interludes (182) that Bernard repeats (189, 245, 273, 284). Although Woolf also may treat mysticism ironically, in writing *The Waves* she insists that she "must come to terms with these mystical feelings."[66] Her desire for meaning struggles with her atheistic disbelief.[67] Although her six mature speakers in *The Waves* hold a decidedly secular Hampton Court Conference, their anxious self-examination embodies an attempt similar to Donne's, and to Woolf's, to define meaningful individuality as well as to deal with its loss or nonexistence in something indefinably larger.

The six speakers in *The Waves,* therefore, are aspects not only of one life, not only of one national history, but also of human individuality endlessly constructing and asserting itself against the relentless rhythms and cycles of the natural world. Bernard's evocation of the "six-sided flower; made of six lives" recalls the carnation on the restaurant table in London at Percival's "last supper" with them. In youth perhaps a traditional erotic symbol, it has become "Marriage, death, travel, friendship, . . . town, and country; children and all that; a many-sided substance cut out of this dark; a many-faceted flower" that blazes "for a moment" before "[i]t is over. Gone out" (229). The flower is also part of a secular eucharist, a ritual repeated in memory of one who was a willing sacrifice to the rule of Britannia by devotees whose gender roles have also been cast by the same authoritarian goddess, herself a construction of the patriarchy.[68]

Following this commemoration of their last supper with Percival, Bernard begins his summing up with these ritualistic words: "This, for the moment, seems to be my life. . . . I would break it off as one breaks off a bunch of grapes. I would say, 'Take it. This is my life'" (238). Source of the eucharistic wine, the bunch of grapes also suggests both unity and multiplicity. Although he moves toward his conclusion in like fashion, Bernard does not invest his ceremony or inevitable death with divine authority: "I have tried to break off this bunch and hand it to you; but whether there is substance or truth in it I do not know." Nor does he know whether the rite of giving and remembering his life is even necessary, whether indeed he is "one and distinct" from his friends or "all of them" (288). The sensuous words of *The Waves* as a whole become, on one level, a complex "life," a revolutionary auto/biography, a ritual, an offering, an attempt to communicate the experience not only of individual but also of communal living, aging, and dying. Bernard's more inclusive perspective is a partial and tentative resolution to the painful individuation of the six characters as they are socialized into the self-consciousness of distinctions: gender, sexual preference, class, ethnicity. His awareness of his own complexities and incorporation in his own fluid self-image of the other speakers also points toward a possible healing of the schisms within and between societies. As such, Bernard's summation anticipates the education in self-awareness of the patriarchy that is one impetus for *Three Guineas* (1938).

Yet Woolf is criticized for allowing a male speaker to sum up and to assume the feminine characteristics necessary for androgyny.[69] Certainly her six speakers can be grouped in a number of ways other than by sex or gender.[70] I would argue too that Bernard's awareness of a "double capacity to feel, to reason" (77) — those abilities traditionally associated with femininity and masculinity — is, like Woolf's portrait of Donne in "Donne after Three Centuries," a revision of Eliot's celebration of the unified sensibility of the metaphysical poets. Says Bernard in a parody of oversimplification that simultaneously exposes his own egotism, "But 'joined to the sensibility of a woman' (I am here quoting my own biographer) 'Bernard possessed the logical sobriety of a man'" (76). Not only in Bernard, who is "many Bernards" (260), but also in Louis, who realizes that his life is a fusion of "many lives" (168), and in Neville, who is "immeasurable" (214), Woolf undoes Eliot's Donne with his neatly unified duality of intellect and emotion. Showing us masculine speakers aware not only of androgyny but of their own multiplicity as well, she probes further to examine, as some have pointed out, the verbal processes by which a "self" is communally defined, blurred, and dissolved.[71] Bernard, for instance, is, like Donne, self-consciously enamored of figurative language, responsible in fact for "nearly forty percent" of the "over eleven hundred examples of metaphor, simile, personification, metonymy and synecdoche" in the text.[72] Does word play become the meaning for which Woolf's speakers search? Or, is there a pun on Donne's name (in Donne's own style) as well as a criticism of verbosity when ultimately Bernard says he is "done with phrases" (287, 295)?

It may be coincidental that one of Woolf's early names for Bernard was "John."[73] It is not coincidental that in the second holograph draft Bernard mentions Donne as a writer with a distinctive voice:

> ℭ   If I have to wait I read; if I wake in the night I feel along the book-
> case & pull out some volume. Thus I accumulate . . . here in my
> head a vast conglomeration; . . . a mass, from which now & then I
> break off whoever it may be—Horace Walpole or Donne, & hold
> him . . . in my hand, & say That's Horace going to call on Madame
> Du Deffand; or thats Shakespeare. How strange the certainty & the
> recognition are![74]

Donne's presence in the draft is related to Woolf's earlier conclusion that he is among those enduring writers of the past whose individuality and multiplicity guarantee their contemporary appeal. The revised passage pushes Bernard's eclectic tastes even further and suggests an alternate literary tradition:

> ℭ   If I have to wait, I read; if I wake in the night, I feel along the shelf
> for a book. . . . there is a vast accumulation of unrecorded matter
> in my head. Now and then I break off a lump, Shakespeare it may
> be, it may be some old woman called Peck; and say to myself . . . ,
> "That's Shakespeare. That's Peck"—with a certainty of recognition
> and a shock of knowledge which is endlessly delightful. (272–73)

Peck, as familiar to Bernard as Shakespeare, emerges as a distinctive individual voice. In part because such literary voices, female as well as male, reverberate in his thoughts, Bernard does not always know whether he is "one person" or "many people" (276).

That which contains and transcends Bernard's complex individuality in *The Waves* is matriarchal and democratic. Donne's poetic cosmology, however vigorously he sometimes flaunts it (as in "The Sunne Rising"), is patriarchal and aristocratic, presided over by a "Sunne" usually gendered masculine and later, puns fully exploited, by the "Sonne" who is Christ.[75] Although Woolf's sun imagery in interludes 1, 3, 4, and 5 of *The Waves* has been variously explained,[76] her cosmology is figured feminine.[77] The sun rises *"as if the arm of a woman couched beneath the horizon had raised a lamp and flat bars of white, green and yellow, spread across the sky like the blades of a fan"* (7). The woman becomes a *"girl who had shaken her head and made all the jewels . . . with sparks of fire in them dance,"* who *"now bared her brows and with wide-opened eyes drove a straight pathway over the waves"* (73). Although the pronoun used with "the sun" in the next interlude is "its," the green mattress that couches the sun returns, with the girl: *"The sun had risen to its full height. . . . as if a girl couched on her green-sea mattress tired her brows with water-globed jewels that sent lances of opal-tinted light falling and flashing"* (148). In his final soliloquy, however, Bernard acknowledges the feminine facets of himself when he blends the feminine sun of the interludes with the more traditional masculine personification: "Day rises; the girl lifts the watery fire-hearted jewels to her brow; the sun levels *his* beams straight at the sleeping house" (291, my emphasis).

Just as Woolf's essay on Donne, projected in about 1924, was to be written from the perspective of an obscure woman, one of her early ideas for *The Waves,* in 1926, was to present the "semi mystic very profound life of a woman," an anonymous "she" who is timeless.[78] Like the woman with the lamp of the interludes, the lady writing at Elvedon is a possible vestige of this "she." So is the general description in the first holograph draft that identifies the pervasive wave imagery with maternity:

> Many mothers, & before them many mothers, & again many moth-
> ers, have groaned, & fallen. . . . Like one wave succeeding another. . . .
> And all these waves have been the prostrate forms of mothers, in
> their nightgowns, with the tumbled sheets about them holding up,
> with a groan, as they sink back into the sea.[79]

Certainly it is significant that the nine sections of the published version and the corresponding nine interludes echo the nine months from conception to birth and that Percival's death coincides with the birth of Bernard's son (153). So, we assume, as Bernard dies, a woman gives birth to someone else, and the wavelike rhythms of death and life continue.

We do not have in Donne's poetry Anne Donne's perceptions of her husband or of bearing twelve children, any more than we have Lady Bedford's perspectives. Dusinberre thinks Woolf identified with lines in Donne's poems, and especially in his prose, filled with "images of female experience such as child-birth and breast-feeding," the results of his living in "unusual proximity with wife and children."[80] Woolf nowhere cites such lines. She does note down, from Edmund Gosse's biography, Donne's descriptions of his domestic life with "many children" (in a letter to his friend Henry Goodyer) as a "prison" and a "hospital."[81] Perhaps Donne's conflicted experience of maternity and domesticity as Gosse describes it parallels Woolf's vicarious and ambivalent experience of her sister Vanessa's and results in similar imagery.[82] Ignoring Susan's husband in *The Waves,* Woolf does give us her maternal speeches: "I shall lie like a field bearing crops in rotation," she says, and "My children will carry me on; their teething, their crying, their going to school and coming back will be like the waves of the sea under me" (131–32). Just as Woolf balances the vision of the female sun in the interludes with the Darwinian struggles for survival its beams illuminate (see 73–74, for example), so she gives us Susan's voice when she is "sick of the body, . . . sick . . . of the unscrupulous ways of the mother who protects, who collects under her jealous eyes . . . her own children, always her own" (191).

Within these unidealized natural cycles in *The Waves,* Woolf's speakers age. Already in her pre-1925 notes she selects from elegy 9 ("The Autumnall") an example of the lines "of great beauty" that appear in Donne's elegies: "I shall ebbe out with them, who home-ward goe." Here the speaker of the poem opts for the company of an aging woman over that of "growing beauties." Woolf also quotes the first lines from the poem: "No *Spring,* nor *Summer* Beauty hath such grace, / As I have seen in one *Autumnall* face." Returning to the images of tides and seasonal cycles in a later notebook, she again quotes the last line of the poem, which apparently suggests an image of her own, "the lady who goes in and out like a fitful lamp behind an elaborate globe."[83] Whatever the associational sequence, Woolf was intrigued with Donne's treatment of the life cycle of a woman in "The Autumnall" and linked it with that of woman, lamp, and globe and her feminine cosmology in *The Waves.*

"If we love things long sought, *Age* is a thing / Which we are fifty yeares in compassing," Donne also writes in "The Autumnall" (1:92–94, lines 33–34).

In this poem he provides a man's graphic view of an aging woman and, although piling on the compensations, still details wrinkles, loss of "voluptuousnesse," "slacke" skin, mouths like "holes," and missing teeth. We do not get the woman's view of her own aging process and its effects on her relationships with men. Through Jinny, therefore, Woolf fills in another blank among the multiple subject positions of poets like Donne. "But look—there is my body in that looking glass. How solitary, how shrunk, how aged!" Jinny says. "I am no longer young. . . . who will come if I signal?" Whereas Donne combines images of aging and dying with a celebration of maturity, Jinny, imagining the inexorable descent to death, manifests courage. She continues to make up her face, to signal to men, and to "march forward" (193–96). "Now I turn grey; now I turn gaunt," she says, "But I am not afraid" (222).

If the male speaker(s) in the Donne poems that Woolf knew celebrate both variety in women (elegy 17, "Variety") and sexual conquests (elegy 19, "Going to Bed"), so Woolf in *The Waves* gives one such woman a voice.[84] Again it is Jinny. "I have only to hold my hand up," she says, and "men, how many, have . . . come to me." If "All things doe willingly in change delight, / The fruitfull mother of our appetite" (1:113–16, lines 9–10), so Jinny is "volatile for one, rigid for another, angular as an icicle in silver, or voluptuous as a candle flame in gold" (221–22), not only because of men's variety but also because of her own multiplicity and role-playing ability. In "The Extasie," the interplay of two lovers' hands and eyes takes them beyond their bodies, and their two souls create a unity of "mixt soules" (1:51–53, line 35). Jinny's vocabulary is secular and sensual, but she too describes unifying transports that she calls "ecstasy": "The torments, the divisions of your lives have been solved for me night after night," she says, "sometimes only by the touch of a finger under the tablecloth as we sat dining—so fluid has my body become, forming even at the touch of a finger into one full drop, which fills itself, which quivers, which flashes, which falls in ecstasy" (221). Unlike the lover in Donne's "The Relique," though, "after a furious conflagration," Jinny says, "we have sunk to ashes, leaving no relics, no unburnt bones, no wisps of hair to be kept in lockets" (222). The one "greater soul" hanging between the lovers in "The Extasie" (line 44) mends the "defects of lonelinesse." So does the unity between Bernard and Susan, who, as children, "sit together close" and, like the lovers in "A Valediction: Forbidding

Mourning" who "melt, and make no noise" of lamentation (1:49–51, line 5), "melt into each other with phrases" and, to distract Susan from her unhappiness, "make an unsubstantial territory" (16).

The latter geographical image, recalling the world-generating and world-dominating heterosexual lovers of Donne's poems, also materializes in a number of other passages in *The Waves*. In Neville, Woolf not only creates a satirist like Donne ("Let me denounce this piffling, trifling, self-satisfied world" [70]); she also gives a voice to the kind of man Donne mocks in his satire 1 as, according to her early notes, "more or less sodomitic."[85] As love "makes one little roome, an every where" in "The Good-Morrow" (1:7–8, line 11), so Neville says to (or about) one of his male lovers: "to sit with you, alone with you . . . in this firelit room, you there, I here, is all. The world ransacked to its uttermost ends, and all its heights stripped and gathered of their flowers holds no more" (177–78). As the lovers in "The Sunne Rising" tell the sun, "This bed thy center is, these walls, thy spheare" (1:11–12, line 30), so Neville's room is made splendid by love's presence and seems to him "central, something scooped out of the eternal night" (178–79).

Again and again the speakers in *The Waves* evoke the Donne-like figures of perceptually expanding and contracting, dividing and uniting globes or worlds. The "globe, yea world" formed by each tear in Donne's "Valediction: of Weeping" (1:38–39, line 16), as well as the lover/speaker, are threatened with inundation. Donne's "search for something whole, something lasting," " —unity again," "becoming one—a persistent idea," "his desire for oneness": these phrases punctuate Woolf's notes on his poems taken at the time of the completion of *The Waves*.[86] So Bernard, for example, repeats the word "globe"—metaphorically as both verb and noun—to suggest unity, lost as quickly as perceived. For him, "[i]deas break a thousand times for once that they globe themselves entire" (157–58). In his final monologue, like Prospero as well as like Donne, Bernard unsuccessfully tries to describe "this globe, full of figures" that is his life, this hypothetical "solid substance, shaped like a globe," this fragile and easily broken "crystal, the globe of life as one calls it" (238, 251, 256).

Aware of multifaceted, unity-seeking writers like Donne and creating her alternate "portrait of the aging artist," Woolf splits her creative protagonist somewhat arbitrarily but manageably into six (as opposed to sixty or six hundred) different facets, each of which must be acknowledged and leavened by the others. "We are creators," says Bernard at the end of the going-away dinner for Percival, who "add to the treasury of moments" (146). In *The Waves* Woolf gives equal time to forms of creativity traditionally dismissed as "feminine." To devalue Jinny's seductive arts (painting her face, dressing her body, moving it in a dance, and using it to signal men), Susan's domestic arts (growing trees and fruit, making ponds, kneading and baking bread, raising children), and Rhoda's arts of evasion and escape (into distant imaginary worlds of pillars, pools, and swallows and ultimately into death by a suicidal leap) would be to impose the very hierarchical values Woolf's novel challenges. Conversely, Neville, the poet who likes the Latin classics and worries about his inhibitions and his facility (83); Louis, the businessman trying "to make a steel ring of clear poetry that shall connect the gulls and the women with bad teeth" (128); and Bernard, the phrase-maker and storyteller who cannot finish his stories, are not exempt from criticism. Woolf's adoption in Bernard's final monologue of a masculine subject position is an indication of her own multiplicity as well as an examination of creativity that is depersonalized. So, too, Bernard finds consolation after Percival's death in painting and Rhoda in music rather than in Woolf's own medium, writing. Creative activity, as Woolf says in one of the last essays she wrote, is the only way "we overcome dissolution and set up some stake against oblivion."[87]

Ultimately, as Beverly Schlack points out, it is Bernard—in contrast to Neville—who shares Donne's recognition (in the *Devotions*) that "[n]o man is an island, entire of itself; every man is a piece of the continent, a part of the main; . . . any man's death diminishes me, because I am involved in mankind; and therefore never send to know for whom the bell tolls; it tolls for thee."[88] "Far away a bell tolls, but not for death," Neville both echoes and denies when he is young and in college (81). When Percival dies, however, Louis recognizes that "all deaths are one death" (170). So Bernard's life, like Donne's and Woolf's, is inseparable from the lives of others. "But now Percival is dead, and Rhoda is dead; we are divided. . . . Yet I cannot find any obstacle separating us. . . . As I talked I felt, 'I am you'" (288–89).

In the end, when Bernard declares that "in me the wave rises" again and then rides against a personified Death with his spear couched, Donne is once again nudging Woolf's pen. Bernard has "hauled himself up" from the depression of the previous pages and hurled himself upon his adversary, just as Donne, writing from Mitcham in 1608 to his friend Goodyer, also plucked himself up and defied a personified and threatening Death. Donne spoke, in the letter Woolf would have found quoted in Gosse's biography, of his melancholy and longing for "the next life," yet roused himself to exclaim, "I would not that death should take me asleep. I would not have him merely seize me, and only declare me to be dead, but win me, and overcome me. When I must shipwreck, I would do it in a sea . . . not in a sullen weedy lake, where I could not have so much as exercise for my swimming."[89] Bernard, like Donne, uses the masculine imagery of combat to present death as the ultimate enemy. The inevitable victor in the obvious sense, death in another sense is defeated by the defiance of an individual so multifaceted as to become a community of individuals, imaged in these passages by the rhythmic waves, or by the magnitude of the sea. "Thoughts of suicide chronic," Woolf had written about a younger Donne in her notes on Gosse's biography; "his faint hold on life, & desire to die."[90] She responds here to Gosse's description of Donne's *Biathanatos*, "in which he defended the thesis that 'self-homicide is not so naturally sin that it may never be otherwise.'"[91] When Woolf committed suicide by drowning a decade after finishing *The Waves*, perhaps one of Donne's texts, or the conclusion of *The Waves*, was again in her thoughts.

By the time Woolf wrote *The Waves*, then, she was in full command of her common reader's voices, and her voices as a common writer—critical, questioning, experimental—as well. No longer do her university-educated, male characters attempt to educate her female ones, whose varied soliloquies contribute equally to the constructions of multiple and communal human and artistic identity. Yet John Donne's "I's" are among the many, past and present, in Woolf's text. He is not responsible, as Woolf pivots on her fiftieth year into her last experimental decade, for her emphasis on multiplicity and the processes of self-definition, but her knowledge of his life and work reinforces these preoccupations. Other readers can recognize Woolf's Donne, whether she treats him up front in "Donne after Three Centuries" or submerges him in *The Waves*. At the same time, he is done to a turn in the dialogic oven of Woolf's own multifaceted personality and tastes.

◠ Notes

I owe a great debt to my colleague Louise Schleiner, whose idea it was to collaborate on this article and whose work on the piece in its early stages was invaluable. Although, unfortunately, illness and absence prevented her from continuing the collaboration, I learned much from her about intertextual studies and about Donne's social and intellectual milieu. Louise also originally detected some of the echoes of Donne in *The Waves* that remain in this piece and suggested the relevance of the Hampton Court Conference. I also wish to thank Sally Greene for her editorial suggestions and, for helpful comments on a late draft, Beth Rigel Daugherty and my colleague Stanton J. Linden.

1. Woolf, *The Diary of Virginia Woolf,* edited by Anne Olivier Bell and Andrew McNeillie, 5 vols. (New York: Harcourt Brace Jovanovich, 1977–84), 3:203 (7 November 1928); Woolf, *The Waves* (1931; reprint, New York: Harcourt Brace Jovanovich [Harvest], 1978); Woolf, "Donne after Three Centuries," in *The Second Common Reader* [1932], edited by Andrew McNeillie (New York: Harcourt Brace Jovanovich [Harvest], 1986), 24–39.

2. Woolf, *The Letters of Virginia Woolf,* edited by Nigel Nicolson and Joanne Trautmann, 6 vols. (New York: Harcourt Brace Jovanovich, 1975–80), 4:397 (27 October 1931).

3. Carolyn G. Heilbrun, "Virginia Woolf in Her Fifties," in *Hamlet's Mother and Other Women* (New York: Ballantine, 1990), 91–92; Juliet Dusinberre, *Virginia Woolf's Renaissance: Woman Reader or Common Reader?* (Iowa City: University of Iowa Press, 1997), 2, 39, 232.

4. Leslie Stephen, "John Donne," *National and English Review* 34 (1899): 595–96, 604; Woolf, *Moments of Being,* edited by Jeanne Schulkind [1976], 2d ed. (New York: Harcourt Brace Jovanovich [Harvest], 1985), 59; Donne, "A Valediction: Forbidding Mourning," in *The Poems of John Donne,* edited by Herbert J. C. Grierson, 2 vols. (Oxford: Clarendon Press, 1912), 1:49–51, line 24; parenthetical references to Donne's poems are to this edition. Cf. S. P. Rosenbaum, *Edwardian Bloomsbury,* vol. 2 of *The Early Literary History of the Bloomsbury Group* (New York: St. Martin's, 1994), 389.

5. Lytton Strachey to Virginia Woolf, 8 November 1912, in Leonard Woolf and James Strachey, eds., *Virginia Woolf and Lytton Strachey: Letters* (New York: Harcourt Brace 1956), 54.

6. Woolf to Strachey, 26 December 1912, in Woolf, *Letters,* 2:15.

7. Strachey, "The Lives of the Poets" (1906), in *Literary Essays* (New York: Harcourt Brace, 1949), 94–99, 97; Desmond MacCarthy, "John Donne" (1908), in *Criticism* (London: Putnam, 1932), 47; T. S. Eliot, "The Metaphysical Poets" (1921), in *Selected Essays* [1932], rev. ed. (New York: Harcourt, Brace, and World, 1964), 241–50,

247. After publishing his essay, MacCarthy talked about writing a biography; see Woolf, *Letters,* 1:498 (21 May 1912); Woolf, *Diary,* 3:19 (14 May 1925).

As Deborah Larson points out in *John Donne and Twentieth-Century Criticism* (Rutherford, N.J.: Fairleigh Dickinson University Press, 1989), 91, both Rupert Brooke (whom Woolf also knew) and Grierson himself preceded Eliot in describing Donne's combination of intellect and emotion. So did Leslie Stephen, who in "John Donne" notes Donne's "combination of syllogism and sentiment" (601). They define positively what Donne's more immediate successors, like Samuel Johnson in his famous comments on metaphysical wit in *Lives of the Poets* (1779), define negatively.

8.   Woolf, *Three Guineas* (1938; reprint, New York: Harcourt, Brace, and World [Harvest], 1966), 4.

9.   Woolf, *The Voyage Out* (1915; reprint, New York: Harcourt, Brace, and World [Harvest], 1968), 172, 154, 164, 163–64. Dusinberre, in *Virginia Woolf's Renaissance,* 69–70, notes the traditional masculine assumption that Donne is too difficult for women readers. In Melymbrosia *by Virginia Woolf: An Early Version of* The Voyage Out, edited by Louise A. DeSalvo (New York: New York Public Library, 1982), Hewet recommends taking George Meredith's *Modern Love* or John Donne's poems on the expedition to Monte Vista because "it would be nice to read something difficult aloud" (86).

10.   See Susan Stanford Friedman, "Virginia Woolf's Pedagogical Scenes of Reading: *The Voyage Out, The Common Reader,* and Her 'Common Readers,'" *Modern Fiction Studies* 38 (1992): 113–16.

11.   Woolf, *Jacob's Room* (1922; reprint, New York: Harcourt Brace Jovanovich [Harvest], 1978), 161.

12.   In *Virginia Woolf's Reading Notebooks* (Princeton, N.J.: Princeton University Press, 1983), Brenda Silver outlines Woolf's note-taking on Donne. The manuscripts, in the Berg Collection at the New York Public Library and in the Monk's House Papers at the University of Sussex library, are available on microfilm. They will be documented in the text by collection (Berg or Sussex) and by notebook or section number. The "savagery" passage is at Sussex B2e.

The notebooks in the Berg Collection are not numbered chronologically. Notebook 19 contains jottings on Donne from prior to 1925, whereas those in notebooks 8, 11, and 20 belong to the period of around 1931.

13.   Dusinberre's chapter on Woolf and Donne in *Virginia Woolf's Renaissance* is a recent exception, but she posits more identification than dialogue and excludes Woolf's prose fiction from her discussion. In *Women Writers of the English Renaissance* (New York: Twayne, 1996), Kim Walker notes Woolf's mention of Lady Pembroke and Lady Bedford as possible "poets of merit" in the essay on Donne as a way of modifying the dominant view precipitated by *A Room of One's Own* that Woolf thought women writers virtually invisible before Aphra Behn (192). In general, how-

ever, Walker sees Woolf's female literary history as something recent feminist literary historians of the Renaissance have had to challenge.

14. Woolf, "A Letter to a Young Poet" (1932), in *The Death of the Moth and Other Essays*, edited by Leonard Woolf (1942; reprint, New York: Harcourt Brace Jovanovich [Harvest], 1974), 208–26, 212.

15. While Woolf was becoming more interested in Donne, Eliot appears to have been losing his early enchantment. See David McWhirter, "Woolf, Eliot, and the Elizabethans: The Politics of Modernist Nostalgia," chap. 10 of this volume, esp. note 18 and accompanying text.—*Ed.*

16. See Silver, *Reading Notebooks*, 21, 222, 228.

17. The Woolfs owned Grierson's *Poems of John Donne; Devotions upon Emergent Occasions Together with Death's Duell by John Donne* (London: Simpkin, Marshall, Hamilton, Kent, and Co., n.d. [1926]); *John Donne* (London: Ernest Benn, 1927); *The First Anniversarie: An Anatomie of the World* and *The Second Anniversarie: Of the Progress of the Soul,* facsimile edition of the British Museum copy of the 1621 edition (London: Noel Douglas, 1926); and *Poems of John Donne,* edited by E. K. Chambers (London: George Routledge and Sons, 1896?). These books are in the Leonard and Virginia Woolf Library and Bloomsbury Collection, Manuscripts, Archives, and Special Collections, Holland Library, Washington State University, Pullman, Washington.

18. Woolf, "The Intellectual Imagination" (1919), in *The Essays of Virginia Woolf,* 4 (of 6) vols. to date, edited by Andrew McNeillie (London: Hogarth Press, 1986–94), 3:134–36, 135; "Romance and the Heart" (1923), in *Essays,* 3:365–68, 367.

19. Strachey, "The Old Comedy" (1913), in *Literary Essays* (New York: Harcourt, Brace, 1949), 47–52, 47; Woolf, *Diary,* 2:168 (18 February 1922); Woolf, "Donne after Three Centuries," in *The Second Common Reader,* 24–25.

20. See Diane Filby Gillespie, *The Sisters' Arts: The Writing and Painting of Virginia Woolf and Vanessa Bell* (Syracuse, N.Y.: Syracuse University Press, 1988), 155–56; Woolf, *A Room of One's Own* (1929; reprint, with a foreword by Mary Gordon, New York: Harcourt Brace Jovanovich [Harvest], 1989), 99.

21. Ruth Porritt, "Surpassing Derrida's Deconstructed Self: Virginia Woolf's Poetic Disarticulation of the Self," *Women's Studies* 21 (1992): 328–29.

22. Woolf, *A Room of One's Own,* 56, 102.

23. Woolf, "Notes on an Elizabethan Play," in *The Common Reader: First Series,* edited by Andrew McNeillie (New York: Harcourt Brace Jovanovich [Harvest], 1984), 48–57, 57; Woolf, "Poetry, Fiction, and the Future" (1927), reprinted as "The Narrow Bridge of Art," in *Granite and Rainbow,* edited by Leonard Woolf (1958; reprint, New York: Harcourt Brace Jovanovich [Harvest], 1975), 11–23, 19.

24. Woolf, "On Being Ill" (1926), in *Essays,* 4:317–36, 324. Woolf's ownership of an edition that included Donne's *Devotions upon Emergent Occasions* (dated the same year

as the publication of "On Being Ill"; see note 17 above) suggests that, although it is Donne's poetry that Woolf says appeals to the senses of the sick, her essay might also be read as another revisioning of his work, this time his prose meditations on illness. Both Donne and Woolf image the body as a world and express astonishment at its sudden transformation by illness and at its mortality. Both describe the isolation of the patient from other people and ordinary activities. Both use their meditations on illness as occasions for the exercise of their wit, yet the tone of each piece is completely different. There is a self-dramatizing, self-pitying, self-lacerating tone in Donne's meditations anticipatory of Leslie Stephen's—one impetus, perhaps, for Woolf's lighter, less personal touch. Although she does not mention the *Devotions* in "On Being Ill," Woolf does allude to one of them in *The Waves* (see p. 235 in this chapter).

25. Woolf, Sussex B2e; "English Prose" (1920), in *Essays*, 3:171–76, 171; Woolf, "The Weekend" (1924), in *Essays*, 3:414–16.

26. Woolf, "Indiscretions" (1924), in *Essays*, 3:460–65, 463. Although in one of the three black-and-white engravings in Grierson the eyes are almost closed, none contains features that adequately explain to me the reference to "narrow *Chinese* eyes" (emphasis mine).

27. Dusinberre, *Virginia Woolf's Renaissance*, 77, 66.

28. Woolf, Berg 19, quoting Donne, *Poems*, 1:119–21, lines 25, 26–28.

29. Alternate, possibly self-mocking titles emphasize Woolf's ambivalence. The essay appeared in *Vogue* in England (1924) with the title "Indiscretions" and the subtitle (quoting Blake) "'Never Seek to Tell Thy Love, Love That Never Told Can Be'—But One's Feelings for Some Writers Outrun All Prudence." The *Vogue* New York reprint (1925) was titled "Indiscretions in Literature: Wherein Our Affections or Disaffections for Writers Come Imprudently Forth" (see *Essays*, 3:464 n. 1).

30. Woolf, *Diary*, 2:202 (26 September 1922). As Dusinberre notes (*Virginia Woolf's Renaissance*, 67), when Woolf quotes line 27 in "The Elizabethan Lumber Room," America is "not merely a land on the map, but symbolised the unknown territories of the soul." Dusinberre thinks Woolf "might have added" "—and the body." I think it equally notable that she did not. For an overview of the mixed reactions to Donne's love poems, see Larson, 137–44.

31. See Silver, *Reading Notebooks*, 63, 73, 114.

32. Woolf, *Diary*, 4:44 (19 September 1931), cf. 4:45 (21 September 1931); 4:70 (3 February 1932); 4:72–73 (4 February 1932).

33. Woolf to Ethel Smyth, 5 February 1932, *Letters*, 5:16; Woolf to Ottoline Morrell, 8 February 1932, *Letters*, 5:16

34. These identifications have been suggested by many readers. Doris Eder, however, in "Louis Unmasked: T. S. Eliot in *The Waves*," *Virginia Woolf Quarterly* 2, no. 1/2 (1975): 13–27, was probably the first to develop the connection between Louis and Eliot. She also mentions the Neville–Lytton Strachey and Percival–Thoby Stephen connections.

35. Woolf, "Donne after Three Centuries," in *The Second Common Reader*, 24–25 (see note 1 above). Subsequent references included parenthetically in the text are to this edition.

36. MacCarthy, 48; Woolf, *Diary*, 3:312 (20 August 1930); Dusinberre, *Virginia Woolf's Renaissance*, 74.

37. Woolf's notes on Gosse's biography are at Berg 20.

38. Woolf, "A Sketch of the Past" (1940), in *Moments of Being*, 64–159, 147. Woolf follows Gosse, who says that "from the very first Donne was a rebel against the poetic canons and tendencies of the age" (Edmund Gosse, *The Life and Letters of John Donne*, 2 vols. [New York: Dodd, Mead, 1899], 1:19), a passage she copied into her reading notebook (Berg 20). An exception was the kind of satire Donne wrote, which, as Alvin Kernan points out in *The Cankered Muse: Satire of the English Renaissance* (New Haven, Conn.: Yale University Press, 1959), is consistent with that of his contemporaries.

Woolf agrees with MacCarthy about Donne's legacy to Browning and Meredith; see MacCarthy, "John Donne," 44. Dusinberre, emphasizing Donne's Catholic upbringing and secret marriage, not his poetry, notes that Woolf "liked Donne because he belonged to her band of outsiders." *Virginia Woolf's Renaissance*, 71.

39. Woolf, "Recent Paintings by Vanessa Bell" (1930), excerpted as "Vanessa Bell by Virginia Woolf" in *The Bloomsbury Group: A Collection of Memoirs, Commentary, and Criticism* [1975], rev. ed., edited by S. P. Rosenbaum (Toronto: University of Toronto Press, 1995), 205; Woolf, *The Waves*, 271.

40. Woolf, "*The Tunnel*" (1919), in *Essays*, 3:10–12, 12.

41. "Dorothy Osborne's *Letters*" (1928), in *The Second Common Reader*, 60.

42. Berg 8.

43. Recent controversial but plausible commentary on Donne, however, suggests that he asserted himself and maintained his masculine dignity in his poems to the aristocratic ladies on whom, in a reversal of gender roles, he was a "beggarly dependant" by parading his knowledge and by recasting himself as a "lover" of a woman in whom he had only a business interest; see John Carey, *John Donne: Life, Mind, and Art* (New York: Oxford University Press, 1981), 78–80.

44. "Poetry, Fiction, and the Future," reprinted as "The Narrow Bridge of Art," in *Granite and Rainbow*, 19–20.

45. Woolf assumes, like most readers before Helen Gardner published her edition of the *Divine Poems* in 1952, that Donne's religious poems were written after his ordination in 1615 rather than before. See note 64 below.

46. Woolf, "Dorothy Osborne's *Letters*," in *The Second Common Reader*, 59.

47. Recent research and the availability of more early women's writings are filling this gap in literary history. See, for instance, Walker; Barbara K. Lewalski, "Lucy, Countess of Bedford: Images of a Jacobean Courtier and Patroness," in *Politics of Dis-*

course: The Literature and History of Seventeenth-Century England, edited by Kevin Sharpe and Steven N. Zwicker (Berkeley: University of California Press, 1987); and especially Louise Schleiner, *Tudor and Stuart Women Writers* (Bloomington: Indiana University Press, 1994).

48. Woolf, "The Patron and the Crocus" (1924), in *The Common Reader,* 206–10, 206–7, 208–10.

49. See Woolf, "Am I a Snob?" in *Moments of Being,* 204–20, 209, 220.

50. See, e.g., *Diary,* 3:146 (4 July 1927).

51. On Woolf's appropriations, see Susan Raitt, *Vita and Virginia: The Work and Friendship of V. Sackville-West and Virginia Woolf* (Oxford: Clarendon Press, 1993), 34–35, 38–40, 137. Donne, who as rector of Sevenoaks preached in the chapel of Knole, Vita's ancestral home, was part of the Sackville family history Woolf uses in her mock biography; see Madeline Moore, "Virginia Woolf's *Orlando:* An Edition of the Manuscript," *Twentieth Century Literature* 25 (1979): 343.

52. Woolf, *The Waves,* 17 (see note 1 above). Subsequent citations included parenthetically in the text are to this edition.

53. Woolf, "Donne after Three Centuries," in *The Second Common Reader,* 33.

54. Clare Hanson, *Virginia Woolf* (New York: St. Martin's, 1994), 142.

55. Woolf, "The Pastons and Chaucer," in *The Common Reader,* 3–22, 7.

56. Joseph Allen Boone, "The Meaning of Elvedon in *The Waves:* A Key to Bernard's Experience and Woolf's Vision," *Modern Fiction Studies* 27 (1981–82): 630; Pamela Caughie, *Virginia Woolf and Postmodernism: Literature in Quest and Question of Itself* (Urbana: University of Illinois Press, 1991), 49.

57. Woolf, *To the Lighthouse* (1927; reprint, with a foreword by Eudora Welty; New York: Harcourt Brace Jovanovich [Harvest], 1989), 160.

58. See Lyndall Gordon, *Virginia Woolf: A Writer's Life* (New York: Norton, 1984), 219; Jean Moorcroft Wilson, *Virginia Woolf: Life and London: A Biography of Place* (New York: Norton, 1988), 93, 156–57; Susan Squier, *Virginia Woolf and London: The Sexual Politics of the City* (Chapel Hill: University of North Carolina Press, 1985), 84.

59. Woolf, *A Passionate Apprentice: The Early Journals, 1897–1909,* edited by Mitchell A. Leaska (New York: Harcourt Brace Jovanovich, 1990), 174.

60. See Schleiner, 107–10.

61. Woolf, *Diary,* 3:324, 324 n. 6 (22 October 1930).

62. Woolf, *A Passionate Apprentice,* 174.

63. Kathy Phillips, *Virginia Woolf against Empire* (Knoxville: University of Tennessee Press, 1994), 154–55.

64. Helen Gardner challenges the assumption (which Woolf accepts) that Donne wrote his Holy Sonnets after his ordination; see Gardner's edition of *John Donne: The Divine Poems* [1952], 2d ed. (Oxford: Clarendon Press, 1959), vi. Dennis Flynn, how-

ever, raises enough questions about Gardner's evidence and offers enough conflicting evidence of his own to make biographical readings of the Holy Sonnets risky, at best. See "'Awry and Squint': The Dating of Donne's Holy Sonnets," *John Donne Journal* 7 (1988): 35–45.

65. Woolf, *Diary*, 3:113 (30 September 1926).

66. On the irony in Woolf's mysticism, see Val Gough, "With Some Irony in Her Interrogation: Woolf's Ironic Mysticism," in *Virginia Woolf and the Arts: Selected Papers from the Sixth Annual Conference on Virginia Woolf*, edited by Diane F. Gillespie and Leslie K. Hankins (New York: Pace University Press, 1997), 85–90; the quote is from Woolf's *Diary*, 3:203 (7 November 1928).

67. See Makiko Minow-Pinkney, "'How then does light return to the world after the eclipse of the sun? Miraculously, frailly': A Psychoanalytic Interpretation of Woolf's Mysticism," in *Virginia Woolf and the Arts: Selected Papers from the Sixth Annual Conference on Virginia Woolf*, edited by Diane F. Gillespie and Leslie K. Hankins (New York: Pace University Press, 1997), 90–98, 97.

68. See Keith Booker, "Tradition, Authority, and Subjectivity: Narrative Constitution of the Self in *The Waves*," *Literature, Interpretation, Theory* 3 (1991): 38; Jane Marcus, "Britannia Rules *The Waves*," in *Decolonizing Tradition: New Views of Twentieth-Century "British" Literary Canons*, edited by Karen R. Lawrence (Urbana: University of Illinois Press, 1992), 140, 145.

69. See, e.g., Eileen Sypher, "*The Waves*: A Utopia of Androgyny?" in *Virginia Woolf: Centennial Essays*, edited by Elaine K. Ginsberg and Laura Moss Gottlieb (Troy, N.Y.: Whitston, 1983), 187–213.

70. See Bonnie Kime Scott, *Postmodern Feminist Readings of Woolf, West, and Barnes*, vol. 2 of *Refiguring Modernism* (Bloomington: Indiana University Press, 1995), 31.

71. Caughie, 48–49; Tracey Sherard, "Voyage through *The Waves*: Woolf's Kaleidoscope of the 'Unpresentable,'" in *Virginia Woolf and the Arts: Selected Papers from the Sixth Annual Conference on Virginia Woolf*, edited by Diane F. Gillespie and Leslie K. Hankins (New York: Pace University Press, 1997), 127–29.

72. James Haule, "Virginia Woolf under a Microscope," *Woolf Studies Annual* 3 (1997): 152.

73. As pointed out by J. W. Graham in "Point of View in *The Waves*: Some Services of Style," *University of Toronto Quarterly* 39 (1969–70): 199.

74. J. W. Graham, ed., *Virginia Woolf: The Waves: The Two Holograph Drafts* (Toronto: University of Toronto Press, 1976), 705.

75. In "To the Countesse of Bedford" ("You have refin'd mee"), Donne flatters the noble lady alighting from her chariot at night as creator, sun-like, of "an artificiall day" (line 24, in Donne, *Poems*, 1:191).

76. J. Marcus, in "Britannia Rules *The Waves*," 155, for instance, associates the lady

with the lamp not only with Britannia but also with the prayers to the sun from the Hindu *Rig Veda,* a suggestion Patrick McGee, in "The Politics of Modernist Form: Or, Who Rules *The Waves?" Modern Fiction Studies* 38 (1992): 632, finds unconvincing.

77. See, e.g., Madeline Moore, *The Short Season between Two Silences: The Mystical and the Political in the Novels of Virginia Woolf* (Boston: George Allen and Unwin, 1984), 27.

78. Woolf, *Diary,* 3:118, 229–30 (23 November 1926).

79. Graham, *Virginia Woolf,* 7.

80. Dusinberre, *Virginia Woolf's Renaissance,* 72.

81. Gosse, 1:187; Woolf, Berg 20.

82. See Gillespie, 47, 49–53, 203.

83. Donne, *Poems,* 1:92–94, lines 49–50, 1–2; Woolf, Berg 19, 11. Following Izaak Walton, biographers agree that this poem was written for Magdalen Herbert but disagree about the dating of the poem as well as about Donne's and Mrs. Herbert's exact ages when it was written; cf. R. C. Bald, *John Donne: A Life* (New York: Oxford University Press, 1970), 119, with Carey, 81–82. Whether or not Mrs. Herbert was fifty is perhaps insignificant, for, as Carey says, in this poem as in others, Donne "has cut loose from reality" (82).

84. Although Woolf does mention (Berg 8) "To the Lady Bedford" ("You that are she and you"), a poem in which the speaker consoles one woman for the loss, through death, of her intimate friendship with another woman, nowhere does she mention "Sapho to Philaenis," a poem usually read as one in which Donne creates a female voice to describe the superiority of love between women to heterosexual love. Annette Oxindine, reading Rhoda in *The Waves* as a suppressed Sapphic figure, contends that "Woolf's fear of being labelled a lesbian, and therefore not being taken seriously, substantially affects the composition process of *The Waves*—her self-described 'very serious' work"; see "Sapphist Semiotics in Woolf's *The Waves:* Untelling and Retelling What Cannot Be Told," in *Virginia Woolf: Themes and Variations: Selected Papers from the Second Annual Conference on Virginia Woolf,* edited by Vara Neverow-Turk and Mark Hussey (New York: Pace University Press, 1993), 172.

85. Woolf, Berg 19.

86. Berg 8.

87. Woolf, "'Anon' and 'The Reader,'": Virginia Woolf's Last Essays," edited by Brenda Silver, *Twentieth Century Literature* 25 (1979): 403.

88. Quoted in Beverly Ann Schlack, *Continuing Presences: Virginia Woolf's Use of Literary Allusion* (University Park: Pennsylvania State University Press, 1979), 111.

89. Gosse, 1:191.

90. Woolf, Berg 20.

91. Gosse, 1:207.

10

~~~

Woolf, Eliot, and the Elizabethans
The Politics of Modernist Nostalgia

~ David McWhirter

*I*n the introduction to her anthology *Tradition and the Talents of Women,* Florence Howe remarks that Virginia Woolf and T. S. Eliot were both "consciously tastemakers" and "creators of culture"—"scholars, readers of the past with a purpose." Why, then, she goes on to ask, is Woolf still largely disregarded as a critic, while Eliot was almost instantaneously acknowledged as a central voice in twentieth-century criticism? As Howe suggests, the canonization of Eliot as critic, and of *his* "tradition," presumably reflects the institutional tastemaking power of the male academicians whom Eliot overtly addressed in his lectures and essays; Woolf, whose affection for Eliot did not preclude her gently mocking him for possessing the "pedagogic" mien of an "American schoolmaster," in contrast cultivated a more diverse, less empowered audience of "common readers."[1] Writing to Julian Bell in 1935 when he accepted a chair of English, Woolf wondered: "But why teach English? . . . all one can do is herd books into groups . . . and thus we get English Literature into A B C; one, two, three; and lose all sense of what its about."[2] The literary history Woolf

constructs, while certainly purposeful, is thus more eclectic, less insistent on a
single narrative line of cultural and literary historical development. Eliot's
clearly defined, highly selective "ideal order" of "individual talents" offers a
neater and perhaps a more marketable package than the frank heterogeneity
of Woolf's tradition—a tradition that embraces whole historical periods (the
nineteenth century), genres (the novel), and categories of writers (notably
women) that Eliot basically dismisses.[3]

I want to keep this last point in mind in turning to my consideration of
Woolf and Eliot's mutual, lifelong engagement with Elizabethan literature and
culture—a fascination persistently manifested in both writers' literary as well
as critical texts. For the Elizabethan age, in certain basic respects, means something very different to each writer. For Eliot, at least in his published criticism,
it means primarily Spenser and Sidney, the playwrights, a select group of
Anglican divines, and those "late Elizabethan[s]," the metaphysical poets; for
Woolf, as Alice Fox shows in her comprehensive study *Virginia Woolf and the
Literature of the English Renaissance,* the Elizabethan cultural landscape is in-
habited not only by the writers anointed by Eliot, but also by many others
found in what she once called "The Elizabethan Lumber Room":[4] prose writers
like Hakluyt, Raleigh, Burton, and Nashe; chroniclers like Hollinshed and William Harrison; and, perhaps most telling, a range of less conventionally "literary" figures encountered by Woolf in letters, diaries, and commmonplace
books—one Philip Henslowe, for example, the owner and manager of a playhouse in Southwark, or Elizabethan women such as Elizabeth Hardwick, Anne
and Mary Fytton, and Lady Anne Clifford.[5] Setting aside her work on *The
Waves,* Woolf writes in her diary: "Now, with this load dispatched, I am free to
begin reading Elizabethans—the little unknown writers, whom I, so ignorant
am I, have never heard of, Puttenham, Webbe, Harvey."[6] That these "little
unknown writers" are especially prominent in "Anon," the manuscript remains
of the history of English literature Woolf was working on at the time of her
death, suggests the ever-growing complexity and diversity of *her* Renaissance;[7]
Eliot's list of sanctioned writers became, if anything, even more restricted as
his thinking became increasingly bound up with notions of legitimacy, orthodoxy, and heresy.

Nevertheless, what is most immediately striking is the degree to which
both Woolf and Eliot tended to valorize the Elizabethans—especially the dra-

matists—as the last outpost of a purportedly premodern ethos, as exemplars of a vital sensibility grounded in a culture that was still largely uncorrupted by the chaos of modern history and the agonizing self-consciousness of modern bourgeois individualism. Thus, in her 1927 essay "Poetry, Fiction, and the Future" (republished posthumously as "The Narrow Bridge of Art"), Woolf parallels Eliot in calling for the development of modern literature along lines defined by a genre that she admits "seems dead beyond all possibility of resurrection to-day": "not the form of lyric poetry," but "the form of the drama, of the poetic drama of the Elizabethan age."[8] Just as Eliot praised "[t]he poets of the seventeenth century" and their predecessors "the dramatists of the sixteenth"—those writers, in other words, who predate the "dissociation of sensibility"—for their possession of "a mechanism of sensibility which could devour any kind of experience," so Woolf praises the Elizabethans' "attitude toward life" as "a view which, though made up of all sorts of different things," allows them to express themselves "freely and fully," to turn "[w]ithout a hitch . . . from philosophy to a drunken brawl; from love songs to an argument; from simply merriment to profound speculation." Like Eliot, Woolf sees the Elizabethans as free from what she elsewhere calls "the cramp and confinement of personality": "they never make us feel that they are afraid or self-conscious, or that there is anything hindering . . . the full current of their minds."[9]

For both Woolf and Eliot, it should be emphasized, the Elizabethans were not only the last premoderns, but also the first moderns: they are crucial because they embody both the last vestiges of a cultural ethos that now seems irretrievably lost and the beginnings of the modernists' own cultural predicament. As Richard Halpern argues in his recent study *Shakespeare among the Moderns*, "[m]odernism's historical allegory" of the late sixteenth and early seventeenth centuries is less "a salvific project" than "a juxtaposition of losses; only in the early modern period does it find a sufficiently dark reflection of its own catastrophes."[10] Thus, Eliot in a sense looks through or behind the "anarchism," "dissolution," and "decay" he regrettably sees as marring the Elizabethan plays[11] in order to discover the lingering aura of *Everyman* or even of Dante—this last, of course, the greatest of impersonal poets, whose *Commedia* embodies, Eliot asserts, not just a unified sensibility but "the assumption of an ideal unity in experience, the faith in an ultimate rationalization and harmonization of experience, the subsumption of the lower under the higher, an ordering of the world more or less Aristotelian."[12] Analogously, Woolf, while lamenting that Spenser, for example, was self-consciously aware of himself as an individual artist as Chaucer and Langland were not, is still able to discern behind the Elizabethan playwright the figure of "Anon"—that "impersonality" or "generality" that "gave us the ballads" and "the songs," that "common voice" that "can say what everyone feels."[13] Differences in critical purpose already alluded to reemerge here: where Eliot longs for the unity of an "ideal," hierarchical "ordering," Woolf wants to recover the "generality" of a "common voice." But in the broadest terms, both writers construct the Renaissance as "early modern" in something like our contemporary sense.[14] For Eliot, thought and feeling were permanently and disastrously dissociated by Milton and the Civil War, a bit of royalist and Anglo-Catholic historiographic sleight-of-hand exposed by Frank Kermode more than forty years ago in *Romantic Image*;[15] for Woolf, the villain is mainly the printing press, but the general contours of the story remain the same: "[t]he book after Shakespeare takes the place of the play," the audience is replaced by the bourgeois reader, and "Anon is dead for ever."[16]

Woolf and Eliot are thus participants in what Kermode describes as a pervasive modernist or symbolist historiography, one that posited "the notion of a pregnant historical crisis . . . because it explained in a subtly agreeable way the torment and division of modern life." The actual history marshaled to support Eliot's thesis was, as Kermode notes, characteristically "feeble," but the real issue is less that "there was not . . . a particular and far-reaching catastrophe in the seventeenth century, than that there was, in the twentieth, an urgent need to establish the historicity of such a disaster." Searching for "a serenely single-minded period" against which to measure contemporary chaos, modernists—Kermode cites Pound's valorization of Cavalcanti over Petrarch, as well as "the medievalism or Byzantinism of Hulme and the Decadents, of Yeats and Henry Adams"—ranged through history only to find that "however far back one goes one seems to find the symptoms of dissociation": "if we were to pursue the dissociation back into the past," says Kermode, "we should find ourselves in Athens"[17]—or, one might add, in Pound's Provence or Cathay, in Gauguin's Tahiti, or even in the Sanskrit-speaking world of *The Waste Land*'s conclusion. The impossibility of recovering such serenity *in history* helps to explain why Eliot, who had once located the "disaster" in the eighteenth century, *after* the metaphysicals, had by 1927 pushed the fall from unity back to the collapse of medieval accord: "The end of the sixteenth century is an epoch when it is particularly difficult to associate poetry with systems of thought or reasoned views of life. . . . It seemed as if, at that time, the world was filled with broken fragments of systems, and that a man like Donne merely picked up, like a magpie, various shining fragments of ideas as they struck his eye." Eliot's Donne, already reduced to a mere "magpie," by 1931 embodies an unmistakable "fissure between thought and sensibility,"[18] and the moment of dissociation has been set back three hundred years to the death of Dante. Sharon Stockman has recently suggested that Woolf's thinking about the Renaissance follows a similar trajectory. Woolf, she argues, increasingly abandoned her early valorization of the Elizabethans as constituting "an Edenic world of pure and unsullied order" for a view of the Renaissance "as a time of violent materiality rather than of transcendent promise": "Woolf's Elizabethans (and Eliot's)," she concludes, "comprise a myth that didn't work in the end."[19]

As Stockman's remarks indicate, the "implicit parallel with the Fall" that Kermode sees as standing behind the varied manifestations of this modernist historiography[20] signals its core, if contradictory, agendas: the attempt to locate the moment of the fall is simultaneously an effort to recover an imagined, implicitly prehistoric cultural unity *and* a rehearsal of modernity's inevitable expulsion into what Eliot once called the "contrived corridors" of history.[21] This is what Perry Meisel means when he argues that modernism persistently enacts "the loss of something primary that it wishes to regain." And the manner in which Woolf and Eliot appropriate the Elizabethans would appear to signal their mutual complicity in what Meisel identifies as the central "myth of the modern"—a nostalgia for origins that, he argues, is really "the retroactive production of a lost primacy by means of evidence belatedly gathered to signify the presence of its absence."[22] Woolf and Eliot, in other words, belatedly invest the Elizabethans with a myth of original coherence and plenitude, the aura of an undissociated golden age, thereby justifying the aesthetic revolutions of modernism as a quest to regain a cultural wholeness and unity that have been lost.

But despite the striking similarities in Woolf's and Eliot's appropriations of the Elizabethans, I want to argue that each participates in the modernist "tradition of return" in order to further widely divergent ideological aims.[23] Stockman, it seems to me, seriously misreads the nature of both Woolf's early investments in, and her later revisions of, the Renaissance: for the unity of

Woolf's Elizabethan ethos, as I have already suggested, is more inclusive, less idealized and ordered than Eliot's—in part because it is more historicized, less eager to discover in its historical reconstruction "a pattern / Of timeless moments" that can be "redeemed from time,"[24] and also because it is informed by twentieth-century political agendas that differed substantially from Eliot's conservative aims. If Woolf, like Eliot, constructs early modernity as a scene of loss, her sense of *what has been lost* is by no means identical to her contemporary's. Eliot's historiography is ultimately aimed at invalidating the forms of historical knowledge and critique to which modernity gives rise; Woolf's is part of her effort, described in *A Room of One's Own,* to reconstruct history in order to "supplement" and "re-write" it.[25]

For Eliot, the Elizabethans' comprehensiveness—their "amalgamating" and harmonizing sensibility—reflects the residual, underlying structure of a medieval cultural unity rooted in the eternal truths of divine and natural law.[26] Eliot's nostalgic vision of the dancing villagers in part 1 of "East Coker" may serve here to suggest how he imbues the Elizabethan period with a kind of ideological closure, especially regarding gender, that Woolf decidedly resists. Drawing on the language of his own Elizabethan ancestor, Thomas Elyot, Eliot writes that "If you do not come too close" you can

> see them dancing around the bonfire
> The association of man and woman
> In daunsinge, signifying matrimonie—
> A dignified and commodious sacrament.
> Two and two, necessarye coniunction,
> Holding eche other by the hand or the arm
> Which betokeneth concorde.[27]

As Andrew Ross remarks in *The Failure of Modernism,* this "historical fantasy"—"Merrie England and all of its effects"—is in truth a negation of history aimed at excluding the "historical Other, while selecting an ancestral Same," and so at "inculcating the pastoral values of a classical conservatism."[28] For Eliot, this hierarchized "concorde," and the regressive social vision and cultural politics it implies, are rooted not only in "sacrament," but also in nature, in the "rhythm" of "the living seasons" to which, he tells us, the dancing villagers keep time.[29] What is revealed *is*, in other words, an ordering more or less Aristotelian—a hypostatized historical moment that seeks to halt history prior to modernity's various dissociations: the civil war, the rise of parliamentary democracy, and the dissolution of stable class hierarchies; the shift from the relative stasis of rural agriculture to an urban capitalist economy; religious division and its effects, including the exile of Eliot's Puritan ancestors to America; the desacralization of the marital relation; and the rise, dated by Woolf at the end of Eliot's disastrous eighteenth century, of the middle-class woman writer.[30] Eliot, resisting these changes, in effect ends by refusing history altogether. Just as "only those who have personality and emotions know what it means to want to escape from these things," so "[a] people without history / Is not redeemed from time."[31] The purpose of history, in other words, is to facilitate an escape from its "cunning passages" and "contrived corridors." Thus, in a related epiphany from "Burnt Norton"—another of the Elizabethan places that provide titles for the *Four Quartets*—Eliot moves "[d]own the passage" of the manor house and "[i]nto our first world," into the garden where he hears, rather than sees, "the hidden laughter / Of children in the foliage."[32] Through an auditory hallucination that recalls Derrida's reading of Rousseau's nostalgic longing for the living speech of a time impossibly prior to the belatedness of writing,[33] Eliot reaches through and beyond history in an effort to hear the "unheard music"[34] made by Adam and Eve in an unfallen world. The canonical expulsions and exclusions through which Eliot increasingly defined *his* Renaissance might well be understood as a reflection of his belief that writing itself, even when properly contained as the provenance of a select, aristocratic few, is at best a necessary evil.

For Eliot, then, the Elizabethan age is predominantly a moment of catastrophic loss; but while Woolf too constructs this history as loss—"[t]he poet," she mourns, "is no longer a nameless wandering voice," part of nature, but a "word conscious" writer like "ourselves . . . very old, with a knowledge of all good and evil" and "already corrupt in this fresh world"[35]—she also celebrates it as a narrative of exuberant, expansive, and unruly possibility, a disorderly fecundity signaled by the very proliferation of writing—and of writers and written forms—that Eliot implicitly deplores. "Writing," as Walter Ong has argued, undoubtedly "introduces division and alienation," but it also facilitates "a higher unity" and "greater openness." "It intensifies the sense of self and fosters more conscious interaction between persons. Writing is consciousness-raising."[36] Thus, the Elizabethan Orlando, Woolf tells us, had penned, before he was twenty-five, "some forty-seven plays, histories, romances, poems; some in prose, some in verse; some in French, some in Italian; all romantic, and all long"[37]—a generic catalog as diverse as the gallery of "little unknown writers" in whom Woolf locates her polyphonic Elizabethan ethos. Indeed, in praising the Elizabethans, especially the culture of the Elizabethan playhouse, Woolf valorizes the noisy multiplicity in which Eliot finds the beginnings "of anarchism, of dissolution, of decay."[38] She celebrates a unity that is anything but hierarchized and monological—something more akin to Bakhtin's conceptualization of carnival or the novel's polyphonic wholeness, where everything is comprehended as part of "an uninterrupted movement into a real future, as a unified, all-embracing and unconcluded process."[39]

Where Eliot finds and approves an art reflecting a fixed, totalizing cultural and societal structure—a naturalized theocracy of sorts—Woolf finds an aesthetic and cultural form (the Elizabethan play) that apprehends wholeness without imposing ideological closure, a communal, democratic ethos premised, as she argues in "Anon" and elsewhere, on a loosening, rather than a hardening, of class and gender distinctions. The Elizabethan scenes in *Orlando* are suggestive here: during the "carnival of the utmost brilliancy" staged on the frozen Thames during the Great Frost, courtiers mingle with commoners—"apprentices; tailors; fishwives; horse dealers; cony catchers; starving scholars; maid-servants in their whimples; orange girls; ostlers; sober citizens; bawdy tapsters; and a crowd of little ragamuffins"—to watch a puppet-show performance of *Othello*.[40] One also thinks of Woolf's fascination with cross-dressing in the Elizabethan theater, as well as of her remark, in her essay "The Niece of an Earl," that the Elizabethan age was "far more elastic" with respect to class distinctions than her own.[41] The latter point is especially central to "Anon," where Woolf muses at length on the implications of a cultural form that made it "possible for the gentry and the commons to sit together in one house."[42] As Brenda Silver has argued, moreover, Woolf views the displacement of the manor house—so crucial to Eliot's hierarchized Elizabethan ideal—by what she calls "the other house," the playhouse, as figuring an alternative, more open model of community.[43] Anon's move from the manor house—where he sang "at the back door" and was "despised" if "tolerated" by the "master and mistress"[44]—to the less stratified, more fluid social arena of the playhouse adumbrates for Woolf a history of both regrettable loss *and* welcome transformation.

All of this, of course, is another kind of "historical fantasy," as the Virginia Woolf who imagined Judith Shakespeare, and who read in Trevelyan that disobedient Elizabethan daughters were "liable to be locked up, beaten and flung about the room," would have been the first to admit.[45] But although Woolf's history may be as partial and overdetermined as Eliot's, the ideological imperatives of her Elizabethan *nostos* are far removed from Eliot's hierarchized unity. While Eliot listens for echoes of Dante's patriarchal authority amid the Elizabethan "chaos," Woolf discerns in the playwrights a still-vital embodiment of Anon's androgynous, "common voice."[46] In *A Room of One's Own*, she had remarked that "Anon, who wrote so many poems without signing them, was often a woman."[47] A few months before her death, she would describe, in the notes and drafts that were to have been the first chapter of her "Common History book," a genealogy for the Elizabethan theater that contrasts strikingly with Eliot's: "Anon"—who is "sometimes man; sometimes woman"—"used the outsiders privilege to mock the solemn, to comment upon the established. The church men *[feared]* and hated the anonymous singer," and though they attempted to "press" Anon into their "service," he "left the church, and staged his pageant in the churchyard, or later was given a pitch for his drama in the market place."[48]

Woolf's alternative reading of the Elizabethans in fact finds a particularly resonant expression in her staging of the pageant—a midsummer festival not unlike the dance of the villagers in "East Coker"—in *Between the Acts*. Many critics have linked this novel with the project of reviving the poetic play outlined in "The Narrow Bridge of Art," a project for which Woolf, in striking contrast to Eliot, found the most appropriate vehicle in "the precious prerogatives of the democratic art of prose."[49] Woolf herself referred to *Between the Acts* as her "Elizabethan play,"[50] and the pageant is imbued throughout with the carnivalesque inclusiveness she typically attributes to the Elizabethans. Consisting of a motley combination of song, dance, masque, and dramatic parody (including a send-up of a late Shakespearean romance), the pageant is performed by amateur actors on an open-air stage that, like Shakespeare's Globe, collapses the illusion of the fourth wall and elides distinctions between actors and spectators: here, as in the Elizabethan playhouse, "half the work of the dramatist" is done by the audience.[51]

The pageant's linear narrative of English history, from its prehistoric beginnings up to "The Present Time[:] Ourselves," *is* punctuated by the appearance
of an anonymous chorus of dancing villagers, who pass in the background
singing that *"the earth is always the same."*[52] And many critics of various persua-
sions—including a number of feminist critics—have seen these "choral interludes" as evidence of Woolf's belief in "a timeless world" of communal values,
a world where historical nonessentials such as "costume and name" change,
"but the people beneath," nature and human nature, "remain the same."[53]
Woolf in fact incorporates this interpretation of the pageant—a vision of history *sub specie aeternitatis*—into her novel in the figure of the Reverend Streatfield, the village clergyman. In his closing remarks as the audience's "representative spokesman," Streatfield points to the fact that the actors play multiple
roles from different historical eras in order to support his reading of the pageant
as an affirmation of the underlying truth that "'[we] act different parts; but are
the same.'"[54]

The idea that Streatfield is Woolf's "spokesman" as well as the audience's
is to some extent sanctioned by his interpretation's affinities with "Anon," a
text Woolf began writing "between the acts" of her novel-in-progress, and one
at least intermittently marked by her nostalgia for the premodern values of a
"fresh world" where human history still followed paths barely distinguishable
from nature's cycles, "roads now faded in the mind."[55] It was "Anon," she tells
us, "who gave voice to the old stories":

> At Christmas the mummers acted Anons old play; and the boys
> came singing his wassailing song. The road led to the old graves, to
> the stones where in time past the English had done sacrifice. The
> peasants still went that way by instinct, in spring and summer and
> winter. The old Gods lay hidden beneath the new. It was to them
> led by Anon that they did worship, in their coats of green leaves,
> . . . enacting their ancient parts.[56]

One catches echoes of *The Waste Land* here, or even of Jessie Weston's *From
Ritual to Romance:* "The old Gods lay hidden beneath the new." But if Woolf
at moments undoubtedly participates in Eliot's brand of modernist nostalgia—one that evokes a timeless world of eternal values and that is in effect a

negation of historical knowledge—I would argue that the pageant in *Between the Acts* functions more consistently as a transgressive communal ritual that serves to disrupt the social and cultural categories that oppress and distort the novel's characters and that have produced the present historical nightmare: the year 1939, when the novel's events take place *and* when Woolf herself is writing the novel. If the pageant, in other words, is "Elizabethan" for Woolf in its vestigial reference to a lost "common voice," it is equally so in its clamorous polyvocality and inclusiveness.[57]

The counter to the Reverend Streatfield in *Between the Acts* is Miss La Trobe, the vaguely foreign, classless, lesbian outsider who is the pageant's author and director. Referred to by her audience as "'Miss Whatshername,'" Miss La Trobe pointedly chooses, at the end of the day, "'to remain anonymous'"; and she uses Anon's "outsiders privilege" to satirize the wholly historical forces— capitalism, imperialism, racism, and sexism—that are inseparable from the fascism and war they have produced.[58] She provides, if you will, another, less sanguine view of "Merrie England and all of its effects." Where Streatfield, like Eliot, believes that we "act different parts; but are the same," La Trobe suggests that we are different, but made—tragically made—to act the same limited, tired, destructive and self-destructive parts. And in rewriting England's history, using, as she says, *"words of one syllable, without larding, stuffing or cant,"* La Trobe is also attempting to discover in that history the possibility of and resources for resisting its current, ominous trajectory, a way to *"break the rhythm and forget the rhyme,"* to change its destructive plot. Asking *"how's this wall, the great wall, which we call, perhaps miscall, civilization, to be [re]built,"* La Trobe draws on the Elizabethan poetic playwright's free and full comprehensiveness not only to expose history's tyrannies and hypocrisies, but also to recover its alternative and suppressed potentialities:

> All the same here I change (by way of the rhyme mark ye) to a loftier strain—there's something to be said: for our kindness to the cat; note too in today's paper "Dearly beloved by his wife"; and the impulse which leads us—mark you, when no one's looking—to the window at midnight to smell the bean. Or the resolute refusal of some pimpled dirty little scrub in sandals to sell his soul. There is such a thing—you can't deny it. What? You can't descry it? All you can see of yourselves

is scraps, orts and fragments? Well then listen to the gramophone affirming. . . .[59]

What I want to suggest, of course, is that the Reverend Streatfield, whose articulation of his faith in a transcendent unity outside of history is ironically "severed" and "cut in two" by the "zoom" of German bombers passing overhead, may in fact *be* T. S. Eliot.[60] Woolf's diaries indicate that Eliot, and "East Coker" in particular, were very much on her mind as she was writing *Between the Acts*. In December of 1940 she remarks on her own "growing detachment from the hierarchy, the patriarchy. When Desmond [MacCarthy] praises East Coker, & I am jealous, I walk over the marsh saying, I am I; & must follow that furrow, not copy another." Eliot's poetry (*The Waste Land* as well as *Four Quartets*) is perhaps the most frequent source of allusions in Woolf's novel. But the degree to which Woolf engages Eliot in order to critique and even parody his work has never been sufficiently noticed. In another diary entry from 1939, Woolf comments that the failure of *A Family Reunion*—it proved, Woolf writes, that Eliot was "a monologist" rather than "a dramatist"—helped her to "confirm a new idea of mine—that I'm evolving in PH [Poyntz Hall, the working title of *Between the Acts*] about the drama."[61]

That the pageant in *Between the Acts*—staged, it is worth noting, at a manor house (Poyntz Hall) for the purpose of raising funds to bring electric lighting to the local village church—is in part Woolf's deliberate response to her friend's own efforts to revive the poetic drama is confirmed by Woolf's suggestively negative reactions to Eliot's *The Rock*, a pageant commissioned by the Church of England in 1933 to support a number of church restoration projects. Writing to Quentin Bell in December 1933, Woolf notes that "Tom is writing a pageant to be acted at Sadlers Wells in the spring . . . in order to collect one quarter of a million to build forty six churches in the suburbs. 'Why' asked Leonard. And Tom merely chuckled. I rather think his God is dwindling. But he likes clerical society, and was going to call on the Vicar of Clerkenwell." In a subsequent letter to Stephen Spender, Woolf expresses her somewhat stupefied "disappoint-[ment]" with *The Rock's* "dogmatism" and "cheap farce": "He seems to me to be petrifying into a priest—poor old Tom."[62]

The Rock in fact displays Eliot's nostalgia at its most reactionary. Valorizing the village church rooted in "the pleasant countryside" as against "the timekept

City, / Where the River flows, with foreign flotations," Eliot proceeds to denounce everything from modern urban sanitation methods to subsidized hous-
ing, even as he recommends—apparently in all seriousness—a national program of church-building as the answer to depression-era unemployment.[63] The
ahistorical fantasy embodied in the dancing villagers of "East Coker" is pre-
figured here, as Eliot evokes an organic community "[c]ontrolled by the rhythm
of blood and the day and the night and the seasons"[64] in order, as John Cooper
remarks, "to interrogate and attack the progressive mandarinate, the liberals and
reformers of society, 'who write innumerable books; being too vain and distracted for silence: seeking every one after his own elevation, and dodging his
emptiness.'"[65] "What we call history," in Eliot's dismissive phrase, *is* in fact
dismissed in *The Rock* as nothing but the "weariness of men who turn from
GOD" to the false "grandeur" and "glory" of their own "mind[s]" and "action[s]":

> To arts and inventions and daring enterprises,
> To schemes of human greatness thoroughly discredited,
> Binding the earth and the water to your service,
> Exploiting the seas and developing the mountains,
> Dividing the stars into common and preferred,
> Engaged in devising the perfect refrigerator,
> Engaged in working out a rational morality,
> Engaged in printing as many books as possible,
> Plotting of happiness and flinging empty bottles,
> Turning from your vacancy to fevered enthusiasm
> For nation or race or what you call humanity.[66]

The chorus in Woolf's pageant, as in Eliot's, laments modern capitalism's
market speculations and environmental depredations, as well as the "fevered
enthusiasm" that has given rise to Mussolini and Hitler.[67] But Woolf does not
share Eliot's desire to flee from the noise of too "many books" and the "litter
of Sunday newspapers" or his dogmatic rejection of the "[k]nowledge of
speech" for the knowledge found in a "silence" in which only one voice (God's,
or maybe Eliot's) remains.[68] Rather, like her character Isa in *Between the Acts,*
who cannot forget the newspaper account she has read of a brutal rape committed by members of the Royal Guard at Whitehall, Woolf remains in history:

"That," Isa and Woolf both know, "was real."[69] After voicing her bewilderment at *The Rock* to Spender, Woolf continues: "What about politics? Even I am shocked by the last week in Germany into taking part," an engagement that "means reading the newspapers" alongside the works of T. S. Eliot.[70]

As *The Rock* suggests, Eliot's persistent return to the Elizabethan playwrights, like Woolf's, is inseparable from the modernist project of reviving poetic drama. But as R. Peacock argues in a perceptive essay, Eliot's Elizabethan play is "a very distilled conception"—one that has "the beauty" (and the limitations) "of an ideal paradigm" and that "is in danger of ending with an apotheosis not of drama but of one type of play, the play of ultimate reconciliation, like Shakespeare's later works." The poetic drama for Eliot, in other words, is a "drama-poem-rite" aimed at retrieving the lost order, peace, and presence of an ideal unity.[71] By the 1930s, when Eliot began to concentrate on writing for the theater, he had already renounced what he once praised in the metaphysicals—their capacity to form "new wholes" by "constantly amalgamating disparate experience"—in favor of what he would later describe as "a kind of mirage of the perfection of verse drama. . . . To go as far in this direction as it is possible to go . . . seems to me the proper aim of dramatic poetry."[72] But that perfection can be achieved only by purging the Elizabethans' regrettably "impure art" of everything—of the contingencies of history; of the clamor of other voices; of prose, and, ultimately, it would seem, of language itself—that exposes this "mirage" for what it is:[73] an impossible, deeply nostalgic dream of an art that claims, by "imposing a credible order on ordinary reality," to reach "some perception of an order *in* reality."[74]

If *Between the Acts* is Woolf's own attempt to revive the poetic drama, it should also be understood as a conscious revision of Eliot's nostalgic project. Streatfield, with his clerical collar and his ironic plea for funds to restore "illumination" to "our dear old church," may not be Eliot in any direct sense.[75] But Woolf, in depicting Streatfield as "an intolerable constriction, contraction, and reduction to simplified absurdity," is surely echoing her affectionate dismissals of "poor old Tom": "He wasn't such a bad fellow; the Rev. G. W. Streatfield; a piece of traditional church furniture; a corner cupboard; or the top beam of a gate, fashioned by generations of village carpenters after some lost-in-the-mists-of-antiquity model."[76] Woolf's fullest response to Eliot comes when the actors gather on stage at the pageant's conclusion, "each declaim[ing] some phrase or fragment from their parts."[77] For the resulting chaos is less a reflection of a fragmented modernity than an image of the wholeness of historical process, less a bitter echo of the end of *The Waste Land,* or of the horrified vision of *The Rock,* than a parody of Eliot's nostalgia for a lost, hierarchized coherence and stability. The pageant's "constantly evolving heteroglossia," in which, as Bakhtin puts it, "any direct word and especially that of the dominant discourse is reflected as something more or less bounded, typical and characteristic of a particular era, aging, dying, ripe for change and renewal," even spills over the edge of the play's frame, reabsorbing Streatfield's "authorized" interpretation into the dispersing crowd's decentered interpretive polyphony:[78]

> The aeroplanes, I didn't like to say it, made one think. . . . No, I thought it much too scrappy. Take the idiot. Did she mean, so to speak, something hidden, the unconscious as they call it? But why always drag in sex. . . . That's the bell. Ding dong. Ding . . . Rather a cracked old bell . . . And the mirrors! Reflecting us . . . I called that cruel. One feels such a fool, caught unprotected . . . There's Mr. Streatfield, going, I suppose to take the evening service. He'll have to hurry, or he won't have time to change. . . . He said she meant we all act. Yes, but whose play? Ah, that's the question! And if we're left asking questions, isn't it a failure, as a play? I must say I like to feel sure if I go to the theatre, that I've grasped the meaning . . . Or was that, perhaps, what she meant? . . . Ding dong. Ding . . . that if we don't jump to conclusions, if you think, and I think, perhaps one day, thinking differently, we shall think the same?[79]

In this last "scrap" of interpretation we can discern, I think, Woolf's embrace of Bakhtin's cathartic recognition that "the ultimate word of the world"—"The Word" so assiduously sought by Eliot—"has not yet been spoken, the world is open and free, everything is still in the future and will always be in the future."[80]

What Woolf recovers from the Elizabethan past is not a vision of a unity that transcends and denies history, but an image or "pattern" of a culture that she finally saw as celebrating difference and dialogue, and the lineaments of a literary form that might be reinvented in order to voice the multiplicitous possibilities for rereading, and hence for rewriting, history.[81] And Woolf's "historical fantasy" of the Renaissance, elaborated throughout her career, is finally self-conscious in a way Eliot's is not—or perhaps in a way that he consistently sought to disguise. The Elizabethan age signals the death of Anon; but it also marks, for Woolf, the birth of the reader, a figure (as she tells us in one of her last extant fragments) who "develop[s] faculties that the play left dormant." Among those faculties must surely be numbered *historical consciousness:* it is only the birth of the reader that allows us to shape and reshape history at all. Woolf's valorization of the past thus ultimately differs from Eliot's in that it acknowledges what Eliot's evades and represses: the truth, as she writes in "Anon," that "[t]here never was . . . a time when men and women were without memory; There never was a young world." The wholeness she attributes to the Elizabethan ethos is the still open potentiality of humanly made history, not the closed, completed unity of a world before the fall. With the birth of the reader, "[w]e are in a world where nothing is concluded."[82]

Eliot shapes the Elizabethan canon to fit the contours of his historiographic desire through repeated gestures of expulsion, excision, and purification. Woolf, if anything, exaggerates that canon's heterogeneity and generic instability, even as she revels in its unwieldy, chaotic historicity—the inclusiveness and "characteristic . . . extravagance," described in one of her earliest essays on the Elizabethans, that are capable of comprehending a "jumble of seeds, silks, unicorns' horns, elephants' teeth, wool, common stones, turbans, and bars of gold, these odds and ends of priceless value and complete worthlessness."[83] But it is Woolf's resistance to Eliot's "mirage" of an Elizabethan age severed from history that ultimately dictates her more productive response to what Meisel defines as the central "crisis" of modernism: "not only the fact of coming late, but of knowing it all too well." Recognizing "the myth of the modern for what it is—a reaction-formation that provides as many advantages as it does restrictions"[84]—Woolf is also able to discover in the Elizabethans a flexible vehicle for engaging the real historical crises of her time, crises from which Eliot sought a refuge far less "real" than the "Unreal City"[85] he loathed.

Woolf's already belated Elizabethans are precursors of the modern subject described by Foucault, who "finds himself" simultaneously "dispossessed of what constituted the most manifest contents of his history" and strangely "interwoven in his own being with histories that are neither subordinate to him nor homogeneous with him." And Woolf's pageant, modeled like her novel and her historiographic project as a whole on the "impure art" of her beloved Elizabethans, situates itself within this "ambiguous" and multiplicitous historicity.[86] As Melba Cuddy-Keane has recently shown, key elements in Woolf's historical practice—"[t]he significance that she accords to unpublished and noncanonical works; her hybrid conflation of literary, social, and economic history; her focus on historical questions rather than on historical patterns; and perhaps most importantly, her situating of literary judgments in terms of an historical text and an historical reader—all contribute to a sense of history that is various, multiple, dynamic, and complexly interrelational."[87] Anticipating postmodernity's incredulity toward metanarratives, historical and otherwise, Woolf's construction of the Renaissance refuses the lure of modernist nostalgia in order to explore more fully a human subject who was, in Foucault's words, "already beginning to recover in the depths of his own being, and among all the things that were still capable of reflecting his image (the others have fallen silent and folded back upon themselves), a historicity linked essentially to man himself." Can this "history ever be anything but the inextricable nexus of different times, which are foreign to him" (Woolf, whose modern reader has learned to read not only "what is on the page" but "what is not written," would surely add, "to her") "and heterogenous in respect to one another?"[88] Resisting Eliot's backward-looking nostalgia for dehistoricized origins, Woolf's historicity, by "thinking differently," reaches toward an always unconcluded future.

⸺ Notes

I wish to thank the anonymous Renaissance scholar-reader for Ohio University Press, whose comments on this essay were especially helpful in supplementing its author's primary expertise in twentieth-century literature.

1. Florence Howe, "Introduction: T. S. Eliot, Virginia Woolf, and the Future of 'Tradition,'" in *Tradition and the Talents of Women,* edited by Florence Howe (Urbana: University of Illinois Press, 1991), 4; Virginia Woolf, *The Diary of Virginia Woolf,* edited by Anne Olivier Bell and Andrew McNeillie, 5 vols. (New York: Harcourt Brace Jovanovich, 1977–84), 2:302 (5 May 1924).

2. Quoted in Quentin Bell, *Virginia Woolf: A Biography* (New York: Harcourt Brace Jovanovich, 1972), 2:173 n.

3. T. S. Eliot, "Tradition and the Individual Talent" (1919), in *Selected Essays* [1932], rev. ed. (New York: Harcourt, Brace, and World, 1964), 3–11, 5.

4. T. S. Eliot, "The Metaphysical Poets" (1921), in *Selected Essays*, 241–50, 241; Woolf, "The Elizabethan Lumber Room," in *The Common Reader: First Series*, edited by Andrew McNeillie (New York: Harcourt Brace Jovanovich [Harvest], 1984), 39–47.

5. Alice Fox, *Virginia Woolf and the Literature of the English Renaissance* (Oxford: Clarendon Press, 1990), passim. For a good sense of the range of Woolf's reading, see especially chap. 3, "The Variety of Elizabethan Literature."

6. Woolf, *Diary*, 3:270 (8 December 1929). Suggestively, Woolf's essay on Gabriel Harvey ("The Strange Elizabethans," in *The Second Common Reader* [1932], ed. Andrew McNeillie [New York: Harcourt Brace Jovanovich, 1986], 9–23), was inspired by her reading of his commonplace book and his marginal notations in other books he had owned. (For further discussion of this essay, see Sally Greene, "Entering Woolf's Renaissance Imaginary: A Second Look at *The Second Common Reader,*" in *Virginia Woolf and the Essay,* edited by Beth Carole Rosenberg and Jeanne Dubino [New York: St. Martin's, 1997], 81–95.—*Ed.*)

7. Woolf, "Anon," in "'Anon' and 'The Reader': Virginia Woolf's Last Essays," edited by Brenda Silver, *Twentieth Century Literature* 25 (1979): 356–441.

8. T. S. Eliot, "The Metaphysical Poets," 247; Woolf, "Poetry, Fiction, and the Future" (1927), reprinted as "The Narrow Bridge of Art," in *Granite and Rainbow,* edited by Leonard Woolf (1958; reprint, New York: Harcourt Brace Jovanovich [Harvest], 1975), 11–23, 12.

9. T. S. Eliot, "The Metaphysical Poets," 247; Woolf, "The Narrow Bridge of Art," 14; Woolf, "How It Strikes a Contemporary" (1923), reprinted (slightly revised) in *The Common Reader,* 231–41, (238).

10. Richard Halpern, *Shakespeare among the Moderns* (Ithaca, N.Y.: Cornell University Press, 1997), 9.

11. T. S. Eliot, "Four Elizabethan Dramatists: A Preface to an Unwritten Book" (1924), in *Selected Essays,* 91–99, 98. Eliot's "unwritten book" was to have focused on Webster, Tourneur, Middleton, and Chapman as instances of "great literary and dramatic genius" marred by "chaos" and "discord." To the "impure art" of the Elizabethans, Eliot contrasts *Everyman:* "in that one [English] play only, we have a drama within the limitations of art" (98, 96, 93).

12. T. S. Eliot, "Donne in Our Time," in *A Garland for John Donne,* edited by Theodore Spencer (1931; reprint, Gloucester, Mass.: Peter Smith, 1958), 8.

13. Woolf, "Anon," 390–92, 397, 382. As Barbara Apstein points out, Woolf's insistence on Chaucer's "artlessness" is itself an oversimplification: "Woolf see[s] Chaucer as relatively simple and straightforward, with no suggestion of the complexities and ironies which have absorbed the attention of later generations of critics." Barbara Apstein, "Chaucer, Virginia Woolf, and *Between the Acts,*" *Woolf Studies Annual* 2 (1996): 118–19.

14. For a discussion of the significance of contemporary criticism's terminological

preference for "early modern" over "Renaissance" as it relates to Woolf's construction of the period, see Sally Greene, "Michelet, Woolf, and the Idea of the Renaissance," chap. 1 of this volume.

15. Kermode, *Romantic Image* (New York: Random House, 1957), 138–47. For T. S. Eliot's discussion of Milton and the Civil War, see "Milton II" (1947), in *On Poetry and Poets* (London: Faber and Faber, 1957), 146–61, 148, 152–53.

16. Woolf, "Anon," 384, 424 n. 103. Although Woolf thus echoes some of the lingering medievalism that characterizes Eliot's ambivalence about the Renaissance, she decidedly does not share her contemporary's emerging view of the period as one of moral disintegration. In this respect, Woolf's developing response to Eliot, as outlined in the pages that follow, offers a suggestive parallel to Pater's earlier revision of Ruskin's moral disapproval of the Renaissance; see Greene, chap. 1 of this volume.

17. Kermode, 140–43.

18. T. S. Eliot, "Shakespeare and the Stoicism of Seneca" (1927), in *Selected Essays*, 107–20, 118; "Donne in Our Time," 8. See also Kermode, 147. (Kermode places Eliot's disillusionment with Donne in the context of the tercentenary celebrations of Donne's life, which is also the context of Woolf's essay on Donne, an essay that culminated years of interest. For discussion of "Donne after Three Centuries" as well as further discussion of the Woolf-Eliot connection, see Diane F. Gillespie, "Through Woolf's 'I's': Donne and *The Waves*," chap. 9 of this volume.—*Ed.*)

19. Sharon Stockman, "Virginia Woolf and the Renaissance: The Promise of Capital and the Violence of Materialism," *Clio* 24 (1995): 241, 245, 250.

20. Kermode, 141.

21. T. S. Eliot, "Gerontion" (1920), in *The Complete Poems and Plays, 1909–1950* (1952; reprint, New York: Harcourt, Brace, and World, 1971), 21–23, 22.

22. Perry Meisel, *The Myth of the Modern: A Study in British Literature and Criticism after 1850* (New Haven, Conn.: Yale University Press, 1987), 1, 229. In his comprehensive study of *imitatio* in the Renaissance era, Thomas Greene points out that the Elizabethans themselves were caught up in the same kind of historiographic myth-making; their own myth of the modern, expressed in "ubiquitous imagery of disinterment, resurrection, and renascence," required both a sense of disjunction and the possibility of recovery, "the myth of medieval entombment" and a belief in "the loss of a remote, prestigious past that might nonetheless be resuscitated." Greene cites Spenser's "Ruines of Time" and Jonson's *Golden Age Restored* as Elizabethan examples of what was in effect an "effort to exchange one recent past for another, distant one"—a "hazardous mythologization" that Greene views as "a local version of a situation universally human. The past always reaches us across a space which we want to deny. It reaches us incomplete, and in attempting to make it whole we merely create a new incompleteness." See Thomas M. Greene, *The Light in Troy: Imitation and Discovery in Renaissance Poetry* (New Haven, Conn.: Yale University Press, 1982), 3, 33–35.

23. Jeffrey Perl, *The Tradition of Return: The Implicit History of Modern Literature* (Princeton, N.J.: Princeton University Press, 1980).

24. T. S. Eliot, "Little Gidding" (1942), in *Four Quartets* (1943), collected in *Complete Poems and Plays*, 138–45, 144.

25. Woolf, *A Room of One's Own* (1929; reprint, with a foreword by Mary Gordon, New York: Harcourt Brace Jovanovich[Harvest], 1989), 45.

26. T. S. Eliot, "The Metaphysical Poets," 247.

27. T. S. Eliot, "East Coker" (1940), in *Four Quartets*, collected in *Complete Poems and Plays*, 123–29, 123–24.

28. Andrew Ross, *The Failure of Modernism: Symptoms of American Poetry* (New York: Columbia University Press, 1986), 59.

29. T. S. Eliot, "East Coker," 124.

30. Woolf, *A Room of One's Own*, 63–65.

31. T. S. Eliot, "Tradition and the Individual Talent," 10–11; "Little Gidding," 144.

32. T. S. Eliot, "Gerontion," 22; "Burnt Norton" (1941), in *Four Quartets*, collected in *Complete Poems and Plays*, 117–22, 117–18, 122.

33. Jacques Derrida, *Of Grammatology*, translated by Gayatri Chakravorty Spivak (Baltimore: Johns Hopkins University Press, 1976).

34. T. S. Eliot, "Burnt Norton," 118.

35. Woolf, "Anon," 390, 385.

36. Walter J. Ong, *Orality and Literacy: The Technologizing of the Word* (London: Methuen, 1982), 179. Ong carefully and consistently resists the nostalgic valorization of orality exemplified by Eliot: "Orality is not an ideal, and never was. . . . Literacy opens possibilities to the word and to human existence unimaginable without writing" (175).

37. Woolf, *Orlando: A Biography* (1928; reprint, New York: Harcourt Brace Jovanovich [Harvest], 1973), 77.

38. T. S. Eliot, "Four Elizabethan Dramatists," 98.

39. Mikhail Bakhtin, *The Dialogic Imagination*, edited by Michael Holquist, translated by Caryl Emerson and Michael Holquist (Austin: University of Texas Press, 1981), 30. (For further consideration of the affinity between Woolf and Bakhtin, see Melba Cuddy-Keane, "The Rhetoric of Feminist Conversation: Virginia Woolf and the Trope of the Twist," in *Ambiguous Discourse: Feminist Narratology and British Women Writers*, edited by Kathy Mezei [Chapel Hill: University of North Carolina Press, 1996], 137–61.—*Ed.*)

40. Woolf, *Orlando*, 34, 56.

41. Woolf, "The Niece of an Earl" (1928), in *The Second Common Reader*, 214–19, 218.

42. Woolf, "Anon," 392.

43. Brenda Silver, "Virginia Woolf and the Concept of Community: The Elizabethan Playhouse," *Women's Studies* 4 (1977): 294.

44. Woolf, "Anon," 383.

45. Woolf, *A Room of One's Own,* 42.

46. Woolf, "Anon," 382.

47. Woolf, *A Room of One's Own,* 49.

48. Woolf, *Diary,* 5:318 (12 September 1940); "Anon," 383. In the passage from "Anon" the italics are Woolf's; the square brackets indicate editor Brenda Silver's uncertainty about Woolf's manuscript.

49. Woolf, "The Narrow Bridge of Art" (see note 8 above), 20.

50. Woolf, *Diary,* 5:356 (26 February 1941).

51. Woolf, "Notes on an Elizabethan Play" (1925), reprinted (revised) in *The Common Reader,* 48–57, 50.

52. Woolf, *Between the Acts* (1941; reprint, New York: Harcourt Brace Jovanovich [Harvest], 1970), 178, 125.

53. Nora Eisenberg, "Virginia Woolf's Last Word on Words: *Between the Acts* and 'Anon,'" in *New Feminist Essays on Virginia Woolf,* edited by Jane Marcus (Lincoln: University of Nebraska Press, 1981), 256–57. Other critics who read the pageant along these lines include Marilyn Zorn, "The Pageant in *Between the Acts,*" *Modern Fiction Studies* 2 (1956): 2; and Richard Lyons, "The Intellectual Structure of Virginia Woolf's *Between the Acts,*" *Modern Language Quarterly* 38 (1977): 153–54.

54. Woolf, *Between the Acts,* 190, 192.

55. Woolf, "Anon," 385, 406 n. 12.

56. Ibid., 384.

57. Streatfield's nostalgic interpretation, in its emphasis on the totalizing and unifying effects of the pageant's choric voice, tends to elide what Apstein, following Ong, identifies as the pageant's "secondary orality." As Ong explains, secondary orality is "not antecedent to writing and print as primary orality is, but consequent upon and dependent upon writing and print." As an instance of secondary orality akin to such modern media as radio and television, the pageant fosters "a communal sense" that is considerably less monological, more self-conscious and historicized, than the primary orality for which Streatfield, like Eliot, longs. See Apstein, 128, 130; Ong, 171, 136.

58. Woolf, *Between the Acts,* 197, 194.

59. Ibid., 187, 188.

60. Ibid., 193.

61. Woolf, *Diary,* 5:347 (29 December 1940), 5:210 (22 March 1939).

62. Woolf to Bell, 3 December 1933, and to Spender, 10 July 1934, *The Letters of Virginia Woolf,* edited by Nigel Nicolson and Joanne Trautmann, 6 vols. (New York: Harcourt Brace Jovanovich, 1975–80), 5:256, 5:315.

63. T. S. Eliot, "Choruses from *The Rock,*" in *Complete Poems and Plays,* 96–114, 96–97.

64. Ibid., 113.

65. John Xiros Cooper, *T. S. Eliot and the Ideology of* Four Quartets (Cambridge: Cambridge University Press, 1995), 70, quoting T. S. Eliot, "Choruses from *The Rock,*" 105.

66. T. S. Eliot, "Choruses from *The Rock*," 107, 104.

67. Woolf, *Between the Acts*, 187.

68. T. S. Eliot, "Choruses from *The Rock*," 104, 102, 96.

69. Woolf, *Between the Acts*, 20.

70. Woolf, *Letters*, 5:315.

71. R. Peacock, "Eliot's Contribution to Criticism of Drama," in *The Literary Criticism of T. S. Eliot*, edited by David Newton-Molina (London: Athlone Press, 1977), 107.

72. T. S. Eliot, "The Metaphysical Poets," 241–50, 247; "Poetry and Drama" (1951), in *On Poetry and Poets*, 72–88, 87.

73. T. S. Eliot, "Four Elizabethan Dramatists," 96.

74. T. S. Eliot, "Poetry and Drama," 87. Eliot remarks in this essay that "a mixture of prose and verse in the same play is generally to be avoided" (73)—a dictum Woolf deliberately violates by mixing her pageant's poetry with her novel's prose.

75. Woolf, *Between the Acts*, 190, 193.

76. Ibid., 190.

77. Ibid., 185.

78. Bakhtin, *The Dialogic Imagination*, 60.

79. Woolf, *Between the Acts*, 199–200.

80. Bakhtin, *Problems in Dostoevsky's Poetics*, edited and translated by Caryl Emerson (Minneapolis: University of Minnesota Press, 1984), 166.

81. In her diary entry for 26 July 1940 (*Diary*, 5:306), written on a "transient, changing, warm, capricious summer evening," Woolf acknowledged the "pressure of suggestions—about Culture patterns"—she had received from reading Ruth Benedict's *Patterns of Culture* (1934).

82. Woolf, "Anon," 429, 385, 429.

83. Woolf, "The Elizabethan Lumber Room, 43, 39.

84. Meisel, *The Myth of the Modern*, 229.

85. T. S. Eliot, *The Waste Land* (1922), in *Complete Poems and Plays*, 37–55, 39.

86. Foucault, *The Order of Things: An Archaeology of the Human Sciences*, translated by Alan Sheridan (New York: Random House, 1970), 368–69.

87. Melba Cuddy-Keane, "Virginia Woolf and the Varieties of Historicist Experience," in *Virginia Woolf and the Essay*, edited by Beth Carole Rosenberg and Jeanne Dubino (New York: St. Martin's, 1997), 61. Cuddy-Keane's argument, like my own, views Woolf's "pluralistic" and "nontotalizing" historicism as anticipating the concerns of late twentieth-century theory; she also usefully reads Woolf's emerging historiographic thinking in light of the nineteenth century's "long history of unease with traditional [historical] practice" (62–63). For a more modest—and less compelling—assessment of Woolf's historicism, see Sabine Hotho-Jackson, "Virginia Woolf on History: Between Tradition and Modernity," *Forum for Modern Language Studies* 27 (1991): 293–313.

88. Foucault, *The Order of Things*, 369; Woolf, "Anon," 429.

Bibliography

Abbott, Reginald. "What Miss Kilman's Petticoat Means: Virginia Woolf, Shopping, and Spectacle." *Modern Fiction Studies* 38 (1992): 193–216.

Abel, Elizabeth. "Narrative Structure(s) and Female Development: The Case of *Mrs. Dalloway*." In Bloom, *Virginia Woolf*, 243–64.

Adelman, Janet. *Suffocating Mothers: Fantasies of Maternal Origins in Shakespeare's Plays, "Hamlet" to "The Tempest."* New York: Routledge, 1992.

Allen, Judith. "Those Soul Mates: Virginia Woolf and Michel de Montaigne." In *Virginia Woolf: Themes and Variations: Selected Papers from the Second Annual Conference on Virginia Woolf,* edited by Vara Neverow-Turk and Mark Hussey, 190–99. New York: Pace University Press, 1993.

Apstein, Barbara. "Chaucer, Virginia Woolf, and *Between the Acts*." *Woolf Studies Annual* 2 (1996): 117–33.

Armstrong, Isobel. "Textual Harassment: The Ideology of Close Reading, or, How Close Is Close?" *Textual Practice* 9 (1995): 401–20.

Arnold, Janet. *Queen Elizabeth's Wardrobe Unlock'd.* Leeds, Eng.: W. S. Maney, 1988.

Baker, Nicholson. *The Size of Thoughts.* New York: Vintage, 1996.

Bakhtin, Mikhail. *The Dialogic Imagination.* Edited by Michael Holquist. Translated by Caryl Emerson and Michael Holquist. Austin: University of Texas Press, 1981. Four essays that originally appeared in *Voprosy literatury i estetiki* (Moscow, 1975).

———. *Problems in Dostoevsky's Poetics.* Edited and translated by Caryl Emerson. Minneapolis: University of Minnesota Press, 1984. Originally published as *Problemy poetiki Dostoevskogo* (Moscow, 1963).

Bald, R. C. *John Donne: A Life.* New York: Oxford University Press, 1970.

Barbour, Reid. *Deciphering Elizabethan Fiction.* Newark: University of Delaware Press, 1993.

Barthes, Roland. "Michelet, Today." 1972. Reprinted in *The Rustle of Language,* translated by Richard Howard, 195–207. Berkeley: University of California Press, 1989. Originally published as *La bruissement de la langue* (Paris: Éditions du Seuil, 1984).

————. "La Sorcière." 1959. Reprinted in *Critical Essays,* translated by Richard Howard, 103–15. Evanston: Northwestern University Press, 1972. Originally published as *Essais critiques* (Paris: Éditions du Seuil, 1964).

————. *S/Z.* Paris: Éditions du Seuil, 1970.

Beer, Gillian. *Virginia Woolf: The Common Ground.* Ann Arbor: University of Michigan Press, 1996.

Bell, Ilona. "Milton's Dialogue with Petrarch." *Milton Studies* 28 (1992): 91–120.

————. "The Role of the Lady in Donne's *Songs and Sonnets.*" *Studies in English Literature 1500–1900* 23 (1983): 113–30.

Bell, Quentin. *Virginia Woolf: A Biography.* 2 vols. New York: Harcourt Brace Jovanovich, 1972.

Belsey, Catherine. *John Milton: Language, Gender, Power.* Oxford: Blackwell, 1988.

Benjamin, Walter. "The Storyteller." 1936. In *Illuminations,* edited and with an introduction by Hannah Arendt, translated by Harry Zohn, 83–109. New York: Schocken Books, 1969. Originally published as *Illuminationen* (Frankfurt: Suhrkamp Verlag, 1955).

Bergeron, David Moore. *Shakespeare's Romances and the Royal Family.* Lawrence, Kans.: University Press of Kansas, 1985.

Berry, Philippa. *Of Chastity and Power: Elizabethan Literature and the Unmarried Queen.* New York: Routledge, 1989.

Besserman, Lawrence, ed. *The Challenge of Periodization: Old Paradigms and New Perspectives.* New York: Garland, 1996.

Bloom, Harold. "Feminism as the Love of Reading." *Raritan* 14, no. 2 (1994): 29–42.

————, ed. *Virginia Woolf.* New York: Chelsea House, 1986.

Booker, Keith M. "Tradition, Authority, and Subjectivity: Narrative Constitution of the Self in *The Waves.*" *Literature, Interpretation, Theory* 3 (1991): 33–55.

Boone, Joseph Allen. "The Meaning of Elvedon in *The Waves:* A Key to Bernard's Experience and Woolf's Vision." *Modern Fiction Studies* 27 (1981–82): 629–37.

Boose, Linda. "The Father and the Bride in Shakespeare." *PMLA* 97 (1982): 325–47.

Booth, Alison. *Greatness Engendered: George Eliot and Virginia Woolf.* Ithaca, N.Y.: Cornell University Press, 1992.

Borges, Jorge Luis. "The Library of Babel." In *Labyrinths: Selected Stories and Other Writings,* edited by Donald A. Yates and James E. Irby, with a preface by André Maurois, 51–58. New York: New Directions, 1964.

Bowlby, Rachel. Introduction to *A Woman's Essays: Selected Essays,* vol. 1 (London: Penguin, 1992). Reprinted in *Virginia Woolf: Introductions to the Major Works,* edited by Julia Briggs, 249–77. London: Virago, 1994.

————. *Still Crazy after All These Years: Women, Writing, and Psychoanalysis.* New York: Routledge, 1992.

————. *Virginia Woolf: Feminist Destinations.* Oxford: Blackwell, 1988.

Boyd, Elizabeth. "Luriana Lurilee." *Notes and Queries* 10 (1963): 380–81.

British Museum. *A Guide to the Use of the Reading Room.* London: By Order of the Trustees, 1924.

Brower, Reuben. "Something Central Which Permeated: *Mrs. Dalloway.*" In Bloom, *Virginia Woolf,* 7–18.

Browne, William. *Circe and Ulysses: The Inner Temple Masque.* Edited by Gwyn Jones. [London]: Golden Cockerel Press, 1954.

Bruno, Giordano. *The Ash Wednesday Supper.* Edited and translated by Edward A. Gosselin and Lawrence S. Lerner. Hamden, Conn.: Archon Books, 1977. Originally published as *La Cena de le Ceneri* (1584).

———. *De Umbris Idearum* [1582]. Edited by Rita Sturlese. Firenze: Leo S. Olschki, 1991.

Bullen, Arthur Henry, ed. *The Poems of William Browne of Tavistock.* London: Lawrence and Bullen; New York: Scribner, 1894.

Bullen, J. B. *The Myth of the Renaissance in Nineteenth-Century Writing.* Oxford: Clarendon Press, 1994.

Burckhardt, Jacob. *The Civilization of the Renaissance in Italy* [1878]. 2d ed., revised and translated by S. G. C. Middlemore. New York: Oxford University Press, 1945. Originally published as *Die Cultur der Renaissance in Italien* (1860).

Cafarelli, Annette Wheeler. "How Theories of Romanticism Exclude Women: Radcliffe, Milton, and the Legitimation of the Gothic Novel." In *Milton, the Metaphysicals, and Romanticism,* edited by Lisa Low and Anthony John Harding, 84–113. Cambridge: Cambridge University Press, 1994.

Caramagno, Thomas. *The Flight of the Mind: Virginia Woolf's Art and Manic-Depressive Illness.* Berkeley: University of California Press, 1992.

Carey, John. *John Donne: Life, Mind, and Art.* New York: Oxford University Press, 1981.

Carruthers, Mary. *The Book of Memory: A Study of Memory in Medieval Culture.* Cambridge: Cambridge University Press, 1990.

Caughie, Pamela L. *Virginia Woolf and Postmodernism: Literature in Quest and Question of Itself.* Urbana: University of Illinois Press, 1991.

Cave, Terence. "Problems of Reading in the *Essais.*" In *Montaigne: Essays in Memory of Richard Sayce,* edited by I. D. McFarlane and Ian MacLean, 133–66. Oxford: Clarendon Press, 1982.

Chartier, Roger. *The Order of Books.* Stanford, Calif.: Stanford University Press, 1994.

Childress, Diana T. "Are Shakespeare's Late Plays Really Romances?" In *Shakespeare's Late Plays: Essays in Honor of Charles Crow,* edited by Richard C. Tobias and Paul G. Zolbrod, 44–55. Athens: Ohio University Press, 1974.

Connerton, Paul. *How Societies Remember.* Cambridge: Cambridge University Press, 1989.

Cooper, John Xiros. *T. S. Eliot and the Ideology of* Four Quartets. Cambridge: Cambridge University Press, 1995.

Creighton, Mandell. *Queen Elizabeth* [1896; rev. ed., 1899]. New York: Longmans, Green, 1927.

Crook, J. Mordaunt. *The British Museum.* New York: Praeger, 1972.

Cuddy-Keane, Melba. "The Rhetoric of Feminist Conversation: Virginia Woolf and the Trope of the Twist." In *Ambiguous Discourse: Feminist Narratology and British*

Women Writers, edited by Kathy Mezei, 137–61. Chapel Hill: University of North Carolina Press, 1996.

———. "Virginia Woolf and the Varieties of Historicist Experience." In *Virginia Woolf and the Essay,* edited by Beth Carole Rosenberg and Jeanne Dubino, 59–77. New York: St. Martin's, 1997.

Dale, Peter Allan. "Beyond Humanism: J. A. Symonds and the Replotting of the Renaissance." *Clio* 17 (1988): 109–37.

Dasenbrock, Reed Way. *Imitating the Italians: Wyatt, Spenser, Synge, Pound, Joyce.* Baltimore: Johns Hopkins University Press, 1991.

de Grazia, Margreta. "*Fin-de-Siècle* Renaissance England." In Fins de Siècle: *English Poetry in 1590, 1690, 1790, 1890, 1990,* edited by Elaine Scarry, 37–63. Baltimore: Johns Hopkins University Press, 1995.

de Grazia, Margreta, Maureen Quilligan, and Peter Stallybrass. Introduction to *Subject and Object in Renaissance Culture,* edited by Margreta de Grazia, Maureen Quilligan, and Peter Stallybrass, 1–13. New York: Cambridge University Press, 1996.

de Lauretis, Teresa. *Technologies of Gender.* Bloomington: Indiana University Press, 1987.

Derrida, Jacques. *Of Grammatology.* Translated by Gayatri Chakravorty Spivak. Baltimore: Johns Hopkins University Press, 1976. Originally published as *De la grammatologie* (Paris: Éditions de Minuit, 1967).

DeSalvo, Louise A. "A Portrait of the *Puttana* as a Middle-Aged Woolf Scholar." In *Between Women: Biographers, Novelists, Critics, Teachers, and Artists Write about Their Work on Women,* edited by Carol Ascher, Louise A. DeSalvo, and Sara Ruddick, 35–53. Boston: Beacon Press, 1984.

———. "Shakespeare's 'Other' Sister." In *New Feminist Essays on Virginia Woolf,* edited by Jane Marcus, 61–81. Lincoln: University of Nebraska Press, 1981.

———. "Virginia, Virginius, Virginity." In *Faith of a (Woman) Writer,* edited by Alice Kessler-Harris and William McBrien, 179–89. Westport, Conn.: Greenwood, 1988.

———. *Virginia Woolf's First Voyage.* Totowa, N.J.: Rowman and Littlefield, 1980.

———, ed. Melymbrosia *by Virginia Woolf: An Early Version of* The Voyage Out. New York: New York Public Library, 1982.

DiBattista, Maria. *Virginia Woolf's Major Novels: The Fables of Anon.* New Haven, Conn.: Yale University Press, 1980.

Dimock, Wai Chee. "A Theory of Resonance." *PMLA* 112 (1997): 1060–71.

Donne, John. *The Poems of John Donne.* Edited by Herbert J. C. Grierson. 2 vols. Oxford: Clarendon Press, 1912.

———. *Poetry: Authoritative Texts and Criticism.* Edited by Arthur L. Clements. New York: Norton, 1992.

Donoghue, Dennis. *Walter Pater: Lover of Strange Souls.* New York: Knopf, 1995.

Dowling, David. Mrs. Dalloway: *Mapping Streams of Consciousness.* Boston: Twayne, 1991.

Dubrow, Heather. *Echoes of Desire: English Petrarchism and Its Counterdiscourses.* Ithaca, N.Y.: Cornell University Press, 1995.

DuPlessis, Rachel Blau. "'Amor Vin—': Modifications of Romance in Woolf." In *Virginia Woolf: A Collection of Critical Essays,* edited by Margaret Homans, 115–35. Englewood Cliffs, N.J.: Prentice Hall, 1993.

Dusinberre, Juliet. "Virginia Woolf and Montaigne." *Textual Practice* 5 (1991): 219–41.

———. *Virginia Woolf's Renaissance: Woman Reader or Common Reader?* Iowa City: University of Iowa Press, 1997.

Eder, Doris L. "Louis Unmasked: T. S. Eliot in *The Waves.*" *Virginia Woolf Quarterly* 2, no. 1/2 (1975): 13–27.

Eisenberg, Nora. "Virginia Woolf's Last Word on Words: *Between the Acts* and 'Anon.'" In *New Feminist Essays on Virginia Woolf,* edited by Jane Marcus, 253–66. Lincoln: University of Nebraska Press, 1981.

Eliot, George. *Romola* [1862–63]. Edited by Andrew Brown. New York: Oxford University Press, 1994.

Eliot, T. S. *The Complete Poems and Plays, 1909–1950.* 1952. Reprint, New York: Harcourt, Brace, and World, 1971.

———. "Donne in Our Time." In *A Garland for John Donne.* 1931. Edited by Theodore Spencer, 3–19. Reprint, Gloucester, Mass.: Peter Smith, 1958.

[———]. "The New Elizabethans and the Old." *Athenaeum,* 4 April 1919, 135–37.

———. *On Poetry and Poets.* London: Faber and Faber, 1957.

———. *Selected Essays* [1932]. Rev. ed. New York: Harcourt, Brace, and World, 1964.

Engel, William E. "Mnemonic Criticism and Renaissance Literature: A Manifesto." *Connotations* 1 (1991): 12–33.

English, James. *Comic Transactions: Literature, Humor, and the Politics of Community in Twentieth-Century Britain.* Ithaca, N.Y.: Cornell University Press, 1994.

Erler, Mary C. "Sir John Davies and the Rainbow Portrait of Queen Elizabeth." *Modern Philology* 84 (1987): 359–71.

Estrin, Barbara. *Laura: Uncovering Gender and Genre in Wyatt, Donne, and Marvell.* Durham, N.C.: Duke University Press, 1994.

Ezell, Margaret J. N. *Writing Women's Literary History.* Baltimore: Johns Hopkins University Press, 1993.

Fentress, James, and Chris Wickham. *Social Memory.* Oxford: Blackwell, 1992.

Ferguson, John. "A Sea Change: Thomas De Quincey and Mr. Carmichael in *To the Lighthouse.*" *Journal of Modern Literature* 14 (1987): 45–63.

Ferguson, Margaret W., Maureen Quilligan, and Nancy J. Vickers, eds. *Rewriting the Renaissance: The Discourses of Sexual Difference in Early Modern Europe.* Chicago: University of Chicago Press, 1986.

Ferguson, Wallace. *The Renaissance in Historical Thought: Five Centuries of Interpretation.* Cambridge, Mass.: Riverside Press, 1948.

Fernald, Anne E. "*A Room of One's Own,* Personal Criticism, and the Essay." *Twentieth Century Literature* 40 (1994): 165–89.

Fleishman, Avrom. *Virginia Woolf: A Critical Reading.* Baltimore: Johns Hopkins University Press, 1975.

———. "Virginia Woolf: Tradition and Modernity." In *Forms of Modern British Fiction,* edited by Alan Warren Friedman, 133–63. Austin: University of Texas Press, 1975.

Flynn, Dennis. "'Awry and Squint': The Dating of Donne's Holy Sonnets." *John Donne Journal* 7 (1988): 35–45.

Forster, E. M. *Aspects of the Novel.* New York: Harcourt, Brace, 1927.

———. *The Longest Journey.* 1907. Reprint, New York: Vintage, 1962.

———. *A Room with a View.* 1908. Reprint, New York: Vintage, n.d.

Foucault, Michel. *Language, Counter-Memory, Practice: Selected Essays and Interviews.* Edited by Donald F. Bouchard. Translated by Donald F. Bouchard and Sherry Simon. Ithaca, N.Y.: Cornell University Press, 1977.

———. *The Order of Things: An Archaeology of the Human Sciences.* Translated by Alan Sheridan. New York: Random House, 1970. Originally published as *Les mots et les choses: une archéologie des sciences humaines* (Paris: Gallimard, 1966).

Fox, Alice. "Literary Allusion as Feminist Criticism in *A Room of One's Own.*" In McNees, 2:199–214.

———. *Virginia Woolf and the Literature of the English Renaissance.* Oxford: Clarendon Press, 1990.

Frame, Donald. *Montaigne in France 1812–1852.* New York: Columbia University Press, 1940.

Friedman, Susan Stanford. "Virginia Woolf's Pedagogical Scenes of Reading: *The Voyage Out, The Common Reader,* and Her 'Common Readers.'" *Modern Fiction Studies* 38 (1992): 101–25.

———. "Weavings: Intertextuality and the (Re)Birth of the Author." In *Influence and Intertextuality in Literary History,* edited by Jay Clayton and Eric Rothstein, 146–80. Madison: University of Wisconsin Press, 1991.

Friedrich, Hugo. *Montaigne* [1949]. Translated by Robert Rovint. Paris: Gallimard, 1968.

Froula, Christine. "The Daughter's Seduction: Sexual Violence and Literary History." In *Feminist Theory in Practice and Process,* edited by Micheline R. Malson, Jean F. O'Barr, Sarah Westphal-Wihl, and Mary Wyer, 139–62. Chicago: University of Chicago Press, 1989.

———. "Out of the Chrysalis: Female Initiation and Female Authority in Virginia Woolf's *The Voyage Out.*" In *Virginia Woolf: A Collection of Critical Essays,* edited by Margaret Homans, 136–61. Englewood Cliffs, N.J.: Prentice Hall, 1993.

———. "Virginia Woolf as Shakespeare's Sister: Chapters in a Woman Writer's Autobiography." In *Women's Re-Visions of Shakespeare,* edited by Marianne Novy, 123–42. Urbana: University of Illinois Press, 1990.

Gardner, Helen, ed. *John Donne: The Divine Poems* [1952]. 2d ed. Oxford: Clarendon Press, 1959.

Gilbert, Felix. *History: Politics or Culture? Reflections on Ranke and Burckhardt.* Princeton, N.J.: Princeton University Press, 1990.

Gilbert, Sandra, and Susan Gubar. *Madwoman in the Attic: The Woman Writer and the Nineteenth-Century Literary Imagination.* New Haven, Conn.: Yale University Press, 1979.

Gillespie, Diane Filby. *The Sisters' Arts: The Writing and Painting of Virginia Woolf and Vanessa Bell.* Syracuse, N.Y.: Syracuse University Press, 1988.

Gordon, Lyndall. *Virignia Woolf: A Writer's Life.* New York: Norton, 1984.

Gorris, Marleen, dir. *Mrs. Dalloway.* With Vanessa Redgrave, Natascha McElhone, Rupert Graves, and Michael Kitchen. First Look Pictures, 1997.

Gosse, Edmund. *The Life and Letters of John Donne.* 2 vols. New York: Dodd, Mead, 1899.

Gossman, Lionel. *Between History and Literature.* Cambridge, Mass.: Harvard University Press, 1990.

Gough, Val. "With Some Irony in Her Interrogation: Woolf's Ironic Mysticism." In *Virginia Woolf and the Arts: Selected Papers from the Sixth Annual Conference on Virginia Woolf,* edited by Diane F. Gillespie and Leslie K. Hankins, 85–90. New York: Pace University Press, 1997.

Graham, J. W. "Point of View in *The Waves:* Some Services of Style." *University of Toronto Quarterly* 39 (1969–70): 193–211.

———, ed. *Virginia Woolf:* The Waves: *The Two Holograph Drafts.* Toronto: University of Toronto Press, 1976.

Grant, Michael, and John Hazed. *Gods and Mortals in Classical Mythology.* Springfield, Mass.: G. and C. Merriam, 1973.

Green, A. Wigfall. *The Inns of Court and Early English Drama.* 1931. Reprint, New York: Benjamin Blom, 1965.

Greene, Sally. "Entering Woolf's Renaissance Imaginary: A Second Look at *The Second Common Reader.*" In *Virginia Woolf and the Essay,* edited by Beth Carole Rosenberg and Jeanne Dubino, 81–95. New York: St. Martin's, 1997.

———. [Sarah L. Greene.] "Reading Woolf Reading the Renaissance: Tracing an Elizabethan Modern's Search for Peace." Ann Arbor, Mich.: Dissertation Abstracts International, 1996.

Greene, Thomas M. *The Light in Troy: Imitation and Discovery in Renaissance Poetry.* New Haven, Conn.: Yale University Press, 1982.

Grierson, Herbert J. C. *Cross Currents in English Literature of the XVIIth Century* [1929]. Rev. ed. London: Chatto and Windus, 1958.

Guth, Deborah. "'What a Lark! What a Plunge!': Fiction as Self-Evasion in *Mrs. Dalloway.*" *Modern Language Review* 84 (1989): 18–25.

Halbwachs, Maurice. *On Collective Memory.* Edited and translated by Lewis A. Coser. Chicago: University of Chicago Press, 1992. Also published as *Les Cadres sociaux de la mémoire* (Paris: Presses Universitaires de France, 1952) and as *La topographie légendaire des évangiles en terre sainte* (Paris: Presses Universitaires de France, 1941).

Halpern, Richard. *Shakespeare among the Moderns.* Ithaca, N.Y.: Cornell University Press, 1997.

Hannay, Margaret P. *Philip's Phoenix: Mary Sidney, Countess of Pembroke.* New York: Oxford University Press, 1990.

Hanson, Clare. *Virginia Woolf.* New York: St. Martin's, 1994.

Harris, P. R. *The Reading Room.* London: British Museum, 1979.

Harris, Wendell V. "Ruskin and Pater—Hebrew and Hellene—Explore the Renaissance." *Clio* 17 (1988): 173–85.

Haule, James M. "Virginia Woolf under a Microscope." *Woolf Studies Annual* 3 (1997): 143–59.

Hazlitt, William Carew, ed. *The Whole Works of William Browne, of Tavistock, and of the Inner Temple.* 2 vols. London: Whittingham and Wilkins, 1868–69.

Heilbrun, Carolyn G. "Virginia Woolf in Her Fifties." In *Hamlet's Mother and Other Women,* 90–113. New York: Ballantine, 1990.

———. *Writing a Woman's Life.* New York: Norton, 1988.

Hill, Katherine. "Virginia Woolf and Leslie Stephen: History and Literary Revolution." *PMLA* 96 (1981): 351–62.

Hoffmann, Anne Golomb. "Demeter and Poseidon: Fusion and Distance in *To the Lighthouse.*" *Studies in the Novel* 16 (1984): 182–96.

Hogan, Patrick Colm. *Joyce, Milton, and the Theory of Influence.* Gainesville: University Press of Florida, 1995.

Homer. *The Odyssey.* Trans. Robert Fitzgerald. Garden City, N.Y.: Doubleday, 1963.

Hotho-Jackson, Sabine. "Virginia Woolf on History: Between Tradition and Modernity." *Forum for Modern Language Studies* 27 (1991): 293–313.

Howe, Florence. "Introduction: T. S. Eliot, Virginia Woolf, and the Future of 'Tradition.'" In *Tradition and the Talents of Women,* edited by Florence Howe, 1–33. Urbana: University of Illinois Press, 1991.

Hull, Suzanne. *Chaste, Silent, and Obedient: English Books for Women, 1475–1640.* San Marino, Calif.: Huntington Library, 1982.

Hussey, Mark. *The Singing of the Real World.* Columbus: Ohio State University Press, 1986.

Hutton, Patrick H. "The Art of Memory Reconceived: From Rhetoric to Psychoanalysis." *Journal of the History of Ideas* 48 (1987): 371–92.

Jankowski, Theodora A. "'The Scorne of Savage People': Virginity as 'Forbidden Sexuality' in John Lyly's *Love's Metamorphosis.*" In *Renaissance Drama* (1993): 123–53.

Jay, Karla. *The Amazon and the Page.* Bloomington: Indiana University Press, 1988.

Jensen, Emily. "Clarissa Dalloway's Respectable Suicide." In *Virginia Woolf: A Feminist Slant,* edited by Jane Marcus, 162–79. Lincoln: University of Nebraska Press, 1983.

Johnston, Georgia. "Women's Voice: *Three Guineas* as Autobiography." In *Virginia Woolf: Themes and Variations: Selected Papers from the Second Annual Conference on Virginia Woolf,* edited by Vara Neverow-Turk and Mark Hussey, 321–28. New York: Pace University Press, 1993.

Kelly, Joan. *Women, History, and Theory: The Essays of Joan Kelly.* Chicago: University of Chicago Press, 1984.

Kendrick, Christopher. "Milton and Sexuality: A Symptomatic Reading of *Comus.*" In *Re-Membering Milton: Essays on the Texts and Traditions,* edited by Mary Nyquist and Margaret W. Ferguson, 43–73. New York: Methuen, 1988.

Kermode, Frank. *Romantic Image.* New York: Random House, 1957.

Kernan, Alvin. *The Cankered Muse: Satire of the English Renaissance.* New Haven, Conn.: Yale University Press, 1959.

Kerrigan, William, and Gordon Braden. *The Idea of the Renaissance.* Baltimore: Johns Hopkins University Press, 1989.

Kingsley, Charles. *Westward Ho!* 1855. Reprint, New York: Dodd, Mead, 1941.

Knapp, Jeffrey. "Elizabethan Tobacco." In *New World Encounters,* edited by Stephen Greenblatt, 272–312. Berkeley: University of California Press, 1993.

Kunz, George Frederick. *Rings for the Finger.* 1917. Reprint, New York: Dover, 1973.

Lanyer, Aemilia. *The Poems of Aemilia Lanyer:* Salve Deus Rex Judaeorum. Edited by Susanne Woods. New York: Oxford University Press, 1993.

Larson, Deborah Aldrich. *John Donne and Twentieth-Century Criticism.* Rutherford, N.J.: Fairleigh Dickinson University Press, 1989.

Lee, Hermione. *Virginia Woolf.* London: Chatto and Windus, 1996; New York: Knopf, 1997.

Lee, Sidney. *A Life of William Shakespeare.* London: Macmillan, 1898.

———, ed. *Elizabethan Sonnets.* 2 vols. [1877–90]. Rev. ed. Westminster: Archibald Constable, 1904.

Levin, Carol. *The Heart and Stomach of a King: Elizabeth I and the Politics of Sex and Power.* Philadelphia: University of Pennsylvania Press, 1994.

Lewalski, Barbara Kiefer. "Lucy, Countess of Bedford: Images of a Jacobean Courtier and Patroness." In *Politics of Discourse: The Literature and History of Seventeenth-Century England,* edited by Kevin Sharpe and Steven N. Zwicker, 52–77. Berkeley: University of California Press, 1987.

———. *Writing Women in Jacobean England.* Cambridge, Mass.: Harvard University Press, 1993.

Limon, Jerzy. *The Masque of Stuart Culture.* Toronto: Associated University Presses, 1990.

Lodge, David. *Small World: An Academic Romance.* New York: Macmillan, 1984.

Logan, George M., and Gorden Tesky, eds. *Unfolded Tales: Essays on Renaissance Romance.* Ithaca, N.Y.: Cornell University Press, 1989.

Low, Lisa. "'Two figures in dense violent night': Virginia Woolf, John Milton, and the Epic Vision of Marriage." *Woolf Studies Annual* 1 (1995): 68–88.

Lyons, Richard. "The Intellectual Structure of Virginia Woolf's *Between the Acts.*" *Modern Language Quarterly* 38 (1977): 149–66.

MacCarthy, Desmond. "John Donne." 1908. Reprinted in *Criticism,* 36–60. London: Putnam, 1932.

Marchi, Dudley M. "Virginia Woolf Crossing the Borders of History, Culture, and Gender: The Case of Montaigne, Pater, and Gournay." *Comparative Literature Studies* 34 (1997): 1–30.

Marcus, Jane. "Britannia Rules *The Waves*." In *Decolonizing Tradition: New Views of Twentieth-Century "British" Literary Canons,* edited by Karen R. Lawrence, 136–62. Urbana: University of Illinois Press, 1992.

———. *Virginia Woolf and the Languages of Patriarchy.* Bloomington: Indiana University Press, 1987.

Marcus, Leah S. *Puzzling Shakespeare: Local Reading and Its Discontents.* Berkeley: University of California Press, 1988.

———. "Renaissance/Early Modern Studies." In *Redrawing the Boundaries: The Transformation of English and American Literary Studies,* edited by Stephen Greenblatt and Giles Gunn, 41–63. New York: Modern Language Association, 1992.

McConnell, Frank D. "'Death among the Apple Trees': *The Waves* and the World of Things." In Bloom, *Virginia Woolf,* 53–65.

McCutcheon, Elizabeth, ed. and trans. "Sir Nicholas Bacon's Great House *Sententiae.*" *English Literary Renaissance Supplements* 3 (1977).

McGee, Patrick. "The Politics of Modernist Form: Or, Who Rules *The Waves?*" *Modern Fiction Studies* 38 (1992): 631–50.

McNees, Eleanor, ed. *Virginia Woolf: Critical Assessments.* 4 vols. East Sussex, Eng.: Helm Information, 1994.

Meisel, Perry. *The Absent Father: Virginia Woolf and Walter Pater.* New Haven, Conn.: Yale University Press, 1980.

———. *The Myth of the Modern: A Study in British Literature and Criticism after 1850.* New Haven, Conn.: Yale University Press, 1987.

Mendelson, Edward. "The Death of Mrs. Dalloway: Two Readings." In *Textual Analysis: Some Readers Reading,* edited by Mary Anne Caws, 272–80. New York: Modern Language Association Publications, 1986.

Mepham, John. "Mourning and Modernism." In *Virginia Woolf: New Critical Essays,* edited by Patricia Clements and Isobel Grundy, 137–56. London: Vision; Totowa, N.J.: Barnes and Noble, 1983.

Michelet, Jules. *Histoire de France.* 17 vols. Paris: Chamerot, 1835–67.

———. *Renaissance et Réforme. Histoire de France au XVIe siècle.* With a preface by Claude Mettra. Paris: Robert Laffont, 1982. Originally published as vols. 7–10 of *Histoire de France* (Paris: Chamerot, 1855–56).

Mikalachki, Jodi. "The Masculine Romance of Roman Britain: *Cymbeline* and Early Modern English Nationalism." *Shakespeare Quarterly* 46 (1995): 301–22.

Miller, J. Hillis. "Mr. Carmichael and Lily Briscoe: The Rhythm of Creativity in *To the Lighthouse.*" In *Modernism Reconsidered,* edited by Robert Kiely, 167–89. Cambridge, Mass.: Harvard University Press, 1983.

————. "*Mrs. Dalloway:* Repetition as the Raising of the Dead." In Bloom, *Virginia Woolf,* 169–90.

Miller, Naomi J., and Gary Waller, eds. *Reading Mary Wroth: Representing Alternatives in Early Modern England.* Knoxville: University of Tennessee Press, 1991.

Milton, John. *John Milton: Complete Poems and Major Prose.* Edited by Merritt Y. Hughes. Upper Saddle River, N.J.: Prentice Hall, 1957.

Minow-Pinkney, Makiko. "'How then does light return to the world after the eclipse of the sun? Miraculously, frailly': A Psychoanalytic Interpretation of Woolf's Mysticism." In *Virginia Woolf and the Arts: Selected Papers from the Sixth Annual Virginia Woolf Conference,* edited by Diane F. Gillespie and Leslie K. Hankins, 90–98. New York: Pace University Press, 1997.

Montaigne, Michel de. *Essais.* Edited by Alexandre Micha. 3 vols. Paris: Garnier Flammarion, 1969.

————. *The Essays of Montaigne.* Translated by E. J. Trechmann. 2 vols. London: Oxford University Press, 1927.

Moore, Madeline. *The Short Season between Two Silences: The Mystical and the Political in the Novels of Virginia Woolf.* Boston: George Allen and Unwin, 1984.

————. "Virginia Woolf's *Orlando:* An Edition of the Manuscript." *Twentieth Century Literature* 25 (1979): 303–55.

Mowat, Barbara. *The Dramaturgy of Shakespeare's Romances.* Athens: University of Georgia Press, 1976.

Mumby, Frank. A. *The Girlhood of Queen Elizabeth.* Boston: Houghton Mifflin, 1909.

Neely, Carol Thomas. *Broken Nuptials in Shakespeare's Plays.* New Haven, Conn.: Yale University Press, 1985.

————. "Constructing the Subject: Feminist Practice and the New Renaissance Discourses." *English Literary Renaissance* 18 (1988): 5–18.

Nicolson, Nigel. *Portrait of a Marriage.* New York: Athenaeum, 1973.

Nora, Pierre. "Between Memory and History: *Les Lieux de Mémoire.*" Translated by Marc Roudebush. *Representations* 26 (1989): 7–25.

Ong, Walter J. *Orality and Literacy: The Technologizing of the Word.* London: Methuen, 1982.

Orgel, Stephen. *The Jonsonian Masque.* Cambridge, Mass.: Harvard University Press, 1965.

Orr, Linda. *Jules Michelet: Nature, History, and Language.* Ithaca, N.Y.: Cornell University Pres, 1976.

Osborn, E. B. *The New Elizabethans: A First Selection of the Lives of Young Men Who Have Fallen in the Great War.* London: John Lane, 1919.

Ovid. *The Metamorphoses.* Translated by Mary M. Innes. London: Penguin, 1955.

Oxindine, Annette. "Sapphist Semiotics in Woolf's *The Waves:* Untelling and Retelling What Cannot Be Told." In *Virginia Woolf: Themes and Variations: Selected Papers from the Second Annual Conference on Virginia Woolf,* edited by Vara Neverow-Turk and Mark Hussey, 171–81. New York: Pace University Press, 1993.

Pater, Walter. *Gaston de Latour* [1896]. Edited by Gerald Monsman. Greensboro, N.C.: ELT Press, 1995.

———. *The Renaissance: Studies in Art and Poetry.* Edited by Donald L. Hill. Berkeley: University of California Press, 1980.

Peacock, R. "Eliot's Contribution to Criticism of Drama." In *The Literary Criticism of T. S. Eliot,* edited by David Newton-Molina, 89–110. London: Athlone Press, 1977.

Perl, Jeffrey. *The Tradition of Return: The Implicit History of Modern Literature.* Princeton, N.J.: Princeton University Press, 1980.

Petrarch's Lyric Poems. Translated by Robert Durling. Cambridge, Mass.: Harvard University Press, 1976.

Pettet, E. C. *Shakspeare and the Romance Tradition.* London: Staples Press, 1949.

Phillips, Kathy J. *Virginia Woolf against Empire.* Knoxville: University of Tennessee Press, 1994.

Porritt, Ruth. "Surpassing Derrida's Deconstructed Self: Virginia Woolf's Poetic Disarticulation of the Self." *Women's Studies* 21 (1992): 323–38.

Potter, Sally, dir. *Orlando.* With Tilda Swinton and Quentin Crisp. United Artists, 1993.

Prest, Wilfred R. *The Inns of Court under Elizabeth I and the Early Stuarts: 1590–1640.* Totowa, N.J.: Rowman and Littlefield, 1972.

Raitt, Susan. *Vita and Virginia: The Work and Friendship of V. Sackville-West and Virginia Woolf.* Oxford: Clarendon Press, 1993.

Raleigh, Walter. "The Age of Elizabeth." In *Shakespeare's England,* vol. 1, 1–47. Oxford: Clarendon Press, 1916.

Reed, John R. "The Victorian Renaissance Self." *Clio* 17 (1988): 187–208.

Rogat, Ellen Hawkes. "A Form of One's Own." In McNees, 2:184–97.

Rosenbaum, S. P. *Edwardian Bloomsbury.* Vol. 2 of *The Early Literary History of the Bloomsbury Group.* New York: St. Martin's, 1994.

———, ed. *Women and Fiction: The Manuscript Versions of* A Room of One's Own. Oxford: Blackwell, 1992.

Ross, Andrew. *The Failure of Modernism: Symptoms of American Poetry.* New York: Columbia University Press, 1986.

Ruotolo, Lucio. "*Mrs. Dalloway:* The Unguarded Moment." In *Virginia Woolf: Revaluation and Continuity,* edited by Ralph Freedman, 141–60. Berkeley: University of California Press, 1980.

Ruskin, John. *The Works of John Ruskin.* 39 vols. New York: Longmans, Green, 1903–12.

Sackville-West, Victoria. *Knole and the Sackvilles.* London: William Heinemann, 1934.

———, ed. *The Diary of the Lady Anne Clifford.* 1923. Reprint, New York: G. H. Doran, 1977.

Sainte-Beuve, Charles-Augustin. *Les Grands Ecrivains français. XVIe siecle: Les prosateurs.* Paris: Garnier, 252.

Scarisbrick, Diana. *Rings: Symbols of Wealth, Power, and Affection.* New York: Harry N. Abrams, 1993.

Schlack, Beverly Ann. *Continuing Presences: Virginia Woolf's Use of Literary Allusion.* University Park: Pennsylvania State University Press, 1979.

Schleiner, Louise. *Tudor and Stuart Women Writers.* Bloomington: Indiana University Press, 1994.

Schoenbaum, S. *Shakespeare's Lives* [1970]. Rev. ed. New York: Oxford University Press, 1991.

Schwartz, Beth C. "Thinking Back through Our Mothers: Woolf Reads Shakespeare." *ELH* 58 (1991): 721–46.

Schwartz, Murray M., and Coppélia Kahn, eds. *Representing Shakespeare: New Psychoanalytic Essays.* Baltimore: Johns Hopkins University Press, 1980.

Scott, Bonnie Kime. *Postmodern Feminist Readings of Woolf, West, and Barnes.* Vol. 2 of *Refiguring Modernism.* Bloomington: Indiana University Press, 1995.

Sedgwick, Eve Kosofsky. *Between Men: English Literature and Male Homosocial Desire.* New York: Columbia University Press, 1985.

Shakespeare, William. *Cymbeline.* Edited by J. M. Nosworthy. 1955. Reprint, New York: Routledge [Arden], 1996.

———. *The Norton Shakespeare.* Edited by Stephen Greenblatt, Walter Cohen, Jean E. Howard, and Katharine Eisaman Maus. New York: Norton, 1997.

———. *The Sonnets.* Edited by G. Blakemore Evans. Cambridge: Cambridge University Press [New Cambridge Shakespeare], 1996.

Shawcross, John. *John Milton: The Self and the World.* Lexington: University Press of Kentucky, 1993.

Sherard, Tracey. "Voyage through *The Waves:* Woolf's Kaleidoscope of the 'Unpresentable.'" In *Virginia Woolf and the Arts: Selected Papers from the Sixth Annual Conference on Virginia Woolf,* edited by Diane F. Gillespie and Leslie K. Hankins, 125–33. New York: Pace University Press, 1997.

Showalter, Elaine. *A Literature of Their Own.* Princeton, N.J.: Princeton University Press, 1979.

Silver, Brenda R. "Virginia Woolf and the Concept of Community: The Elizabethan Playhouse." *Women's Studies* 4 (1977): 291–98.

———. *Virginia Woolf's Reading Notebooks.* Princeton, N.J.: Princeton University Press, 1983.

Smith, Hallett. *Shakespeare's Romances.* San Marino, Calif.: Huntington Library, 1972.

Solomon, Julie Robin. "Staking Ground: The Politics of Space in Virginia Woolf's *A Room of One's Own* and *Three Guineas.*" In McNees, 2:251–63.

Somerset, Anne. *Elizabeth I.* New York: Knopf, 1991.

Spalding, Frances. *Vanessa Bell.* New Haven, Conn.: Ticknor and Fields, 1983.

Spiller, Michael. *The Development of the Sonnet: An Introduction.* New York: Routledge, 1992.

———. *The Sonnet Sequence: A Study of Its Strategies.* New York: Twayne, 1997.

Squier, Susan M. *Virginia Woolf and London: The Sexual Politics of the City.* Chapel Hill: University of North Carolina Press, 1985.

Stephen, Leslie. *English Literature and Society in the Eighteenth Century.* 1903. Reprint, New York: Barnes and Noble, 1955.

———. *George Eliot.* London: Macmillan [English Men of Letters], 1902.

———. "John Donne." *National and English Review* 34 (1899): 595–613.

Stockman, Sharon. "Virginia Woolf and the Renaissance: The Promise of Capital and the Violence of Materialism." *Clio* 24 (1995): 231–50.

Strachey, Lytton. *Elizabeth and Essex: A Tragic History.* New York: Harcourt, Brace, 1928.

———. *Literary Essays.* New York: Harcourt, Brace, 1949.

Strong, Roy C. *Gloriana: The Portraits of Queen Elizabeth I.* London: Thames and Hudson, 1987.

Sypher, Eileen B. "*The Waves:* A Utopia of Androgyny?" In *Virginia Woolf: Centennial Essays,* edited by Elaine K. Ginsberg and Laura Moss Gottlieb, 187–213. Troy, N.Y.: Whitston, 1983.

"Teaching Judith Shakespeare." *Shakespeare Quarterly* 47, no. 4 (1996).

Tillyard, E. M. W. *The Elizabethan World Picture.* 1943. Reprint, New York: Vintage, n.d.

Tremper, Ellen. "'The Earth of Our Earliest Life': Mr. Carmichael in *To the Lighthouse.*" *Journal of Modern Literature* 19 (1994): 163–71.

Tyler, Lisa. "'Nameless Atrocities' and the Name of the Father: Literary Allusion and Incest in Virginia Woolf's *The Voyage Out.*" *Woolf Studies Annual* 1 (1995): 26–46.

Uffelman, Larry F. *Charles Kingsley.* Boston: Twayne, 1979.

Vickers, Nancy. "Diana Described: Scattered Woman and Scattered Rhyme." *Critical Inquiry* 8 (1981): 265–79.

Walker, Kim. *Women Writers of the English Renaissance.* New York: Twayne, 1996.

Walpole, Horace, Lord Orford. *Anecdotes of Painting in England.* 1761. Reprint, World Library of Standard Works. London: Ward, Lock, and Co., 1879.

Wang, Ban. "'I' on the Run: Crisis of Identity in *Mrs. Dalloway.*" *Modern Fiction Studies* 38 (1992): 177–91.

Warner, Eric. *Virginia Woolf: The Waves.* Cambridge: Cambridge University Press, 1987.

Wells, H. G. *The Outline of History* [1920]. 3d ed. London: Macmillan, 1924.

Weston, Jessie. *From Ritual to Romance.* Garden City, N.Y.: Doubleday, 1957.

White, Hayden. *Metahistory: The Historical Imagination in Nineteenth-Century Europe.* Baltimore: Johns Hopkins University Press, 1973.

———. *Tropics of Discourse: Essays in Cultural Criticism.* Baltimore: Johns Hopkins University Press, 1978.

Wilson, Jean Moorcroft. *Virginia Woolf: Life and London: A Biography of Place.* New York: Norton, 1988.

Woolf, Leonard. *The Journey Not the Arrival Matters: An Autobiography of the Years 1939 to 1969.* Vol. 5 of *The Autobiography of Leonard Woolf.* 1969. Reprint, New York: Harcourt Brace Jovanovich [Harvest], 1975.

———. "Montaigne." Review of *The Essays of Montaigne,* translated by E. J. Trechmann. *Nation and Athenaeum,* 17 September 1927, 778.

Woolf, Leonard, and James Strachey, eds. *Virginia Woolf and Lytton Strachey: Letters.* New York: Harcourt, Brace, 1956.

Woolf, Virginia. "'Anon' and 'The Reader': Virginia Woolf's Last Essays." Edited by Brenda Silver. *Twentieth Century Literature* 25 (1979): 356–441.

———. *Between the Acts.* 1941. Reprint, New York: Harcourt Brace Jovanovich [Harvest], 1970.

———. *The Captain's Death Bed and Other Essays.* Edited by Leonard Woolf. 1950. Reprint, New York: Harcourt Brace Jovanovich [Harvest], 1978.

———. *The Common Reader: First Series.* Edited by Andrew McNeillie. New York: Harcourt Brace Jovanovich [Harvest], 1984. Originally published as *The Common Reader* (London: Hogarth Press, 1925).

———. *The Complete Shorter Fiction of Virginia Woolf.* Edited by Susan Dick [1985]. 2d ed. New York: Harcourt Brace [Harvest], 1989.

———. *The Death of the Moth and Other Essays.* Edited by Leonard Woolf. 1942. Reprint, New York: Harcourt Brace Jovanovich [Harvest], 1974.

———. *The Diary of Virginia Woolf.* Edited by Anne Olivier Bell and Andrew McNeillie. 5 vols. New York: Harcourt Brace Jovanovich, 1977–84.

———. *The Essays of Virginia Woolf.* 4 (of 6) vols. to date. Edited by Andrew McNeillie. London: Hogarth Press, 1986–94.

———. *Granite and Rainbow.* Edited by Leonard Woolf. 1958. Reprint, New York: Harcourt Brace Jovanovich, 1975.

———. Introduction to *Mrs. Dalloway,* v–ix. New York: Modern Library, 1928. Originally published in 1925.

———. *Jacob's Room.* 1922. Reprint, New York: Harcourt Brace Jovanovich [Harvest], 1978.

———. *The Letters of Virginia Woolf.* Edited by Nigel Nicolson and Joanne Trautmann. 6 vols. New York: Harcourt Brace Jovanovich, 1975–80.

———. *The London Scene.* New York: Random House, 1975.

———. *The Moment and Other Essays.* Edited by Leonard Woolf. 1947. Reprint, New York: Harcourt Brace Jovanovich [Harvest], 1975.

———. *Moments of Being.* Edited by Jeanne Schulkind [1976]. 2d ed. New York: Harcourt Brace Jovanovich [Harvest], 1985.

———. *Mrs. Dalloway.* 1925. Reprint, with a foreword by Maureen Howard, New York: Harcourt Brace [Harvest], 1990.

———. *Night and Day.* 1919. Reprint, New York: Harcourt Brace Jovanovich [Harvest], 1973.

———. *Orlando: A Biography.* 1928. Reprint, New York: Harcourt Brace Jovanovich [Harvest], 1973.

———. The Pargiters: *The Novel-Essay Portion of* The Years. Edited by Mitchell A. Leaska. 1977. Reprint, New York: Harcourt Brace Jovanovich [Harvest], 1978.

———. *A Passionate Apprentice: The Early Journals, 1897-1909.* Edited by Mitchell A. Leaska. New York: Harcourt Brace Jovanovich, 1990.

———. "Recent Paintings by Vanessa Bell." 1930. Excerpted as "Vanessa Bell by Virginia Woolf" in *The Bloomsbury Group: A Collection of Memoirs, Commentary, and Criticism* [1975]; rev. ed., edited by S. P. Rosenbaum, 201-5. Toronto: University of Toronto Press, 1995.

———. *A Room of One's Own.* 1929. Reprint, with a foreword by Mary Gordon, New York: Harcourt Brace Jovanovich [Harvest], 1989.

———. *The Second Common Reader* [1932]. Edited by Andrew McNeillie. New York: Harcourt Brace Jovanovich [Harvest], 1986.

———. *Three Guineas.* 1938. Reprint, New York: Harcourt Brace Jovanovich [Harvest], 1966.

———. *To the Lighthouse.* 1927. Reprint, with a foreword by Eudora Welty. New York: Harcourt Brace Jovanovich [Harvest], 1989.

———. *The Virginia Woolf Manuscripts: From the Henry W. and Albert A. Berg Collection at the New York Public Library.* Microform. 21 reels. Woodbridge, Conn.: Research Publications International, 1993.

———. *The Virginia Woolf Manuscripts from the Monks House Papers at the University of Sussex.* Microform. 6 reels. Brighton, Sussex, Eng.: Harvester Microform, 1985.

———. *The Voyage Out.* 1915. Reprint, New York: Harcourt, Brace, and World [Harvest], 1968.

———. *The Waves.* 1931. Reprint, New York: Harcourt Brace Jovanovich [Harvest], 1978.

———. *The Years.* 1937. Reprint, New York: Harcourt, Brace, and World [Harvest], 1969.

Wroth, Mary. *The Poems of Lady Mary Wroth.* Edited by Josephine A. Roberts. Baton Rouge: Louisiana State University Press, 1983.

Wyatt, Jean M. "The Celebration of Eros: Greek Concepts of Love and Beauty in *To the Lighthouse.*" *Philosophy and Literature* 2 (1978): 160-75.

———. "*Mrs. Dalloway:* Literary Allusion as Structural Metaphor." *PMLA* 88 (1973): 440-51.

Yates, Frances A. *The Art of Memory.* 1966. Reprint, London: Pimlico, 1992.

Zorn, Marilyn. "The Pageant in *Between the Acts.*" *Modern Fiction Studies* 2 (1956): 31-35.

Zwerdling, Alex. *Virginia Woolf and the Real World.* Berkeley: University of California Press, 1986.

Contributors

REGINALD ABBOTT is an instructor in English at Georgia Perimeter College. Other essays of his on Woolf have appeared in *Modern Fiction Studies* (1992) and *Animals and Women: Feminist Theoretical Explorations,* edited by Carol J. Adams and Josephine Donovan (1995).

KELLY ANSPAUGH, a lecturer in English at the Ohio State University, Lima, has published analyses of Woolf's work in *Twentieth Century Literature* (1994) and the *Joyce Studies Annual* (1996).

ANNE E. FERNALD is an assistant professor of English at Purdue University, where she teaches courses in modern British fiction. She has published essays on Woolf in *Twentieth Century Literature* (1994) and *Virginia Woolf and the Essay,* edited by Beth Carole Rosenberg and Jeanne Dubino (1997).

DIANE F. GILLESPIE is a professor of English at Washington State University. She is author of *The Sisters' Arts: The Writing and Painting of Virginia Woolf and Vanessa Bell* (1988); co-editor of *Julia Duckworth Stephen: Stories for Children, Essays for Adults* (1987); editor of *The Multiple Muses of Virginia Woolf* (1993) and the Shakespeare Head edition of Woolf's *Roger Fry: A Biography* (1995); and co-editor of *Virginia Woolf and the Arts: Selected Papers from the Sixth Annual Conference on Virginia Woolf* (1997).

SALLY GREENE is an independent scholar affiliated with the University of North Carolina, Chapel Hill. Her essays on Woolf and the Renaissance have appeared in *Virginia Woolf and the Essay,* edited by Beth Carole Rosenberg and Jeanne Dubino (1997), and *Virginia Woolf and the Arts: Selected Papers from the Sixth Annual*

Conference on Virginia Woolf, edited by Diane F. Gillespie and Leslie K. Hankins (1997). She is guest editor of a special issue of *Women's Studies: An Interdisciplinary Journal,* "Virginia Woolf in Performance," forthcoming in 1999.

DIANA E. HENDERSON, an associate professor of literature at the Massachusetts Institute of Technology, is the author of *Passion Made Public: Elizabethan Lyric, Gender, and Performance* (1995). Her work-in-progress, "Uneasy Collaborations: Transforming Shakespeare Across Time and Media," will include a more extensive discussion of *Mrs. Dalloway.*

REBECCA LAROCHE is an assistant professor of English at the University of Colorado, Colorado Springs. Other portions of her project on the English Renaissance love sonnet and the erotic formation of literary history are found in *Shakespeare's Sonnets: Critical Essays,* edited by James Schiffer (1998), and forthcoming in the journal *Genre* (1999).

LISA LOW is a professor of English at Pace University. She is author of a number of essays on seventeenth-century literature and is co-editor of *Milton, the Metaphysicals, and Romanticism* (1994). Her work-in-progress, "Unkind Masters," details the relationship between John Milton and Virginia Woolf.

NICOLA LUCKHURST is a lecturer in French at Somerville and Brasenose Colleges, Oxford. Her doctoral thesis, "Structure and Science in Proust's *A la recherche,*" is shortly to appear from Oxford University Press. She has also written on the relationship between Bloomsbury and Vogue magazine and has co-edited a collection of Stéphane Mallarmé's letters, entitled *Stéphane Mallarmé. Correspondance: compléments et suppléments* (1998).

DAVID MCWHIRTER is an associate professor of English at Texas A&M University. He is author of *Desire and Love in Henry James: A Study of the Late Novels* (1989) and editor of Henry James's *New York Edition: The Construction of Authorship* (1995). His essay on *Between the Acts* as tragicomedy appeared in *English Literary History* in 1993; he is working on a book-length study of tragicomic modes in literary modernism.

Index